I0755900

Ecclesia semper reformanda est

The church is always reforming

The church is always reforming

Ecclesia semper reformanda est

A *festschrift* on ecclesiology in honour of Stanley K. Fowler on his seventieth birthday

EDITORS

DAVID G. BARKER

MICHAEL A.G. HAYKIN

BARRY H. HOWSON

www.joshuapress.com

Published by
Joshua Press Inc., Kitchener, Ontario, Canada
Distributed by
Sola Scriptura Ministries International
www.sola-scriptura.ca

Cover and book design by Janice Van Eck

The publication of this book was made possible by the generous support of Heritage College & Seminary, Cambridge, Ontario, Canada.

Library and Archives Canada Cataloguing in Publication

Ecclesia semper reformanda est = the church is always reforming : a festschrift on ecclesiology in honour of Stanley K. Fowler on his seventieth birthday / editors David G. Barker, Michael A.G. Haykin, Barry H. Howson.

Essays.
Issued in print and electronic formats.
ISBN 978-1-894400-75-6 (hardback).—ISBN 978-1-894400-74-9 (paperback).—ISBN 978-1-894400-76-3 (html).—ISBN 978-1-894400-77-0 (pdf)

1. Fowler, Stanley Keith, 1946-. 2. Theology. 3. Christianity—History. I. Fowler, Stanley Keith, 1946-, honouree II. Barker, David G., 1951-, editor, author III. Haykin, Michael A. G., editor, author IV. Howson, Barry H (Barry Hamlin), editor, author V. Title: Church is always reforming.

BR50.E23 2016 260 C2016-905131-5
C2016-905132-3

To **Stanley K. Fowler**, lover of Christ and his Word, theologian *par excellence* and dear friend—with deep thanksgiving to God for you.

Contents

Foreword ix
BY RICK REED

Contributors xi

Stanley K. Fowler: A biographical sketch xv
BY DARRYL DASH

Biblical

1 Hannah's song, a new world order and the right side of history 3
BY STEPHEN G. DEMPSTER

2 People of God in the Hebrew Bible 33
BY TERRY GILES

3 The church as community: Foundational biblical theological insights and some implications 49
BY BYRON WHEATON

4 The church and imprecations in the Psalms: The place of the call to curse in the life of the church today 65
BY DAVID G. BARKER

Theological

5 The church in God's program of salvation: A Baptist perspective 91
BY TERRANCE L. TIESSEN

6 The recovery of a sacramental ontology as the basis for developing a sacramental theology of baptism 115
BY CRAIG A. CARTER

7 Come let us read together: The role of the church in reading Scripture for Christian ethics 137
BY GUENTHER (GENE) HAAS

8 Introduction to New Testament distinctives of worship 157
BY DOUGLAS A. THOMSON

Historical

9 The sacrament of baptism among the first Baptists 189
BY ANTHONY R. CROSS

10 Christian community in German pietism: Gottfried Arnold and Johanna Eleonora Petersen on the church, with special attention to the place of women 213
BY DOUGLAS H. SHANTZ

11 "To reconcile a Trinity of persons with the Scripture unity of God": Edward Sharman and his quarrel with Andrew Fuller 235
BY MICHAEL A.G. HAYKIN

Practical

12 "For the good of the Baptist interest": The work of the Particular Baptist associations 253
BY JAMES M. RENIHAN

13 Reviewing recent trends in congregational worship: It is time for a mid-course correction 273
BY GRANT GORDON

14 What does a sixth-century Catholic pope have to say to twenty-first century evangelical pastors? An examination of Gregory the Great's *Pastoral Care* 295
BY BARRY H. HOWSON

Afterword 327
BY HEINZ G. DSCHANKILIC

Stanley K. Fowler's publications 331

Foreword

BY RICK REED

"Scholars in service of the church." That's a phrase Stan Fowler has used to describe the ministry of the faculty at Heritage Seminary. It's a phrase that fits him perfectly. Over the course of his life Stan has served Christ and his church through his scholarship. Blessed by God with a sharp mind and steel-trap memory, Stan has used his gifts well.

He initially pursued a career in the field of mathematics, switching to theology after sensing God's call on his life. While pastoring a congregation in downtown Toronto, he was invited to teach a theology course at Central Baptist Seminary. He and his students realized he had found the sweet spot of his ministry calling: being a scholar in service of the church.

For the past twenty-three years, Stan has taught God's Word at Heritage Seminary, equipping many pastors and ministry leaders. In his theology courses and personal counsel, he helps students apply biblical truth to difficult pastoral issues.

Stan's ministry isn't limited to helping seminary students. He is often contacted by pastors and denominational leaders seeking help in thinking through challenging theological and pastoral issues. Those who call him know they will receive counsel that is biblically faithful and pastorally wise. They also know Stan will speak to an emotionally-charged situation in a godly and gracious way.

Although he is a stellar theologian, he's anything but a stuffy one. His interests are wide and varied. Named after the famous St. Louis Cardinal baseball slugger, Stan Musial, he has developed a passion for a variety of sports. He's quick to remind anyone of the professional quarterbacks who graduated from beloved *alma mater*—the Purdue Boilermakers. Perhaps most amazing to me is the way he and his wife, Donna, share a passion for riding the wildest rollercoasters they can find.

In honour of his seventieth birthday a collection of his colleagues have come together to honour him through the publication of this *festschrift*. The articles they have written gravitate to the themes that have dominated Stan's life and ministry: Christ, Scripture and Christ's church. Several recent books have highlighted the role of the "pastor as theologian." This book honours the service of a man who exemplifies the "theologian as pastor."

It's with joy that I invite you to read these articles and to thank God for Stan Fowler, a dear friend, mentor and colleague—a scholar in service of the church.

Contributors

DAVID G. BARKER (Th.D. Grace Theological Seminary) is presently a part-time professor at Heritage College & Seminary. He has served at Heritage since 1978 and taught in the areas of Old Testament and pastoral studies. He has most recently served as vice president—academics and student affairs, and seminary dean.

CRAIG A. CARTER (Ph.D., University of St. Michael's College, Toronto) currently serves as professor of theology at Tyndale University College in Toronto, Ontario, and as part-time theologian-in-residence at Westney Heights Baptist Church, Ajax, Ontario. He completed a Ph.D. under John Webster at the Toronto School of Theology and is the author of two books and a number of articles.

ANTHONY R. CROSS (Ph.D., University of Keele) is a member of the faculty of theology and religion, University of Oxford.

DARRYL DASH (D.Min., Gordon-Conwell Theological Seminary) is pastor Liberty Grace Church, a new church in Liberty Village, Toronto, Ontario. He is also director of the Advance Church Planting Institute in Toronto.

STEPHEN G. DEMPSTER (Ph.D., University of Toronto) is professor of religious studies at Crandall University, Moncton, New Brunswick. His specialty is the field of Old Testament/Hebrew Bible studies with a particular interest in biblical theology and canon.

HEINZ G. DSCHANKILIC (B.Th., Central Baptist Seminary) is a contributing author to Particular Baptist Press and Joshua Press. He currently serves as executive director at Sola Scriptura Ministries International, Kitchener, Ontario.

TERRY GILES (Ph.D., Michigan State University) teaches biblical studies in the Department of Theology at Gannon University. He is author of several books, most recently on the Samaritan Pentateuch and the oral prehistory of the book of Ruth.

GRANT GORDON (Th.M., D.Min., Princeton Theological Seminary) is ordained with the Fellowship of Evangelical Baptist Churches in Canada and served as pastor for eighteen years. He then became director of supervised ministry at Tyndale Seminary, Toronto, and lecturer in Baptist history. For fifteen years, he then served as transitional pastor in numerous churches. Now retired, he pursues his interest in researching and writing in church history.

GEUNTHER (GENE) HAAS (Th.D., University of Toronto) is professor of religion and theology, Redeemer University College, Ancaster, Ontario.

MICHAEL A.G. HAYKIN (Th.D., Wycliffe College/University of Toronto) is professor of church history and biblical spirituality at The Southern Baptist Theological Seminiary (since 2008) and director of The Andrew Fuller Center for Baptist Studies. A 16-volume critical edition of the works of Andrew Fuller is being published under his editorship by Walter de Gruyter. His present areas of research include eighteenth-century British Baptist life and thought, as well as Patristic trinitarianism and Baptist piety.

BARRY H. HOWSON (Ph.D., McGill University) is vice president—academics and student affairs, and College & Seminary dean at Heritage College and Seminary, Cambridge, Ontario. He teaches in the areas of theology and church history.

RICK REED (D.Min., Trinity Evangelical Divinity School) has been the president of Heritage Baptist College and Theological Seminary, Cambridge, Ontario, since 2013. Prior to that, he served as pastor in churches in the U.S.A. and Canada. His most recent pastoral ministry, before coming to Heritage, was as lead pastor of the Metropolitan Bible Church in Ottawa, Ontario.

JAMES M. RENIHAN (Ph.D., Trinity Evangelical Divinity School) is dean and professor of historical theology at the Institute of Reformed Baptist Studies, Escondido, California. He also serves as a pastor at Christ Reformed Baptist Church, Vista, California.

DOUGLAS H. SHANTZ (Ph.D., University of Waterloo) is professor of Christian thought in the Department of Classics and Religion at the University of Calgary. He is author of articles, reviews and books on early modern German Protestantism. His recent publications include *An Introduction to German Pietism* (Johns Hopkins, 2013) and *A Companion to German Pietism, 1660–1800* (Brill, 2014).

DOUGLAS A. THOMSON (M.T.S., Ontario Theological Seminary; M. Mus., University of Hartford; D.W.S., Webber Institute for Worship Studies) is director of the music program at Heritage College where he has served for twenty-three years. He has also been the worship director at a number of churches for over thirty years, and is presently serving at Benton Street Baptist Church, Kitchener, Ontario.

TERRANCE L. TIESSEN (Ph.D., Ateneo de Manila University) is professor emeritus of systematic theology and ethics at Providence Theological Seminary, Manitoba.

BYRON WHEATON (Ph.D., Westminster Seminary) has served for thirty-five years in pastoral ministry and theological education. He has taught a variety of bible and theology courses in different Bible colleges and seminaries in the United States, Singapore, Malaysia and Canada. He is currently an adjunct professor at Heritage Seminary, Cambridge, and Ryle Theological College, Ottawa.

Stanley K. Fowler: A biographical sketch

BY DARRYL DASH

Stanley Keith Fowler was born on July 29, 1946, in Oakland City, a small town in southern Indiana known for coal mining. He was born to Donald and Virginia Fowler and named after Stan Musial ("Stan the Man"), outfielder and first baseman for the St. Louis Cardinals. Stan has one brother, Steven Fowler, born in 1949.

Stan moved to Indianapolis, Indiana, in 1956, and then to the suburb of Brownsburg, Indiana a year later. He attended Bethesda Baptist Church in Brownsburg, Brownsburg Public School, and Brownsburg High School. He graduated from Brownsburg as valedictorian and attended university on a National Merit Scholarship.

When Stan was in the fifth grade, he met Donna Sue Bishop. When he was fifteen, he began dating Donna. Their relationship continued throughout high school, and later as they attended different universities. Stan attended Purdue University beginning in 1964 to pursue a Bachelor of Science degree in mathematics with a minor in philosophy, while Donna studied nursing.

Stan and Donna wrote letters to each other throughout university. Stan once returned a letter to Donna with grammatical corrections. He thought it would be funny. Somehow, their relationship survived. As university continued, they felt that they were not ready to get married, and found it difficult to continue their relationship. They broke up, but then realized that neither one of them was happy. Stan and Donna married on June 15, 1968, shortly after he graduated.

Stan was on track to become a life insurance actuary, completing three of the seven exams. He also enjoyed philosophy, and found that the further you get in math, the closer you get to philosophy. While at university, he attended a church near the school and became close to his pastor, Pastor Shaw.[1] He developed an interest in reading philosophical works and, eventually, decided to abandon his plans to become an actuary. A former professor became angry at him, believing that he had thrown away a promising and lucrative career.

In 1968, Stan began studies at Dallas Theological Seminary. While writing his thesis, he realized that he disagreed with aspects of dispensational theology. He raised these issues in his thesis, making some of his professors nervous. Nevertheless, he was allowed to graduate.

Stan completed the Master of Theology in 1972. He had one child (Charissa) and another on the way (Timothy). He decided to postpone doctoral studies because of his growing family. Later, his family joked that he waited until he had four children and a full-time job to complete his schooling.

In 1972, the family moved back to Indiana, and Stan became pastor of Emmanuel Baptist Church in Bloomington, close to Indiana University, then a church of 150 to 200 people. He loved living in the city, and enjoyed the stimulation and constant change associated with university students. The church continued

---

[1] Later on, while pastoring in Indiana, Stan conducted the funeral for Pastor Shaw who had encouraged him in ministry.

Stan as a young student

to grow. One wife had dragged her reluctant husband to church, praying that God would work in his life and that he would connect with the pastor. A small traffic accident between this couple and Stan and Donna led to an opportunity to develop this relationship.

The Bloomington Church had been aware of Stan's position on dispensationalism. When the General Association of Regular Baptist Churches (GARBC) passed a position statement requiring all pastors to affirm their agreement with dispensational theology, Stan knew that he could not sign this statement.

While pastoring in Indiana, Stan wrote an article which was published in one of the evangelical journals. Pastor Ed Mawhorter, a fellow American who had moved north of the border, contacted Stan after reading the article and suggested that Stan would be happier in the Canadian theological climate. He recommended that he consider a church within the Fellowship of Evangelical Churches in Canada. Stan agreed, and he attended the Fellowship Convention in Niagara Falls where he made several contacts. He received a call to Portage la Prairie in Manitoba and also considered Wishing Well Acres Baptist Church[2] in Scarborough but did not accept positions in either church. He came to a mutual agreement with the leadership at Emmanuel and completed his ministry in Bloomington in 1977 after he accepted a call to Runnymede Baptist Church in Toronto in January 1978. Runnymede Baptist was formerly pastored by Gordon Brown, an influential Baptist leader in Canada, and dean of Central Baptist Seminary.

Stan jokes that he came to Canada as a theological refugee.

Stan and Donna arrived in Canada with three children: Charissa, Timothy and Daniel. A fourth child, Paul, was born during Stan's tenure at Runnymede.

While pastoring at Runnymede, Stan began to teach part-time at Central Baptist Seminary in Scarborough. Michael Haykin, then professor of church history at Central and now professor of church history at The Southern Baptist Theological Seminary, recalls meeting Stan in the second-floor chapel of seminary, and sensing an instant connection. He recognized that Stan was dif-

---

2 Now GracePoint Baptist Church.

Stan and Donna Fowler with Charissa, Timothy and baby Daniel. Their fourth child, Paul, came later. Photo *circa* early seventies.

ferent from other part-time faculty, who were primarily practitioners. Stan, he says, was deeply intellectually driven. They began a friendship that continued for years as they worked together.

In 1985, Stan resigned from Runnymede to begin full-time doctoral studies at Wycliffe College, University of Toronto. He became a member of Richview Baptist Church in Etobicoke. He also served as an itinerant preacher and interim pastor in various churches. Occasionally, these churches would pursue him further, wanting him to become their pastor.

In 1987, Stan joined the full-time faculty of Central Baptist Seminary as professor of theology. In 1989 he became dean, and paused his doctoral studies. He participated in seminary life and showed his sense of humour at the annual orientation retreat, in which students and faculty reenacted the parables of Jesus with comedic twists.

When the seminary faced a financial crisis, Stan played a pivotal role. In 1989, he first suggested the idea of a merger with London Baptist Seminary in London, Ontario. Jack Hannah, chairman of the board of Central, and later president, regularly consulted with Stan. The seminary's crisis escalated, and the school was left leaderless. Stan became leader of a three-person steering committee composed of himself, Roy Lawson (General Secretary of the Fellowship) and Ted Flemming.

The situation was dire, but Jack Hannah recalls some funny moments. He and Stan prepared an idea and presented it to Roy Lawson without mentioning the source of the idea. "Anyone with any sense would realize that was a stupid idea," Lawson pronounced. Hannah also remembers the Paul Simon song that would come up when he (Jack), Stan and Roy Lawson worked together:

> You just slip out the back, Jack
> Make a new plan, Stan
> You don't need to be coy, Roy

Hannah says that from a human perspective, Stan is the reason that Central survived the crisis. Haykin says that Stan's leadership was crucial during this period. His phlegmatic personality gave a sense of stability when the future of the seminary was at stake.

Stanley K. Fowler

Stan's daughter, Charissa Redlich, agrees with this assessment of his personality. She credits Stan with being even-keeled, honest without being cynical, and able to say hard things without being judgemental. He searches for the truth, she says, regardless of the party line.

Throughout his ministry, Stan was always involved as a father. He attended most of his sons' baseball games. At the height of a stressful situation, he adjusted his schedule and made time for his family.

Stan also maintained other interests. He became a Toronto Blue Jays fan when he moved to Toronto in 1978 and also enjoys basketball, football, hockey, tennis, golf and soccer. He attended a World Series game in Toronto in 1992 with his father, which was a meaningful experience. He is fiercely competitive, and he enjoys theme parks.

In 1992, Donna was diagnosed with serious, invasive breast cancer. Surgery took place in November, the same week as the Fellowship Convention. Stan, usually a fixture at these events, remained at the hospital with Donna. Ed and Mary Mawhorter visited at the hospital, and many friends let them know that they had prayed corporately during the Convention for her health. Donna recovered and resumed her career in nursing.

In 1993, Central Baptist Seminary merged with London Baptist Seminary to form Heritage Theological Seminary. Stan was one of only a few members of faculty who made the transition. He moved to Kitchener, Ontario, and commuted to London until the school moved to its permanent location in Cambridge. He missed Toronto, but he enjoyed Kitchener, which reminded him of Bloomington, Indiana. He attended the Kitchener-Waterloo Symphony, and occasionally travelled back to Toronto for Blue Jays games. He became a member of Grandview Baptist Church in Kitchener, and joined a small group.

According to Haykin, some of the faculty members of London Baptist were initially wary of the Central Baptist faculty. As they got to know Stan, their concerns dissipated. David Barker remembers travelling to a conference with Stan during the height of the open theism controversy. Stan spoke eloquently for hours about the nuances of the debate. Barker credits Stan with one of the sharpest theological minds he has encountered.

Stan was appointed academic dean of Heritage when it merged. In 1996, Stan took a one-year study leave to complete his studies at Wycliffe. He graduated with a Doctor of Theology in 1998. His thesis became the basis for his book *More Than a Symbol: The British Baptist Recovery of Baptismal Sacramentalism*, published in 2002. Haykin says that this book has been widely reviewed and quoted, and has contributed to a sacramental turn in the Baptist understanding of baptism.

Stan stepped aside as academic dean in 2011 and focused his energies on teaching.[3]

According to Redlich, Stan's passion is focused theological discussion in the church. Haykin comments that Stan's greatest contribution has been through the classroom, in which he has influenced a large number of pastors over thirty years. He is a churchman, says Haykin, who has both pastoral experience and theological insight and is therefore able to see how theological trends will work themselves out within the church.

Stan has written in Fellowship publications and has been consulted in the Fellowship on theological issues. Hannah comments that Stan has shown a real loyalty to the Fellowship, and has had a positive impact, calling the Fellowship to be theologically driven.

Stan has travelled extensively to teach in Europe, Brazil and Uganda, and has presented papers at many theological conferences in North America.

Stan became a Canadian citizen in 2014. He now has six grandchildren, to whom he is affectionately known as Papa: Joanna, Sarah, Rebekah, Noah, Ethan and Christopher.

Stan Fowler continues to teach at Heritage.

---

3 He had been in and out of the dean's chair over his years at Heritage Seminary.

Biblical

1

Hannah's song, a new world order and the right side of history

BY STEPHEN G. DEMPSTER

It is no accident that the song of Hannah appears near the beginning of the books of Samuel.[1] There it provides a lens through which to see and evaluate the vast amount of historical material contained in these volumes. It was not haphazardly placed in this textual location but it was selected intentionally to provide a contextual frame for the various sources and stories set within the parameters of these books. While the time period spans the tumultuous period in Israel at the turn of the second millennium B.C. (1050–980), these books—one book in the Hebrew Bible—are anything but a dispassionate

[1] 1 Samuel 2:1–10. I would like to thank Matthew Maguire, one of my students, for helping me formulate the title of this essay. I would also like to thank Professor Gregg Finley, a historian at St. Stephen's University, for his helpful comments with an earlier draft of this paper.

chronicling of events and times. What is found here is a sophisticated historiography, which highlights certain events and actors while placing others in the shadows. And the writer does not leave us very long in doubt as to what is the key determining principle for the selection of events for his history. It is a song of thanksgiving of a once hapless Hebrew woman, who has discerned in the resolution of her personal pain, suffering and frustration, a future resolution to the pain, suffering and frustration of the world. In short, she sees the coming of a new world order.

This thanksgiving poem is a masterpiece of early Hebrew poetry, but it was not chosen as an introduction to this historical work primarily because of its literary beauty; it was selected for its hermeneutical value, to provide the fundamental key to understanding the historical events for which it provides a framework. These historical events could be simply viewed as isolated facts strung in succession, but the poem presents the fundamental pattern for understanding these events so that the reader will "connect the dots." Or one could say that it presents a "grid" which supplies the conceptual apparatus for understanding the subsequent historical and literary data. This grid establishes polarities worked out in the early history of Israel: pride and humility, strength and weakness, satiety and hunger, fertility and sterility, wealth and poverty and life and death. But this grid does not present these in a neutral way; it reorients them to show that there is a movement from *the way things are* to *the way things will be* with YAHWEH governing history. The radical reorientation, sings Hannah, is not just one historical option of many. Hannah is granted a glimpse of a coming new world order which is the goal of history. She is thus able to see the right side of history!

If the biblical scope is opened well beyond the books of Samuel, Mary is heard, in the New Testament in her magnificent Magnificat, loudly echoing Hannah's song about the right side of history.[2] Thus, in a time of ecclesiological decline in the West, when many are saying the church is on the wrong side of history, it may be helpful to consider Hannah's song and its implications.[3] I thus am

---

2 Luke 1:46–55.

3 As I was writing this essay a letter to the editor in our local newspaper was published arguing that the recent referendum in Ireland in favour of same-sex marriage

honoured to dedicate this paper to Stan Fowler for his personal friendship and for his commitment to the church of Jesus Christ.

The historian and his sources

There is not much explicit information within the books of Samuel about the author and his sources. Tradition has associated the authorship of these books with Samuel the prophet, with help from the later prophets, Gad and Nathan. [4] But there is no firm evidence for such a view. The book does seem to have some literary integrity defining it from the other books with which it is associated in the Hebrew Bible. Although it once seems to have been part of a great historical work stretching from Joshua to 2 Kings, the so-called Deuteronomic History, it has been given its own literary boundary by being delimited to two books. [5] It seems also to have a distinctive style separating it

---

is an example of Martin Luther King's statement about the moral arc of the universe being long but bending toward justice. Recently John Lloyd has written that the Catholic Church is married to the wrong side of history, and its counterattacks on secularism are analogous to the barbarians at the gates! (http://blogs.reuters.com/john-lloyd/2013/01/04/a-church-married-to-the-wrong-side-of-history/; accessed May 9, 2016)

4 See e.g. 1 Chronicles 29:29. The records referred to here are probably other "extra-biblical" books to which the Chronicler is referring his readers. See also the Babylonian Talmud (*Baba Bathra* 14b) which mentions in one section that Samuel wrote the books of Samuel, Ruth and Judges, whereas in another (*Baba Bathra* 15a) it states that since Samuel died long before the books of Samuel were completed, Gad and Nathan finished them. This seems to be relying on a particular interpretation of 1 Chronicles 29:29.

5 Of course there is only one book in the early Hebrew Bible (the first time it was divided into 2 books in Hebrew Bibles was in the Bomberg Bible first printed in 1525), and this was divided into two in the Greek Bible and labelled First and Second Reigns, thus becoming more closely related to the next two books, Third and Fourth Reigns (First and Second Kings). The separation into two volumes in the Greek Bible was probably due to reasons of convenience, but the result linked Samuel more closely to Kings. Before Martin Noth's famous study there were various theories of authorship of this material. The most popular was that the historical material represented a continuation of the sources of the Pentateuch which had been edited by a Deuteronomic group of editors, not to be confused with those responsible for the D source. It was Martin Noth's thesis that the book of Deuteronomy was to be separated from the Pentateuch to provide a theological framework for the historical material in Joshua to 2 Kings. Noth believed that a person, whom he named the Deuteronomist, provided an introduction to an already existing corpus of law in Deuteronomy (chs. 1–3) and then through a process of selection and redaction of sources and the composition of important transitional links and speeches, he wrote a coherent account of Israel's history approximately identical to the account in Joshua to 2 Kings. The work was called

from the other works of this history, so simply to characterize it as the third volume of a four volume history is probably not accurate. Nevertheless, it is apparent that the author(s) did not see himself as writing history in a historical vacuum. One does not have to read long before becoming aware of a long historical tradition which can be traced back to a belief in YAHWEH as Creator, and the patriarchs' descent into Egypt on the one hand,[6] and a prophecy about the priesthood of Eli which is fulfilled in the book of Kings on the other.[7] Moreover, literarily the conjunction at the beginning of the book and the one at the beginning of Kings presupposes a linguistic sequence for the work. Thus the literary and historical context for the book stretches ahead to the Babylonian exile and then back to the conquest, and even further beyond that to the creation of the world itself! And in terms of the Christian canon, the book's future trajectory reaches into the New Testament and even further to the final goal of history, the new heavens and new earth.

The author(s) could have been an individual or part of a team of writers connected to various locations within Israel. The book received its final form probably during the exile. One recent author has dubbed the final author of this material the world's first major historian.[8] In this essay most of the study focuses on the books of Samuel, and then this focus will be expanded to consider their wider canonical context.

There are a few details that we can infer about the author(s). A variety of sources were used: narrative accounts,[9] lists,[10] poems[11]

---

the Deuteronomistic History. See Martin Noth, *Überlieferungsgeschichtliche Studien. Die sammelnden und bearbeitenden Geschichtswerke im Alten Testament*, 2nd ed. (Tübingen: Max Niemeyer, 1957).

6 1 Samuel 2:8.

7 1 Samuel 2:27–36; 1 Kings 2:27.

8 John Van Seters, *In Search of History: Historiography in the Ancient World and the Origins of Biblical History* (New Haven and London: Yale University Press, 1983), 362.

9 There were major blocks of narrative that the historian had at his disposal; on these see below. The question of whether the author "mechanically" arranged these sources or creatively rewrote them is a question that needs further study, but in my judgement the latter is more likely. See the discussion in Robert Polzin, *Samuel and the Deuteronomist: A Literary Study of the Deuteronomic History. Part Two: 1 Samuel* (Bloomington: Indiana University Press, 1993), 9–15.

10 2 Samuel 8:16–18, 21:15–22, 23:8–39.

11 1 Samuel 2:1–10, 2 Samuel 1:19–27; 3:33–34; 22; 23:1–7.

other books.[12] He respected his sources so much that he would sometimes provide explanations for his audience rather than changing the sources, whether oral traditions or written texts. When his source used an ancient expression no longer understood in his own time, the author clarified the meaning. For example, as soon as the source described Saul and his servant going to visit a seer, there is the explanation: "In Israel in days gone by, when someone wished to consult God, he would say, 'Let us go to the seer.' For what is nowadays called a prophet used to be called a seer" (1 Samuel 9:9). [13] Sometimes these explanations are more theological than informative. When Eli's evil sons did not listen to their father's rebuke, the author added the reason for their callous behaviour "for the LORD wanted to kill them" (1 Samuel 2:25). Moreover, the reason why Absalom chooses the advice of Hushai over that of Ahithopel was because the LORD had determined to frustrate the good advice of Ahithopel in order to bring disaster on Absalom (2 Samuel 17:14).[14]

Not only do these explanatory comments reveal something about the methodology of the author, his perspective can also be seen from the sources he selects as well as the comments he makes.[15] From his explanatory guidance it is obvious that he is not a "fan" of the priesthood of Eli. And in the choice of sources which have been edited, a Davidic orientation is strong. There are six main blocks of material. Chapters 1-3 of 1 Samuel deal with traditions concerning Shiloh; chapters 4-6 the ark narrative, an account of the "fortunes of the ark during one particularly

---

12 2 Samuel 1:18 (*The Book of Yashar*).

13 Some scholars may view this simply as a gloss, updating the historian's work.

14 See further 1 Samuel 17:50.

15 The question of how much of the history contains sources and how much was composed by the author has been raised afresh by John Van Seters. Noth believed that most of the Deuteronomistic History was composed of sources the final author had at his disposal. He pieced these together and redacted them in such a coherent fashion that Noth can call the final product truly the work an author not a redactor. See Noth, *Überlieferungsgeschichtliche Studien*, 11. Van Seters argues that most of what Noth considers sources should be considered composition by the Deuteronomist. Yet in order to maintain this position Van Seters has to eliminate material which does not seem to be consistent with his Deuteronomist's perspective. Thus 2 Samuel 9–20 with its focus on David's faults has to go! I find this methodology problematic. On this whole question see also note 3 above.

troubled period in the history of Israel."[16] The transition to kingship unifies the material in chapters 7–15, as does the emergence of David and his rise to prominence in 1 Samuel 16–2 Samuel 8. The material from 2 Samuel 9–20 is largely known as the Succession Narrative, a text which is concerned with the succession to David's throne.[17] Finally, various dischronologized sources are arranged in an appendix to the narrative in 2 Samuel 21–24.

There is a Davidic interest in at least 1,122 of these 1,504 verses! This is even true when Saul is still king. For fifteen chapters of narrative the regnant Saul is largely ignored while his servant-turned-fugitive, David of Bethlehem, takes centre stage in the historiography.[18] What takes place in the caves in the wilderness is more important for the historiographer than what occurs in the royal palace at Gibeah! Moreover in the appendices which are added to the book of Samuel (2 Samuel 21–24), the concern is blatantly Davidic: two plagues that happened during his reign (2 Samuel 21:1–14; 24:1–25)—one specifically caused by Saul and remedied by David, and the other both caused and remedied by David—two lists of Davidic warriors (2 Samuel 21:15–22; 23:8–39) and two Davidic poems (2 Samuel 22; 23:1–7). This Davidic focus is accentuated by the apologetic thrust of some of the material. The author takes pains to stress that David did not take Saul's life even when afforded the perfect opportunity (1 Samuel 24, 26). David also distances himself from the death of Saul (2 Samuel 1), his relatives (2 Samuel 4) and his military personnel (2 Samuel 3:26–39). When Abner, the military commander of the house of Saul was assassinated by Joab, David's military chief, the author states repeatedly that David had no complicity (2 Samuel 3:21, 23, 26, 28, 36, 37).

Such Davidic concern and royal apologetic imply that there were other competing versions of events whose perspective the author did not share. A glimpse of one version can be found in the mouth of a Saulide supporter, whose views are presented

---

16 Robert P. Gordon, *I & II Samuel: A Commentary, Library of Biblical Intepretation* (Grand Rapids: Zondervan, 1988), 24.

17 The classic statement is by L. Rost, *The Succession to the Throne of David* (Sheffield: Almond Press, 1982).

18 1 Samuel 18 to 2 Samuel 1.

during the description of David's flight from Jerusalem because of the coup of Absalom. In the midst of his flight David encounters an unsympathetic Shimei, who shares a different perspective than the historiographer but who is still allowed to speak nonetheless. He curses the king: "Get out! Get out, you murderous scoundrel! The LORD has taken vengeance on you for the blood of the house of Saul whose throne you took, and he has given the kingdom to your son Absalom. You murderer! See how your crimes have overtaken you!" (2 Samuel 16:7–8). This shows very clearly that there was an anti-Davidic and a pro-Saulide reading of history in ancient Israel, a reading which was so pervasive, it fueled the later rebellions of Absalom and Sheba.[19]

Although it is obvious that the author/historiographer does not share this perspective of events, it is clear that he is also not a mere propagandist for the Davidic empire, offering as it were a "royal" reading of events, a reading that is self-serving, intending to support uncritically the institution of the monarchy.[20] This is too reductionistic.[21] It fails to take into account the fact that a significant part of the material is pre-Davidic and concerns important events which are not just mere background: the birth of Samuel, the fall of the house of Eli, the birth of kingship and the rise and rejection of Saul (1 Samuel 1–15). These events seem important in their own right.[22] Moreover, David, when he does appear on the scene, is clearly not a heroic figure in the traditional sense. In fact his debut is clearly inauspicious as it is marked by the weakness of youth. From his culture's perspective, from his father's perspective, even from the prophet Samuel's

---

19 2 Samuel 15–18, 20.

20 This view is often found. For example, in his writings, Walter Brueggemann pits a royal (Davidic) and a covenantal view (Moses) against each other. See Walter Brueggemann, *The Prophetic Imagination* (Philadelphia: Fortress Press, 1978). While Brueggemann does make some significant points, he tends to overstate his case in my judgement.

21 Pun intended. James Barr writes (with tongue not too firmly in cheek) that for Brueggemann "almost everyone who has ever said anything about anything [regarding the Hebrew Bible] is a reductionist except for the Hebrew Bible." James Barr, *The Concept of Biblical Theology: An Old Testament Perspective* (Minneapolis: Fortress Press, 1999), 546.

22 This is quite different than the Chronicler's history where the first ten chapters are background for David's arrival. The Chronicler has history waiting for this moment of David's arrival.

perspective, he was regarded as the one least likely to succeed as king; he is more of a musician than a warrior-king, a simple shepherd-boy (1 Samuel 16). Although he does become a successful warrior and later a king, it is not because of any physical attributes. He spends most of his warrior years running from Saul, surrounded by vagabonds and criminals; he has to act like a raving maniac to escape the clutches of a Philistine king (1 Samuel 21:10–15). Abigail prevents him from murdering her husband in a fit of rage (1 Samuel 25).

And of course his lust eventually leads him to murder Bathsheba's husband, Uriah (2 Samuel 11). Not to be forgotten are the royal scandals of Tamar and Amnon, the murder of Amnon, the rebellion and death of Absalom, and the suppression of Sheba's revolt. This material is anything but the stuff of dynastic propaganda. I cannot imagine for one minute a royally sponsored recent history of the English monarchy devoting such attention to the affairs of Charles and Diana and the scandals of the grandchildren. The Israelite historiographer is not sitting in the court of the kings of Judah. He sits in a higher one. His perspective is not political but rather theological.[23]

The song of Hannah—the historian's lens

This specific perspective of the historiographer is seen by the choice to begin the history with a poetic source, the song of a woman profoundly thankful for the intervention of God in her own personal history.[24] The writer chooses to present this song

---

23 It seems to me that this is where a work such as John Van Seters' *In Search of History* fails. In this work 2 Samuel 9–20 cannot be part of the Deuteronomistic Historiography because it is too critical of David. Is it possible that the perspective of the historiographer has been wrongly identified? Robert Polzin makes an important point. Scholars often start with a presupposition about the text and proceed to construct an original hypothetical text the meaning of which actually contradicts the text as it is found in the document. See Polzin, *Samuel and the Deuteronomist*, 3–4. This is not to say that this historiography should be judged by modern historical standards. For an important discussion on this matter see Rachelle Gilmour, *Representing the Past: A Literary Analysis of Narrative Historiography in the Book of Samuel* (Leiden: Brill, 2011).

24 Scholars who argue that the books of Samuel are not history because of the use of narrative art and therefore are an imaginative re-enactment of history for ideological or entertainment purposes confuse modern standards with ancient ones. Even modern historians use their imaginations and can occasionally entertain. Purely factual

in its entirety at the beginning of his historical work, because it sets the tone for everything to follow. This lens through which Hannah sees her own personal history is used by the historian to view his nation's past. With this lens he was able to zoom in on which sources were important and which were not, which figures would become part of the foreground and which would be set in the background, which events would become central and which would be peripheral. He begins his work with this beautiful piece of poetry not for aesthetic reasons but for theological ones. He saw that this song not only anticipated his nation's history; it determined it. It offered a transcendent, prophetic perspective on all the subsequent events during the tumultuous years to follow.

Literary and historical context of the song of Hannah

The historical context provided in the historian's sources is situated near the end of the period of the judges during a time of political and moral chaos. The Philistines threatened the nascent Israelite nation on its western border, with their superior political organization and military technology (1 Samuel 4). The one unifying thread in the Israelite nation was its faith, and this had fallen on hard times as the opening chapters of Samuel describe in detail the corruption of the priesthood. Yet the description of such corruption and consequent oppression is delayed by the historian until he supplies the immediate context for Hannah's Song. The text of the first chapter of Samuel focuses on a childless woman, one of two wives of a husband named Elqanah, abject in her miserable condition,

---

histories are not histories! They can be a catalogue of events or chronicles but certainly as Gilmour (*Representing the Past*, 1–28) argues, historiography involves a view of causation, meaning and significance. Everyone has to have a starting point! For those who do not regard biblical narrative as history because of the role of imagination see Robert Alter, "Sacred History and Prose Fiction," in *The Creation of Sacred Literature: Composition and Redaction of the Biblical Text*, ed. Richard Elliott Friedman (Berkeley: University of California Press, 1981), 7–24.; because of entertainment purposes, see David M. Gunn, *Story of King David: Genre and Interpretation* (Sheffield: JSOT Press, 1978); because of the primacy of divine causation see Ernest Nicholson, "Story and History in the Old Testament," in *Language, Theology and the Bible*, ed. Samuel E. Balentine and John Barton (Oxford: Clarendon Press, 1994), 135–150. In my judgement while there are elements of truth in all these works, they are reductionistic, and they impose modern categories on ancient documents.

and whose annual pilgrimage to the sanctuary with the family in which her childlessness is conspicuous for all to see, is a prime opportunity for her fertile, rival-wife to humiliate her publicly. In fact the text colourfully describes Peninnah's assault on Hannah, using imagery which suggests Hannah would "thunder" in rage (1 Samuel 1:6). Finally, on one occasion, Hannah, completely broken and no longer able to endure the torment, rushes to the sanctuary in her tears and grief and bares her soul to God, asking him to "remember" her humiliation and give her a child (1 Samuel 1:9–11). She promises that if her request is granted she will loan the child to the sanctuary as long as he lives. The conclusion of the matter is that Hannah is "remembered" by YAHWEH. She becomes pregnant and bears a child whom she names Samuel (because the name sounds like the Hebrew word for "a request" or "loan"). After she weans her son, she presents him to the Lord at the sanctuary, loaning him back to God. Because of the dramatic reversal in her own life, from humiliation to exaltation, from death to life, she is described as singing the song which the historian finds so important to include in its entirety.

The structure and theme of the song

The song is a general thanksgiving song consisting of three stanzas (1 Samuel 2:1–3, 4–8b, 8c–10). The first stanza expresses Hannah's exultation in YAHWEH for having been saved from her miserable condition. Only YAHWEH, the giver of life, could effect this salvation, so he is described as uniquely the Holy One, the solid rock upon which one can rely. Consequently there is no ground whatsoever for human boasting, speech that is bombastic and arrogant. God knows every human situation and weighs actions.

Stanza 1: Boast only in Yahweh (verses 1–3)

My heart thrills in YAHWEH!
  My horn has been raised by YAHWEH!
My mouth speaks against my enemies!
  For I rejoiced in your salvation.
There is no Holy One like YAHWEH!
  For there is no one like You!
  No rock like our God!

Do not boast saying "High, High!"
  So that arrogance comes out of your mouth.
For YAHWEH is a God of knowledge,
  By him actions are weighed.

Three points emerge as significant in the first stanza. First, speech that is bombastic is termed "high, high" (*gĕbōhâ gĕbōhâ*).[25] These words become extremely important in the narrative to follow, because being tall represents a view of reality which is opposed to God.[26] The tall one is the strong one and therefore the proud one, as he or she frequently trusts in his or her own strength. Secondly, Hannah uses the metaphor of a raised horn to describe her salvation. The animal's horn is a symbol of strength, and it raises its horn as a sign of victory in battle. If it raises its horn on its own, it is a symbol of pride (cf. Psalm 75:4–5). Note that Hannah says that she is victorious only because it is YAHWEH who has raised her horn. The glory belongs to him. There is no ground for human praise—only thanksgiving. Thirdly, the section closes by providing an apt introduction to the second stanza: God is a God of justice—he is aware of the human situation—a God of knowledge and he weighs actions.[27] Nothing escapes his notice. No situation is too hidden from his gaze, and the assumption is that he will act.

Stanza 2: Yahweh, the shaper of history (4–8b)

MILITARY	MILITARY/SOCIAL
The mighty bowmen are confounded,	YAHWEH kills and YAHWEH gives life,
The exhausted acquire strength.	He brings down to Sheol and resurrects.

---

25 Note the similarity of this word to two others that are extremely important in the narrative to follow: Gibeah (*gib'â*), the place of Saul's birth, and Gilboa (*gilbōa'*), the place of his death.

26 Polzin, *Samuel and the Deuteronomist*, 34.

27 There is a question of whether the verb "weigh" (*nitkĕnû*) should be translated "weigh" or "balance." In the context the best sense would be the traditional "weigh" as it affords a nice parallel to the previous stich: God is a God of knowledge. He therefore understands whether actions stem from proud or humble motives. It is unnecessary to look for a less common meaning. Cf. P. Kyle McCarter Jr, *I Samuel*, Anchor Yale Bible (New Haven: Yale University Press, 1995), 72.

ECONOMIC The full hire themselves out for something to eat, The hungry cease from the land.	**ECONOMIC** Yahweh impoverishes and enriches, He humbles; he also exalts.
SOCIAL/POLITICAL The barren woman has seven children The fertile woman laments her losses.	**SOCIAL/POLITICAL** He raises from the dust the poor one From the ash heap, the needy To make them dwell with princes, To inherit a glorious throne.

The second stanza (4–8b) describes this God of knowledge as moving into action and shaping history by reversing the status quo, humbling the proud and exalting the humble. The once powerful are humbled while the once weak are exalted. The stanza is balanced into two approximately equal halves, which depict the same sequence of reversals in three particular spheres: military, economic and social/political. In each half the social/political sphere of begetting children is the climactic one, which completely concurs with the literary context of Hannah who is expressing gratitude for her child. The second stanza, however accelerates the reversal process by specifying a reversal on every line, not every two lines as in the first section. It is almost as if the poet is emphasizing the fact that this world order is coming.[28] Finally the agent of the reversal is explicitly identified in the second half. YAHWEH is the one who is doing the saving and judging within history. This message, of course, is the supreme proof for the premise of the first stanza: since there is no one like YAHWEH, there is no ground for human pride. Why should anyone boast in being given life, in being brought up from the grave, in being wealthy, in being exalted, raised from the dust to be on a throne? Rather, the proper response is rather thanksgiving. If one wants to boast, then boast only in YAHWEH.

But the message of this stanza should not be lost on the hearer or reader, for this text essentially contains a philosophy of history

---

28 Note that the final reversal in the second section is doubly positive as opposed to containing a negative and positive outcome: there is only exaltation.

in a nutshell. Any presently established order should not presume that it will be secure forever. Immanent historical forces whether they be military, economic or social/political do not have the last word. The strong, the rich, the life-bearers do not "call the shots" on the historical scene. It may appear as if they do. They may attempt to define and manage reality and shape history with their speech, their military technology, their economic ledger, their human resources, but they will inevitably and finally fail. They are on the wrong side of history because they trust in their own resources rather than YAHWEH.

Stanza 3: Yahweh's goal for history (verses 8c–10)

To YAHWEH belong the foundations of the earth;
He supports the world with them.
He guards the feet of his devoted ones;
But the wicked will perish in darkness,
Since not with strength is a man strong.
YAHWEH—his enemies collapse.
Against them he thunders in the heavens
YAHWEH will bring justice to the ends of the earth.
He will give strength to his king
And raise the horn of his Messiah

This stanza shows that YAHWEH can act the way he does in history because he is the Creator of the world: the pillars upon which he laid the world belong to him. This picture of ancient cosmology is especially relevant, since YAHWEH can knock the foundations down as well as put them up again. Creation/nature and history are inseparably linked. This is clearly shown in the next verse where human foundations—the feet of the faithful ones—are supported by YAHWEH. This stanza indicates that the process of historical reversal initiated by YAHWEH is headed in a specific direction with a clearly defined goal. This goal shows the right side of history as YAHWEH's faithful ones are supported in the order of history by the one who supports the natural order. The wicked thus perish in the pre-creation darkness.[29] To be on the right side of history means the exclusion of human strength

---

29 Genesis 1:2.

and power (*kî lō' bĕkōaḥ yigbar 'îš*).[30] No longer does Hannah speak of her personal salvation from personal enemies but of YAHWEH's enemies, against whom he will thunder as Penninah had caused Hannah "to thunder."[31] As YAHWEH has raised Hannah's horn to deliver her from personal injustice, he will one day raise his Messiah's horn to bring about universal justice. Hannah then is caught up in something far more profound than she realizes. Her personal salvation is part of a cosmic salvation as she somehow "discerned in her own individual experience the general laws of the divine economy and its signification in relation to the whole history of the kingdom of God." [32]

The historical narrative through the lens of the song of Hannah

The writer clearly sees in the birth of Samuel and the exaltation of Hannah over Penninah an outworking of the divine program for history, the making of a new world order. Little people matter. Hannah has been given a glimpse through her own personal experience of something international, to which her song bears witness. And bear witness it does, as the revolution is about to begin. In the ensuing narrative the young boy Samuel is pointedly contrasted with the corrupt priesthood, who literally get fat from the offerings of the sanctuary worshippers as they use their strong-arm tactics to exploit and oppress (1 Samuel 2:11–17). This intentional literary contrast by the historian identifies explicitly the strong and the weak, the rich and the poor, the proud and the humble. But the reversal is coming as anticipated in some of the prophetic sources which the historian utilizes. The prayer of desperation of Hannah which led to the birth of Samuel has started the historical "ball" rolling; Eli's house will soon be decimated and in the end go begging for bread. The historian uses the first statement by a prophet in the narrative to spell out more clearly the historical revolution stimulated by Hannah's prayer: "Those who honour me I will honour; those who despise

---

30 Cf. Psalm 33:16–17 and 145:10.

31 Many recent commentators point out the relationship between 1 Samuel 1:6 and 1 Samuel 2:10.

32 Auberlen, cited in C.F. Keil and Franz Delitzsch, *Commentary on the Old Testament: The Books of Samuel* (Grand Rapids: Eerdmans, 1971), 29.

me will meet with contempt" (1 Samuel 2:30). The source which describes young Samuel's vision of God in the night and old Eli's blindness and deafness is effectively placed next in sequence (1 Samuel 3). The epistemological hegemony of the Elide priesthood has been shattered by a new word from God. The managers of Israelite "reality" will soon be managed. A new order has begun. The next source, which describes the Philistine victories over the Israelites in which the ark is taken and priesthood destroyed, show YAHWEH at work humbling and exalting (1 Samuel 4). The *coup de grâce* is blind, old, obese Eli falling and breaking his neck and his fertile daughter-in-law dying with her newborn baby, whom she appropriately names "No-Honour" (1 Samuel 4:21). The strong and the proud in Israel have come tumbling down and nothing can put them together again.

But it is equally clear that it has not been Philistine strength and their god which have been responsible for victory. After Philistine exaltation, their capture of the ark leads to their humiliation. They place it in their temple, where it takes second position to Dagon, the great pagan grain god. But the next day Dagon has fallen down before YAHWEH in worship. The stubborn Philistines do not get the picture and reinstall Dagon to his "rightful" place; but the following day he has fallen and lost his head and hands in the process, condemned to a worse fate than old Eli's collapse and subsequent broken neck (1 Samuel 5:1-5). The triumphant Philistines are again subdued as they experience the plagues brought about by the presence of God. They send the ark back to the Israelites and experience relief (1 Samuel 5:6-6:12). They have learned the truth of Hannah's words: YAHWEH kills and YAHWEH revives. The Israelites learn the same lesson again when the people of Bethshemesh play fast and loose with the ark and are struck down. The response of the survivors "Who can stand before YAHWEH, this Holy God?" (1 Samuel 6:20) echoes the words of Hannah, "There is no one Holy like YAHWEH!" (1 Samuel 2:2).

The next chapters narrate the history of the transition to kingship in ancient Israel. After an initial victory over the Philistines in which they are defeated by YAHWEH's thunder in a storm (1 Samuel 7:10 cf. 1 Samuel 2:10), the people however do not get the point and want a human king who will fight their battles for them. The sources used by the historian which indicate the choice of Saul for king seem to contain different emphases, some pro- and some anti-monarchical. In my judgement these can be reconciled by the people's reason for a king: it is rooted in the desire to be like the other nations and have the king's own strength be responsible for a strong government and military success (1 Samuel 8:5, 20). The so-called pro-monarchical sources need to be read in this light.[33] YAHWEH gives them the person they want, one who is strong and tall, a superb warrior (1 Samuel 10:17ff; 11). Read through the lens of the song of Hannah, one should be naturally suspicious of anyone who is tall and naturally strong. Note that though the song itself anticipates a king, it will be YAHWEH who will empower him (1 Samuel 2:10).[34]

Consequently Saul's demise happens just as rapidly as his rise. It begins with disobedience rather than submission, and as a result he loses the kingship *de facto*. In a subsequent battle against the Philistines, he and his many warriors become fearful, while his son, Jonathan, and an armor bearer, strike the first blow while voicing the theology of the song of Hannah: "Nothing can stop the Lord from winning a victory, by many or by few" (1 Samuel 14:6).[35] In the ensuing battle, Saul and his warriors' exhaustion and Jonathan's renewed strength continue to echo Hannah's themes (1 Samuel 14:27ff).

Shortly thereafter, David is introduced, but his bearing is a studied contrast to Saul. Even to the prophet Samuel, he is the least likely candidate of Jesse's sons to replace Saul. Samuel learns over again an aspect of his mother's philosophy of history: "Do not look at his outward appearance or the height of his stature (*'el-gĕbōah qômātô*) for I have rejected him; not as people see do I see for they look at the outward appearance but YAHWEH looks upon the heart" (1 Samuel 16:7). The people have had their choice for king but now it is YAHWEH's turn. Consequently David

---

33 The historian has given the anti-monarchical sources the narrative priority.

34 Note that although Saul is naturally strong, while he is a legitimate king he receives his strength from the Spirit of YAHWEH (1 Samuel 10:10; 11:6; cf 16:14 where the Spirit leaves him and he is afflicted with an evil spirit and 19:23 where the Spirit cripples Saul's innate physical power in order to protect David).

35 Note also the use of the word *māṣûq* in 1 Samuel 14:5 which is an echo of 2:8! The impregnable obstacle serves to remind Jonathan of the Creator.

is not tall (*gĕbōah*); he is the opposite: small (*qāṭān*), a mere shepherd (1 Samuel 16:11). Surely in this text there is an implied contrast not only to David's taller brothers who are not selected but to the tallest man in Israel who has recently been rejected.[36]

The next two stories essentially indicate who the real king of Israel is. While the tall Saul rules *de jure*, the small David rules *de facto*. The Spirit of God is now with David, and an evil spirit is with Saul, and David the musician shepherd is fetched to exorcise the evil spirit with his musical ability (1 Samuel 16:14–23). It is the shepherd boy David who maintains Saul's sanity and therefore his *de jure* kingship. Secondly, the next story of the encounter with Goliath exalts the small David while abasing the tall Saul and the gigantic Philistine even more. The story is one long sustained meditation on the outworking of Hannah's philosophy of history: the abasement of the mighty and the exaltation of the humble. When Goliath is described, the first thing noted is his height (1 Samuel 17:4). The daunting physical description which follows occupies four complete verses (4-7)![37] But the most important part of the description is the bombastic speech, which defies the army of Saul (1 Samuel 8-10). One can hear in the background the warning of Hannah: Do not multiply speech, saying 'High, High,' so that arrogance comes out of your mouth" (1 Samuel 2:3). When David is juxtaposed to Goliath in the narrative, the first physical quality noted is his smallness (*qāṭān* v. 14), which automatically disqualifies him from fighting in the army. He is a mere messenger boy whose main job is to stay home and look after the sheep. But David's main concern is for YAHWEH's reputation that Goliath has tarnished with his bombastic speech. This is the shepherd boy's main motivation for entering the challenge. Before the climactic encounter with Goliath the writer humorously indicates the truth that "not by strength is a man strong" (1 Samuel 2:9). David is described

---

36 This comparison is made explicit in the ensuing narrative as the anointed David is endowed with the Spirit while simultaneously the Spirit withdraws from Saul and he is reduced to a raving maniac (1 Samuel 16:13–23).

37 Note that this "descriptive overkill" has a didactic purpose: "All this is mentioned to show that the Philistine was protected as well as possible, so that the assailant would have no possible opening." Hans Wilhelm Hertzberg, *First and Second Samuel: A Commentary*, trans. J.S. Bowden (Philadelphia: Westminster Press, 1964), 149.

trying on Saul's armour (1 Samuel 17:38-39). The equipment does not fit—not only does it not fit David's physique but also YAHWEH's economy! In the actual encounter the speech of Goliath is the epitome of trust in self while David's is reliance on God. Goliath's subsequent collapse and death is not lost on the narrator who concisely comments, "David was stronger than the Philistine with a sling and stone. He smote the Philistine and killed him without holding a sword" (1 Samuel 17:50). Like Dagon his god before him, Goliath also comes tumbling down in another historical reversal.[38] And all the Philistine horses and all the Philistine men cannot put Goliath back together again.

David's elevation and Saul's abasement continue as the heir apparent to the throne, Jonathan, recognizes David's destiny and confers on him his royal robe and weapons (1 Samuel 18:1ff). David is the real heir, and the crown prince knows it. Israelite society joins David's retinue as the women praise his battle exploits much more than Saul's (1 Samuel 18:7). The next chapters deal with Saul's constantly frustrated efforts to murder David. David, outmanned and outarmed, always seems to evade Saul. The strong are abased and the weak gain new life. He and his hungry warriors are fed with bread taken from the sanctuary (1 Samuel 21). On another occasion, he is trapped, surrounded, and as good as dead, with Saul closing in for the kill. Then, news comes that the Philistines are ravaging the Israelite countryside (1 Samuel 23:27). As Saul retreats and David is spared, one cannot help but hear Hannah's words: YAHWEH kills and YAHWEH revives, YAHWEH brings down to the grave and YAHWEH brings up (1 Samuel 2:6) Further development of these themes is seen in the account of the rich and proud Nabal who refuses to feed David's hungry warriors; he is killed by YAHWEH while his wife feeds the hungry army to their full (1 Samuel 25). Finally David has to settle with the Philistines to escape Saul's wrath (1 Samuel 27).

The section comes to a conclusion when Saul and his sons collapse on the hills of Gilboa with the defeat of the Israelite army (1 Samuel 31). This defeat is presaged by Saul's attempt to gain information through occultic means from the dead Samuel

---

38 "Goliath is prostrated like Dagon before the ark (1 Samuel 5:1–5) and will likewise suffer decapitation (17:51)." Gordon, *I & II Samuel*, 158.

about the impending battle with the Philistines (1 Samuel 28).[39] To be driven to such lengths is the ultimate humiliation. When Samuel rises from the grave to announce a prophecy of doom, the reader is not to admire the necromancer's skill but to read this in the light of the song of Hannah: *Yahweh* brings down to the grave and *Yahweh* brings up.[40] When Saul hears the news he collapses the full length of his *height* (1 Samuel 28:20) for "there is no strength left in him" (1 Samuel 28:20 cf. 1 Samuel 2:9). Yahweh has brought up from the grave the dead Samuel to bring down the tall Saul, who is alive and well. This collapse of the mighty Saul and his lack of strength anticipates his collapse on the hills of Gilboa the next day, and this collapse resounds in David's lament when he hears the news. Repeatedly in this dirge we hear the words: How are the mighty fallen! .... How are the mighty fallen! How the war weapons have perished! These words function as drum beats which pound on the theme of Hannah's song (2 Samuel 1:19, 25).

These examples should suffice to show the importance of the piece of poetry with which the historiographer begins his work. Throughout the second book of Samuel the same motifs keep appearing. When David himself begins to act like a power hungry king and legitimate his kingship by bringing back the Ark while ignoring divine strictures, he is publicly humbled (2 Samuel 6:1–10).[41] When he repents, he throws aside his dignity to the wind and dances with elated abandon before the ark in a processional, humbling himself before an audience of servant girls, and thereby offending his proud and aloof wife, Michal, the daughter of the tall Saul. To her reproach David retorts that he would gladly endure humiliation in his own eyes and be held in honour by those whom his wife views as human riff-raff. He who has

39 On the entire encounter see my popular article, Stephen G. Dempster, "What's Up with the Witch of Endor?" June 15, 2015 (https://www.thegospelcoalition.org/article/whats-up-with-the-witch-of-endor; accessed May 9, 2016].

40 Note Gordon's perceptive comment: "The part played by the spirit-rapper in the interview is not so much as mentioned…moreover Samuel speaks as a prophet, not as a ghost, and the seance becomes the occasion for a sermon" (*I & II Samuel*, 196). In fact this necromancer seems shocked by the turn of events.

41 See Donald F. Murray, *Divine Prerogative and Royal Pretension: Pragmatics, Poetics and Polemics in a Narrative Sequence about David* (2 Samuel 5:17–7:29) (Sheffield: Sheffield Academic Press, 1998), 112–156.

made himself low is now being honoured.[42]

When David decides to honour God by building a house (temple) for him, God builds one for him (dynasty) in the Davidic covenant, and the proud Michal will not provide a descendant for the throne.[43] When David begins to act like any other king by committing adultery with Bathsheba and murdering her husband, he is humbled by YAHWEH in an extraordinary manner (2 Samuel 11–12).

The question of the identity of the successor to David on the Israelite throne can be seen through the same frame of these polarities. He will be the least likely candidate from a human perspective. When Amnon's lust leads to oppression of the weak, he is abased (2 Samuel 13). When the handsome and popular Absalom enlists the services of David's peerless counselor, Ahithopel, in a *coup d'état*, it is not long before the extraordinary brilliance of the sage is brought to nothing by a mercenary soldier working for David (2 Samuel 16-17). Ahithopel is next seen probably hanging from a tree which portends the fate of the charismatic Absalom who is literally "hoisted by his own petard" (2 Samuel 17:23, 18:8-15).[44] Sheba leads an unsuccessful revolution and has to flee to a distant city only to be decapitated (2 Samuel 20). One by one, possible successors to the kingship have been eliminated. Who will the next ruler be? Although the book of Samuel does not explicitly answer this question, it presents a clue in a few lines tucked away in the veritable mass of content. After the loss of the child of adultery due to God's judgement, the humbled and repentant David comforts his wife and loves her tenderly instead of lustfully:

> Then David comforted his wife Bathsheba, and he went to her and slept with her. She gave birth to a son, and they named him Solomon. The LORD loved him; and because the LORD loved him, he sent word through Nathan the prophet to name him Jedidiah (2 Samuel 12:24-25).

---

42 Note the echoes of 2 Samuel 6:22 and 1 Samuel 2:7–8.

43 Note the strong link between 2 Samuel 6:23 and the entirety of 2 Samuel 7.

44 In this example it is Absalom's physical appearance, in many ways the reason for his celebrity status in ancient Israel, which actually causes his demise. His stunning locks of hair hoist him in the air resulting in his capture and execution (2 Samuel 18:9).

This touching detail buried obscurely in the narrative focuses on comfort and tenderness and above all YAHWEH's love for the child. This is the only example of YAHWEH's naming of a child in Samuel, and he names it with a name which combines David's with His own. Yet who could have imagined this narrative seed sown from the union of David and Bathsheba would result in the future king of Israel? The high are abased and the low are exalted in YAHWEH's scheme of things!

The highly structured appendices with which the books conclude (2 Samuel 21-24) reinforce the same themes, but perhaps nowhere more than in the final chapter which provides a foundation story for the location of the future temple's construction. Here David experiences in his own person both the abasement of his pride and his own elevation by YAHWEH. His hubris in taking a census leads to divine judgement on the nation, but he chooses the judgement to come directly from the hand of YAHWEH and upon himself and his house, and to be directed away from the people who are like helpless sheep. David is no longer a king who "counts" numbers from the perspective of hubris and pride; now he "counts" only on divine mercy.[45]

Hannah's song and the historiography of Joshua to 2 Kings

As mentioned before, the Song of Hannah begins the books of Samuel, which is now in the biblical canon part of a narrative sequence which extends from Joshua to 2 Kings, the conquest to the exile. Although the other volumes have different emphases there are some similarities with the perspective used in Samuel. The conquest of Canaan in Joshua is not made by human power, but by a trust in divine power as the fallen fortress of Jericho attests (Joshua 6). In the book of Judges, the noted individuals are often weak figures who are used by YAHWEH to accomplish great feats. The left-handed Ehud accomplishes a great victory (Judges 3:12–30); Deborah and Jael triumph over Jabin and Sisera (Judges 4–5); Gideon wins a battle with three hundred men (Judges 6); Jepthah, the son of a prostitute, wins the day against the Ammonites (Judges 11). Samson, the strong one, would seem to contradict

---

45 Walter Brueggemann, *Power, Providence, and Personality: Biblical Insight Into Life and Ministry* (Louisville: Westminster John Knox Press, 1990), 102.

this pattern, but he is only strong because of the Spirit of YAHWEH (Judges 13–16). In the book of Kings, it is Solomon and not Adonijah who becomes the next king. In Solomon's humility he receives great wisdom, but in his idolatry and intermarriage, his reliance on strength and power, he causes the dissolution of the kingdom. The northern kingdom is destroyed for its autonomy and idolatry, and the southern kingdom is also destroyed about a century later for the same.[46]

The fact that the historian ends his work with Judah on the ash-heap in Babylonian exile may well signal hope for his exilic audience. From such places thrones of glory are fashioned. What confirms this is his conclusion of the history with the notice that the Davidic monarch is granted release from prison to sit at the Babylonian king's table (2 Kings 25:27–30). This is far more than just the last piece of historical evidence to which the historiographer had access.[47] This becomes nothing less than a lightning rod of hope. Humiliation is at an end and exaltation has begun.[48] Jehoiachin is now on the right side of history.

Hannah's song and the canon of Scripture

When the context of Hannah's Song is extended to include the entire biblical canon, it fits neatly into a key biblical theme of the reversal of fortune begun by YAHWEH in the Torah and continued throughout the rest of Scripture. The way things are after the Fall begins to be reversed to the way things will be in the economy of YAHWEH in a process that begins in Genesis 4 and ends in Revelation 21-22. The younger Abel is preferred over the older Cain in what becomes a standard configuration realized again and again in people like Isaac, Jacob, Joseph, Judah, Moses, Gideon and David. It comes to classic expression in the coming of the Servant of the Lord who is despised and rejected, yet chosen by

---

46 What stems the tide in the Southern Kingdom are a number of significant reforms, one of which leads to a victory over the Assyrians against stupendous odds. In language reminiscent of David's victory over the Philistine Goliath, Hezekiah successfully overcomes the Assyrian Goliath (2 Kings 18–19). Note the similar language: 1 Samuel 17:36, 46; 2 Kings 19:16, 19.

47 Cf. Noth, *Überlieferungsgeschichtliche Studien*, 108. See now the definitive study on this point: James R. Critchlow, *Looking Back for Jehoiachin: Yahweh's Cast-Out Signet*, Africanus Monographs (Eugene: Wipf & Stock Publishers, 2013).

48 Cf. Isaiah 40:1–3.

God.[49] This is the stone which the builders rejected becoming a precious cornerstone in the building of God's kingdom.[50] The coming birth of this stone comes not to the rich and the powerful but to a humble, peasant virgin, in the small town of the small David.[51] When she finds out that she is to be the mother of the Messiah, she, like Hannah, her ancient forbearer, also celebrates nothing less than a new world order in which the rich, the powerful and the prideful are swept away before the humble and the hungry in the coming of a new world order:

> He has performed mighty deeds with his arm;
> he has scattered those who are proud in their
> inmost thoughts.
> He has brought down rulers from their thrones
> but has lifted up the humble.
> He has filled the hungry with good things
> but has sent the rich away empty.[52]

The kingdom of this servant is where the first are last and the last first, where those who serve rule and those who rule serve.[53] Thus it is not a coincidence that the servant of all is lifted high on the cross.[54] Here is learned something of the essential character of God, that he the Great One humbles himself to take the form of a servant and die for others and from this great humiliation he is finally exalted to that place above every other name and before whom every knee will bow as history is brought to its dramatic conclusion.[55] And this same kenotic mind is urged upon Christians,[56] as these "other stones that the builders reject" are included in the grand temple project of heaven and earth.

---

49 Isaiah 52:13–53:12.
50 Psalm 118:22–23.
51 Luke 2:1–5.
52 Luke 1:51–53.
53 Mark 10:35–45.
54 John's dramatic irony is thus to the point: the Son of Man is exalted in the supreme place of humiliation (John 3:14; 8:28; 12:32, 34). For further reflection on this important theme see the fine treatment by Jeremy R. Treat, *The Crucified King: Atonement and Kingdom in Biblical and Systematic Theology* (Grand Rapids: Zondervan, 2014).
55 Philippians 2:5–11.
56 Philippians 2:4.

> Brothers and sisters, think of what you were when you were called. Not many of you were wise by human standards; not many were influential; not many were of noble birth. But God chose the foolish things of the world to shame the wise; God chose the weak things of the world to shame the strong. God chose the lowly things of this world and the despised things—and the things that are not—to nullify the things that are, so that no one may boast before him. It is because of him that you are in Christ Jesus, who has become for us wisdom from God—that is, our righteousness, holiness and redemption. Therefore, as it is written: "Let the one who boasts boast in the Lord" (1 Corinthians 1:26–31).

Historiography: ancient and modern

The ancient Israelite historian stressed both immanent and transcendent factors in his understanding of the historical process. To be sure the immanent factors that captured his attention in his sources were quite different from those that would seem to be significant in the vision of modern historiographers. It is not that the Israelite historian is naïve. He is aware of economic and political factors. For example during the time of the Philistine domination of the Israelites he notes that the Israelites were dependent on the Philistine blacksmiths for the sharpening of their tools and that only Jonathan and Saul had (iron) weapons (1 Samuel 13:19-22). Modern scholarship stresses that the Philistine monopoly on iron at the beginning of the Iron Age resulted in a technological advantage over the Israelites, which led to the domination of the latter.[57] The Israelite historiographer, however, is no proponent of technocracy, the view that the rise and fall of civilizations is dependent on technological discoveries. His brief note, which he adds to his source, actually emphasizes the opposite. The military victory of the Israelites which follows

---

[57] John Bright, *A History of Israel*, 4th ed. (Louisville: Westminster John Knox Press, 2000), 185. "The later Philistine monopoly on iron (1 Samuel 13:19–21), which apparently cut off Kenites from a supply of the metal and presumably from knowledge of how to work it, was a critical threat to the survival of Israel" [Norman Gottwald, *Tribes of Yahweh: A Sociology of the Religion of Liberated Israel, 1250–1050 BCE* (Sheffield: Bloomsbury T&T Clark, 1999), 321].

this note comes despite their technological inferiority.[58] It results from the courage and faith of Jonathan.

For the Israelite author(s), the immanent factors that shape history are people like Jonathan with courage and faith, people like desperate Hannah pleading for a child to end her misery, people like pure and innocent Samuel maintaining that condition while surrounded by corruption and injustice, people like David overlooked by everyone *except God*. One is reminded of Pascal's statement that it is in prayer that human beings are given the dignity of causality.[59] Negatively, the shaping of history is not found with the Penninahs of the world, the Elis, the Sauls, the Goliaths, the tall ones. This historiographer is against giants and on the side of the weak and lowly.[60] Giants seem imposing on a limited snapshot of the historical process before they "bite the dust." Neither can the shaping of history be reduced to economics or power-politics, and that which takes place in the back rooms of palaces and temples by the so called movers and shakers of society. According to the Israelite historian, a domestic squabble became the seedbed for the harvest of an historical crop of almost unparalleled proportions in the Old Testament.

But what makes these immanent factors—the humble and the lowly—important for the Israelite historian is the looming transcendent factor—YAHWEH. It is the nature of YAHWEH as a moral and personal God beyond history. This YAHWEH has a specific goal for the historical process and his prophetic word will achieve that goal, bringing down the strong, exalting the weak until his

58 "This parenthetical notice serves not only to portray the restrictions imposed by Philistine rule but also to emphasize the importance of divine help in the Israelite victory described below" (McCarter, *I Samuel*, 238).

59 Blaise Pascal, *Pensees*, ed. A. J. Krailsheimer (New York: Penguin Classics, 1995), VII. 513. "Why God has established prayer. 1. To communicate to his creatures the dignity of causality." For the historiographer it remains a fact that the great catalyst for historical change in the book of Samuel starts with a woman's broken-hearted cry for a child in the midst of a domestic squabble. The broken-hearted and frightened David, fleeing imminent death from his own son, utters a prayer that God frustrate the flawless counsel of Ahithopel (2 Samuel 15:31). Ahithopel and Absalom end up abased while David reclaims kingship. Out of David's deep desire to build a house for God because it is only appropriate, God builds a house for him (2 Samuel 7).

60 See the insightful study by Taylor Murray, *Against Giants* (Dallas: Redeeming Press, 2014).

king will bring about universal justice and shalom. To be on his side is to be on the right side of history.

In my judgement contemporary Christian historiographers are not that much different from the ancient Israelite historiographer, although they do lack the inspiration which guided the ancient Israelite in his own writing and in the selection and redaction of sources at his disposal. As David Bebbington has written:

> The Christian historian cannot write in the manner, say, of the writer of the Second book of Kings. He lacks the inspiration that gave the biblical historians their special insight. The first lesson the Christian historian must learn is humility.[61]

But nonetheless Christian historians do have the illumination of the Holy Spirit to which they need to be attuned. If prayer gives human beings the dignity of causality, then perhaps prayer gives human beings the dignity of perceiving causality in history. To understand YAHWEH's ways one must know YAHWEH's heart. There can be no substitute for dependence upon God of which prayer is a powerful indication.

Secondly, for the Christian historiographer, there can be no substitute for training one's mind to think in categories supplied by the Magnificats of the Old and New Testaments, the songs of Hannah and Mary. This is what the Israelite historiographer did with the song of Hannah. His assessment of his sources, his selection of sources, his redaction of the same, his own compositions and reflections betray a powerful *thinking through* of the history of the nation in the light of the categories of the Song. This is in no way mechanical. Who would have thought that the necromancer of Endor would be used by YAHWEH to bring Samuel up from the grave? This historiography is the result of a creative reflection on the sources through the lens of Hannah's Song. If this is true for Israelite historiography, how much more should it be for Christian historiography. Who would have thought that Jesus of Nazareth was the Christ of God? Who would have thought that crucifixion would lead to resurrection?

---

61 David Bebbington, *Patterns in History: A Christian Perspective on Historical Thought* (Vancouver: Regent College Publishing, 1990), 183.

How would a contemporary historiography look as a result of these principles. Hans Frank, one of the few penitent Nazis at Nuremburg, illustrates the relevance of this understanding:

> Many things have become clear to me in the loneliness of this cell. Hitler represented the spirit of evil on earth and recognized no greater power than his own. God watched this band of heathens puffed up with their puny power and then simply brushed them aside in scorn and amusement. I tell you the scornful laughter of God is more terrible than the vengeful lust of men! ... Here are the would-be rulers of Germany each in a cell like this, with four walls and a toilet, awaiting trial as ordinary criminals. Is this not proof of God's amusement with men's sacrilegious quest for power?[62]

On the ash-heap after being on top of the world, Frank is able to distinguish reality from illusion. The liberation of the extermination camp at Sobibor began with the cry of a baby.[63] More recently, who would have thought in the 1980s that the Iron Curtain would be torn down, that Corazon Aquino would acquire power after the murder of her husband in cold blood in the Philippines, that there would be a worldwide audience for Nelson Mandela's funeral in 2013 and that the person who was the poster boy for LiveStrong, Lance Armstrong, would collapse in humiliation.

What would Canadian historiography look like when viewed through Hannah's eyes. In the late 1990s the Canadian news magazine, *Maclean's*, gathered together historian Jack Granatstein and a coterie of pundits to determine 100 of the most important Canadians. While conceding that the list was somewhat arbitrary because "importance" can be defined differently,[64] *Maclean's* ranked Henry Morgentaler ahead of Tommy Douglas.[65] K.C Irving with his international financial influence ranked tenth while Jean Vanier with his international spiritual influence did

---

62 Robert E. Conot, *Justice at Nuremberg* (New York: Harper & Row, 1983), 81

63 Richard Rashke, *Escape from Sobibor* (Chicago: University of Illinois Press, 1995), 166–167.

64 Jack Granatstein, "100 Canadians," *Maclean's* (July 1, 1998): 14–15.

65 Interestingly, Tommy Douglas was voted the "Greatest Canadian" six years later in a poll held by the Canadian Broadcasting Corporation.

not even make the list. In fact "spirituality" does not even make the grade as a factor for assessing importance.[66] Father Brebeuf, the Jesuit missionary, was ranked not for his Christianity and martyrdom but for his keen anthropological observations.[67] A Christian historiography would certainly give a different assessment of what is meant by importance.

There might well be a different assessment of the significant events as well. The prosperity that Canada has enjoyed for many years has led to its boasting in its status as one of the most coveted places to live in for material standards of living. Has this led Canadians to be more thankful and humble? Could the periodic economic and political crises, over the last two decades, the near loss of Quebec in a referendum, the growing internal threats of terrorism be ominous signs on the horizon? And as far as the church goes, one wonders if western churches with their emphasis on prosperity and numbers, and their abandonment of historic orthodoxy, has led to their decline when compared to the rapid growth of the church in the two-thirds world among the poor and the destitute, for whom the Scriptures are alive and God is a living reality.[68]

Conclusion: Hannah, historiography and the right side of history

One of the translators of the Hebrew Bible into Greek for a Jewish audience in Egypt in the third century B.C. added the following words near the end of the song of Hannah from the prophet Jeremiah:[69]

---

66 It is interesting that the spirituality of the top Canadian on *Maclean's* list is at least acknowledged. Granatstein, "100 Canadians," 16.

67 Granatstein, "100 Canadians," 22.

68 Philip Jenkins, *The Next Christendom: The Coming of Global Christianity* (New York: Oxford University Press, 2011). My own limited personal experience in Africa and India affirms many of the insights of Jenkins' work.

69 McCarter remarks that this is "a remarkable intrusion" (*1 Samuel*, 70). There is some evidence that there may be a slightly different Hebrew Vorlage which the translator followed, but there are still significant additions (cf. 4QSama): Theodore J. Lewis, "The Textual History of the Song of Hannah: 1 Samuel 2:1–10," *Vetus Testamentum* 44 (1994): 43; Steven Weitzman, *Song and Story in Biblical Narrative: The History of a Literary Convention in Ancient Israel* (Bloomington: Indiana University Press, 1997), 122–123.

"Let not the wise man boast in his wisdom,
Let not the rich man boast in his wealth,
Let not the strong man boast in his strength,
But let him that boasts boast in this that he knows me:
That I do covenant love, justice and righteousness in the world.
For in these things I delight,"
says YAHWEH (Jeremiah 9:23–24).

While the Septuagint translator may be guilty of not following the letter of the law in faithfully rendering his original text here, surely he has captured its spirit. Jeremiah and Hannah sing a duet in perfect harmony teaching that in the end the power of riches, wisdom and might, the substance of so much historiography, are actually on the wrong side of history, while the weakness of covenant love, justice and righteousness teach about the One in whom to place faith.[70] For it is these qualities which ultimately determine who will be on the right side of history in YAHWEH's new world order.[71]

After finishing this essay, I could not help but note the relevance of the remarks by the late Archbishop of Chicago, Cardinal Francis George, to a group of struggling priests worried about the secularization of western culture:

> I expect to die in bed, my successor will die in prison and his successor will die a martyr in the public square. His successor will pick up the shards of a ruined society and slowly help rebuild civilization, as the church has done so often in human history.... The world divorced from the God who created and redeemed it inevitably comes to a bad end. It's on the wrong side of the only history that finally matters.[72]

---

70 This sentence rephrases the following words of Walter Brueggemann: "Jeremiah asserts that the power of riches, wisdom and might, the substance of the royal history, is a poor match against *hesed*, *mishpat* and *sedaqah* in determining what will finally shape history." See Walter Brueggemann, "The Epistemological Crisis of Israel's Two Histories (Jer. 9:22–23)," in *Israelite Wisdom: Theological and Literary Essays in Honor of Samuel Terrien*, ed. John G. Gammie (Missoula: Scholars Press, 1978), 97.

71 Cf. Psalms 113 and 136.

72 Tim Drake, "Cardinal George: The Myth and Reality of 'I'll Die in My Bed'," *National Catholic Register* (http://www.ncregister.com/blog/tim-drake/the-myth-and-the-reality-of-ill-die-in-my-bed/; accessed March 10, 2016).

2

People of God in the Hebrew Bible

BY TERRY GILES

Introduction

Commonly used, the "people of God" is a discriminatory term, designed to separate those on the inside from those on the outside; those who are people "of God" and those who are not. The line, separating the two groups, is a perceived relationship to God, defined by the insider. Sometimes, the label, "people of God," functions as a projection: people like me are the people of God and people not like me are obviously not the people of God.[1] In all cases, when self-pronounced, the claim seems more than just a little presumptuous. More, the term is often used to emphasize the

[1] Claimants make the pronouncement, either for themselves (People of God; pogpgh.org; accessed November 22, 2014) or for those they favour (Jerry Falwell, CNN interview, November 21, 1982).

supposed moral and ethical inferiority of those outside the group. The people of God enjoy a privileged position due to their enhanced intimacy with the deity. Unlike other constructed forms of self-identification referencing ethnic, political or religious affiliation, the identifier "people of God" involves a social orientation of ultimate importance. The "people of God" label claims divine legitimacy and with it a level of certainty that grants authority to perform what might otherwise be considered extreme acts. And when used as legitimacy for untoward actions directed at the outsider, the claim provides a sense of absolute moral certitude that can have disastrous results. It's a we/they designation that has had horrible consequences.[2]

Within theological reflection, the "people of God" designation is generally made without explanation, as if it were self-evident.[3] Used to signify some part of a Jewish or Christian community, the "people of God" label relies upon an appropriation of biblical texts, often without a literary or historical analysis in support of that appropriation. Even among those aware of sociological theory and the processes involved in self-definition among social movements,[4] there is, all too frequently, an uncritical acceptance that one or another of these movements has, in fact, a special relationship to deity.[5] The following seeks a partial remedy to

---

2 In the summer and fall of 2014 the ISIS group has been quite willing to demonstrate what appears, for those outside the group, to be an extreme authority in videotaped beheadings.

3 N.T. Wright's well received *The New Testament and the People of God* (Leicester: InterVarsity Press, 2004) provides an example. Although the Christian community is described in the title of the book as "people of God," only "people of the land," a reference to a portion of the ancient Israelite population, finds definition in the book. Lawrence Wills describes what he believes to be the extent of the identities created, "The Bible, directly or indirectly, defines identity for most of the people in the world." Lawrence Wills, *Not God's People: Insiders and Outsiders in the Biblical World* (New York: Rowman and Littlefield, 2008), 2.

4 See Fredrik Barth, *Ethnic Groups and Boundaries: The Social Organization of Culture Difference*, Scandinavian University Books (Bergen: Universitetsforlaget, 1969); Erving Goffman, *Frame Analysis: An Essay on the Organization of Experience* (New York: Harper Colophon, 1974), 21; David Snow and Robert Benford, "Ideology, Frame Resonance and Participant Mobilization," *International Social Movement Research* (1988)1:197–200; Robert Benford and David Snow, "Framing Processes and Social Movements: An Overview and Assessment," *Annual Review of Sociology* 26 (2000): 614.

5 Howard Clark Kee, *Who Are the People of God? Early Christian Models of Community* (New Haven: Yale University Press, 1995), 5–16.

this lack of analysis by surveying the use of the "people of God" label and offering observations about the nature of that use in the Hebrew Bible.

The people of God in the Hebrew Bible

The "people of God" claim is reciprocated and codified in one of the few great creedal statements of the Hebrew Bible:

> Hear, O Israel: the LORD our God is one LORD (Deuteronomy 6:4).

The claim of exclusivity ("our God") presupposes that other people groups make analogous claims referencing other deities. As stated in Deuteronomy 6, the claim is more a disclosure about group identity then about the nature of the LORD. When the social characteristics of the insider group change, so too does the definition of the people of God.[6] This fluidity of referent is observable throughout the Hebrew Bible. For the very ethnically aware Ezra, Nehemiah and those supporting their plan of social reconstruction, the people of God were those who could prove their lineage and separate themselves from the people of the land (Ezra 10:11). Alternately, the writer of Isaiah 19 submits ethnicity to other, perhaps, in his estimation, more important, characteristics determinative of the people of God when he confidently states that:

> In that day Israel will be the third with Egypt and Assyria and the LORD of hosts will declare, "Blessed be Egypt my people, and Assyria the work of my hands, and Israel my heritage" (Isaiah 19:24–25).

---

6 And so "the people of God" can be a select religious group, political or national unit given heightened status by connection to the Divine. Perhaps illustrated by Christopher J. H. Wright's recent *Old Testament Ethics for the People of God* in which the "people of God" refers first to Israel and then the Christian church. Christopher J.H. Wright, *Old Testament Ethics for the People of God* (Leicester: InterVarsity Press, 2004). The insider/outsider dichotomy has even been used to warn of global economic depression. David Wilkerson, *God's Plan To Protect His People in the Coming Depression* (New York: Wilkerson Trust Publications, 1998).

It isn't just the passage of time that causes fluidity in the description of a people of God. Equally, Abraham, Abimelech of Gerar (Genesis 20) and Hagar (Genesis 16 and 21) can have unmediated communication with God, apparently without raising any question about insider or outsider status among either the characters of the story or the reading audience.

This variableness means that the appellation "people of God" to a social group is not a self-evident objective fact, universally recognized, but requires immersion into a set of assumptions and cognitive conventions that are shared between communicants.[7] That is, the "people of God" designation is the kind of label that is only evident and only makes sense to insiders. As the assumptions and conventions of the group change (the cognitive givens that make up the frame of reference for insiders), so too, changes the identity of the people of God. Within the Hebrew Bible, social groups labeled the "people of God" change. The characteristics that determine insiders and outsiders are not constant but shifting, constructed designations that require group consensus before they assume the appearance of established fact.[8]

The "people of God" designation, and its semantic equivalents (my people, your people), does not appear uniformly across the Hebrew Bible. In fact, the label doesn't appear as often as one might expect.[9] In narrative, the "people of God" label tends to cluster around the Exodus from Egypt (particularly the plague narratives) and Solomon's temple dedication (both in 1 Kings 8

---

7 Benedict Anderson, *Imagined Communities: Reflections on the Origin and Spread of Nationalism* (London: Verso, 1991), 7.

8 See Jonathan Smith, "What a Difference a Difference Makes," in *To See Ourselves as Others See Us: Christians, Jews, "Others" In Late Antiquity,* ed. Jacob Neusner and Ernst Frerichs (Chico: Scholars Press, 1985), 16. John Goldingay, *Theological Diversity and the Authority of the Old Testament* (Grand Rapids: Eerdmans, 1987), 59, recognizes the changing nature of the social group to which the label is given, but is much more generous, applying it more freely than does the biblical literature, even though he recognizes the label is first used only in Exodus 3 (Goldingay, *Theological Diversity*, 64). Similarly, H. J. Kraus applies the label indiscriminately, even when not so used by the biblical writers. H. J. Kraus, *The People of God in the Old Testament* (London: Lutterworth Press, 1958). Lawrence Wills is more on track when he writes, "the construction of the Other is much more complicated.... These complications reveal ambiguities of identity and vast differences among biblical texts that are often assumed to speak with one voice" (Wills, *Not God's People*, 1).

9 Despite Goldingay's claim that the people of God is, "one of the most prominent themes in the Bible" (Goldingay, *Theological Diversity*, 59).

and 2 Chronicles 6 and 7).[10] The label is also found in select Psalms and in the prophets (Isaiah, Jeremiah, Ezekiel and scattered throughout the Twelve).

Exodus narrative

The first appearance of the label "people of God"[11] or its variants is in Exodus 3:7 and 10. There is no doubt that the referent is the earlier mentioned people of Israel (Exodus 2:23, 25) and so the label is applied to a pre-existing social group defined ethnically and perhaps culturally—but certainly not religiously.[12] In the conversation between God and Moses, only God refers to the Israelites as people of God, and not consistently. The people of God need to be introduced to the LORD by Moses, and convinced by Moses that the LORD, the "God of the fathers," has come to honour his covenant and end the oppression of his people. Oddly, despite the objections raised by Moses in his conversation with the LORD in Exodus 3, when he and Aaron actually speak to the leaders of the people of Israel, no claim of divine ownership is made (Exodus 4:29–31). It isn't until Moses confronts the Pharaoh (Exodus 5, throughout the plague narrative, and spoken to the leaders of Israel in Exodus 6:7) that the repeated directive "let my people go" functions to highlight, not the special status of this ethnic social group, but the superiority of the LORD while contending with Pharaoh. After having fled Egypt and arriving at Mt. Sinai, the status of the people of Israel as the people of God is described as provisional, conditioned

10 Interestingly, the label is not used in the patriarchal stories, although Christopher Wright argues that, "In the patriarchal context the people of God is primarily a community called out of the sociopolitical environment and given a new identity and future by the promise of God." Wright, *Old Testament Ethics for the People of God*, 220. Wright's assessment illustrates the way in which the changing cognitive context of the speaker (in this instance Christopher Wright), can have a fluid effect on the nature of the group, absorbing into the group, (the "people of God") those previously not so designated (the patriarchs). A caution to this appropriation can be found in Arnold Ehrhasdt, "A Biblical View of the People of God," *American Ecclesiastical Review* 159 (1968): 127–128.

11 There are variants in the title given to deity (LORD, LORD of Hosts, God of Heaven, God Almighty, God of Israel) when appearing in the "people of God" label. An examination of the significance those variations may have on the identity of the social group is not included in this paper.

12 Anthony Smith offers a description of the function of group narrative in creating identity. Anthony Smith, *The Ethnic Origins of Nations* (Oxford: Blackwell, 1986), 192.

upon obeying the voice of the LORD and keeping covenant with him (Exodus 19:5–6).[13] When that covenant is broken (Exodus 32:7–14), through Aaron's leadership in worship of the golden calf, the LORD calls Israel "stiff-necked" and "this people" (Exodus 32:9–10) leaving it up to Moses and the narrator to employ the "your people" or "his people" identifier (Exodus 32:11,12,14)[14] in an effort to dissuade the Divine anger.[15] Moses acknowledges that the people of God possess no special quality deserving of the label, but it is only the presence of the LORD that makes a difference.

> Is it not in thy going with us, so that we are distinct, I and thy people, from all other people that are upon the face of the earth? (Exodus 33:16)

As a result of Moses' pleading, the LORD relents and promises his continuing presence and covenant with *your* [Moses'] people (Exodus 34:10).

Twice the "people of the LORD" designation appears in Numbers (Numbers 11:29; 16:41). In Numbers 11:29, Moses deflects a potential threat to his leadership by expressing a wish that the LORD's presence would be immediate and that all Israel (people of the LORD) would be prophets. In Numbers 16:41, the term "people of the LORD" is used in an accusation directed toward Moses. Korah and a substantial number of Israel's leadership object to the authority that Moses has gathered to himself, claiming that:

---

13 So also in the covenant formula, Leviticus 26:12. See Brevard Childs, *Biblical Theology of the Old and New Testaments* (Minneapolis: Fortress Press, 1992), 138. Childs contends that the people of the LORD tradition is closely allied to the covenant at Sinai. In truth, the people of the LORD tradition begins development in the plague narrative of Exodus (and also in the Psalm 78 and Psalm 105 rendition of the plague narrative). Childs goes too far when he states that "the term [people of God] is thus not an ideal or theological construct but refers primarily to an empirical people, indeed to a nation." (Childs, *Biblical Theology of the Old and New Testaments,* 138). It is more accurate to say that the term is an ideological construct selectively applied to an empirical people. The "people of God" label is used as a motivator for obeying the law or keeping covenant: Deuteronomy 14:2, 21; 21:8; 26:15, 18, 19; 27:9; 28:9; 29:13. Once, the "people of God" label is found in the law codes (Leviticus 26:12) to distinguish between lending practices to the poor of Israel and those not of "my people."

14 Paraphrased and applied to a different event in Deuteronomy 9:26, 29.

15 See also Deuteronomy 9:12.

> You have gone too far! For all the congregation are holy, every one of them, and the LORD is among them (Numbers 16:3).

In the ensuing confrontation, Korah and a number of his fellows are killed, swallowed by the earth. The next day, the congregation accuses Moses and Aaron, saying:

> You have killed the people of the LORD (Numbers 16:41).

The LORD takes the side of Moses and threatens to "consume them in a moment" (Numbers 16:45). Once again, Moses intervenes, and total annihilation is averted even though over 14,000 meet their doom. The lesson is clear, the "people of Israel" and the "people of the LORD" may overlap but are not the same.

Deuteronomy

In the book of Deuteronomy and the literature in the Deuteronomic vein, the designation "people of God" takes a different turn. Here, "people of God" and "people of Israel" are much more likely, but not always,[16] to be interchangeable.[17] The "people of

---

16 In 2 Kings 11:17 and 2 Chronicles 23:16, Jehoiada leads the people of Israel in a covenant renewing their identity as "the LORD's people."

17 See Judges 5:11. Terry Giles and William Doan, *Twice Used Songs: Performance Criticism of the Songs of Ancient Israel* (Peabody: Hendrickson, 2009), 75–83. Also, Judges 20:2; 1 Samuel 9:16, 17; 12:22; 2 Samuel 1:12; 3:18; 7:10–11, 23–24. The interchangeableness of "people of God" and "people of Israel" can also be seen in corresponding passages: 1 Chronicles 17:6, 7, 9, 10, 21, 22; Ruth 1:6; 1 Kings 3:8, 9 (2 Chronicles 1:10, 11); 6:13; 16:2; 2 Kings 20:5. Similarly, 1 Chronicles 11:2; 23:25; 2 Chronicles 31:8, 10; 35:3; 36:16. In 2 Samuel 5:2 the elders of Israel's tribes approach David with an offer of the monarchy. In their presentation, they quote the LORD's pronouncement that David "shall be shepherd of my people Israel" and so cast David in a unique and special relationship to the LORD. Bringing to mind the pleas of Moses in Exodus 32 and 33, David pleads for Divine mercy on "thy people" in 1 Chronicles 21:17. 2 Chronicles 36:23 deserves special notice. Cyrus, an outsider, claims the LORD's favour and command to build a temple in Jerusalem. In so doing, he commissions the return to Jerusalem of "his people" with the wish that "the LORD his God be with him." Here, the relationship between God and people is affirmed without a necessary elevated status given to the people. Cyrus remains an outsider even though using the "people of God" motif (2 Chronicles 36:23). That Cyrus did not imply a unique quality to the Israelites seems clear by his devotion to Marduk and similar rebuilding efforts permitted to other people groups and cults. James Pritchard, *Ancient Near Eastern Texts Relating to the Old Testament* (Princeton: Princeton University Press, 1969), 315–316.

God" label appears infrequently in Deuteronomy, outside the Deuteronomic Code. Twice, in the sermonic introduction to the book (Deuteronomy 4:20; 7:6),[18] the designation is motivational support for exclusive loyalty to the LORD. The "people of God" motif appears three more times in the Song of Moses (Deuteronomy 32: 9, 36, 43),[19] also used to encourage loyalty to the LORD.[20] The song, composed by the LORD, makes God's presence immediate and offers hope for restoration despite the assumed acts of infidelity committed by the people of the LORD. As a group, the song describes the people of the LORD bounded by ethnicity and common origin narrative but transcending religious affiliation and moral character.

Solomon's temple designation

In Deuteronomic literature, the "people of God" designation is frequently used to comment on Israel's uniqueness or special status.[21] Solomon's temple dedication is the narrative representing the second major cluster of "people of God" usage, both in 1 Kings 8 and 2 Chronicles 6 and 7. Although significant differences exist between the Kings and Chronicles account, the function of the "people of God" designation is the same. The label given to the people of Israel, under the monarchy of David and Solomon, religiously centred on the temple in Jerusalem.[22] Like the Song of Moses, in Deuteronomy 32, no assumption is made of continued religious fidelity or moral behaviour as essential characteristics of the group. Rather, ethnicity (with the "foreigner" as the outsider) or nationality (with "enemy" as the outsider), seem to be the constants by which "people of God" is defined.

---

18 The idea of a special people also appears in Deuteronomy 10:15.

19 A near parallel to verse 9 is found in Isaiah 19:24 with a very different referent in mind.

20 See the introduction to the Song in Deuteronomy 31:19–22. Giles and Doan, *Twice Used Songs*, 108–109.

21 2 Samuel 7:23.

22 That other members of Israel understand the "people of God" label in very different terms is clear. Robert Anderson and Terry Giles, *Tradition Kept: The Literature of the Samaritans* (Peabody: Hendrickson, 2005), 161.

Psalms

Given that the preponderance of usage for the term "people of God" in Samuel, Kings and Chronicles appears in divine speech, prayers or liturgical settings, we might expect to find the term frequently appearing in the Psalms—and we would be wrong. Of the 150 psalms appearing in the Hebrew Bible, only 27 contain a reference to the "people of God" or its semantic equivalent.[23] In all but one instance, the "people of God" term, or its equivalent, refers to Israel, identifiable by having territory, enemies, a political form,[24] and a corporate narrative that emphasizes the exodus from Egypt, consequent wilderness wandering and conquest of Canaan,[25] illustrating God's choice of his people (Psalms 33, 111). The "people of God" label is used in prayers for blessing (Psalms 3, 14, 28, 79), calls for divine deliverance (Psalms 53, 80), lament for tragedy (Ps. 60), complaints against evildoers (Psalms 83, 94), warning of divine judgement (Psalms 50, 78) and hope for restoration and divine forgiveness (Psalms 85, 106). There is an implicit recognition that religious infidelity is a very real possibility, if not a present reality (Psalms 50, 106), among the people of God.

The single occurrence of the "people of God" label, not referring to Israel, likens all nations to the "people of the God of Abraham" (Psalm 47:9), asserting that God is king over all nations (Psalm 47:8). Although it is not unique in its description of God's universal claim over all humanity (Psalm 117), Psalm 47 does discriminate between the "pride of Jacob whom he loves" (Psalm 47:4) while at the same time acknowledging that:

> God reigns over the nations;
> God sits on his holy throne.
> The princes of the peoples gather as the people of the God of Abraham (Psalm 47:8–9).

---

23 Spread evenly among the five books: Psalms 3, 14, 28, 33, 47, 50, 53, 60, 68, 72, 77, 78, 79, 80, 83, 85, 94, 95, 100, 105, 106, 111, 125, 135, 136, 148, 149.

24 The people of God are subjects of a Davidic king (Psalm 72:2) and are able to enter gates and courts, presumably of the temple in Jerusalem (Psalm 100:4).

25 The exodus narrative, wandering and conquest are prominent in Psalms 77, 78, 95, 105, 106, 135, 136.

Prophets

a) Isaiah

In Isaiah, the people of God are overwhelmingly equated with Israel, defined ethnically and politically[26] or a remnant of Israel sometimes described as house of Jacob or known by the predominant city—Jerusalem or Zion. As equated with Israel, the people of God are able to go into exile, to be restored from exile, to be distinguished among the nations, to host a foreigner, to have rulers and to claim a common narrative of God's redemptive acts in the Exodus from Egypt.[27]

Throughout Isaiah, there is a ready acknowledgement of moral failings and religious infidelity that do not negate the people of God status, even though the people are sent into exile and dispersed among nations. Yet, there are other instances where moral behaviour[28] and not ethnicity or nationality provides the defining quality for the people of God (Isaiah 65:9) and where the leaders of the nation, because of their oppression of the general population or poor among the population, seem to stand in opposition to the people of God (Isaiah 3:12, 15; 10:2).

Isaiah recognizes that Assyria and Egypt[29] as well as a number of other nations,[30] have been oppressors of the people of God. Nevertheless, in a surprising turn, these consummate outsiders, Egypt and Assyria in particular, are destined to become insiders and share in Israel's favoured status.

> In that day Israel will be the third with Egypt and Assyria, a blessing in the midst of the earth, whom the LORD of hosts has blessed, saying, "Blessed be Egypt my people, and Assyria the work of my hands, and Israel my heritage" (Isaiah 19:24–25).

---

26 Less frequently, Israel is described in explicitly religious terms (Isaiah 56:3–8; 63:18).

27 Isaiah 1:3; 3:12, 15; 5:13, 25; 10:2, 24; 11:11, 16; 14:32; 30:26; 32:13, 18; 40:1; 43:20, 21; 47:6; 49:13; 51:4, 16, 22; 52:4, 5, 6, 9: 53:8; 56:3; 57:14; 58:1; 60:21; 63:8, 11, 14, 18; 64:9; 65:10, 19, 22.

28 Ernest Nicholson, *God and His People: Covenant and Theology in the Old Testament* (Oxford: Clarendon Press, 1986), argues that this emphasis on morality in the eighth century prophets marked a significant transition in the understanding of the LORD and the character of "his people" (Nicholson, *God and His People*, 208–209).

29 Isaiah 11:16; 47:6; 52:4.

30 Isaiah 11:11.

Here, in chapter 19 and in chapter 56, Isaiah looks to the future and breaks the insider/outsider boundaries of the people of God. Ethnicity and religious identity will give way to "keeping justice" and "doing righteousness" as the notable characteristics of the people of God (Isaiah 56:1). The foreigner (the outsider) who keeps justice, does righteousness, keeps the Sabbath and keeps his hands from doing evil need never say, "The LORD will surely separate me from his people" (Isaiah 56:3) for the LORD says of these people:

> these I will bring to my holy mountain, and make them joyful in my house of prayer; their burnt offering and their sacrifices will be accepted on my altar; for my house shall be called a house of prayer for all peoples (Isaiah 56:7).

In this future vision, religious ritual and affiliation alone are not enough to define the people of God.

> Is not this the fast that I choose:
> to loose the bonds of wickedness,
> to undo the thongs of the yoke,
> to let the oppressed go free,
> and to break every yoke?
> Is it not to share your bread with the hungry,
> and bring the homeless poor into your house;
> when you see the naked, to cover him,
> and not to hide yourself from your own flesh?
> Then shall your light break forth like the dawn,
> and your healing shall spring up speedily;
> your righteousness shall go before you,
> the glory of the LORD shall be your rear guard.
> Then you shall call, and the LORD will answer;
> you shall cry, and he will say, "Here I am" (Isaiah 58:6–9).

b) Jeremiah

Like Isaiah, Jeremiah's use of the "people of God" label is almost exclusively to refer to Israel or a portion of Israel, identifiable ethnically or nationally. Divine complaints describe the religious infidelity of "my people,"[31] followed by predictions of God's judgement[32] and restoration[33] of Israel, Israel and Judah (Jeremiah 30:3) and the descendants of Jacob (Jeremiah 33:26). The Exodus from Egypt narrative is woven into the accusations and complaints as a way of describing the people of God.[34] Like Isaiah, Jeremiah singles out the religious leaders (prophets and priests) of the people of God for special condemnation.[35]

On several occasions, and reminiscent of usage in Deuteronomy,[36] identity as the people of God is connected to Israel's fidelity to God's command:

> But this is the command I gave them, "Obey my voice, and I will be your God and you shall be my people" (Jeremiah 7:23).[37]

Although, for Jeremiah, religious infidelity does not negate the identity as people of God (Jeremiah 7:12), the Jeremiah 7:21–34 passage uses the "people of God" designation in the context of religious fidelity. When that fidelity is abandoned, Israel becomes "this nation" (Jeremiah 7:28) or "the sons of Judah" (Jeremiah 7:30) occupying Judah and Jerusalem.

c) *Ezekiel*

Ezekiel uses the term "people of God" or a semantic equivalent exclusively for the nation of Israel, identifiable by opposing nations,[38] occupying a defined territory[39] and recipients of a future covenant of peace.[40] The people of God have prophets,[41]

---

31 Jeremiah 2:11; 5:26; 8:7, 19; 12:14 (includes a conditional promise of blessing on Israel's neighbours—but those neighbours remain outside the people of God); 13:11; 15:7; 18:15.

32 Jeremiah 4:11; 7:12; 9:1, 2, 7; 12:14.

33 Jeremiah 31:7; 32:38; 50:4–6.

34 Jeremiah 11:4; 13:11; 18:15; 32:21.

35 Jeremiah 5:31; 6:14; 8:11; 23:2, 13, 22, 27, 32.

36 Deuteronomy 26:18; 27:9–10; 28:9; 29:13 and similar to Deuteronomy 4:20.

37 See also Jeremiah 11:4; 30:22, 31:33; 32:38.

38 Ezekiel 25:14; 36:20; 38:14, 16.

39 Ezekiel 36:8, 12; 38:16.

40 Ezekiel 34:30.

41 Ezekiel 13:9, 10, 18, 19, 21, 23; 14:9, 11.

priests,[42] and princes[43] who sometimes act despicably and stand in danger of divine judgement. Ezekiel offers a vision of a future restoration that includes moral behaviour as a defining characteristic of the people of God (Ezekiel 11:20; 36:27–28; 37:23, 27) in a manner similar to Jeremiah 7:23. Although not always explicit, this moral expectation is presupposed in all of the accusations, laments, and divine complaints registered against the people of God in Ezekiel.

d) The Twelve

Many of the same themes and usages for the "people of God" label found in Isaiah, Jeremiah and Ezekiel are also found in the Book of the Twelve. The "people of God" motif is used to refer to Israel, or a portion of Israel (be it Judah, Jerusalem or a future remnant), warning of impending judgement,[44] expressing a lament or prayer for divine mercy[45] or a hope for future restoration.[46] The people of God are recognizable by surrounding nations who risk divine judgement for maltreatment of Israel.[47] The national and religious leaders of the people of God are condemned for their abusive and often deceptive leadership.[48] And the Exodus narrative is employed to describe the past beneficence of the LORD directed toward his people.[49]

Perhaps the most recognizable use of the "people of God" label is in Hosea and the symbolic names given to the prophet's son (Hosea 1:9–10). The baby is named "Not my people" symbolizing the divine separation from a group: the house of Jehu, the kingdom of Israel, house of Israel, house of Judah and people of Israel (expressed also in 11:7). That condition is not permanent, however, as a future reunion between God and people is envisioned (Hosea 2:23; 6:11).

One occurrence of the label in Zechariah deserves special notice.

---

42 Ezekiel 44:23.

43 Ezekiel 45:8–9; 46:18.

44 Amos 7:8, 15; 8:2; 9:10; Micah 6:2–3.

45 Joel 2:17; Micah 1:9; 7:14.

46 Joel 2:18, 19, 26, 27; Amos 9:14; Zechariah 8:7–8; 13:9.

47 Joel 3:2; Obadiah 13; Zephaniah 2:8–9.

48 Hosea 4:6, 8, 12; Micah 2:4, 8, 9; 3:3, 5.

49 Micah 6:5; Habakkuk 3:13.

> And many nations shall join themselves to the LORD in that day, and shall be my people; and I will dwell in the midst of you, and you shall know that the LORD of hosts has sent me to you. And the LORD will inherit Judah as his portion in the holy land, and will again choose Jerusalem (Zechariah 2:11–12).

Along with similar usages in Isaiah 19 and Psalm 47, the expansiveness of the people of God matches the expansiveness of the LORD. As the perception of God changes from a nationalistic and territorial deity to a universal Lord of all creation, so too, expand the potential boundaries for the people of God.

Concluding observations

The Hebrew Bible is a collection of documents written by and for a community, connected in various ways over the span of hundreds of years.[50] At times, that community is bound and known to outsiders by ethnicity, nationality, occupation of a particular territory, religious cultus or common narrative. Occasionally, the community or parts of the community are called "people of God." Overwhelmingly, the "people of God" is a term for insiders describing insiders, emphasizing responsibilities or aspects of the group that come into greater relief when defined in relationship to the Deity. Unlike ethnicity, nationality, religious affiliation—characteristics that can be recognized by insiders and outsiders alike—the "people of God" label requires a heightened degree of shared cognitive framing. Even when coterminous with a social entity (ie. national Israel) it is a concept not equally recognized by insiders and outsiders. That is, the surrounding nations could recognize Israel as a social entity, and perhaps even as the people of the LORD (understanding the LORD as a national or territorial deity) but would not recognize them as the people of God in the sense of a unique relationship to a monotheistic deity who exerts claim and ownership over all people and territories.

---

50 And so it may not be coincidental that the "people of God" label does not occur in the Hebrew Wisdom literature, a collection more international in authorship and scope even though moral character and divine approval and blessing are frequent themes.

The "people of God" label is frequently applied to a previously identifiable social group, marking that group for special, even divinely sanctioned, privilege or responsibility. In the biblical text, the "people of God" label becomes more prominent during periods of social transition.[51] The national origin tradition in the Exodus, the elevation of Jerusalem and the Jerusalem cult, the dissolution of national identity, particularly at the hand of the Babylonians, and a projected restoration of national identity, all serve as occasions for biblical writers to apply the label. The term bridges and connects previously disparate social groups, or portions of those groups, even when separated by time or space, by subordinating (but not erasing) previously recognized group identifiers (ethnicity, nationality, religious affiliation), in favour of a more outstanding identity.[52] Use of the label allows present group members to reach into the past or the future to create social continuity and appropriate desired group characteristics. The "people of God" label allows a sense of group continuity when more observable boundaries fail. This observation makes the Isaiah 19 and Zachariah 2 passages all the more remarkable and surprising.

In the biblical literature, the "people of God" designation is conditioned by the nature of the possessive deity. As the perception of God expanded beyond that of a nationalistic or territorial deity, so also, expanded the scope of God's people. In the plague narratives, the God of Israel is distinguished from the gods of Egypt (Exodus 12:12; Numbers 33:4)—and so too, the LORD's people are segregated from the Egyptians. In the temple dedication accounts, most usages in the sixth-century prophets, and the majority of the psalms, the LORD's influence is centred on

---

51 Contr., Goldingay, who claims, "God's people is a clearly defined social entity" (Goldingay, *Theological Diversity*, 60). It is more accurate to say that the "people of God" designation is a theological construct frequently, but not always, applied to a defined social entity. Paul Hanson comes close to this position when he asserts "a triadic notion of community" characterized by righteousness, compassion and worship. Paul Hanson, *The People Called: The Growth of Community in the Bible* (San Francisco: Harper and Row, 1986), 70–74.

52 E. J. Schnabel, also equates Israel with the "people of God" designating the outsider as "non-Israelite" or "foreigner," and noting only two inclusive exceptions (Isaiah 42:1, 6–7; 49:6; 51:4–5 and 66:18–21). "Israel, the People of God, and the Nations," *Journal of the Evangelical Theological Society* 45 (2002): 39–41.

Israel but extends to the surrounding nations, bringing them into the orb of "God's people," conditioned by their treatment of Israel. Occasionally, a vision of a monotheistic LORD of the universe finds expression in the Hebrew Bible. When this happens, the people of God encompass all nations. Wherever God is present, in a manner anticipated by Moses (Exodus 33:16), there are his people.

In contemporary usage, the "people of God" label is, all too often, a way to absolutize discrimination: calling upon God to confirm our choices by damming the outsider. In the Hebrew Bible, usage of the label begins as a way of demarcating insiders from outsiders, a way to separate between people. The "people of God" label moves, however, from particular to general, enveloping more and more in its sweep. The label ends as a way to unify, to express solidarity of all people, while still recognizing less important national, ethnic and religious identifications. The people of God admit, often imperfectly, an ultimate devotion to the God of all creation—a devotion that binds in solidarity all humanity and favours the poor and weak.

The Hebrew Bible is clear. The people of God are dependent upon the presence of God. More than a label of privilege, the designation "people of God" in the Hebrew Bible is a call to accountability—a call to be and do better.

3

The church as community: Foundational biblical theological insights and some implications

BY BYRON WHEATON

Recently, I was reading a book which discussed some research concerning the reasons young people leave the church. As I was reflecting on the data being presented, it struck me that our author never really said what "the church" was that these young people were leaving. Was it "organized religion" that he was referring to as the church? Or was it some buildings on the corner of XY street? Or was it some programming? What is "the church?" It is necessary that if we are going to involve ourselves in discussion about the church we should make some attempt to understand what we mean by it. I want to propose that the biblical notion of the "church" is that of *a community of people, bound to God and to one another by their faith in Christ Jesus, and giving expression to that faith by their obedience to their Lord.* It is the formation of this community of people that is the object of redemptive history. Does Scripture support this?

For many, knowing what Scripture teaches about the church would mean immediately consulting the New Testament, examining the letter to the Ephesians or perhaps Corinthians. Of course those would be helpful texts. But to enter on the discussion at that point would be to short-circuit it. I want to suggest that we should begin our thinking into the nature of the church in the Old Testament, because the church emerges in the context of redemptive history. It is part of the unfolding of God's purposes over time, and like most of what is realized in the plan of God, it is anticipated in the earlier story.

The faith community in the Old Testament story

Perhaps you might object that the Old Testament story appears to be largely about the nation of Israel. Are we then to assume that the church and Israel are equivalent? Not at all! If we read the text closely, we will discover that the story is not so much about Israel the nation, as it is first about "the family" of Abraham. When God first came to Abraham in Genesis 12 and summoned him to leave his country, his kindred and his father's house, he promised to make him a great nation. At first glance this would seem to point toward a political entity. Subsequently in Genesis 17, Abraham is told that he will be the father of many nations. How are we to understand this? Will Abraham father a number of different political entities? That of course could be possible, and indeed it was the case that Abraham was the father of both Isaac and Ishmael who both developed into nations. But the expression "many nations" seems to point more to a multitude of people than it does to particular political entities.[1]

Other parallel terms like "descendants" and "seed" or "offspring" are used to speak of those in Abraham's community, clarifying the idea intended. This language points beyond a particular ethnic and political entity to a community that bears

---

[1] John H. Sailhammer, "Genesis" in *The Expositor's Bible Commentary,* vol. 2, ed. Frank E. Gabelein (Grand Rapids: Zondervan, 1990), 2:138, writes, "God's part of the covenant consists of two promises: abundant descendants (verses 4–6) and eternal faithfulness (verses 7–8). ...The promise of abundant descendants is memorialized in the change of Abram's name to 'Abraham.'"

Abraham's likeness. Bruce Waltke writes with regard to the notion of "seed": "The kind of humans in view extends beyond racial distinction and physical features into character, behavior and most important, spiritual proclivity."[2] If this is the case, then the focus of the narrative is not so much a story about an ethnic and political nation "Israel," but about a people who share the spiritually distinctive qualities of their father.

This is supported by the fact that Abraham was a new initiative of God to redeem his people in the progress of redemption.[3] In counterpoint to the acts of defiance and hubris described in Genesis 11 that bring on God's judgement, God intervened to take out of that community of rebellion one whom he would transform into a source of blessing to the nations. That one, unlike Adam who rebelled, had to be a person of faith. So, instead of God finding a person in whom faith is already operative, he formed a person of faith from one who was an idol worshipper by calling him and shaping him through the experiences of life to which he subjected him. The stories of Abraham show the emergence of this one who can trust God both for the land his offspring will occupy and for the offspring who will occupy it. His descendants must be like him in this main characteristic.[4]

Israel formalized as a people at Sinai

Abraham's descendants went to Egypt and lived there until they became so large in number that they were perceived to pose a threat to the existence of the Egyptians. This led to their enslavement and subsequently to the Pharaoh's decision to eliminate them by destroying all baby boys born to Israelite parents. God saw the afflictions of his people and came to rescue them.[5] He called Moses to lead his offensive against the Pharaoh. Moses returned to Egypt calling the people to trust God to deliver them. Using the powers supposedly under the control of Egypt's gods, YAHWEH ravaged the nation and the country. Humbled as he was

---

2 Bruce K. Waltke, with Charles Yu, *An Old Testament Theology* (Grand Rapids: Zondervan, 2007), 321.

3 John H. Sailhammer, "Genesis" in *Expositor's Bible Commentary*, 2:111–112

4 See Byron Wheaton, "Focus and Structure in the Abraham Narratives," *TrinJ* 27 (Spring 2006): 143–162, where I demonstrate this development in Abraham's life.

5 Exodus 3:7–8.

under God's power, Pharaoh consented to let the people go. Further resistance led by Egypt's armies was quashed at the Red Sea. Israel, and many other non Israelite people who left Egypt with them,[6] then journeyed to Sinai to worship God. During this journey, the people faced other challenges including lack of food and water. These served to teach them that the principle characteristic of their lives as a people was to trust YAHWEH. Israel's emergence in the context of the supernatural intervention of God was intended to produce a community of faith.

At Sinai, God would formalize this mixed multitude as his people by making a covenant with them. Before making the covenant, God described the nature of the people he wished to form in a message he gave Moses to relay to Israel:

> You yourselves have seen what I did to the Egyptians and how I bore you on eagles' wings and brought you to myself. Now therefore, if you will indeed obey my voice, and keep my covenant, you will be my treasured possession among all peoples, for all the earth is mine; you shall be to me a kingdom of priests and a holy nation. This is what you shall speak to the people of Israel.[7]

Dumbrell describes this passage as Israel's vocation.[8] In what did it consist? It entailed being a people in relationship to God, to others and to their world.

First, they were to be a "treasured possession." In common usage, this word points to that which is the king's personal possession.[9] It is often used of God's relationship to Israel to designate the special relationship which they have with him.[10] As the text itself indicates, though God owns all things, Israel is a unique possession among that holding. As a community, Israel's special relationship with God will express itself in their being a

---

6 Exodus 12:38

7 Exodus 19:4-6; unless otherwise indicated, all quotations are from *The Holy Bible, New International Version* (Nashville: Holman, 1986).

8 W.J. Dumbrell, *Covenant and Creation: A Theology of the Old Testament Covenants* (Nashville: Nelson, 1984), 85).

9 Cf. 1 Chronicles 29:3; Ecclesiastes 2:8.

10 Deuteronomy 7:2; 14:6; 26:18; Psalm 135:4.

people who worship God only. The covenant stipulations that followed this text included a great deal of specific protocol about how they were to approach God and to live in his presence.

Second, they were described as a "kingdom of priests" or perhaps a "priestly kingdom." The role of the priest was to mediate God and his grace to the community. That, as the existence of the priesthood in Israel showed, could be done actively as the priests participated in enabling the worshipper to bring his worship to God. It also could be done passively as the priesthood modelled for the people what living a holy life entailed.[11] So, as a community, Israel had a task with respect to other nations that involved bringing them to observe and experience the grace of God. One aspect of this was to model what living under God's good rule would look like. Moses described this task as follows:

> See, I have taught you decrees and laws as the Lord my God commanded me, so that you may follow them in the land you are entering to take possession of it. Observe them carefully, for this will show your wisdom and understanding to the nations, who will hear about all these decrees and say, "Surely this great nation is a wise and understanding people." What other nation is so great as to have their gods near them the way the LORD our God is near us whenever we pray to him? And what other nation is so great as to have such righteous decrees and laws as this body of laws I am setting before you today?[12]

Finally, Israel was to be a "holy nation." This too stressed the role of separation to God. But beyond that it also pointed toward Israel's relationship with the world as a sanctifying presence. The word used here is the Hebrew term *goy* which indicates that the people are being referred to in their corporate character as a nation. As a community living under the rule of God, they were to demonstrate holiness in every sphere of their lives. That, too, is elaborated as the holiness code is spelled out. How they dressed, how they ate, how they plowed their fields, how they

11 Dumbrell, *Covenant and Creation*, 90, stresses this role.

12 Deuteronomy 4:5–8.

related to the natural world and much more was included in the prescriptions for holiness that were provided.

So God related to Israel as a community and described their function in collective terms. As W.J. Dumbrell points out, the nation "will affect her world by being the vehicle through whom the divine will is displayed."[13] That is why, before giving this description of the people, God insisted that Israel must be obedient to his commands. They could only realize their purpose by conformity to his will. Thus their obedience would express their faithfulness to God and to his covenant calling. The history of Israel unfolds how well they complied with this calling.[14]

The failure of Israel to be a people of faith and the formation of a replacement community

Reading through Israel's history makes it quite plain that the nation did not adhere to this vocation, and consequently, the covenant curses fell upon Israel just as Moses had warned and the prophets predicted. The summary statement accounting for Israel's exile, given by the Deuteronomist, drives this point home:

> But they would not listen [to the warnings of the prophets] and were as stiff-necked as their ancestors, who did not trust in the LORD their God. They rejected his decrees and the covenant he had made with their ancestors and the statutes he had warned them to keep. They followed worthless idols and themselves became worthless. They imitated the nations around them although the LORD had ordered them, "Do not do as they do."...So the LORD was very angry with Israel and removed them from his presence. Only the tribe of Judah was left, and even Judah did not keep the commands of the LORD their God. They followed the practices Israel had introduced. Therefore the LORD rejected all the people of Israel; he afflicted them and gave them into the hands of plunderers, until he thrust them from his presence.[15]

---

13 Dumbrell, *Covenant and Creation*, 90.

14 Dumbrell, *Covenant and Creation*, 80.

15 2 Kings 17:14–15, 18–20.

The removal of the northern kingdom of Israel by the Assyrians in 722 B.C. and the exile of the south in 603 B.C., again in 597 B.C. and in 586 B.C. when the temple was destroyed and the city of Jerusalem burned, brought this judgement to culmination.

However, the prophets also argued that God would not be frustrated in his purposes but that he would have a people for his special possession. Evidence of this came as early as the ninth century B.C. when God corrected Elijah, who lamented that only he was left of God's faithful followers, by informing him that there are still 7,000 who had not bowed the knee to Baal.[16] Later, Isaiah predicted a day when Israel would be taken into exile but later a remnant would be returned who would fully trust the Lord. Hosea spoke of a time coming when God would bring some of his people back into the wilderness to purify them again and to reconcile them to himself so that their relationship had the character of a faithful husband and wife once more.[17]

But the prophets did not stop with simply the promise of the restoration of some from among the people of Israel. They spoke of a new age when the peoples from all over the earth would come to worship, know and obey God. Perhaps Isaiah's prophecy says it best,

> In that day there will be a highway from Egypt to Assyria. The Assyrians will go to Egypt and the Egyptians to Assyria. The Egyptians and Assyrians will worship together. In that day Israel will be the third, along with Egypt and Assyria, a blessing on the earth. The LORD Almighty will bless them, saying, "Blessed be Egypt my people, Assyria my handiwork, and Israel my inheritance."[18]

Thus in the developed theology of the Old Testament, the people of God are a community drawn from every nation who are marked by their obedience to and love for the LORD their God.

---

16 1 Kings 19:18.

17 Isaiah 10:20–22; Hosea 2:14–20; cf. Jeremiah 31:1–9.

18 Isaiah 19:23; cf. Isaiah 2:2–4; Micah 4:1–2.

Faith community in the New Testament accounts

Jesus and the formation of a community of faith

It is precisely this community that Jesus began to form as he started his public ministry. He chose out of the nation of Israel, twelve men to be with him and to join him in his ministry.[19] With the exception of Judas, these men formed the foundation of Jesus' new community. It is not marked by being a national entity but by being a cohort of faithful followers of Jesus. In fact, Jesus condemned the nation and its leadership because they remained unrepentant as were their fathers.[20] The disciples of Jesus were shaped by the teaching of Jesus and obeyed his commandments. He defined those who make up his family as those who "do the will of my Father in heaven."[21]

Jesus' focus in developing this community during his earthly ministry was among the people of Israel, or what he calls, "the lost sheep of the house of Israel."[22] But there are hints of a larger horizon for his kingdom. Even as he spoke of Israel as his focus, he responded to the needs of a woman from the region of Tyre and Sidon because of her great faith. Earlier he had healed the servant of a centurion and had remarked on the faith of this Roman:

> I tell you, with no one in Israel have I found such faith. I tell you, many will come from the east and west and recline at table with Abraham, Isaac and Jacob in the kingdom of heaven while the sons of the kingdom will be thrown into outer darkness.[23]

That Jesus drew a distinction between the sons of the kingdom who would be rejected and those who came from outside who would be included is most striking. In the parable of the tenants,

---

19 Mark 3:13–15.

20 Matthew 11:20; 23:37–38. Some theologians argue that it was not until the triumphal entry when Israel rejected the Messiah that God's redemptive focus shifted to the Gentiles. But Jesus' condemnation of the nation and its leadership for their unbelief is a constant refrain throughout his preaching ministry and indicates that his calling out of a faithful "remnant" is part of his work from the beginning of his public ministry.

21 Matthew 12:50.

22 Matthew 15:24.

23 Matthew 8:10–12.

Jesus described how the "kingdom of God [would] be taken away from you [Jews] and given to a people producing its fruits."[24] Those who make up the kingdom will be distinguished not by their *ethnicity* but by their *obedience*. Finally just before the events of Jesus' death and resurrection, some Greeks came to Philip asking to see Jesus. Philip and Andrew approached Jesus with this request but Jesus responded that though he would not be distracted from his imminent "glorification" by this request, "I, when I am lifted up from the earth, will draw all people to myself."[25] Clearly the future Jesus perceived involved people from every nation who would follow him. That is fully articulated in the Great Commission when the disciples are sent into the whole world to make disciples.[26]

The apostolic contribution to the community of faith

The disciples understood their calling to further Jesus' work of building an obedient, closely knit, multi-ethnic community. The images used of the church by the apostolic writers include "body," "temple," "family" and "bride," terms that point to the church as an organic entity in the closest of relationship to Christ and one another.[27] Peter applied to the church Moses' description of Israel's vocation, "You are a chosen people, a royal priesthood, a holy nation, God's special possession."[28]

The apostles realized that they were entrusted with the task of being Jesus' witnesses in the whole world, beginning in Jerusalem, but going to the ends of the earth.[29] Under the direction of the Spirit, the disciples were led to go into all the world. Paul is converted and commissioned to "carry [Jesus'] name before the Gentiles, and kings, and the children of Israel" and this is what he did.[30] In explaining his work, Paul said that the mystery he was entrusted with communicating was that "the Gentiles are fellow

---

24 Matthew 21:43.
25 John 12:32.
26 Matthew 28:19–20.
27 Cf. Romans 12:5; 1 Corinthians 12:13; Galatians 6:10; Ephesians 2:21; Ephesians 5:27; 1 Peter 2:5.
28 1 Peter 2:9.
29 Acts 1:8.
30 Acts 9:15; 26:19–20.

heirs, members of the same body, and partakers of the promise in Christ Jesus through the gospel."[31] Hence they too are invited to be partners in this community of faith. Paul said to the Galatian (Gentile) Christians, "If you belong to Christ, then you are Abraham's seed and heirs according to the promise."[32] John, in his vision, saw a community drawn from "all tribes and peoples and languages, standing before the throne and before the Lamb."[33]

So the progress of redemption shows that God is creating a community of people—Jew and Gentile—who are marked by their worship and submission to Jesus Christ, and who, in obedience to him, join in realizing his purposes on earth.

Practical implications of the church as a community of faith

Now how should this redemptive goal of a community of faith inform our thinking and practices for ecclesiastical life? It is important that we should ask that question in light of the rampant individualism that marks contemporary Western society and is shaping too much of the church's practices. Here are a few suggestions that I believe to be important in today's church climate.

First, since we are the community of *faith*, there must be a priority to the Word of God in our midst. The preaching and teaching of the Word is the way we experience the presence of the risen Christ. Paul urged Timothy to "devote [himself] to the public reading of Scripture, to preaching and to teaching."[34] That was necessary because "faith comes from hearing the message, and the message is heard through the word of Christ."[35] One of the key contributions of the Reformation was the recovery of the place of the Word in the life of the church. The liturgies included readings from Old Testament, Gospels and Epistles. It is alarming that in so many services of worship today, so little Scripture is read or exposited. This should be of concern for those who wish to be biblically faithful because it indicates that the Word is not central.

---

31 Ephesians 3:6.
32 Galatians 3:29.
33 Revelations 7:9–10.
34 1 Timothy 4:13.
35 Romans 10:17.

Second, it is necessary to insist that because we are created to be a *community* of faith, the community takes precedence over individuality in the life of the local church. The ordinances of the church—baptism and the Lord's supper—are, among other things, means of grace that proclaim and affirm our connection to the body. Baptism is not only a personal confession of faith in Jesus Christ, but it is also a visible sign of the believer's entrance into the community that was baptized by the Spirit at Pentecost. This is the intent of Paul's reference to baptism in 1 Corinthians 12:13, and it is in the context of keeping the unity of the Spirit that Paul says we have "one baptism."[36] Similarly the Lord's table is an event that affirms our unity in Christ. That is why Paul is so disturbed when the Corinthian church's practice of it leads to division.[37] He insists that when we eat we show that we are one because we eat from one loaf.[38] The unity of the body is declared.

Third, because this is true, *commitment* needs to be emphasized. In our setting, commitment usually is expressed as membership. While the New Testament does not command a certain process for this, the notion that believers belonged to a local assembly of believers is clear. For instance, Luke says that "The Lord added to their number daily those who were being saved."[39] Paul can address believers in a community as a distinct body as he does for instance in Corinth where he calls them "the church of God which is in Corinth" or as he does to the believers in Ephesus whom he addresses as "the saints who are in Ephesus."[40] Mark Dever summarizes,

> ...church membership is a biblical idea. It comes, from among other things, Paul's use of the body imagery about the local church. It comes from Christ saving us by his grace and placing us in churches to serve him in love as we serve others. It comes from our mutual obligations as spelled out in Scripture's "together" and "one another" passages."[41]

---

36 Ephesians 4:5.
37 1 Corinthians 12:27–31.
38 1 Corinthians 10:3.
39 Acts 2:47.
40 1 Corinthians 1:2; Ephesians 1:1.
41 Mark E. Dever, *Nine Marks of a Healthy Church* (Washington: IX Marks, 2013), 36.

So, intentional commitment needs to be expected of those who are part of our fellowships.

As a corollary to commitment, *accountability* to the community and its leadership matters. Congregants should expect that people care about what they do. They care because they are interested in the total well-being of each member, but they also care because the health of each part of the body affects the body's health as a whole. Why is it that people are afraid to challenge one another about sinful behaviour or about righteous conduct as if it is none of one's business? This is even more applicable to pastors and elders. Pastoral care is about leadership interacting with congregants for the sake of the individual's well-being but also for the health of the community.

Church discipline is therefore important because the disciplinary process assumes the care of congregants for one another. The Old Testament example of Achan is a powerful testimony to this truth. His actions polluted the nation of Israel and led to their defeat at Ai. God described what had occurred as "Israel has sinned; they have transgressed my covenant that I have commanded them; they have taken some of the devoted things; they have stolen and lied and put them among their belongings."[42] Achan's action is connected to the nation as a whole. It was only by eradicating the family from the community that Israel could be restored to right relationship with God and experience his blessing in victory over the nations. The harshness of the discipline must be understood against the serious corruption that came because of the one's disobedience.

Something similar is in effect in the Corinthian church when Paul urges that the immoral man among the church be disciplined. He uses the illustration of yeast, arguing that as yeast affects the whole lump of dough, so sin affects the whole body of Christ. Then he explicitly says that they are not "to associate with anyone who bears the name of brother if he is guilty of sexual immorality, or greed, or is an idolater, reviler, swindler….Purge the evil person from among you.."[43] The action called for is severe because the holiness of the community before God is a priority.

42 Joshua 7:11.

43 1 Corinthians 5:6–7, 11, 13.

Fourth, the local church must order its life around the interests of the community *as a whole* before the interests of individuals or of groups in the family. Too many people "shop" for a church home, looking for a certain mix of programs and experiences that will leave them "spiritually satisfied." Many pastors and church leaders fall prey to this expectation and seek to include in the life of their church an array of "offerings" that will satisfy the most demanding of "shoppers." This only subverts the priority of the community and exalts the individual.

Positively, leadership must teach the place of the community and urge members to see the priority of the body in their lives. Just as a healthy marriage requires the marriage partners to submit their personal interests to the greater interest of the marriage relationship, so individuals must submit their personal interests to the well-being of the body. "Cultivating the priority of the local congregation in the lives of individual members will help curb our selfish individualism and create an atmosphere of humble servanthood."[44]

Fifth, the local church should endeavour to reflect and promote a *multi-generational, multi-cultural fellowship*. Many church planting gurus argue that the most effective church plants are those that are homogeneous. So we end up with church communities that are all about young people or young professionals or white middle-class suburbanites or whatever. While it is not always possible, local church leadership needs to try to build communities that represent the diversity of the kingdom—a body of people who are from different social strata and from the variety of ethnicities and language groups that are represented in the society of which each local church is a part. As Mark Dever and Paul Alexander point out, this kind of love challenges a market-niched world with something that is radically different and fulfills Jesus intention that the world would know we are his disciples by our love one for another.[45]

---

44 Mark Dever and Paul Alexander, *The Deliberate Church: Building Your Ministry on the Gospel* (Wheaton: Crossway, 2005), 111.

45 Dever and Alexander, *The Deliberate Church*, 111. Note how in the book of Acts the church grew as it overcame ethnic differences and included different ethnic groups into its number.

Sixth, because we are a coherent unit, we must give attention to obey Jesus' command to *love one another.*[46] That suggests that intentional effort must be expended to nurture true fellowship among the people. That fellowship must not be determined by social cohesiveness but determined by spiritual reality. That is what John says in his first epistle when he reminds us that our fellowship is in the Word, in obedience; it is with the triune God and with one another.[47] Paul, using other language, speaks of living "in harmony with one another" and keeping "the unity of the Spirit in a bond of peace."[48]

Seventh, this corporate idea needs to inform *how we do worship.* James Torrance has pointed out that worship is not something we initiate but "is the gift of participating through the Spirit in the incarnate Son's communion with the Father."[49] Gathered worship is the collective voice of the assembly, not only in the moment but also in terms of its past and its future. The use of worship expressions like the creeds, hymns and the prayers of the church shaped over the millennia connects the contemporary community with the saints already in the presence of the Father, who are worshipping under the direction of the Son. As well, the use of multi-generational and multi-ethnic community worship resources enables the contemporary believing community to reflect that solidarity with the church in the world in their worship experience.

Finally, the church must seek a *corporate expression of our service to our world.* Being a loving, obedient community is itself a powerful witness of the gospel to a fragmented and alienated world. But beyond that, it is important that the church collectively serve in its world. While we affirm that individuals who make up the church be salt and light in their world, the church needs to complement individual actions by creatively and corporately addressing their world with the good news.

---

46 John 13:35; 15:12.

47 1 John 1:3, 7.

48 Romans 12:16; Ephesians 4:3.

49 James B. Torrance, *Worship, Community and the Triune God of Grace* (Downers Grove: IVP, 1996), 20.

Conclusion: a corporate discipleship

If indeed the biblical narrative of redemption has as its end a people who are truly God's special treasure, his royal priesthood and his holy nation, if Jesus Christ died not just to save people from their sins, but to "make [the church] holy, cleansing her by the washing with water through the word, and to present her to himself as a radiant church, without stain or wrinkle or any other blemish, but holy and blameless" (Ephesians 5:26–27), then it is imperative for us to join in that community and to contribute to its being shaped into that glorious church that is a testimony to God's grace and glory. It is time to do discipleship as if the church mattered.[50]

After reminding his readers of the model of community that the triune God provides, Torrance asks,

> Is it not rather [our obligation] to return to the forgotten Trinity—to an understanding of the Holy Spirit who delivers us from a narcissistic preoccupation with the self to find our true being in loving communion with God and one another —to hear God's call to us in our day to participate through the Spirit in Christ's communion with the Father and his mission from the Father to the world—to create in our day a new humanity of persons who find true fulfillment in other-centered communion and service in the Kingdom of God?[51]

If we are to make a difference in enabling the church to become what God intends it to be, we must answer with an emphatic "yes!"

---

50 Cf. James Wilhoit, *Spiritual Formation as if the Church Mattered: Growing in Christ Through Community* (Grand Rapids: Baker, 2008) is one attempt to challenge us to begin thinking about what this might entail.

51 Torrance, *Worship, Community and the Triune God of Grace*, 41.

4

The church and imprecations in the Psalms: The place of the call to curse in the life of the church today

BY DAVID G. BARKER

hat is the voice of the church in the face of brutal persecution, genocide and horrific abuse captured in terms like rape, dismemberment and mass murder. What cry of rage, retaliation and revulsion that we all feel is

---

It is a privilege to contribute to this volume in honour of my friend and colleague, Dr. Stanley K. Fowler. Our conversations over the years have been many and varied. We talked theology (especially eschatology and ecclesiology), ethics, hermeneutics and about many biblical texts. One of our very first conversations, way back in the '80s, was the seeming remote possibility of two seminaries joining forces. Amazingly, they did, and as a result we have worked closely together for almost twenty-five years at Heritage. Stan is one of the finest theologians I know. He has a unique ability to consider the many sides of a biblical, theological, moral or ethical idea, and come to a conclusion that is radically rooted in Scripture, and thoughtfully considered and articulated. Congratulations Stan, and Donna, on this milestone in your life. It has been a joy to journey with you over these last three decades.

legitimized by Christ, the apostles and holy Scripture when such horror is perpetrated, not just against the church, but against humanity and society at large? Is the church called to be passive and non-responsive? Is it simply to take the tact of "Father, forgive them, because they don't know what they are doing" and leave it there? Does Jesus' teaching to love our enemies trump any call for vindication or vengeance? Does being blessed when persecuted imply no voice or action of protest?

At first glance, the mind of Christ would seem to reflect a placid, "So be it, Lord," response, and that would seem to end the conversation. However, several factors indicate that the conversation is not so quickly resolved. One of the first thoughts that comes to mind is the apostle Paul's call to the church to sing to one another in "psalms, hymns and spiritual songs" (Ephesians 5:19; Colossians 3:16). While the reference to "psalms" may not be limited to the Book of Psalms in the Old Testament, it would seem that it cannot mean less. If this is the case, a voice of the people of God in Psalms[1] included what are called "imprecations"—curses. Regularly throughout Psalms, we find statements against enemies such as:

> Break the teeth in their mouths, O God;
> LORD, tear out the fangs of the lions!
> Let them vanish like water that flows away;
> when they draw the bow, let their arrows fall short.
> May they be like a slug that melts away as it moves along,
> like a stillborn child that never sees the sun (Psalm 58:6–8).

> Make them like tumbleweed, my God,
> like chaff before the wind (Psalm 83:13).

> May his days be few;
> may another take his place of leadership.
> May his children be fatherless
> and his wife a widow.
> May his children be wandering beggars;
> may they be driven from their ruined homes (Psalm 109:8–10).

[1] For the purpose of this essay "Psalms" refers to the Book of Psalms, and "psalms" refers to individual or select psalms in the Book of Psalms.

Daughter of Babylon, doomed to destruction,
happy is the one who repays you
for what you have done to us.
Happy is the one who seizes your infants
and dashes them against the rocks (Psalm 137:8-9).

If only you, God, would slay the wicked!
Away from me, you who are bloodthirsty! (Psalm 139:19)[2]

It seems that these were real statements in real situations of brutality, persecution and attack. And the critical point for us is that they were evidently used in the worship life of the first-century church if we can take Paul's remark as inclusive of all the psalms.

So the question arises, "What does the church do with this part of sacred Scripture?" Further, has the new covenant era made such appeals, such prayers, obsolete for the church, whether it uses these psalms directly or not? Is there a place for the church to call out to God for the demise of those harming his, and other, people? Then, in addition, how do we handle to evident violence portrayed in these psalms? Is the prayer and song of God's people today a call to actually smash the heads of our enemies' babies against rocks?

C. S. Lewis was abhorred by such a thought, and wrote:

> In some of the psalms the spirit of hatred which strikes us in the face is like the heat from a furnace mouth. In others the same spirit ceases to be frightful only by becoming (to a modern mind) almost comic in its naiveté.... The hatred is there—festering, gloating, undisguised—and we should be wicked if we in any way condoned or approved it, or (worse still) used it to justify similar passions in ourselves.[3]

Bob Ripley, former pastor of Metropolitan United Church in London, Ontario, and who was recognized as an evangelical

---

2 Other psalms would include Psalms 7:6–9; 12:3; 17:13; 31:17; 35:4; 55:15, 23; 59:11–13; 69:22–28; 70:2–3; 79:6, 12. All Scripture quotations are from the *New International Version* (Grand Rapids: Zondervan, 2011).

3 C.S. Lewis, *Reflections on the Psalms* (London: Harcourt Brace Jovanovich, 1958), 20–22.

during his pastoral ministry, has gone on record that he has abandoned the Christian faith because of several things, but two of them are the "genocide" texts and the imprecations in the psalms.[4] Gordon Wenham quotes the German psychologist Franz Buggle who argues that most people reject the Bible not because God is pictured as creating the world in seven days, but because of his unethical behaviour.[5]

So, how do we come to these texts and use them in the worship of the church, and in the life of piety for the follower of Christ? Should we abandon them and relegate them to a former era of God's covenantal people? Or should we embrace them in some way, and if so, how?

Unsatisfactory answers

John N. Day has helpfully identified three answers that have commonly been brought forward as solutions to the ethical and spiritual issues that the imprecations in the psalms, and elsewhere in the Bible, raise.[6] The first is that these texts are evil emotions and are not to be expressed. C.S. Lewis, mentioned above, represents this perspective. Day answers this perspective by noting that David, the attributed author of many of these psalms,[7] while not by any means morally and spiritually perfect, is a man "after God's own heart" (1 Samuel 13:14), and does show care and forgiveness toward his enemies. Further, Day notes that the purposes and themes found in these psalms reflect high ethical values such as the honour and sovereignty of God, concern for justice and the preservation of the righteous, a con-

---

4 Bob Ripley, *Life Beyond Belief: A Preacher's Deconversion* (London: Binea Press, 2014).

5 Gordon Wenham, *The Psalter Reclaimed* (Wheaton: Crossway, 2013), 136.

6 John N. Day, *Crying for Justice: What the Psalms Teach Us about Mercy and Vengeance in an Age of Terrorism* (Grand Rapids: Kregel, 2005). Day's book is based on his Ph.D. dissertation [John N. Day, "The Imprecatory Psalms and Christian Ethics" (Ph.D. diss., Dallas Theological Seminary, 2001)]. Day has articulated an approach that is very similar to the one affirmed in this article. I highly recommend his book.

7 The preposition *lamedh-sewa* before the name David and others in Psalms probably indicates authorship—a *lamedh auctoris*, see Bruce K. Waltke and M. O'Connor, *An Introduction to Biblical Hebrew Syntax* (Winona Lake: Eisenbrauns, 1990), 206. However, "to" and "for" are the common meanings of the preposition, see Gary D. Pratico and Miles V. Van Pelt, *Basics of Biblical Hebrew*, 2nd ed. (Grand Rapids: Zondervan, 2007), 51. Hence, the descriptor "Davidic" may be the best way to render this phrase.

cern that the enemy would seek God, and an abhorrence of sin. Then, Day makes the point that these psalms are "inspired," and to reject them brings questions about the nature of Scripture. Finally, Day observes that they found a place in the regular worship of God's people, and in the canon—"the book of worship for God's people."[8]

Related to this is the view that these psalms are to be expressed but then relinquished. Day cites Walter Brueggemann who talks about "a way *through* them and not *around* them."[9] Christians are to own these psalms as an expression of their vengeance, but take them to God and relinquish them there. While Brueggemann has been a significant voice in helping the church use the psalms in its authentic and passionate worship and prayer, the notion that these psalms are reflective of an evil expression, especially in the Old Testament, runs counter to the "trans-testamental testimony" of the affirmation and usage of these psalms by Jesus and the New Testament writers.[10]

A second answer Day notes is that the Old Testament in general, and these psalms in particular, reflect a lower moral plane than the New Testament. This tends to be rooted in a dispensational reading of the Bible, and that "the unfolding of revealed truth in the Word of God is accompanied by a similar advancement of morals."[11] Related to this is J. Carl Laney's approach who emphasizes the dispensational distinction between Israel and the church and "the covenantal basis for the curse on Israel's enemies."[12] He roots his conclusion in the Abrahamic covenant, and the statements of "curse those that curse" and "bless those that bless" as applicable to Israel, and not the church. Finally, some appeal to the cross as the final expression of God's justice, and that any expression of imprecation takes on an eschatological and spiritualized focus.[13]

---

8 Day, *Crying for Justice*, 21–25.

9 Walter Brueggemann, *Praying the Psalms* (Winona: Saint Mary's Press, Christian Brothers Publications, 1986), 68, emphasis in original.

10 See Day, *Crying for Justice*, 25.

11 See Roy B. Zuck, "The Problem of the Imprecatory Psalms" (Th.M. thesis, Dallas Theological Seminary, 1957).

12 J. Carl Laney, "A Fresh Look at the Imprecatory Psalms," *Bibliotheca Sacra* 138 (1981): 41–42.

13 Bruce K. Waltke and James M. Houston, with Erika Moore, *The Psalms as Chris-*

Day challenges each of these approaches noting the common and continuing morality between Old and New Testaments ("a difference in degree but not in kind"), an over-distinction between Israel and the church,[14] and the evidence of imprecations on real people in the New Testament.[15] Yes, the apostle Paul teaches the church, "Do not repay anyone evil for evil.... Do not take revenge, my dear friends" (Romans 12:17, 19). But he cites, "If your enemy is hungry, feed him; if he is thirsty, give him something to drink" from Proverbs 25:21–22. Texts such as Exodus 23:4–5, Leviticus 19:17–18 and Proverbs 24:17 emphasize a similar ethic. Paul uses the Old Testament ethic to substantiate his teaching in new covenant ethics. But further, vengeance is not left out of the conversation. Paul instructs the believers to not take revenge, but "leave room for God's wrath" and cites, "'It is mine to avenge; I will repay,' says the Lord" from Deuteronomy 32:35. Imprecation and vengeance, referred back to God, is part of the "moral plane" of the New Testament.

Finally, another approach that Day notes is that the speaker of the psalms is ultimately Jesus Christ. Hence, while David spoke these prayers, he did so as the prototype of Christ who bore the curse and wrath of God. So, as believers today we pray them as participating in Christ, rooted in the cross and the love of God characterized by forgiving one's enemies.[16] However, as Day observes, not all the imprecations in the psalms or elsewhere in Scripture are written or spoken by David, and further, if they can be placed on the lips of Jesus, and thus are part of the "way" of Jesus, the proposal offers no real solution to the issue for the church.[17]

Bruce Waltke and James Houston take the approach that these psalms can be prayed by the church, but not for immediate retri-

---

tian Worship: A Historical Commentary (Grand Rapids: Eerdmans, 2010), 97, reflects this thinking. Also, Tremper Longman III, *How To Read the Psalms* (Downers Grove: InterVarsity, 1988), 139, states, "Since our warfare is against Satan and the spiritual forces of evil, we may call down our curses upon them."

14 Texts such as Romans 2:28–29; 4:9–25; Galatians 3:6–29.

15 Day, *Crying for Justice*, 26–32.

16 This perspective is articulated by James Adams, *War Psalms of the Prince of Peace: Lessons from the Imprecatory Psalms* (Phillipsburg: Presbyterian & Reformed, 1991), 21; and Dietrich Bonhoeffer, *The Psalms: The Prayer Book of the Bible*, trans. J.H. Burtness (Minneapolis: Augsburg, 1970), 18.

17 Day, *Crying for Justice*, 34–35.

bution. They state that "ultimate justice occurs in the eschaton ...and it is appropriate to pray for the destruction of the wicked at that time of judgment and the avenging of the righteous."[18] They also assert that sin and the sinner can be differentiated in this dispensation, and so we can hate the sin and love the sinner. Further, the struggle today is against spiritual powers of darkness, which are conquered by "turning the other cheek and by praying for the forgiveness of enemies through their repentance."[19]

However, Daniel Block makes the comment, "God does in fact hate sin (Deuteronomy 12:31; 16:22), but the Scriptures do not hesitate to use the same verb (*sane'*) to speak of God's disposition toward people: Hosea 9:15; Malachi 1:3; Psalms 5:5; 11:5; Proverbs 6:16–19."[20] While we are engaged in a struggle against the spiritual powers of darkness (Ephesians 6:10–20), the powers are often manifest in real people doing horrific things. Jesus, Peter and Paul did not hesitate to call real people out (Pharisees, Simon Magus, Alexander the metalworker). It is not at all evident that these "call outs" were spoken only in terms of an eschatological hope. That may have been part of the thinking, but "may your money perish with you" (Acts 8:20) seems to have a very "now" implication.

Imprecation as a voice for the church

The thesis of this essay is that the imprecations in the psalms are a legitimate expression of worship and piety for the church. But, furthermore, these voices are critical for the church to use as an expression of its rage against horrific injustice, especially against its own people. Further, they are a passionate and courageous call on God to act. Without these voices, the church is truncated in its prayer and song. Songs of lament are the single largest category of psalms in Psalms, and the church has not done well in bringing these psalms and their voices into the public expression of piety and faith.[21] Inevitably, imprecations are found in

---

18 Waltke and Houston, *The Psalms as Christian Worship*, 97.

19 Waltke and Houston, *The Psalms as Christian Worship*, 97–98.

20 Daniel I Block, *For the Glory of God: Recovering a Biblical Theology of Worship* (Grand Rapids: Baker Academic: 2014), 8, n. 18.

21 There have been many responses to this issue in the last number of years, including Waltke and Houston, *The Psalms as Christian Worship*. A powerful and personal call to

lament psalms. Further, as noted earlier, as a voice of worship, these kinds of expressions are referred back to God. The psalms are the voice of God's people to God, and Paul makes it clear that revenge is not something God's people take on themselves, but rather they embrace Deuteronomy 32:35 and the promise that God will avenge.

However, we also need to understand that these psalms are not merely some kind of psychological, or even spiritual, coping mechanism that has little to do with theological and ethical truth.[22] As will be noted below, these expressions are focused on forces, and representatives of forces, arrayed against God and his manifest kingdom on earth (whether Israel or the church). John Goldingay observes that the painful language in Psalm 137 is not merely the expression of any people who miss their homeland. It is the expression of a people who understand who and what they are as Zion/Jerusalem, and that the call for God to act the way they do is not just an "understandable vitriol" of an exiled people but "an appeal for action in accordance with the declarations that YHWH had given Judah."[23]

Imprecations are dangerous expressions; but the fact is all the psalms are dangerous. They take worshippers and pray-ers places where they are not used to going. Eugene Peterson writes:

> Psalm-prayer also enters into the way-things-are, but finds that the way-things-are is pretty bad. Evil is encountered. Wickedness is confronted. This prayer quickens the pulse and shoots adrenalin into the bloodstream. The people who practice this prayer get excited—they yell and gesture.... Prayer is combat.[24]

The lament psalms calling on God to "Awake, Lord! Why do you sleep? Rouse yourself! Do not reject us forever" (Psalm

---

embrace lament in the psalms is J. Todd Billings, *Rejoicing in Lament: Wrestling with Cancer and Life in Christ* (Grand Rapids: Baker, 2015) where he chronicles his journey with a rare form of incurable cancer.

22 John Goldingay, *Psalms, Baker Commentary on the Old Testament: Wisdom and Psalms*, ed. Tremper Longman III, vol. 3 (Grand Rapids: Baker Academic, 2008), 609, 612.

23 Goldingay, *Psalms,* 609.

24 Eugene Peterson, *Answering God: The Psalms as Tools for Prayer* (San Francisco: HarperCollins, 1991), 95.

44:23), or crying out, "How long, LORD? Will you forget me forever? ...Look on me and answer, LORD my God. Give light to my eyes, or I will sleep in death (Psalm 13:1, 3), or asking "Why LORD, do you reject me and hide your face from me?" (Psalm 88:14), or concluding a psalm with the desperate cry, "You have taken from me friend and neighbor—darkness is my closest friend" (Psalm 88:18), are all dangerous.

Even psalms of praise and thanksgiving are dangerous when spoken, prayed or sung un-nuanced or in painful contexts. To uncritically quote the well-loved Psalm 121, "The LORD will keep you from all harm—he will watch over your life" (verse 7) in the context of deep suffering, grief, loss or brutality can cause this psalm (and many others like it) to become not just disappointing, but dangerous, in that it can lead pious people to not take seriously the brutal realities of life. As Walter Brueggemann says, "The collection of the Psalter is not for those whose life is one of uninterrupted continuity and equilibrium."[25]

So, yes, there is danger in affirming the voice of imprecation for the church, and without nuance or boundaries, such expressions can descend into places that are outside what is appropriate. But, as in so many things in life and faith, the danger of misuse should not marginalize the gifts that God has given for authentic faith and the vulnerable presentation of ourselves to God in worship as living and holy sacrifices (Romans 12:1–2).

The place of the Abrahamic covenant

An often missed or minimized point in dealing with imprecations in Psalms is the fact that the foundation for these imprecations lies in the Abrahamic covenant. God promises to make Abraham a great nation and a blessing, but then states:

> I will bless those who bless you,
> and *whoever curses you I will curse* (Genesis 12:3, emphasis mine).

The imprecations are an act of calling on God to be true to his promise to Abraham and his descendants. A similar expression is found in Deuteronomy 32:35–36,

25 Brueggemann, *Praying the Psalms*, 20.

It is mine to avenge; I will repay.
In due time their [the enemy's] foot will slip.
...The Lord will vindicate his people
and relent concerning his servants.[26]

As noted earlier, J. Carl Laney correctly states that "the fundamental ground on which one may justify the imprecations in the Psalms is the covenantal basis for the curse on Israel's enemies."[27] While he dismisses the use of these expressions in the psalms in the church due to his dispensational understanding of the church and Israel, he correctly identifies this critical point. Imprecations are little more than calling on God to be faithful to his covenant with his people.

For those who see more continuity between Israel and the church, and hear the apostle Paul's description of the church as "Abraham's seed" (Galatians 3:29) as an expression of a single people of God in continuity with Israel, that covenantal promise, and its associated blessings and curses, is central to the life of the church today.[28] So, the Abrahamic covenant lies not only at the foundation of Israel's worship expressions of lament and imprecation but also the church's. This is a crucial point in the discussion, and it is somewhat surprising that it does not play a larger role in the voluminous literature dealing with this issue. It is safe to say that whoever blesses the church will be blessed and whoever curses the church will be cursed. The church brings a voice to call on God to such action, and not just for itself but as an agent of blessing and redemption to the world through Jesus Christ.

Imprecations in the New Testament and the church

So, while there is continuity between Israel and the church with the Abrahamic covenant serving as the promissory base of the people of God, do we actually find imprecation in the literature

26 While the context of this passage is God's judgement by the nations on his people for their spiritual apostasy, it remains a text of hope for vindication as God turns his wrath toward the nations who do not acknowledge the fact that it is the God of Israel who has empowered them to execute his judgement on his people.

27 Laney, "A Fresh Look," 41.

28 See my comments on "Geopolitical implications today" near the end of this chapter.

of the New Testament? Do we find anything in Jesus, Peter, Paul or others? The answer is "yes."

First, we need to remind ourselves that the Old Testament was the Bible of the first-century church, and Paul's reference to singing psalms does not include exceptions of seemingly less fitting expressions of worship and piety. Evidently all of them were to be used in the worship life of the church.

However, a psalm like Psalm 109 is virtually ignored by the church. It is rarely read, and is not included in the lectionary readings.[29] In Acts 1:20, in reference to Judas Iscariot, the apostle Peter cites Psalm 109:8b in his address to the gathered believers in Jerusalem after Christ's ascension,

> Let his days be few;
> may another take his place of leadership.
> May his children be fatherless,
> and his wife a widow (Psalm 109:8–9).

Clearly Peter sensed no aversion to bringing that voice into the new covenant community as part of what it was to be that community rooted in Jesus Christ. It further demonstrates that Psalms was known by the founders of the first-century church, and all the psalms contained therein were available for public proclamation.

The apostle John records the martyrs in the book of Revelation crying out, "How long, Sovereign Lord, holy and true, until you judge the inhabitants of the earth and avenge our blood?" (Revelation 6:10). The words come directly from the Song of Moses in Deuteronomy 32:43 in which God promises to "avenge the blood of his servants." Further, it is significant to note that the saints in heaven refer directly to "the song of God's servant Moses and of the Lamb" as they celebrate Christ's actions in bringing justice to the earth (Revelation 15:3). While the actual-

---

29 W. Sibley Towner talks about a "canon within a canon" in which the liturgical church hymnals select psalms that resonate in genre with, and have more significant meaning for, the contemporary singing church, W. Sibley Towner, "Without Our Aid He Did Us Make," in *A God So Near: Essays in Old Testament Theology in Honor of Patrick D. Miller*, ed. Brent A. Strawn and Nancy R. Bowen (Winona Lake: Eisenbrauns, 2003), 17–34.

ization of the judgements is eschatological, the saints were using these texts to speak to their present reality.

The cry "How long?" is well-known in the psalms. In Psalm 13:1–2 the psalmist cries out four times, "How long…how long…how long…how long?" The psalmist questions in Psalm 79:5, "How long, LORD? Will you be angry forever?" He then moves to an appeal that God "pour out his wrath on the nations that do not acknowledge you," and "make known among the nations that you avenge the outpoured blood of your servants" (Psalm 79:6,10). In Psalm 94 the psalmist cries, "How long will the wicked be jubilant?" But the psalm begins with "The LORD is a God who avenges. O God who avenges, shine forth!" (Psalm 94:1–3). The cry of the martyred saints under the altar is solidly rooted in the imprecatory language of the Old Testament.

Second, the apostle Paul uses imprecation himself. He states in Galatians 1:8–9,

> But even if we or an angel from heaven should preach a gospel other than the one we preached to you, let them be under God's curse. As we have already said, so now I say it again: If anybody is preaching to you a gospel other than what you accepted, let them be under God's curse!

In addition, he said to the Corinthian church, "If anyone does not love the Lord, let that person be cursed. Come, Lord!" (1 Corinthians 16:22).

It is doubtful that this is some kind of apostolic privilege. Rather, he is using the voice given to the first-century church to speak powerfully to the issue of a false gospel or an enemy of the church, and would expect the Galatian church to use similar language.

Third, Peter, the rock upon which Jesus promised to build his church,[30] said to Simon Magus who tried to buy the power of the Holy Spirit, "May your money perish with you, because you thought you could buy the gift of God with money" (Acts 8:20).

---

30 While the confession of Peter in Matthew 16:16 is critical for the church to understand, Jesus' reference to Peter as the rock (*petra*) was a play on his name, Petros. As such, Peter is a synecdoche for the apostolic band commissioned to lay down the foundation for the church (see Matthew 18:18–20; John 20:19–20; Ephesians 2:20; 1 Corinthians 3:9–17).

Expressing imprecation against someone who would profane the work of the Spirit in this way, and seek such power to further aggrandize himself (Acts 8:9), was well within the boundaries of appropriate apostolic (and church) response.

Finally, Jesus himself engaged in a type of imprecation in his woe pronouncements against the Galilean towns of Chorazin, Capernaum and Bethsaida (Matthew 11:21–24; Luke 10:13–15). We should also not avoid his woe pronouncements against religious leaders calling them "whitewashed tombs" among several other rather harsh descriptions (Matthew 23:13–39). In Mark 11:14 Jesus curses a fig tree, and while the fig tree literally suffered the consequence of the imprecation, Jesus clearly had in mind the nation of Israel, and in particular, the temple as the centre of their worship and religion.[31] So, while the imprecation is indirect, it is real, and most interpreters would point to the Roman invasion of A.D. 70 as the fulfilment of the prophetic curses.[32]

It is fascinating that in Luke's story of Jesus cleansing the temple (Luke 19:41–48) Jesus uses the language of Psalm 137:9 to describe the destiny of Jerusalem, "They will dash you to the ground, you and the children within your walls." The Septuagint (LXX) uses the same Greek term in Psalm 137 (*edapiousin*) as Luke uses to render Jesus' words in his text. As noted in the previous section, the New Testament writers were not afraid to bring Old Testament texts into their imprecatory contexts.

In Matthew 11:20–24 and 23:13–39, while using "woe" language rather than imprecation, Jesus invokes judgement upon towns characterized by resistant unbelief. As John Day notes, "Although not identical to imprecation, a close relationship exists between 'woe' and 'curse.'"[33]

---

31 See Day, *Crying for Justice*, 100–103, for a helpful discussion of this event.

32 See C.E.B. Cranfield, *The Gospel According to Saint Mark*, in *The Cambridge Greek New Testament Commentary*, ed. C.F.D. Moule (Cambridge: Cambridge University Press, 1959), 356; Robert H. Stein, *Mark*, in *The Baker Exegetical Commentary on the New Testament*, ed. Robert W. Yarbrough and Robert H. Stein (Grand Rapids: Baker Academic, 2008), 513, 516; William Lane, *The Gospel According to Mark*, in *The New International Commentary on the New Testament*, ed. F. F. Bruce (Grand Rapids: Eerdmans, 1974), 400.

33 Day, *Crying for Justice*, 168, n. 25. His dissertation thoroughly develops this connection, Day, "The Imprecatory Psalms and Christian Ethics," 186–190. See also Zechariah 11:17.

So, while Jesus ministered and served with much messianic privilege, it seems that the Captain of our salvation and the Shepherd of our souls is pointing the way forward in response to forces that are opposed to the kingdom of God and those that represent those forces. It seems that if the Head of the church uses these voices to bring the kingdom near, his body, the church, the entity commissioned to proclaim that kingdom, is endowed with the same voices.

Some boundaries

But, are there boundaries for the church in the use of such evocative and violent language? How do we bring this into harmony with Jesus' words, "You have heard that it was said, 'Love your neighbour and hate your enemy.' But I tell you, love your enemies and pray for those who persecute you" (Matthew 5:43–44)?

First, we need to understand that Jesus statement, "You have heard that it was said," is only partially rooted in the Leviticus 19:18 text that he is citing, namely the "Love your neighbour" part. The second part, "and hate your enemy," is a proverb of the time, not an Old Testament citation. Even the first part of the Leviticus 19:18 text challenges a response of revenge or bearing a grudge.[34] Further, the wisdom teachings of the Old Testament make it clear that grace and mercy extended to an enemy is part of an old covenant people of God ethic (Proverbs 25:21). Jesus is not bringing a radically new ethic to the new covenant. It was already something imbedded in the old covenant life of God's people. As such, it is not appropriate to point to Jesus in our time and declare that imprecatory language is obsolete because of Jesus' superior ethic. He used the language, and built on an established and known kingdom of God ethic.

Second, it seems that imprecations were spoken by recognized representatives of the community. Psalms are regularly attributed to people like David, Asaph, Sons of Korah (Levites) and others.[35] Even the anonymous psalms evidently come from some kind of

34 And yes, it is set in the context of a covenantal neighbour.

35 The psalm titles are recognized by Psalms scholars as being added later to the text, but most would affirm that the titles reflect a tradition that goes back to origins of the psalm in question, see Allan P. Ross, *A Commentary on the Psalms, vol. 1 (1–41)*, Kregel Exegetical Library (Grand Rapids: Kregel Academic and Professional, 2011), 42.

official context (temple, palace). While the community at large sang and prayed these psalms, and certainly may have directed them at personal enemies, the intent was for an official representative of the community (e.g. king, priest, Levite, worship leader, prophet, sage) to speak to God on behalf of the community.[36] This representative notion is furthered by Jesus and the apostles as they spoke imprecations. But Paul makes it clear that "others" (leaders in the church) are building on the foundation the apostles were laying, and need to be very careful in how they build on that foundation (1 Corinthians 3:10–17),[37] in other words, in how they represent the church.

Third, the imprecations are directed toward people and institutional systems and structures that oppose the work and people of God as a nation or community. Isaiah declares, "For the LORD has a day of vengeance, a year of retribution, to uphold *Zion's cause*" (Isaiah 34:8, emphasis mine).[38] The imprecations were not intended to be everyday vendettas against personal enemies or antagonists. Jesus' words, "Love your enemy," come into play at the personal level. David, the psalmist, showed kindness and personal concern against his enemies Saul and Absalom (his son!) with compassion and concern (2 Samuel 1:1–16; 2:5; 16:11–12; 19:12–23). Even in psalms with the harshest imprecations, the psalmists show grace and mercy toward their enemies (e.g. Psalms 35:1,12–13; 109:4–5) indicating that the expression of curse goes beyond personal vendettas. The wisdom teaching of Proverbs 25:21 is directed toward a personal enemy.[39]

But when a system, or a structure (political, economic, military, religious, social and more), or a person representing that

---

36 Erich Zenger notes that in Psalm 109 the Davidic king is made the literary-theological speaker of the psalm, see Frank Lothar Hossfeld and Erich Zenger, *Psalms 3: A Commentary on Psalms 101–150*, in *Hermeneia*, trans. Linda M. Maloney (Minneapolis: Fortress, 2011), 131.

37 In fact, Paul uses imprecatory language to warn those who build on the apostolic foundation (pastors, teachers, leaders in the church) when he says, "If anyone [and the 'anyone' is a reference to those building on the apostolic foundation] destroys God's temple [the church], God will destroy him, for God's temple is sacred, and you [Corinthian church] are that temple" (1 Corinthians 3:16–17).

38 Zenger states concerning Psalm 137 that we have "a protest against the brutality of great powers toward small nations," Hossfeld and Zenger, *Psalms 3*, 523.

39 Longman, *How to Read the Psalms*, 139, makes this point.

system, is arrayed against God and his people, or the representative of his people (i.e. Psalm 109), the people of God (Israel then or the church now) have a voice to call on God to act in protection, vengeance, and vindication. This was more clearly evident in Old Testament Israel, who, as a nation, had defined geopolitical boundaries, and the enemies were other nations with their false religions and militaristic objectives. However, this is not to relegate imprecations in the church to merely spiritual or mystical forces. Real enemies of the church (and society) exist (Simon Magus would fit into this description), and real pain and brutality are felt.

Fourth, it is crucial to understand that the call is for God to act. It is never something that is to be personally enacted out of personal vengeance. Erich Zenger writes about Psalm 137, perhaps the most violent of the imprecations in the psalms:

> Psalm 137 is not the song of people who have the power to effect a violent change in their situation of suffering, nor is it the battle cry of terrorists. Instead, it is an attempt to cling to one's historical identity even when everything is against it. Still more, it is an attempt, in the face of the most profound humiliation and hopelessness, to suppress the primitive human lust for violence in one's own heart, by surrendering *everything* to God—a God whose word of judgment is presumed to be so universally just that even those who pray the psalm submit themselves to it.[40]

However, this does not eliminate the reality that God uses people (his and others) to bring curse (and blessing). This is where things get murky. What does it mean to enact God's vengeance? What does that look like? When we read of Joshua and others conquering Canaanite cities, we certainly cannot think that somehow this was painless and anything less than brutal. We can call on the context of the warfare of the times to provide some justification, but these "genocide" texts are not easily dismissed.[41] When the church uses this voice, and realizes that it

---

40 Erich Zenger, *A God of Vengeance? Understanding the Psalms of Divine Wrath*, trans. Linda M. Maloney (Louisville: Westminster John Knox, 1996), 48. Emphasis in original.

41 See Paul Copan and Matthew Flannagan, *Did God Really Command Genocide:*

may well be the instrument of curse to "take out" forces arrayed against God and his church and kingdom, what does that look like? This is not an easy question to answer.

The church is not a centralized geopolitical national entity like Israel with military and economic structures standing ready to be used. Rather it is a dispersed collection of "outposts" of God's kingdom related to each other in varying degrees of interdependence or autonomy. Thus, it seems that each local church, or perhaps groups of local churches (associations, denominations, fellowships), has the responsibility and privilege to act in response to imprecation as determined by the wisdom of their leaders or communal consensus, and as prompted by the Spirit who makes each local church his temple (1 Corinthians 3:16).

However, the agent is inevitably unnamed. Supplicants never expect to undertake the action of vengeance. We/they know from the prophets and apostles that it is God who recompenses (see Deuteronomy 32:35; Isaiah 63:4; Jeremiah 51:6, 24, 56; Obadiah 15; Romans 12:19; Hebrews 10:30).[42] Giving vengeance over to God is "an act of profound faith."[43]

A critical factor in the discussion of boundaries is that when we read of the brutal violence contained in imprecations in Psalms, we need to understand, first, the poetic nature of the material, and second, the warfare contexts of the songs. The material is poetry, and filled with hyperbole and poetic imagery (lions' fangs, melting slugs, stillborn children, tumbleweed, chaff, and more). These poetic and powerful ways to communicate the pain of loss and injustice are not just immediate, knee-jerk, literal reactions to be passed off as such but are, in fact, carefully crafted, thoughtful, but truly heart-felt and character-forming, poetic expressions of lament and imprecation. Kathleen Scott Goldingay writes,

> Human formation is a process that involves the transformation of day-to-day patterns of thinking, feeling, believing and behaving. Formative practices *such as singing the Psalms*

Coming to Terms with the Justice of God (Grand Rapids: Baker, 2014).

42 Goldingay, *Psalms*, 609.

43 Brueggemann, *Praying the Psalms*, 62.

> change our neurons and create capacity to embrace a new world-view.[44]

They are well-tested, well-rehearsed pictures and ideas that shape our thinking, shape our being and so often voice what we could not otherwise say. But, it is poetry, with all the evocative and emotive language and response such literature contains.

Further, as hard as it is for us to comprehend, and yes wrapped in poetic hyperbole and imagery, the brutality reflected in Old Testament imprecatory language is rooted in the way ancient near-eastern warfare was done. The songs are a product of their times. The writers did not think outside their cultural and historical context. The poet in "The (Babylonian) Curse of Akkad" (2400 B.C.) prays, "May the cattle slaughterer slaughter his wife...may your sheep butcherer butcher his child."[45] It needs to be noted that this is also poetry, and uses the normal literary conventions (hyperbole) characteristic of any poetry. But, it does reflect a practice of warfare of the time, and it helps set the historical context for some of the language and ideas in the imprecations. At the same time, while these reflections go some distance in ameliorating the repulsiveness we feel when we read such texts, they do not fully resolve the issue, and that is part of the reason why the conversation continues into our times.

Finally, we need to understand that when the church uses these expressions, they are, in fact, a call for justice and righteousness. J. Clinton McCann writes:

> [Psalm 109] suggests that evil, injustice and oppression must be confronted, opposed, hated because God hates them. From this perspective, the psalmist's desire for vengeance amounts to a desire for justice and righteousness in self and society.... The anger is expressed, but it is expressed in prayer and thereby submitted to God.... Thus, this vehement, violent sounding prayer is, in fact, an act of non-violence.[46]

---

44 Kathleen Scott Goldingay and John Goldingay, "The Sting in the Psalms, Part 1," *Theology* 117:6 (2014): 408. Emphasis mine.

45 See D.J. Wiseman, *The Vassal Treaties of Esarhaddon* (London: British School of Archaeology in Iraq, 1958), 60–78.

46 J. Clinton McCann, Jr., "The Book of Psalms" in *The New Interpreter's Bible,* ed.

They are legitimate expressions for God's people in their times of deep pain, sense of helplessness and burning anger. These are real and undeniable, and the church does a great disservice to its people when it teaches that they are not the way of Jesus, and that such innate human feelings are to be suppressed or denied. Naming evil and injustice, and calling perpetrators to account, is an important part of restoration and healing. At present, Canadian society is wrestling with the injustices of the past (and present for that matter) against First Nations peoples. A crucial part of the healing is to allow people to tell their stories, and name the pain. Eugene Peterson makes the point that hate should be prayed, not stifled. Apathy, not hate, is the opposite of love.[47] The boundary here is that they are to be directed to God, that they are, in fact, expressions of worship, and in giving such a voice in our worship we remove the impulse to take vengeful action ourselves.

Geopolitical implications today

As noted earlier, a crucial point in understanding the place of imprecation in the church is the centrality of the Abrahamic covenant, "I will bless those who bless you, and whoever curses you I will curse." The call for imprecation by Israel's speakers was a call for God to honour that promise in their founding covenant with their forefather, Abraham.

The question then arises. Who are the inheritors of the Abrahamic covenant today? The answer to that question is wide-ranging and far-reaching. It moves all the way from a Dual-Covenant theology in which God has two covenants, one with Israel and another with the church, to a Supercessionist or Replacement Theology view in which the church has completely replaced Israel. Inbetween are the positions of Classical Dispensationalism, Progressive Dispensationalism, Historical Premillennialism, and Covenant Theology.[48]

Leander E. Keck (Nashville: Abingdon, 1996), 4:1127. Nancy deClaisse-Walford notes this point and quotes McCann in her commentary on Psalm 109. Nancy de-Claisse-Walford, Rolf A. Jacobson, Beth LaNeel Tanner, *The Book of Psalms*, NICOT (Grand Rapids: Eerdmans, 2014), 833.

47 Peterson, *Answering God*, 98.

48 A helpful resource, written and illustrated in an easily understandable way, for

Irrespective of how we may answer this question, based on his statements in Galatians 3:7–9 and Romans 4:11–12, 16–17, it is clear that the apostle Paul believed that in some way the church was a participant in the promises of the Abrahamic covenant. Further, he writes:

> May I never boast except in the cross of our Lord Jesus Christ, through which the world has been crucified to me, and I to the world. Neither circumcision or uncircumcision means anything; what counts is the new creation. Peace and mercy to all who follow this rule—to the Israel of God (Galatians 6:14–16).

Paul clearly identifies the church as "the Israel of God."[49] How modern Israel fits into this today is not the point of the discussion. But it cannot be denied that the church does fall into the domain of "I will bless those who bless you, and whoever curses you I will curse."

This has geopolitical implications. We have often heard that the nations that bless the modern state of Israel will be blessed, and that we need to call on our political leaders to support the nation of Israel for that reason. This may well be true, whether from a theological, historical or purely humanitarian point of view. However, significantly, for the church, which we are, the promise is ours to inherit. Paul calls us "Abraham's children." Hence, we need to call upon our political leaders, and all leaders everywhere, to "bless" the church in order for their nations, organizations and movements to be blessed. This means that we

---

understanding some of these positions is Timothy Paul Jones, *Rose Guide to End-Time Prophecy* (Torrance: Rose Publishing, 2011). Also, Chad Brand, Tom Pratt and Robert L. Reymond, eds., *Perspectives on Israel and the Church: Four Views* (Nashville: B&H Academic, 2015). To engage the conversation on Replacement Theology see Charles D. Provan, *The Church Is Israel Now: The Transfer of Conditional Privilege* (Portland: Ross House Books, 1987), Ronald E. Diprose, *Israel and the Church: The Origin and Effects of Replacement Theology* (Downers Grove: InterVarsity, 2010), Michael J. Vlach, *Has the Church Replaced Israel? A Theological Evaluation* (Nashville: B&H Academic, 2010). A helpful biblical theology that seeks a "middle way" (*via media*) is Peter J. Gentry and Stephen J. Wellum, *Kingdom through Covenant: A Biblical-Theological Understanding of the Covenants* (Wheaton: Crossway, 2012).

49 Galatians 6:16.

call upon presidents, prime ministers and leaders of every sort, to affirm and bless the church, not just as an institution that has a place in society, but as an institution that affirms values, morality, ethics and a spirituality that are not just to be characteristic of the church but are for the good of all humankind. Such values, ethics, morality and spirituality lead to expressions of justice and a civil society that are rooted in the character of God in whose image all people are created. For sure, the church has not always done well as an expression of God-ordained values. Its flaws, foibles and, at times, destructiveness are well-known. But all nations, and all people everywhere, would do well to embrace and bless the church in what it embodies and brings to society and the world.[50]

Reflections on praxis

Of course, the immediate question is one of how do we make this work. What form does it take in the church? The following reflections are offered as a way to begin to think about how we use these voices in the church.

1. Read *all* the psalms publicly, and read all *of* the psalms. The contemporary North American church has failed in this call. Further, learn to read them well. Learn to read them with the passion the poetry evokes. This takes time and practice.
2. Teach on the nature of the various kinds of psalms and the imprecations in some of the psalms. The psalms teach us to pray and give us the broad range of the voices of worship (praise, lament, thanksgiving, trust, wisdom, imprecation and more). Our congregations need to know well what they are and how to use them.
3. Publicly name the horrors of our world. Leaders in the church, and the church itself, are called to speak up for righteousness, justice and mercy. To not name movements and institutions that perpetrate brutal wickedness

50 A popular affirmation of the value of the church is Kevin DeYoung and Ted Kluck, *Why We Love the Church: In Praise of Institutions and Organized Religion* (Chicago: Moody, 2009).

in the world is to give them voice and power.

4. Pray, speak and sing the imprecations as a worship call on God to respond. As noted above, there are boundaries on how they are used and to whom they are addressed, but to not use the voice is to fail to embrace all the gifts that God has given the church.
5. Act in mercy and justice. To pray and not act is hypocritical. The church is called to be an agent of redemption in the world through Jesus Christ. So, while we call out people and movements of violence and brutality, we also need to act in a way that stops such violence, offers the grace and forgiveness of Christ to perpetrators and rescues, protects and brings hope and healing to those victimized by violence and brutality.

Conclusion

Erich Zenger writes:

> ...the good news is:
>
> The stream of events will not run on forever, over blood and victims, goodness, evil, innocence and justice. *God* will put an end to the course of history and will make clear that there is a difference between justice and injustice, and that this difference must be demonstrated. God will seek out the buried victims, the forgotten, starved children, the dishonoured women [and men], and God will find the hidden doers of these deeds. God will gather all of them before God's eternal, holy will for the good, so that all must see how it stands with their lives.[51]

Certainly this is the hope of all who seek a world "put to rights."[52]

Nancy deClaisse-Walford writes:

> Is such language permissible in the context of the biblical text? The overwhelming consensus seems to be "Yes; by all

---

51 Zenger, *A God of Vengeance?* viii. Emphasis in original.

52 A favourite expression of N.T. Wright, see for example, N.T. Wright, *Simply Christian: Why Christianity Makes Sense* (New York: HarperOne, 2006), 3.

> means, yes." People are accused unjustly; goodness is sometimes rewarded with bad; justice is not always served. How should the people of God respond? With silence? With indifference? With long-suffering? Yes—sometimes. And yet at other times, God calls on us to speak out, to protest, and to say, "This is not right!"[53]

Imprecations in the psalms give the church that voice.

---

53 deClaisse-Walford, et al., *The Book of Psalms,* 832–833.

Theological

5

The church in God's program of salvation: A Baptist perspective

BY TERRANCE L. TIESSEN

Baptist theology is essentially an ecclesiology. This was clearly demonstrated in the formation of the 1689 London Baptist Confession where the most significant changes made to the Westminster Confession (1646) appear in the articles regarding the church and its ordinances.[1] Unlike some other denominations, one cannot usually tell the soteriological perspective of a Baptist congregation without further examination. At first sight, it may seem that Baptist distinctives stop with their ecclesiology,[2] but I suggest that a discernible shape is given to Baptist soteriology by

---

1 This can be seen in the tabular comparison of these two confessions at http://www.proginosko.com/docs/wcf_lbcf.html; accessed May 12, 2016.

2 Generally speaking, the Baptist distinctives include an affirmation of regenerate church membership, believer's baptism, congregational polity, local church autonomy and religious freedom (as part of a general freedom of conscience).

entailment of our commitment to believer baptism. In this paper, I will examine the big picture, looking at the role the church plays in God's program of salvation. Mine is a Baptist perspective, but I do not expect that all Baptists would accept it as their own.

The church as a means of grace

Baptists these days are often uncomfortable speaking about "means of grace" and "sacraments." Our roots are in the radical Reformation tradition which moved further from the practices of the Roman Catholic Church than the magisterial reformers did. The immediacy of the believer's relationship with God is highly valued and the Baptist stress on the necessity of conversion through individual or personal faith for salvation can easily foster individualism.[3] Nonetheless, I want to suggest that Baptists need not be afraid of the sacramental language of "means of grace," and that we should affirm that the church is God's primary means of doing his work of grace in the world.[4]

God's intention that the church should be a means of grace is highlighted in Jesus' promise that he would build his church on "this rock" (Peter), and that the gates of hell would "not prevail against it" (Matthew 16:18).[5] Christ "loved the church and gave

---

[3] This was observed by Stephen Duffy, a Roman Catholic priest and professor of theology. He writes: "The Baptist tradition, in which salvation has little to do with receiving sacraments (ordinances) and more to do with preaching and soul winning, seems to emphasize that grace works directly in the individual will in obedient conversion to Jesus Christ as Lord and Savior. The Catholic tradition, on the other hand, strikes a more communal note; salvation is mediated through the church and its sacramental system." Stephen J. Duffy, "Southern Baptist and Roman Catholic soteriologies: A comparative study," *Pro Ecclesia*, Vol. 9, No. 4 (Fall 2000): 445.

[4] Mark Dever sums up well how Baptists should see this matter: "The church itself is a means of grace not because it grants salvation apart from faith but because it is the God-ordained means his Spirit uses to proclaim the saving gospel, to illustrate the gospel, and to confirm the gospel. The church is the conduit through which the benefits of Christ's death normally come." Mark Dever, *The Church: The Gospel Made Visible* (Nashville: IX Marks/B&H Academic, 2012), 74.

[5] Gregg Allison observes the connection within Matthew's narrative between the promise to build the church and Jesus' prediction of his death and resurrection. "It does not seem too far a stretch to say that Jesus' mission of accomplishing salvation and of constructing the church is all of a piece. If this is the case, then the church becomes an agent in the Son's mission to rescue humanity from sin. And Jesus himself prophesied the church and its role in the outworking of salvation." Gregg R. Allison, *Sojourners and Strangers: The Doctrine of the Church*. Foundations of Evangelical Theology (Wheaton: Crossway, 2012), 58. All my quotations of Scripture are from

himself up for her...so that he might present the church to himself in splendor" (Ephesians 5:25, 27), and God "put all things under [Christ's] feet and gave him as head over all things to the church, which is his body, the fullness of him who fills all in all" (Ephesians 1:22–23). This body is constituted by baptism with the Holy Spirit (1 Corinthians 12:13) and is equipped for its ministry in the world by "the grace given to each one of us according to the measure of Christ's gift" (Ephesians 4:7–12, 15–16). It is for this reason that the writer to the Hebrews urged believers to assemble regularly as the church (Hebrews 10:24–25). As with Israel under the Abrahamic covenant, so in the new covenant, God works primarily in and through the covenant community as the renewed people of God, a community in which all the members are regenerate; they all know the Lord (Jeremiah 31:32–34), unlike the situation in the old covenant when "not all Israel was Israel" (Romans 9:6).[6]

The church is so important to God's purposes that it does not come to an end when salvation is complete. It is instrumental in God's bringing his kingdom to realization, but in Romans 8 creation is groaning for the redemption of God's people because it will then be properly stewarded and not abused by vice-regents not doing God's will. The creation of the earth was the context in which humans as the image of God were to thrive and the climax of God's creative work came with the creation of those image bearers. Likewise, in the new earth the dominion of redeemed human beings is not taken away as though the new earth were the final goal. Rather, the people whom God has redeemed through the Son and formed into a worshipping community will then live in perfect harmony with one another because of their perfect fellowship with God. The bride of Christ will be visible in all the glory of her total redemption and sanctification when the entire population of the earth is the body of Christ in right relationship to its head. Certainly, the renewal of the cosmos is a part of the regenerative and restorative work accomplished in

---

the ESV unless otherwise noted, but Scripture citations embedded in quotes from other writers are not changed.

6 Peter J. Gentry and Stephen J. Wellum, *Kingdom through Covenant: A Biblical-Theological Understanding of the Covenants* (Wheaton: Crossway, 2012), 649.

the application of Christ's victory at the cross, but the relationship between God's created image bearers and the physical creation will be essentially the same as it was before sin distorted the exercise of dominion by humans. Thus the formation of the church, body and bride of Christ, is God's primary interest, and the restoration of the earth is putting to rights all that sin had disrupted in the creation, so that it serves as a fitting dwelling place for God and his people in perfectly reconciled harmony (Revelation 21:1–3).[7] Then the church will be "the fullness of him who fills all in all" (Ephesians 1:17–23).

The church and the new covenant

God's saving plan is described in Scripture within the context of God's establishment of covenants, so we cannot properly consider the church's place in God's saving program without looking carefully at its relationship to God's covenants.[8] As Thomas McComiskey observes, "the major periods of redemptive history are governed by great covenantal institutions,"[9] and the church is surely the institution most pertinent to the new covenant (Jeremiah 31:31–34; Isaiah 42:6; 49:6–8; Ezekiel 36:25–27; Joel 2:28–32).[10] Each of the covenants is a further stage in the process of God's self-revelation, without which no one could know God in a saving way.

Throughout the covenants that God established, we see God's intention that human parties whom God had blessed with a covenant relationship should be a blessing. The covenants were a process by which he gave those people a mission, on God's behalf,

---

7 See Stanley J. Grenz, *Theology for the Community of God* (Nashville: Broadman and Holman, 1994), 478.

8 I concur with Peter Gentry and Stephen Wellum that a proper understanding of the biblical covenants "provides the grounding to a Baptist ecclesiology over against other ecclesiologies," and I agree substantially with the position they expound, which they call "progressive covenantalism" (Gentry and Wellum, *Kingdom through Covenant*, 25). Most significant for ecclesiology is the way in which a difference of conviction concerning the continuity/discontinuity between the old and the new covenants leads to pedobaptism in the Reformed churches but believer's baptism among Baptists.

9 Thomas Edward McComiskey, *The Covenants of Promise: A Theology of the Old Testament Covenants* (Grand Rapids: Baker, 1985).

10 As Gregg Allison states, in summing up Paul's point in Ephesians 3:2–11, "the church belongs within the eternal divine counsel as a means of divine revelation" of God's eternal plan (Allison, *Sojourners and Strangers*, 58).

beyond themselves. This was true even before the Fall, in the covenant of creation where God gave humanity the mandate to fill the earth, subdue it and to rule over the rest of creation (Genesis 1:28; cf. 2:15). "The care and keeping of creation is our human mission. The human race exists on the planet with a purpose that flows from the creative purpose of God himself."[11]

Jeffrey Niehaus argues plausibly that even the original covenant of creation was part of "God's overall program of covenants that lead to renewal" because "redemption is implied in creation." As Creator, God has "an ultimate covenantal commitment to restore all that he has created, including a new heavens and earth and a new humanity."[12] Later, God chose Israel in order "to make himself known to the world through her." Israel was to show that "there is none like him in all the earth" (Exodus 8:10; 9:14; 14:4, 18), "the earth is YAHWEH's" (9:29) and "YAHWEH is greater than all the gods" (18:11). Thus YAHWEH used Israel to be an instrument, to be his witness.[13]

It is God's intention that the nations "will self-consciously share in the blessing of Abraham through deliberate appropriation of it for themselves."[14] This purpose does not change in the new covenant when God chooses the church as his primary and normal means of saving revelation. The "multinational vista" stated in God's promises to Abraham "is possible only through Christ," and Paul could therefore "say what he had said to the Galatians: 'You are all sons of God through faith in Christ Jesus. ... If you belong to Christ, then you are Abraham's seed, and heirs according to the promise' (Galatians 3:26, 29)."[15] Before creation, God planned to bring the church into being in the fulness of time, and so "the Son's self-giving and the Spirit's regenerative work were the execution of the Father's eternal plan. Not only were we chosen in Christ 'before the foundation of the

---

11 Christopher J.H, Wright, *The Mission of God: Unlocking the Bible's Grand Narrative* (Downers Grove: IVP Academic, 2006), 65.

12 Jeffrey J. Niehaus, "An Argument Against Theologically Constructed Covenants," *JETS* 50 (2007):272.

13 Seock-Tae Sohn, *The Divine Election of Israel* (Grand Rapids: Eerdmans, 1972), 100; cited by John Walton, *Covenant: God's Purpose, God's Plan* (Grand Rapids: Zondervan, 1994), 28.

14 Wright, *Mission of God*, 219.

15 Wright, *Mission of God*, 220.

world' (Ephesians 1:4, NKJV); Christ himself is spoken of as the Lamb slain from the foundation of the world' (Revelation 13:8, KJV)."[16] The new covenant's ceremonial meal (Matthew 26:16–29; Luke 22:14–20) is given to Jesus' disciples, not simply to the houses of Israel and Judah, but to those who follow Jesus, "regardless of ethnicity, Jew first and, later on, also non-Jew."[17] The "one new man" of Ephesians 2:15 is "a new Adam," and the church "constitutes this new Adam—a renewal of the Adamic role initiated with Abraham and his family."[18]

One of the most exciting features of the covenant is the promise of God's presence among his people. YAHWEH makes them his dwelling place and makes them his people (Leviticus 26:12). The language God uses there is

> replete with echoes of the Genesis portrait of creation under God's blessing (especially fruitfulness and increase) or of the rolling back of the curse (in peace and the absence of danger).... The covenant presence of God will be a return to the intimacy of Eden. Ultimately, God's presence among his people must point to the blessing of his presence in all the earth. And thereby, what would be true for Israel in covenant blessing...would eventually be true for all who would enter into the same blessing through the outworking of God's covenant with Abraham.[19]

We see this covenant blessing picked up in New Testament references to the church as God's dwelling place by his Spirit (Ephesians 2:19–22; 3:6); we are God's new covenant temple, the new covenant fulfilment of the tabernacle in the wilderness and the temple in Jerusalem. For this reason, the presence of Christian congregations in a neighbourhood, provided they are true to the gospel, will be a redemptive instrument of God's own presence in that community. "The presence of God in Israel's tabernacle and temple looked backward to his presence in Eden, and forward

---

16 Michael Horton, *God of Promise: Introducing Covenant Theology* (Grand Rapids: Baker Books, 2006), 80.

17 Gentry and Wellum, *Kingdom through Covenant*, 496.

18 Gentry and Wellum, *Kingdom through Covenant*, 496.

19 Wright, *Mission of God*, 334.

to his ultimate presence among all nations in a renewed creation (Revelation 21–22),"[20] so that the church becomes not only a fulfilment of old covenant institutions but also a foretaste of the consummation of God's redemptive work in the new heavens and new earth. Our ethical distinctness should be "a pointer to the presence of the ethical God, YHWH"[21] in our midst (cf. Leviticus 19:2; cf. Paul's citation of Leviticus 26:12 in 2 Corinthians 6:16–18). Indeed, Paul viewed this presence of God in the church as the very mystery of the gospel (Colossians 1:27). Now we are the temple of God, but ultimately the whole cosmos will be God's temple, and we will serve him in it as kings and priests (Revelation 5:10).[22]

The church's role as proclaimer of God's Word

John Walton has proposed that, in Genesis 12:3,

> the nature of the blessing on the nations is that through Abraham's family, God revealed himself. The law was given through them, the Scripture was written by them, and their history became the public record of God's attributes in action. Then to climax it all, his own Son came through them and provided salvation for the world. Israel was the chosen people of God, not in the sense that they always obeyed or believed; not in the sense that they were all automatically heirs to salvation; but in the sense that they were the instrument, and sometimes the medium, of his own self-revelation. It is expected and proper that the New Testament should emphasize the blessing of salvation through Christ, for that is the ultimate provision of the way that relationship could be achieved. It is the climax and culmination of God's program of revelation.[23]

This being the case, it is not surprising that the New Testament emphasizes the church's role in spreading the gospel and teaching

20 Wright, *Mission of God*, 334.
21 Wright, *Mission of God*, 336.
22 Wright, *Mission of God*, 340.
23 Walton, *Covenant*, 60.

believers so that they are well equipped for service to God both in the church and in the world. (See, for instance, Matthew 28:19–20; Luke 2:29–32; 3:4–6; 24:45–48; Acts 3:18–26; Romans 1:1–6; 10:12–15).

The covenant people are peculiarly raised up by God as missionary instruments in God's program of salvation. This is very evident in God's deliverance of Israel from Egypt.

> Clearly, the motivation from God's point of view was not only the liberation of his enslaved people but this driving divine will to be known to all nations for who and what he truly is. The mission of God to be known is what drives this whole narrative.[24]

This was similarly true of great acts of YHWH which he did after the Exodus.[25] "The whole history of Israel...is intended to be the shop window for the knowledge of God in all the earth. This is the reason the story is to be told from generation to generation.[26]

God's election of Israel was "instrumental, not an end in itself." His purpose was "fundamentally missional, not just soteriological,"[27] and the same must be said concerning God's choosing of the church. Thus Paul argues in Romans 10:4–18 that, ironically,

> Israel's rejection of the gospel is not something strange; rather, it was prophesied in the Scriptures, as the warnings in Deut. 32 and Isa. 65 demonstrate. At the same time Israel's rejection of the gospel is organically, if paradoxically, linked

---

24 Wright, *Mission of God*, 95 (emphasis mine). Gentry and Wellum see an "unmistakable allusion to Jeremiah 16:16 in Matthew 4," where Jesus chooses twelve men "whom he would train as his special agents. Jesus tells Peter and Andrew that "he will use his followers to bring the exiles home." This second stage of return from exile was inaugurated with the coming of Jesus and his ministry. "The new exodus has begun in the person and work of Jesus Christ" (cf. allusion to Isaiah 27:12–13 in 1 Thessalonians 4:13–18). Gentry and Wellum, *Kingdom through Covenant*, 489–491.

25 Those acts include "the crossing of the Jordan (Joshua 4:24), David's victory over Goliath (1 Samuel 17:46), God's covenant with David (2 Samuel 7:26), God's answering prayer in Solomon's temple (1 Kings 8:41–43, 60), God delivering Jerusalem from the Assyrians (2 Kings 19:19; Isaiah 37:20), God bringing Israel back from exile (Isaiah 45:6; Jeremiah 33:9; Ezekiel 36:23). Wright, *Mission of God*, 127.

26 Wright, *Mission of God*, 127, citing Psalm 22:27, 30–31.

27 Wright, *Mission of God*, 263.

> with the promised acceptance of the Gentiles into the people of God.[28]

In turn, Paul saw his Gentile mission as a means for the salvation of Israel (Romans 11:13–14). "When a Gentile joins the eschatological people of God, it is a *creatio ex nihilo*, a creation out of nothing; when a Jew comes to faith in Jesus the Messiah, it is like a resurrection."[29]

Perhaps the most far-reaching beneficial result of the Protestant Reformation, in its impact upon the Christian church, was the priority given to Scripture and the importance of preaching. The radical reformers were particularly vigorous in allowing Scripture to be the supreme authority in the church, and Baptists stand in this tradition. The health of the church, and its effectiveness as God's normal means of doing his work of grace in the world, through developing disciples of Christ within their congregations and proclaiming the gospel to unbelievers, depends to a large extent upon its faithful teaching of God's revealed Word.

The ordinances as means of grace or sacraments

Even Baptists who acknowledge that the church is God's primary and normal instrument for pursuing his saving purposes in the new covenant age are often hesitant to speak of the ordinances (baptism and the Lord's supper) as means of grace or sacraments. This arises from the Protestant rejection of the Roman Catholic belief that the sacraments (of which they now have seven) are effective in and of themselves (*ex opere operato*).

---

28 Eckhard J. Schnabel, *Early Christian Mission. Vol. 2: Paul and the Early Church* (Downers Grove: IVP Academic, 2004), 1314.

29 Schnabel, *Early Christian Mission*, 2:1315. As Christopher Wright observes: "Peter sees the priestly nature of the church as 'declaring the praises' of our exodus God and living in such a way among the nations that they come to glorify God (1 Peter 2:9–12). This is an authentic combination of the missional and ethical reapplication of Exodus 19:4–6. Significantly also, in the only New Testament text to speak of any individual Christian's ministry in priestly terms, Paul describes his evangelistic mission as his 'priestly duty.' Immediately he refers to the same double direction of movement—bringing the gospel to the nations and bringing the nations to God (Romans 15:16). The ethical dimension of the task actually forms an envelope around the whole letter, as Paul twice gives it as his life's work to bring about 'the obedience of faith among the nations' (Romans 1:5; 16:26, author's translation)." Wright, *Mission of God*, 333.

Furthermore, the radical reformers believed that the magisterial reformers had been insufficiently rigorous in their rejection of extra-biblical accretions to Scripture, and this was particularly seen in regard to the ordinances or sacraments. Through the Anabaptists, the memorialist understanding of Ulrich Zwingli also had a significant influence in the formation of the Baptist tradition.[30] The basic question Christians must answer from the Scriptures is whether ordinances/sacraments are solely a testimony by the believer or whether God also says and/or does something in and through them, and if so whether he does it only in response to the believer's faith or regardless of it.

Stanley Grenz observed that some Baptists in the twentieth century were reaffirming "a sacramental significance for the acts of commitment, while retaining the primacy of the designation 'ordinance.'"[31] Grenz himself proposed that, as ordinances, we practice them "as the primary divinely ordained means for us to declare our loyalty to Jesus as Lord," but Christ commanded us to observe them because participation in them is of benefit to us.[32] "Through our participation we not only declare the truth of the gospel, however, we also bear testimony to our reception of the grace symbolized." Thus, "as we affirm our faith in this vivid symbolic manner, the Holy Spirit uses these rites to facilitate our participation in the reality the acts symbolize,"[33] and these ordained means for our expression of loyalty to Christ become "channels of the Holy Spirit at work in our lives."[34]

The Lord's supper

Most Baptists in North America now assume a memorialist understanding of the elements of communion, but "it was not until the end of the eighteenth century that the memorial view became predominant in Baptist churches."[35] *The Second London Confession*

30 As A.H. Strong put it, in a classic Baptist work of the early twentieth century, "By the ordinances, we mean those outward rites which Christ has appointed to be administered in church as visible signs of the saving truth of the Gospel." Augustus H. Strong, *Systematic Theology* (Philadelphia: The Judson Press. 1907), 930.

31 Grenz, *Theology for the Community of God*, 671.

32 Grenz, *Theology for the Community of God*, 671.

33 Grenz, *Theology for the Community of God*, 672.

34 Grenz, *Theology for the Community of God*, 673.

35 Allison, *Sojourners and Strangers*, 385.

of Faith (1689), in paragraph 7 of Article 12, "Of the Lord's supper," stated:

> Worthy receivers, outwardly partaking of the visible elements in this ordinance, do then also inwardly by faith, really and indeed, yet not carnally and corporally, but spiritually receive, and feed upon Christ crucified, and all the benefits of his death; the body and blood of Christ being then not corporally or carnally, but spiritually present to the faith of believers in that ordinance, as the elements themselves are to their outward senses (1 Cor. 10:16, 11:23–26).

Christ is not somehow spiritually present in the elements themselves, any more than he is spiritually present in the written or preached Word, in some sort of substantive way. But Christ has committed himself to these elements, as he has committed himself to the Word, as means through which he ministers grace to those who receive them in faith. Understood in this way, the communion elements are appointed means of grace, just as the Word of God is, and hence they have sacramental significance; they are appointed by our Lord as aids to our faith. In general, the supper symbolizes the Lord's death as the sustaining power of the believer's life. When we eat the bread and drink the cup, we should do so as an act of faith, as a reception of the body and blood of Christ broken and shed for us. We are continuously dependent on the crucified and risen Christ for our spiritual life. But when we eat and drink the body and blood of Christ in faith, we do more than memorialize it, we "participate" in it anew, as Paul explicitly says in 1 Corinthians 10:16. Christ ministers to us by his Spirit, feeding our spirits, nourishing us again with the resurrected life which he obtained through his obedient sacrifice. We partake, with fellow believers, in the meal of the new covenant which Christ established in his blood (Luke 22:20; cf. Jeremiah 31:31–34; Hebrews 8:8–13; 10:16–18).

A mere memorialism does not do justice to 1 Corinthians 11; a careless or unbelieving reception of the elements is serious precisely because those who receive it improperly are spurning Christ who offers himself to us, not simply refusing to remember him.[36] Christ's presence in the supper is not *in* the bread and wine, but by the power of the Spirit who brings about our communion with Christ and his body, the church.[37] It is the *Lord's* supper, not our own.[38] "The fundamental dynamic of God's covenant is operative: God takes the judgement curse to his own heart; those who believe receive instead the covenant blessings through faith, which is, in essence, communion with Christ, crucified, risen and exalted."[39] In John 6:53–56, Jesus speaks of believers eating his flesh and drinking his blood, and a connection is evident between this statement of Jesus and his later words in instituting the new covenant supper. The language seems too strong simply to be interpreted symbolically. "In a spiritual sense, believers 'eat the flesh' and 'drink the blood' of the Son of God."[40] The elements become means by which Christ re-presents himself to us, so that we miss something potentially beneficial to our spiritual lives if we simply remember Christ's death by word and imagination, without the physical act of reception of the elements which Christ himself appointed as means of communion with him and with one another.

Baptism

I find Baptists more likely to speak of the Lord's supper than they are of baptism as a means of grace.[41] The most fundamental

---

36 Note that "the view that the Lord's supper simply commemorates the Lord's sacrificial death has no clear precedent before the sixteenth century." Gregory A. Boyd and Paul R. Eddy, *Across the Spectrum: Understanding Issues in Evangelical Theology* (Grand Rapids: Baker Academic, 2002), 197.

37 Sinclair B. Ferguson, *The Holy Spirit: Contours of Christian Theology* (Downers Grove: InterVarsity Press, 1996), 201.

38 Everett Ferguson, *The Church of Christ: A Biblical Ecclesiology for Today* (Grand Rapids: Eerdmans, 1996), 251: "He sets a table for his people, invites them to it, and presides at the gathering."

39 Ferguson, *The Holy Spirit*, 201.

40 Boyd and Eddy, *Across the Spectrum*, 196.

41 I am intrigued, for instance, by Greg Allison's strong affirmation of the Lord's supper as a means of grace (*Sojourners and Strangers*, 394–398), despite his reluctance to speak of it as a "sacrament," because, in his treatment of baptism, he never gets beyond a memorialist perspective, or at least not beyond an explanation in terms of what the church proclaims, without any indication that God has chosen this Christian practice as a place/event where Christ is ready to do something in the lives of those who participate in faith. But John Hammett's anecdotal experience leads him "to believe that opposition to the word 'sacrament' is weakening among Baptists today"

item of Baptist belief is the conviction that faith must precede baptism, which is itself a visible expression of faith. We are concerned about any return to Rome's belief that baptism itself saves, but we are also leery of fellow Protestants who call the ordinances "sacraments" while continuing to baptize infants, even though they insist on the necessity of faith for salvation. The rise among Baptists of churches which teach that baptism is necessary to salvation further contributes to a nervousness about a sacramental understanding of baptism.

But anti-sacramentalism was not always a feature of the commitment to believer's baptism.[42] Stanley Fowler has made a valuable contribution to Baptist theology by making us aware of important Baptist churchmen and theologians before us who believed that God intends baptism to be a means of grace. Of the seventeenth century, Fowler writes:

> Early Baptist authors consistently argued against any kind of sacramentalism which posits an automatic bestowal of grace through baptism, but they did not deny that baptism has an instrumental function in the application of redemption.... Baptist protests against baptismal regeneration did

[John Hammett, "Believer Baptism: Human Act of Obedience and Divine Means of Grace" (a paper read at the annual meeting of the Evangelical Theological Society in San Diego, Nov. 11, 2014), 2].

42 Jonathan Rainbow explains that, "For Zwingli, baptism was a mere sign. For Hubmaier, it was more than a sign. Baptists historically belong in the high baptismal tradition which sees baptism as the expression and embodiment of the saving work of God, the sacramentum fidei, not just an act of obedience tacked on. Baptists historically have known how to embrace Peter's declaration, 'Baptism now saves you' (1 Peter 3:20), not because they ascribe a crude, magical saving power to the rite as such, but because they consider, on the basis of an open and personal confession, that the person coming to the water believes in Jesus Christ, and that there is an inner reality to which the baptism corresponds. Baptism is not magic, but it is more than a sign. That is the heart of what the Reformation Anabaptists were saying." Jonathan H. Rainbow, "'Confessor baptism': The baptismal doctrine of the early Anabaptists," in *Believer's Baptism: Sign of the New Covenant in Christ*, New American Commentary Studies in Bible and Theology, ed. Thomas R. Schreiner and Shawn D. Wright (Nashville: B&H Publishing, 2006), 196. As Paul Fiddes puts it, sacramentalist Baptists "affirm that God acts in baptism, coming graciously to meet and transform the believer as part of a process of salvation which has already begun." Paul Fiddes, "Baptist Theology," in *The Cambridge Dictionary of Christian Theology*, ed. Ian A. McFarland, David A.S. Fergusson, Karen Kilby, Iain R. Torrance (New York: Cambridge University Press, 2011), 56.

> not necessarily deny that baptism is instrumental in some way in the experience of spiritual rebirth by confessing believers.[43]

In the eighteenth century, however, Baptist theologians less commonly used the term "sacrament" of baptism, which had been used interchangeably with "ordinance," in the seventeenth century.[44] And they seldom called baptism a "seal," which had been common among seventeenth century authors. But Fowler astutely observes that "the way in which baptism functions according to Baptist theology, i.e., as a tangible confirmation of faith and what faith receives, is precisely what the term seal is all about," so the term fell out of favour but the concept did not.[45] In the nineteenth century, much of the Baptist literature was "reactionary, focusing on what does not happen in the baptism of infants and attacking the idea of the automatic conveyance of grace through baptism," and consequently it was common to affirm "a minimalist understanding of what actually happens in the baptismal event."[46]

In a different context from that of the nineteenth century, Baptist sacramentalism was reformulated in the twentieth century,[47] but its key proponents neglected systematic theology and disregarded their own earlier Baptist literature, and this contributed to poor acceptance of their proposals within their own Baptist communities.[48] As a result, Baptists in the twenty-first century (particularly in North America) are reluctant to speak of baptism

---

43 Stanley Fowler, *More Than A Symbol: The British Baptist Recovery of Baptismal Sacramentalism*. Studies in Baptist History and Thought, Vol. 2 (Eugene: Wipf & Stock, 2002), 31–32.

44 Fowler, *More Than A Symbol*, 14.

45 Fowler, *More Than A Symbol*, 56.

46 Fowler, *More Than A Symbol*, 86.

47 Fowler helpfully describes the twentieth-century context in which Baptist sacramentalism was reformulated. Being a minority in England, believer baptists needed to enunciate clearly their denominational identity, "and it was not clear that a purely symbolic view of baptism was sufficient to undergird a distinct denominational existence." Baptists also became more involved in ecumenical discussion, and the exegetical work done by people like Ernest Payne, G.R. Beasley-Murray, Morris West and Neville Clark rediscovered in the New Testament a sacramental understanding of baptism (Fowler, *More Than A Symbol*, 154–155).

48 Fowler, *More Than A Symbol*, 55.

as a means of grace. So it did not surprise me that no writer in the fine collection of essays on believer's baptism edited by Thomas Schreiner and Shawn Wright used the term "sacrament" in regard to the New Testament teaching concerning baptism.[49]

In the foreword to Schreiner and Wright's collection, Timothy George asserts that "the recovery of a robust doctrine of believer's baptism can serve as an antidote to the theological minimalism and atomistic individualism that prevail in many Baptist churches in our culture."[50] I suggest that a classic sacramental position offers just the sort of "robust doctrine" that is needed, and I sometimes hear such a doctrine even from Baptist authors who explicitly reject the term "sacrament" to identify what they describe, for fear that it entails an assertion of intrinsic efficacy. So perhaps we can also say of Baptist theology in the twenty-first century that the concept of sacramentalism is being affirmed in instances where the term is avoided.[51]

---

49 Schreiner and Wright, ed. *Believer's Baptism*. The editors of that volume grant that "Fowler rightly argues that baptism is more than a symbol," but they believe that "the use of the word 'sacramental' is unfortunate since it is liable to a number of different interpretations." Although they perceive that "Fowler's own use of the word may fit with what is argued in this book since he claims that those who are unbaptized but believers may still be saved," they think that his book "suffers from lack of clarity in using the word 'sacramental,'" so that they find it "difficult to determine precisely what he means" ("Introduction," 2, n. 4).

To the contrary, I suggest that it is not hard to discern what Fowler and other Baptist sacramentalists mean by "sacrament" or "means of grace." Fowler writes: "for sacramentalists the confirming/assuring/sealing function of baptism concerns the confirmation that saving union with Christ is here and now a reality, not that such union with Christ has become a reality at some earlier time through some other means" (Fowler, *More Than A Symbol*, 211). And he hears a unified New Testament affirmation that "entrance into the life of the kingdom of God includes repentance, faith and baptism from the human side, and forgiveness of sin and the gift of the Holy Spirit from the divine side, and that baptism is the normal point at which the action of each side is focused" (221). George Beasley-Murray posited that what Baptists mean when they call baptism a sacrament is: "the occasion of God's personal dealing with a man in such a fashion that he henceforth lives a new existence in the power and fellowship of God." George Beasley-Murray, *Baptism in the New Testament* (Grand Rapids: Eerdmans, 1962), 274. Similarly, John Hammett describes baptism as "one of the appointed contexts where God meets obedient faith with blessing." Here, God may give to Christians who receive baptism in faith "strengthening and sustaining grace," though "not, strictly speaking, saving grace" (Hammett "Believer baptism," 7).

50 Timothy George, "Foreword," in Schreiner and Wright, ed. *Believer's Baptism*, xvii.

51 As Fowler said of the eighteenth century (Fowler, *More Than A Symbol*, 56).

In his splendid study of baptism in Luke-Acts, Robert Stein observes that, "In the experience of becoming a Christian, five integrally related components took place at the same time, usually on the same day: repentance, faith, confession, receiving the gift of the Holy Spirit, and baptism."[52] Previously, in discussing the association of baptism with the forgiveness of sins in Acts 2:38, Stein had made the important observation that

> the desire to refute a mechanistic understanding of baptism that leads to the error of baptismal regeneration need not cause us to divide and separate in time and intent these two components of the conversion experience that are intimately associated by Luke and the NT.[53]

When Ananias visited Paul in Damascus he told him: "Rise and be baptized and wash away your sins, calling on his name" (Acts 22:16). Regarding this statement, Stein writes:

> Here 'washing away one's sins,' i.e., the forgiveness of sins, is intimately associated with baptism, and the expression, 'wash away your sins,' suggests that *there is not just a temporal but a causal relationship between baptism and the forgiveness of sins* [emphasis is mine]....
>
> A "repentance-faith-baptism" results in the forgiveness of sins. Luke, who in his Gospel describes John the Baptist as "proclaiming a baptism of repentance for the forgiveness of sin" (3:3), ties baptism and the forgiveness of sins intimately together. This fits well with what Paul says in Ephesians 5:26, which is most simply interpreted, that Jesus gave himself for the church "having cleansed her [a reference to the forgiveness of sins] by the washing of water [a reference to baptism] with the word.
>
> The interconnectedness of repentance, faith and baptism is witnessed to by the fact that they all lead to the forgiveness of sins. It would certainly be wrong to think that Luke believed

---

52 Robert H. Stein, "Baptism in Luke-Acts," in Schreiner and Wright, ed. *Believer's Baptism*, 42.

53 Stein, "Baptism in Luke-Acts," 40.

> these were three separate ways of receiving forgiveness: the "repentance" way, the "faith" way and the "baptism" way. On the contrary, he understood them as all part of the experience of becoming a Christian. This is even more evident on the occasions where these components are paired together in Acts as bringing about the forgiveness of sins: in 2:38 repentance and baptism are placed side by side ("repent and be baptized") as resulting in the forgiveness of sins, and in 26:18 repentance and faith ("turn from darkness to light...by faith in me") are associated together as the necessary response(s) for receiving the forgiveness of sins ("that they may receive forgiveness of sins"). Compare also 5:31–32 where repentance and the forgiveness of sins are mentioned together in 5:31 and the gift of the Holy Spirit and obedience/faith are mentioned together in 5:32. For Luke "repentance" is an example of synecdoche in which "repentance" refers to "repentance-faith-baptism." Similarly, "faith" refers to "faith-repentance-baptism" and "baptism" refers to "baptism-repentance-faith," i.e., a baptism preceded by repentance and faith. Thus one can refer to becoming a Christian as "the day they repented," "the day they believed," "the day they were baptized," "the day they confessed Christ" and "the day they received the Spirit" or, to use Johannine terminology "the day they were born again." All these are interrelated and integral components in the experience of conversion in becoming a Christian, and all take place in Acts on the same day.[54]

When I speak of baptism as a "means of grace," I simply mean to affirm that, in this rite, it is not only the humans involved who are active (whether that be the baptizand or the church) but that we can also expect God to act. As Stein remarks, "becoming a Christian in Acts is a 'trinitarian' affair in which the individual, the church, and God are all intimately involved."[55]

---

54 Stein, "Baptism in Luke-Acts," 41–42.

55 Stein, "Baptism in Luke-Acts," 46. Stein's conclusion makes this point well: "Along with this human response of repentance-faith-confession and the church's baptizing of the individual, *God is also intimately involved in the conversion process* [emphasis mine]. Thus, becoming a Christian involves a 'trinitarian' relationship. In discussing the di-

Contemporary Baptist nervousness about speaking too strongly concerning the effect of *God's* work in baptism was stimulated to some extent by the rise of the Stone-Campbell restoration movement, within the Baptist community. So I read Ardel Caneday's critique of that movement with particular interest, and I was happy to hear, even in that threatening context, an understanding of baptism which gives it significance beyond the mere symbolic. In Paul's first letter to the Corinthians, Caneday sees a recognition by Paul that "some in Corinth are inclined to attribute to baptism a significance that Christ did not give it (1 Corinthians 1:14–15)," and that Paul therefore "subordinates baptizing to preaching the gospel (1:17)," in order "to correct their sacerdotal-born factionalism."[56] Caneday's identification of the Corinthian error as "sacerdotalism," not "sacramentalism" is highly important. If that distinction is kept clearly in mind, speaking of baptism as a "sacrament" is less likely to cause offence.

Accordingly, Caneday goes on to observe that "Paul regards baptism as significant and *not a bare symbol* [emphasis supplied]," in Galatians 3:27: "For as many of you as were baptized into Christ have put on Christ."[57] Noting the great importance of

---

vine role in the conversion process, Luke is less interested in describing the prevenient work of the Spirit in bringing conviction and making possible repentance and faith (see, however, 2:37; 13:48; 16:14) than in describing the coming of the Spirit upon those who repent and believe. Because of the intimate relationship of repentance-faith-confession-baptism, *the additional component of the gift of the Holy Spirit can be associated with any of these four components* [emphasis in original]. In Acts it is associated at times with repentance, at times with faith, at times with baptism. Its association with baptism is such that the receiving of the Spirit can be referred to as 'the baptism of the Holy Spirit' (Matthew 3:11; Mark 1:8; Luke 3:16; John 1:33; Acts 1:5; 11:16; and 1 Corinthians 12:13). The relationship between the coming of the Spirit and baptism, however, should not be understood as automatic (*ex opere operato*) in Acts, because at times the Spirit is portrayed as coming before baptism." Stein, "Baptism in Luke-Acts," 54.

56 A.B. Caneday, "Baptism in the Stone-Campbell Restoration Movement," in Schreiner and Wright, ed. *Believer's Baptism*, 275.

57 Caneday comments: "[Paul] seems to equate all who have put on Christ with all who are baptized into Christ, as though the two were fused as one. To be baptized into Christ by submission to the symbolic washing called for by the gospel is to be clothed with Christ Jesus. This seems remarkable since this statement appears at the pinnacle of Paul's argument against Jewish intruders who have attempted to seduce Christians in Galatia to subject themselves to circumcision of the flesh so that they might become Abraham's children (Galatians 2:16–3:29, esp. 3:6–7,29)." Caneday, "Baptism in the Stone-Campbell Restoration Movement," 276.

Acts 2:38 in any assessment of the Stone-Campbell tradition, Caneday grants that "some in the Stone-Campbell tradition have overstated their case," but he thinks that "evangelical critiques have too often been characterized by strong bias, exaggeration and misrepresentation."[58] As we seek to enunciate in a biblically faithful way *how baptism is a means of grace*, I believe that Caneday's comments on Acts 2:38 are very helpful. Concerning his translation of the text ("Repent and let each of you be baptized on the name of Jesus Christ for the forgiveness of your sins and you will receive the gift of the Holy Spirit") he writes:

> Rejections of this exegetical understanding derive from confusion of the *instrumental cause* and the *efficient cause* of salvation. Expressed another way, the array of interpretations of Acts 2:38 originate from merging the *means* of salvation with its *ground*. The importance of distinguishing the two can hardly be overstated. When we read or hear Acts 2:38, it is easy to confuse the *efficient* and *instrumental* causes of salvation. Out of zeal to enforce Christian baptism, some have mistakenly exalted repentance and baptism to the place of effectual cause. This error of "baptismal regeneration," vesting baptism with effectual cleansing power, invariably diminishes grace. Yet others, excessively fervent to preserve *sola fide*, have committed the opposite error of "creedal (or popularly 'decisional') regeneration," assigning to faith the effectual saving power that belongs only to God's grace. Some who advocate creedal regeneration iso-

Elsewhere, the apostle Paul spoke even more strongly, as Caneday asserts: "Paul more expressly links receiving Christ's saving effects with Christian baptism when he says, 'Or do you not realize that as many as were baptized into Christ Jesus were baptized into his death? We, therefore, were buried with him through baptism into this death with the purpose that just as Christ was raised from the dead through the glory of the Father, in the same manner we also might walk in newness of life' (Romans 6:3–4). As Paul formulates the matter, to be 'baptized into Christ Jesus' is to be 'baptized into his death.' Thus, 'baptism into Christ Jesus' is the means through (*dia*) which the believer is 'buried with him.' This, Paul makes clear when he says, 'Thus, we were buried with him through this baptism into death' (*sunetaphē men auto dia tou baptismatos eis ton thanaton*). So, it seems that for Paul those baptized into Christ Jesus share in the redeeming effects of Christ's death." Caneday, "Baptism in the Stone-Campbell Restoration Movement," 276.

58 Caneday, "Baptism in the Stone-Campbell Restoration Movement," 299.

> late faith from repentance and deny both repentance and baptism any function in our salvation lest they deny *sola fide* and *sola gratia*. Others for the same reason suppress the *proper function of baptism as a means of God's grace* [emphasis mine] and abstract baptism from repentance as separable rather than merely distinguishable. Because they confound *grace* and the *means* of grace, they suppose that to speak of repentance and baptism as *means by which God administers his grace* is tantamount to denying God's redemptive accomplishment in Christ Jesus as the *sole ground of God's gracious, saving act*. Indeed, if one conceptually isolates baptism from repentance, then baptism loses its integral defining connection. The result is that baptism becomes an empty form, ancillary and optional to repentance. For Peter, however, repentance and baptism, though distinguishable, are inseparable—one without the other is unthinkable, especially for the apostles and early Christians.[59]

Caneday then explains Peter's statement that "baptism…now saves you" (1 Peter 3:21) by judicious appeal to this distinction between effectual and instrumental cause.[60] In Acts 22:16, after Paul's encounter with Jesus, Ananias tells him to "rise and be baptized and wash away your sins." An unmistakable connection is made between baptism or washing, and forgiveness or washing away of sins. This might be simply a reference to the symbol (baptism) and the thing symbolized (forgiveness of sins)[61] but, as Fowler notes, "While the reference to invoking the name of the

---

59 Caneday, "Baptism in the Stone-Campbell Restoration Movement," 302–303.

60 Caneday writes: "The final phrase of v. 21, 'through the resurrection of Jesus Christ,' links to the verb 'save.' Thus, in this one verse Peter speaks of both the instrumental and efficient causes of salvation: 'now baptism saves you…through the resurrection of Jesus Christ.' Anyone who is tempted to suppress Peter's assured declaration that baptism's water 'now saves you' and in its place elevate his attached mention of the effectual cause, needs to recall that this 'language concerning the effect of baptism is by no means unparalleled in the New Testament; any view of baptism which finds it a rather embarrassing ceremonial extra, irrelevant to Christian salvation, is not doing justice to New Testament teaching.'" Caneday, "Baptism in the Stone-Campbell Restoration Movement," 305–306, citing R.T. France, "Exegesis in Practice: Two Samples," in *New Testament Interpretation*, ed. I.H. Marshall (Grand Rapids: Eerdmans, 1977), 274.

61 Caneday, "Baptism in the Stone-Campbell Restoration Movement," 306.

Lord indicates that the power at work is that of the Lord, and not baptism *per se*, it is equally clear that this spiritually cleansing power of God is conceived as operative in the context of baptism."[62] Perhaps it was with his own experience in mind that Paul wrote to the Corinthians, "you were washed" (1 Corinthians 6:11), to Titus of "the washing of regeneration" (Titus 3:5) and to the Ephesians of Christ's having cleansed them "by the washing of water with the word (Ephesians 5:26)."[63]

Paul wrote to the Romans: "All of you who were baptized into Christ Jesus were baptized into his death" (Romans 6:3), and to the Galatians: "as many of you as were baptized into Christ have put on Christ" (Galatians 3:27). "For Paul, 'baptism into Christ Jesus' (reflecting the baptismal formula Jesus authorized; *eis*, 'into, unto,' Matt. 28:19) is so integral to being a Christian that to speak of those baptized into Christ is to speak of believers."[64]

---

62 Fowler, *More Than A Symbol*, 159.

63 Of 1 Corinthians 6:11, Caneday observes that Paul "appeals to the Corinthian believers to recall their conversion, signaled by baptism, as the time of their being washed of these contaminants that prevent inheriting God's kingdom. Stein rightly contends that the verb 'you were washed' is not merely a metaphor disconnected from baptism, because Paul attaches the baptismal formula, 'in the name of the Lord Jesus Christ' (Acts 10:48; 1 Corinthians 1:13–15), tightly associating baptism and conversion (Caneday, "Baptism in the Stone-Campbell Restoration Movement," 308, citing Robert Stein, "Baptism and becoming a Christian in the New Testament," *SBJT* 2 (1998):12, and referring also to G.R. Beasley-Murray, *Baptism in the New Testament* (Grand Rapids: Eerdmans, 1962), 162–167. Caneday continues: "That Paul says 'you were washed' instead of 'you were baptized,' accents the actual washing symbolized by the symbolic washing of baptism as Paul's principal concern. Baptism does not wash away sin's filth but 'is the occasion when the Spirit creatively works in the individual." Citing G.R. Beasley-Murray, "Baptism," NIDNTT (Grand Rapids: Zondervan, 1986), 1:153. As D. Garland explains, "That is why this verb appears first, since it marks the beginning of the Christian life, when one is transferred from the sphere of darkness into the power field of the Spirit." Caneday, "Baptism in the Stone-Campbell Restoration Movement," 309, citing D. Garland, *1 Corinthians*, BECNT (Grand Rapids: Baker, 2003), 216.

64 Caneday, "Baptism in the Stone-Campbell Restoration Movement," 310. I note that, in this context, Caneday commends Beasley-Murray's work on baptism in the New Testament because he "has done much to call for serious exegesis and to allow the text to have its full force." Caneday also observes that the exegesis of earlier evangelical scholars on passages like this "was too much guided by the desire to avoid perceived dangers of 'baptismal regeneration' as in the Stone-Campbell tradition," but there is now less suspicion "so that recent commentators on crucial biblical passages find themselves in guarded harmony with their more cautious and articulate counterparts in the Christian Church and Churches of Christ tradition" (Caneday, "Baptism

Thus Caneday criticizes a separation of the symbol from the reality because Paul considered them to be "inseparable but distinguishable" in Romans 6:3–4. In both Romans and Galatians, "Paul argues his case on the assumption that the ritual of baptism is full of significance and is not just a symbol."[65] Baptism into death is the means by which we are buried with Christ, but only if God graciously works in conjunction with the physical act. It is at most an instrumental (not an effectual) cause.[66] But Paul assumes that he is speaking to people for whom the sign and the reality converged when they were baptized; this is why they cannot continue sinning.

Conclusion

Much more could be said about the church's role as God's normal means of grace in the new covenant period, but when the Protestant Reformers spoke about the marks of a true church, the ministry of Word and sacrament was prominent, so I have focused on these means of grace in addressing the theme of the essay. I'm also keenly aware that North American Baptists have tended toward a non-sacramentalist (Zwinglian) understanding of the ordinances, and many are unaware that there is any other way for a Baptist to understand Scripture in this regard. So I thought that it would be beneficial to add another voice to the minority perspective. I have given significant space to the work of Stein and Caneday because it indicates that the essence of a Baptist sacramentalism is more widely affirmed than might ap-

---

in the Stone-Campbell Restoration Movement," 311). Consequently, Caneday observes, "evangelicals tend to agree with Cottrell's restrained comments on Romans 6:3.... This union with Christ is not effected by the ritual itself, either by the water or by the act. It is accomplished by the grace and power of the living God alone. That it happens in the act of baptism is simply a matter of God's free and sovereign choice; he has appropriately designed this event as the occasion for the beginning of this saving union with the Redeemer. It is not wrong to say that water baptism symbolizes or has a metaphorical connection with this saving union (citing J. Cottrell, *Romans* (Joplin: College Press, 1996), 1:383–384).

65 Caneday, "Baptism in the Stone-Campbell Restoration Movement," 313.

66 Baptism is thus analogous to circumcision: "an external sign is meaningless apart from possessing the internal reality to which the sign points, in this case the reality of a heart circumcised by God's Spirit (Romans 2:17–29)." Caneday, "Baptism in the Stone-Campbell Restoration Movement," 312.

pear from the terminology used.[67] Baptists are right to insist that the ordinances do not communicate God's grace automatically, but then nor does the preaching of the Word of God. They are also correct to insist that, although baptism is one of a complex of actions spoken of in the New Testament (somewhat interchangeably) as instrumental in justification and sanctification, without faith it is ineffective as a means of grace. Believer baptism is what the New Testament instructs, but baptism is not dispensable because repentance and faith have occurred. Rather, it is the normal means of expression of that faith, and we should not shrink from giving the biblical language its full force.

God has chosen to make the church the primary instrument of his gracious saving work in the world. As Christ establishes his rule, the church comes into being. In this community God is present by his Spirit, and through its proclamation of the gospel and its obedience to its Lord, God's saving program moves forward. We can expect God's Spirit to work in grace when we act in faith and obedience.

67 Given more space, it would have been very helpful to draw upon the exegetical work of G.R. Beasley-Murray, but I wanted to demonstrate that contemporary evangelicals who do not self-identify as sacramentalist have reached conclusions similar to Beasley-Murray's and have not hesitated to cite him in so doing.

6

The recovery of a sacramental ontology as the basis for developing a sacramental theology of baptism

BY CRAIG A. CARTER

> "Theology that refuses to address questions of ontology can never be more than mythology."[1]

Stan Fowler has made many contributions to the growth of the church and to the progress of the gospel in Canada. One of his many contributions is his book, *More Than a Symbol: The British Baptist Recovery of Baptismal Sacramentalism*,[2] in which he calls for the recovery of a Baptist sacramental theology of baptism. I wish to discuss this book's thesis in this essay because I believe that it is

---

1 David Bentley Hart, *The Beauty of the Infinite: The Aesthetics of Christian Truth* (Grand Rapids: Eerdmans, 2003), 213.

2 Stanley K. Fowler, *More Than a Symbol: The British Baptist Recovery of Baptismal Sacramentalism* (Eugene: Wipf and Stock, 2002).

one of the most significant works of theology produced in Canada in the past few decades, even though its impact has surely fallen short of what the author, and many of us who share his concerns, might wish. Why is Baptist sacramental theology so rare today? I want to suggest that we have lost not only sacramental theology, narrowly defined, but also a sacramental worldview—a sacramental ontology—broadly understood. What needs to change in Baptist theology (and in North American evangelical theology more generally) in order for a truly Baptist and evangelical sacramental doctrine of baptism to be developed is that we need to engage in a process of *ressourcement* and recover a sacramental ontology as the proper context in which a sacramental theology of baptism can be shown to make sense.

Recovering a sacramental theology of baptism

In analyzing this book, one could say that its strength lies in chapters one, three and four, while its weakness lies in chapter two. In chapter one Fowler makes his greatest contribution by recovering the early, Reformed, Baptist theology of the sacraments held by seventeenth-century English Baptists. It is comforting, in an age of widespread semi-Pelagianism and ahistorical, experience-based theology, to know that the roots of our movement were catholic, reformed and biblical. In affirming the action of God in baptism, our Baptist forefathers were one with catholic tradition. Fowler summarizes the seventeenth-century Baptist view of baptism this way:

> Some early Baptists spoke more strongly than others, but there is among them a recurring affirmation that the reception of the benefits of Christ is in some way mediated through baptism.... Christian baptism was for them a human response to the gospel, but this human act of obedience did not exhaust the content of the event.[3]

This kind of baptismal theology allows the Baptist theologian to affirm the heart of the entire orthodox tradition of Christianity from the apostles to the Fathers to the medieval schoolmen to

---

[3] Fowler, *More Than a Symbol*, 32.

the reformers, while simultaneously subjecting elements of that tradition to a scriptural critique. This makes the Baptist movement a valuable part of the "great tradition," rather than a deviant or novel sect. It also enriches the entire Christian tradition by incorporating into the tradition the evangelical critique of mechanical grace without living faith imparted by a sacramental priesthood under the control of a politicized hierarchy. Was that not what the Reformation was all about? And was that not genuinely a call to *reform* of the catholic tradition rather than an innovation or departure from that tradition?

The weakness of the book, however, is found in chapter two. Fowler is, of course, correct in discerning that the twentieth-century British Baptists are the only significant group of Baptist theologians to put much effort into developing a sacramental theology of baptism in the past three centuries, so it is understandable that he would focus on them in this book. But, as Fowler notes, the majority of Baptists in the world live in the United States, and they have been unreceptive to the British attempt to articulate a sacramental theology of baptism. Why is this so? Perhaps the fault lies on both sides.

Fowler notes that the British Baptist effort was marked by a concern for Baptist identity in the context of the early twentieth-century ecumenical movement. This could be described as a concern over how to be good members of the ecumenical movement while rejecting infant baptism. However, as Fowler notes, these Baptist theologians showed only a limited knowledge of the early Baptist tradition and "were more concerned to interact with scholars of other traditions than to interact with earlier Baptist literature."[4] This made it all too easy for other Baptists to dismiss their concerns as liberal and ecumenical, rather than biblical and orthodox. By the dawn of the twentieth century, as Fowler painstakingly demonstrates in chapter one,[5] Baptists gradually had lost contact with the sacramentalism of their founding fathers and increasingly had emphasized baptism as a human response to the gospel, rather than as a divine act of grace. As a result, by the beginning of the twentieth century,

---

4 Fowler, *More Than a Symbol*, 155.

5 See his summaries of these trends in Fowler, *More Than a Symbol*, 53–57 and 86–88.

British Baptist theologians were cut off from the great tradition by their ignorance of their own Baptist roots in Reformed theology and by their preoccupation with dialogue with the liberal theology of the ecumenical movement.

The leaders of the ecumenical movement never managed to extract themselves from the liberal project, that is, the attempt beginning with Friedrich Schleiermacher to restate Christian doctrine within the narrow metaphysical constraints of Enlightenment naturalism. The liberal project involves the rejection of the theological metaphysics of the great tradition in the belief that Christian doctrine can be restated without its metaphysical substratum. The history of the twentieth century, however, demonstrates that the liberal project degenerates into relativism and unlimited pluralism in doctrinal matters coupled with an increasingly myopic preoccupation with the secular and material world in ethical matters. Although the liberal theologians with whom the British Baptists were in dialogue may have come from denominations shaped by sacramental theology, their investment in the liberal project meant that their own sacramental theology was in the process of being undermined by modern historicist and idealist ideas that were inconsistent with the theological metaphysics of the great tradition on which all sacramental theology depends.

Modernity can be defined concisely as the rejection of Christian Platonism.[6] Western modernity can be defined as a movement of thought that began with the rise of *nominalism* in the fourteenth century and then influenced the development of modern science in the sixteenth and seventeenth centuries in a *mechanistic* direction. In the Enlightenment, a philosophical natu-

---

[6] Ancient Platonism can be defined broadly as the movement of philosophy that (1) began in response to the dilemma of being and change posed by Parmenides and Heraclitus; (2) achieved classic expression in the dialogues of Plato; and (3) constituted a tradition in which there was considerable debate within certain defined limits from Aristotle to the Old Academy to the Academic Skeptics to the Middle Academy to Plotinus. See Lloyd Gerson, *Aristotle and Other Platonists* (Ithaca: Cornell University Press, 2005) and especially *From Plato to Platonism* (Ithaca: Cornell University Press, 2013). Augustine was a certain kind of Platonist, namely a *Christian* Platonist, and his version of Christian Platonism summed up the fourth century pro-Nicene position and became the basic Christian theological metaphysics of Christendom for a over a millennium.

ralism triumphed among the intellectual elites of Western Europe. This rejection of the rich tradition of Christian Platonism and the embrace of ancient *materialism* instead led to *skepticism*, *relativism* and eventually *nihilism*.[7] The culture of death in twentieth-century Western Europe and North America is the bitter cultural fruit of this philosophical and spiritual malaise.

While Christianity still exercised a healthy influence over certain parts of Western culture during the nineteenth century, the nihilism of modernity remained largely concealed from view like a cancer growing but not yet manifested by obvious symptoms. The popularity of modernity grew from the fifteenth to nineteenth centuries as it wrapped itself in the garb of science, technology and reason using the rhetorical techniques of sophism, while rejecting true philosophy. By the beginning of the nineteenth century, however, this revival of ancient paganism had seized cultural dominance from Christianity, and Christian theology was in danger of being driven out of the universities and reduced to the status of astrology.

The response of major European theologians from Schleiermacher on was to engage in what can be called "the liberal project." This project was an attempt to carve out a space in which Christianity could continue to exist without accepting complete exile from the commanding heights of culture. The essence of the liberal (or revisionist) project is the acceptance of modern philosophical critiques of the great tradition and the attempt to re-state the essence of Christianity in terms of the metaphysical assumptions of modernity. There was much talk in the nineteenth century about separating the "essence" of Christianity, that is, the indispensable kernel, from the dispensable "husks." Specifically, this meant abandoning the "Hellenistic" theological metaphysics forged in the fourth-century Arian controversy, delivered to the Middle Ages by Augustine and refined by Thomas

---

7 Gerson defines "Ur-Platonism" (that is, the views held in common by all Platonists regardless of their many disagreements on the details, justification and implications of these views) as: anti-nominalism, anti-materialism, anti-mechanism, anti-skepticism and anti-relativism. Note that modernity rejects all five of these positions. (See Gerson, *From Plato to Platonism*, 9–19). "Christian Platonism" is a variation within this general tradition with significant modifications resulting from the incorporation of biblical revelation into the system.

Aquinas. The hope was that perhaps the dogma could be salvaged if the metaphysics was sacrificed. Adolf von Harnack's attack on the ontological implications of creedal orthodoxy was styled as a "de-Hellenization" of the gospel.[8] But the acids of modernity, once unleashed, did not stop with the metaphysics underlying the Trinitarian and Christological dogmas. They quickly began to threaten central doctrines such as biblical inspiration and the virgin birth, sinless life, miracles, atoning death, bodily resurrection, ascension and personal return of our Lord Jesus Christ.

This led to the Fundamentalist-Modernist controversies of the early twentieth century as orthodox theologians like J. Gresham Machen attempted to resist the seemingly inexorable march of heresy. The battle was often waged at the level of exegesis and doctrine, however, without consideration of the philosophical assumptions being presupposed by both sides. For example, arguments over whether Genesis could be reconciled with science failed to be critical enough of the bad metaphysics underlying the conception of "science" shared by all sides in the debate. The liberal project has a conservative as well as a liberal wing, with the primary difference being a judgement as to how much of orthodox dogma can be shoehorned into the narrow space permitted by modern, neo-pagan metaphysics. But as long as the debate is conducted in terms of seeking to determine what can be dispensed with as not essential to Christian faith and as long as the deficient metaphysical dogmas of the Enlightenment itself are not challenged, the long-term outlook for orthodox Christianity in the West is dim. The growth of the nihilistic culture of death in tandem with the decline of Christian faith is the story of the twentieth century in Western culture.

---

8 This attack continues today. See Brian D. McLaren, *A New Kind of Christianity: Ten Questions That Are Transforming the Faith* (San Francisco: HarperOne, 2010), 38ff and N.T. Wright, *Surprised by Hope: Rethinking Heaven, and Resurrection, and the Mission of the Church* (San Francisco: HarperOne, 2008), 88-91. For some inexplicable reason, the nineteenth-century theories of Harnack, which are increasingly seen as outdated and incorrect by serious patristic scholarship, have been discovered by left-wing Evangelicals as if they constituted a set of new and daring ideas. Hans Boersma discusses this unfortunate aspect of Wright's thought and says: "N.T. Wright associates Platonism with Gnosticism without wondering why it is that Christian tradition carefully distinguished between positive and negative elements in the former, while vehemently opposing the latter" [Hans Boersma, *Heavenly Participation: The Weaving of a Sacramental Tapestry* (Grand Rapids: Eerdmans, 2011), 33].

The theological metaphysics of the great tradition is a sacramental ontology in which the Christian doctrine of creation *ex nihilo* is central to a Trinitarian account of how God and the world interact. Basically, the sacramental ontology of the great tradition of Christian orthodoxy consists of the metaphysical presuppositions that were found necessary to articulate the Christian doctrine of God in such a way as to be faithful to the biblical witness and to rule out the neo-Platonism of Arius and the rationalism of Eunomius during the fourth century struggle that produced the Nicene doctrine of the Trinity. The Fathers adopted some aspects of Platonism, modified others and rejected still others outright. But at least Platonism was worth dialoguing with, unlike the nominalism and materialism of the philosophical naturalists, the skepticism of the Epicureans and the irrational relativism of the Sophists.

In the rest of this essay, I wish to describe this sacramental ontology as the coherent set of metaphysical beliefs that developed out of the Nicene doctrine of God and as the framework in which the exegesis of Scripture needs to be done. Fowler's chapter three deals competently with a large number of the most important biblical texts relevant to the discussion of the sacramental nature of baptism, but the metaphysical assumptions of modernity and its rejection of the sacramental ontology integral to the great tradition are not challenged radically enough.

This leads to a number of problems in modern critical interpretation of the Bible, such as a concept of causation in that whatever is caused by man is not caused by God as if causation were a zero sum game, which in turn leads to a dichotomy between divine action and human action and between grace and faith. It then appears that one must sacrifice grace to retain faith or make baptism a mechanical and automatic impartation of grace, if it is to be a matter of grace at all. But sacramental grace need not be conceived as separate from human faith in a sacramental ontology in which human actions can be taken up into, and participate in, divine actions. Modern philosophy begins with a Cartesian dualism between divine and human action and ends by obliterating divine action altogether and Christian theology cannot resist it merely by insisting that both divine and human action should be retained (which is what conservative modernism does). What needs to be affirmed is a different and more biblical kind of relationship between divine and human action, a relationship that is only thinkable within a sacramental ontology.

Recovering a sacramental ontology

Christian sacramental ontology is a view of reality (that is, of *being* or *what is*) that grows out of the attempt to describe the triune God of the Bible and answer questions about how God is known, the divine nature and God's relationship to the world.[9] Any Christian theology proper must deal with the knowledge of God, election, God's attributes, God's triune nature, and God's transcendence, immanence, creation, providence and incarnation. Such issues are not matters of idle speculation; rather, they arise inevitably out of the proclamation of the Christian gospel and the exposition of God's Word. So they are not illegitimate, but necessary, questions, the answers to which inevitably involve the affirmation of certain metaphysical doctrines and the denial of others. Any Christian doctrine of God that does not make explicit the implicit ontological assumptions required to answer these questions coherently is either irresponsible or incomplete.[10]

The deepest and finally authoritative source of a Christian, sacramental ontology is, of course, Holy Scripture. But like the doctrine of the Trinity itself, the elaboration of sacramental ontology was the work of centuries of prayerful reflection on the biblical gospel in conversation with the best of philosophical thought in the culture. Lewis Ayres offers a salutary warning against thinking of individual pro-Nicene theologians as constructing "Christian ontologies" in the sense of proposals grounded in particular philosophies, which take the form of

---

9 Hans Boersma has explored the concept of sacramental ontology in two important books: *Nouvelle Theologie & Sacramental Ontology: A Return to Mystery* (Oxford: Oxford University Press, 2009) and *Heavenly Participation: The Weaving of a Sacramental Tapestry*. On pages 47–51 of the latter book, Boersma gives a concise example of the sort of thing I am talking about. He shows how Gregory of Nyssa drew on Christian Platonism's account of the relationship of universals to particulars in order to argue for the unity of the triune God, rather than tritheism. Boersma calls for a recovery of the Platonist-Christian synthesis through *ressourcement*.

10 Recall the quotation at the head of this essay: "Theology that refuses to address questions of ontology can never be more than mythology" (Hart, *The Beauty of the Infinite*, 213).

systems created by individual authors.[11] He argues that, instead, we should look for "fundamental orientations towards complex ontological questions and at the strategies used to negotiate complex inherited traditions."[12] This is a salutatory warning. What we need is not so much a single, detailed, philosophical system, as a shared tradition of strategies by which trinitarian classical theism is allowed to shape the philosophical and world-view assumptions that drive the process of intellectual life and culture-formation. What I mean by sacramental ontology is actually a shared vision of some key ontological implications of the doctrine of the Trinity, a vision that took shape in the fourth century and grew from there as a living tradition in which there was enough agreement to allow for interesting debates.

There are three main strategies by which trinitarian theism shaped trinitarian ontology in the great tradition. These strategies are visible in fourth-century pro-Nicene theology and they came to flourish in medieval Christendom. They are: metaphysical realism, a sacramental view of creation and the use of analogical language to speak about the mystery of the triune God. Let us briefly consider what each one means.

Metaphysical realism

First, trinitarian ontology rests on the foundation of a realist metaphysics. It recognizes the existence of universals, although it is not wedded to the details of any particular metaphysical system.[13] Individual entities in the world are what they are, and remain what they are, by participating in some way in the *Logos* of the triune God. The flux of historical existence is anchored in the realm of unchanging being where universals exist; the universe is not merely a free-flowing stream of meaningless matter

---

11 Lewis Ayres, *Nicaea and Its Legacy: An Approach to Fourth-Century Trinitarian Theology* (Oxford: Oxford University Press, 2004), 312. The work of John Zizioulas would be an example of the danger against which Ayres is warning here. See John Zizioulas, *Being as Communion* (Crestwood: Saint Vladimir's Seminary Press, 1985) and his many works since then.

12 Ayres, *Nicaea and Its Legacy*, 313.

13 To affirm metaphysical realism is not necessarily to take a position on the classic debate between Plato and Aristotle on the nature of universals and the various historical attempts to find compromise positions between the two. There is much debate with the Platonist tradition on this point, even among Christian Platonists.

behaving randomly or individual entities that have no shared essences. The adoption of this metaphysical position was the result of a conscious, considered decision on the part of the Fathers that the biblical worldview is expressed more faithfully by utilizing certain Platonic concepts (with revision and re-definition as necessary) and decisively rejecting Stoic pantheism and philosophical naturalism. The fourth-century church Fathers did not know very much of Aristotle's philosophy; the Thomistic integration of Aristotelian insights into this picture would come later, but it would be a development not a revolution, an enhancement not a deconstruction.

It should be recognized that Platonic concepts were employed by the Fathers in the service of biblical theology to explain in coherent, philosophical terms what the Bible itself proclaims in narrative, pictorial terms. Their authority for doing so was the example of the apostles themselves in the New Testament.[14] For example, consider Augustine's distinction between the meaning of the word "heavens" in Genesis 1:1 and the meaning of the word "heaven" in Genesis 1:8 in Book XII of *The Confessions*. Augustine thinks that the statement in Genesis 1:1, "In the beginning God created the heavens and the earth," is describing the creation of all created reality including both the physical universe, "the earth," and the spiritual realm, "the heavens."[15] He refers to this spiritual realm described in verse 1 as the "heaven of heavens,"[16] and he describes it as "a kind of creation in the realm of the intellect."[17] The word "heaven" in verses 8–9, however, refers to the expanse that divides the waters below from the waters above and which is contrasted with the earth and the sea. Clearly it is what we call "the sky" and is part of this

---

14 It should also be noted that this move begins, not in the Fathers, but in the Bible itself. The prologue to the Gospel of John interprets Christ using the Stoic term *Logos* and immediately re-defines this term in personal terms, which makes it mean some of what the Stoics meant but also much more.

15 Book XII, ix, 9, in Saint Augustine, *Confessions*, Oxford World Classics, trans. Henry Chadwick (New York: Oxford University Press, 2008), 250.

16 "Heaven of heavens" is Chadwick's translation. The latest and best translation of *The Confessions* by Sister Maria Boulding has "heaven's heaven." See Saint Augustine, *The Confessions*, trans. Maria Boulding, *The Works of Saint Augustine: A Translation for the Twenty-First Century* (Hyde Park: New City Press, 1997/2012), 317.

17 Augustine, *The Confessions*, 317.

physical universe, whereas the heavens contrasted with the earth in verse 1, the "heaven of heavens," is the spiritual realm of created reality—the place where the angels constantly worship the slain Lamb in the presence of the church triumphant. The "heaven of heavens" contains something like Plato's forms or ideas, which are universals, that is, the ideas in which created objects participate and by participating are what they are.[18] Augustine here employs Platonic concepts in his biblical exegesis to assert something rather startling in a Greek context: both the realm of spirit and the material world were created *ex nihilo* by God and continue to exist only by participating in the divine being. So much for a dualism in which God is merely part of the spiritual world! Augustine's God is as closely related to our material world as he is to the spiritual world because both subsist in him and he is transcendent over both. Plato's philosophy as corrected by biblical revelation helps to explain how this is so.

But is it *exegesis* or *eisegesis*? That may depend on whether or not one thinks, as Augustine and all orthodox exegetes in the patristic and medieval eras did, that it is proper to interpret the meaning of a particular biblical passage in the context of the entire canonical witness as a whole. Heaven (Augustine's "heaven of heavens") is not merely a figment of the imaginative speculation of Platonic philosophers and neither is it just a bit of philosophy read into the text by Augustine. Rather, it is a reasonable way of interpreting Genesis 1:1 as teaching the creation of something that the rest of the Bible clearly assumes to exist (and therefore must have been created at some point). For example, when Satan presents himself before the LORD with the sons of God in Job 1, where did that occur? It was not on earth. Was it on another planet? Or is it just a story with no correspondence in reality at all? Well, what about Isaiah's vision of the heavenly throne room in Isaiah 6 or John's vision of heaven in Revelation 4? Are they just mythical stories, made-up tales with a moral? It is apocalyptic language, some say, as if that explained everything.

18 Thomas Aquinas would later strengthen this point by mounting a convincing argument that these ideas actually are in the mind of God. See Gregory T. Doolan, *Aquinas on the Divine Ideas as Exemplar Causes* (Washington: Catholic University of America Press, 2008).

But if there is no heaven, where did the body of Jesus go in Acts 1? Interestingly, we are told that it went up from a mountain and was hidden by a cloud leaving the disciples gazing up into "heaven" (Acts 1:9). The angel (apparently possessed of no Bultmannian sensibilities whatsoever), tells them, "This Jesus, who was taken up from you into heaven, will come again in the same way as you saw him go into heaven" (Acts 1:11). For better or worse, the Bible seems to teach clearly that the space-time continuum we inhabit is not the totality of created reality. In fact, the ancient/modern view that the space-time continuum we inhabit *is* the totality of created reality is a doctrine called philosophical naturalism, which is clearly incompatible with the Biblical doctrine of creation: note, not merely with Platonic metaphysics! There is more than what we can access by means of our five senses; on this point the overwhelming majority of Christians for 2,000 years (and Jews for 2,000 years prior to Christ) are agreed. Shakespeare inhabited this worldview and has Hamlet express it: "There are more things in heaven and earth, Horatio, than are dreamt of in your philosophy."[19] To read philosophical naturalism into one's interpretation of the Biblical text, as Bultmann does, is a highly intrusive and radical example of eisegesis, but to read the text as requiring some sort of metaphysics that makes room for a dual creation with both physical and spiritual realities is to submit to the "plain sense" of the text.

But the exact nature of this spiritual reality is confusing. On the one hand, it appears to be immaterial, which makes perfect sense in that created reality consists of two levels: the material and the spiritual. Of course, these are nice, tidy (and very separate) compartments and modern atheists are eager to keep them as separate as possible while waiting for people to give up believing in the spiritual realm altogether.[20] But just as the human creature is unique in consisting of a mysterious union of the material (the body) and the spiritual (the soul), so there are hints scattered everywhere in the canonical Scriptures that the

---

19 William Shakespeare, *The Tragedy of Hamlet, Prince of Denmark*, Act I, Scene V, in *The Complete Works of William Shakespeare* (London: Abbey Library, 1974), 854.

20 In the meantime, they propagandize ceaselessly insinuating that immaterial = unreal, which from a biblical perspective is complete nonsense.

current rift between the material and the spiritual aspects of created reality is not entirely normal; that interaction between the two realms is actually far more common than we might suspect, and that such interaction would be even more common if it were not for the occurrence of a catastrophe of cosmic proportions in the distant past. In fact, the movement of Jesus' resurrection body from this realm to the other one (and its promised return again) suggests that the spiritual realm is not entirely without a material aspect, just as prayer suggests that this material world is not entirely bereft of the influence of the spiritual world. If philosophical naturalism is a clumsy and hopelessly inadequate philosophical tool for interpreting Scripture, the modernist hard and fast 'nature versus supernature' distinction is only marginally better. Neither materialism nor magic can do justice to the ontology generated by the God of the Bible, and the nature-supernature dualism roams uncomfortably close to mere magic.

As human beings—ensouled bodies/embodied souls—*we* are the point of contact and conflict between the two aspects of God's creation. We have a consciousness of being more than animals, yet we are not simply angelic spirits. It is for us to discover via biblical revelation that the connections, in fact the *interdependence*, between the two realms is vast, complex and integral to the existence of both. A key insight is gained when we come to understand that both are part of created reality and distinct from the Creator. This was a key point in Athanasius' argument against the Arians. God is not a part of the spiritual realm, as opposed to being a part of the material realm. Instead, God is utterly *transcendent* over both the spiritual and the material realm and directly present to both; this is the reason why the Arian idea of Christ as the first created being whose role was to mediate between God and the material world was not only wrong but unnecessary.[21] It is not that God is spirit and therefore in need of a mediator to connect with the material. God actually is transcen-

---

21 Christ is primarily a moral/spiritual mediator—Redeemer—rather than an ontological mediator. Angels can go back and forth between the two ontological spheres of creation, but only Christ is able to overcome the division introduced into creation by the Fall and thus unite sinful humanity and the holy God. Arius conceived of Christ as a kind of "super angel" with a primarily ontological mission rather than as fully divine and one with the Father.

dent and not merely a part of either the spiritual or the material realm; both are his creation, and he is present directly to both. God's *immanence* is the other side of the coin of his transcendence. Transcendence is not merely a cipher for immaterial, but is rather a declaration of the divine freedom, that is, the divine independence of creation (*aseity*). Platonist ideas are used to make this point, but the biblical doctrine of God is very different from the idea of the One in neo-Platonism. The disagreement between Plotinus and the Fathers is conducted within the general range of the Platonic tradition but involves very serious differences, as the Arian debate demonstrates.

Augustine was simply being a typical, biblical Christian in believing that the meaning of this material world is tied up with and, in the end, incomprehensible apart from the spiritual realm of pure spirits, ideas and the divine intellect (referred to in Scripture as the *Logos* or *wisdom* of God). He made use of an existing, more or less philosophically coherent account of the relationship between divine ideas (universals) and particular things in this world to explain the existence, nature and continuation in being of the things of this world; that is, he posited the truth of the Platonic concept of universals. It must be understood, however, that his decision to utilize Platonism was also, at the same time, a decision to *reject* the philosophical naturalism of the Epicureans and the pantheism of the Stoics, which means that he rejected far more Greek philosophy than he ever accepted.[22] And he certainly rejected a good bit of Platonism as well, as the reader of Book VII of *The Confessions* soon learns. This world is radically dependent on God, rather than being autonomous, and Platonism helps us specify something of the nature of this dependence. How can this be regarded as illegitimate unless one proves that every single aspect of Greek philosophical thought—including both sides of contradictory schools of thought—are all false? Are we expected to believe that the Greeks, alone of all the cultures of the world, failed to understand even one single truth

22 One fears that the commonly encountered horror at any sort of hint of "Hellenistic metaphysics" is not really a rejection of *all* Greek philosophy, but rather of certain currently unfashionable Greek views. Regrettably, this usually amounts to embracing the Greeks precisely where they were wrong from a biblical perspective.

about the nature of reality? To argue on exegetical grounds that Augustine was mistaken in accepting this or that particular tenet of Greek philosophy is perfectly legitimate and, in fact, necessary in testing his theology against the standard of Scripture, but to argue that he should have used nothing whatsoever from his culture is to impose a standard on him that no contemporary theologian would be willing to accept. To insist that using an idea from Plato is necessarily selling out the gospel and then to fall on one's face in obeisance to Kantian epistemology or Humean skepticism reflects a disturbing lack of self-awareness, not to mention a need for a remedial course in logic.[23]

Certain Platonic ideas proved to be useful to the Fathers in explicating the gospel and, because of the massive influence of Augustine, continued as a component of orthodox Christian thought well into the middle ages and beyond. Thomas Aquinas summed up the patristic tradition and integrated certain ideas from Aristotle into the basic Christian Platonism of the great tradition. But others in the high middle ages did, in fact, call the "Platonist-Christian synthesis" into question and thereby participated in precipitating a massive cultural crisis known to us as the breakdown of the medieval synthesis and the rise of early modernity. This breakdown involves the rise of nominalism and voluntarism and has been analyzed by many historians.[24] But for well over a thousand years there stood at the heart of the great tradition one kind or another of realist metaphysics for the very good reason that it seemed incontrovertibly to be required by the biblical doctrine of the triune God as Creator.

A sacramental view of creation

Second, a sacramental ontology has a sacramental view of nature. By this I mean what Thomas Howard means in his excellent little book contrasting the medieval and modern worldviews

---

23 The idea that Plato and Aristotle are mostly wrong and that Hume and Kant are mostly right is an astonishingly indefensible position, which explains why it is often presumed but seldom argued. For a sustained argument for, and explanation of, this point see: Edward Feser, *The Last Superstition: A Refutation of the New Atheism* (South Bend: St. Augustine's Press, 2008).

24 See, for example, Louis Dupre, *Passage to Modernity: An Essay in the Hermeneutics of Nature and Culture* (New Haven: Yale University Press, 1993).

when he refers to how, in the medieval worldview, it is only natural for one thing to stand for another. Describing the medieval mind, he writes,

> Nature and politics and animals and sex—these were all exhibitions in their own way of the way things are. This mind fancied that everything meant everything, and that it all rushed up finally to heaven.... So this mind handled all the data of experience as though they were images—cases in point, that is, of each other and of the way things are.[25]

In a sacramental ontology there is a hierarchical unity to reality. A sacramental ontology is not one in which the seven sacraments of the medieval church are the sole means of grace and mediated through a sacramental priesthood, which is itself under the control of the church hierarchy. We must work hard to keep separate in our minds the idea of sacramental ontology from the idea of a hierarchal, sacramental priesthood.

What I mean by a sacramental ontology is that *meaning is inherent in the universe because the universe has been infused with meaning by the Creator and continues to be infused with meaning at every moment.* For Christianity, metaphysical realism makes the world sacramental because the ideas (or universals) posited by the great tradition are not, as in Platonism, impersonal entities existing independently, but rather are ideas in the mind of a personal God who, by his Word, creates all things, upholds all things in existence, preserves the nature of all things, and guides all things to their appointed end.[26] God's Word has ontological reality, not merely an ephemeral, passing, fleeting reality. As the prophet Isaiah puts it, "The grass withers, the flower fades, but the Word of our God will stand forever" (Isaiah 40:8). Without metaphysical realism, the doctrine of the preservation of creation (a sub-section of the doctrine of divine providence), is conceptually incoherent. The point here is simply to emphasize that sacra-

---

25 Thomas Howard, *Chance or the Dance? A Critique of Modern Secularism* (San Francisco: Ignatius Press, 1969), 13.

26 For a study of universals as ideas in the mind of God in the thought of Thomas Aquinas see Doolan, *Aquinas on the Divine Ideas.*

mental ontology, with its realism, is not specifically Roman Catholic in character but rather part of "mere Christianity."[27] The meaning built into the universe by the all-wise Creator means that Christians who study nature and culture can be assured that nature is not merely random chance occurrences of matter and energy of unknown origin, as it is for the ancient and modern atheists,[28] and history is not merely "sound and fury, a tale told by an idiot signifying nothing,"[29] as it is for the postmodern nihilists. But should the meaning inherent in the universe be considered to be natural or supernatural? The sacramental implications of trinitarian ontology make this question difficult to answer in a straightforward manner.

To claim that this meaning is either merely natural or totally supernatural seems to be a case of being asked to choose between two inadequately phrased extremes. Alasdair MacIntyre, in *After Virtue*, argues that modern secularism is nihilistic because it evacuates the material world, including human nature, of all meaning by denying that anything, including human nature, has a *telos* (or end or purpose).[30] Aristotelian teleology can be understood as an implication of a sacramental view of creation and that is why Thomas Aquinas was able to weave it into his theological and philosophical synthesis. MacIntyre concludes that we have a choice between Aristotle and Nietzsche. I would state the dilemma by saying that the nihilism of modernity cannot be escaped without embracing Christ and the spiritual realm as the source of our *telos*; therefore, it is a choice between Nietzsche and Christ.[31] MacIntyre, in *After Virtue*, could be read as implying that there would be no need to recover the Christianized

27 The phrase, of course, is that of C.S. Lewis, who borrowed it from Richard Baxter. The fiction of Lewis and Tolkein is incomprehensible apart from the assumption of a sacramental ontology.

28 See Christopher Hitchens, ed., *The Portable Atheist: Essential Readings for the Nonbeliever* (Philadelphia: Da Capo Press, 2007).

29 William Shakespeare, *The Tragedy of Macbeth*, Act V, Scene V, in *The Complete Works of William Shakespeare* (London: Abbey Library, 1974), 843.

30 Alasdair MacIntyre, *After Virtue : A Study in Moral Theory*, 3rd ed. (Notre Dame: University of Notre Dame Press, 2007), especially chapters 9 and 18.

31 I am not sure that MacIntyre would disagree very strenuously with my way of stating the dilemma. See MacIntyre's *Whose Justice? Which Rationality?* (Notre Dame: University of Notre Dame Press, 1988) and *Three Rival Versions of Moral Inquiry: Encyclopedia, Genealogy and Tradition* (Notre Dame: University of Notre Dame Press, 1990).

Platonism of the great tradition in order to avoid nihilism—so long as one has Aristotle. I would suggest, however, that Aristotle integrated into the Augustinian neo-Platonism of Thomas Aquinas is an adequate alternative to nihilism, but that the pagan Aristotle by himself is too slender a reed on which to lean. I could accept gladly the assertion that the choice is between Nietzsche and Thomas.[32]

The Augustinian interpretation of the great tradition that I am promoting here is more in line with the *Nouvelle Theologie*'s contention that man's *telos* is ultimately the beatific vision and that even our natural end, when understood in the light of our ultimate end, is directed toward God. As Augustine put it: "You have made us for yourself and our heart is restless until it rests in you."[33] Undoubtedly, we have a natural *telos* as neo-Thomism asserts (for example, to reproduce or to grow to maturity) and we also have a supernatural *telos* (for example, to glorify God and enjoy him forever), but what I am resisting is the temptation to keep them in airtight compartments so that the latter can never affect the former. Thus, I am arguing for a relaxing of the stringent division of reality into material and spiritual (natural and supernatural) that has been accepted by both neo-Thomism and Protestant fundamentalism under the secularizing pressure of modernity.[34] In a sacramental ontology it simply is not possible to clearly mark off an area of creaturely autonomy that derives its meaning from human will alone, rather than from divine design. Yet, there is no reason to deny the existence and essential goodness of a purely natural human *telos*. We can have a natural *telos* without having nothing but a natural *telos* and also without our natural *telos* being unaffected in any way by a higher, supernatural *telos*.

---

32 Of course, I interpret Thomas as a Christian Platonist. So, an Augustinian Christian like me, therefore, does not have to become a "card-carrying Thomist," that is, Thomistic on every single point, in order to say that Thomas can represent the great tradition in this way.

33 Book I, i, 1, in Augustine, *Confessions*, 3.

34 Those who are familiar with the work of Henri de Lubac will recognize that I am, at least partially, siding with him in the debate between the neo-Thomists and the adherents of the *Nouvelle Theologie*. Those unfamiliar with this debate would do well to start with two books by Hans Boersma: *Nouvelle Theologie & Sacramental Ontology* and *Heavenly Participation*.

Analogical language for God

Thirdly, because of the realism of sacramental ontology, the method of analogy is the only proper way to express our knowledge of God. To affirm the doctrine of analogy is to say that human language is fit for purpose when it comes to speaking of God. In a sacramental ontology human words about God are not *univocal*, which is to say that there is no one-to-one, exact equivalence in speaking, for example, of a human father and God as our heavenly Father. The meaning of the word "father" applied to God and man is, thus, not identical. But human words about God also are not *equivocal*, which is to say that there *is*, in fact, something common in the concept of a human father and the concept of our heavenly Father. There is some overlap of meaning, which there would not be if they were equivocal. The two concepts (human father and God as Father) are thus neither exactly equivalent nor totally dissimilar. To say this is to say that there is an analogy between the two concepts, which means that we can speak of God analogically. However, in any analogy between the creaturely realm and God the dissimilarity is always greater than the similarity. So we can speak truly about God but not exhaustively. Our statements can be partial truths without being untruths. As T. F. Torrance puts it in a description of how Athanasius conceived of the knowledge of God: "in the very act of *apprehending* something of God, faith is bound to confess that it is incapable of *comprehending* him."[35] In other words, one fact we can apprehend about God is that it is impossible for any finite being to comprehend God. But knowledge of this fact is itself valid knowledge of God.

If the world had not been created the way it was created by God, analogical knowledge of God would not be possible. But given a realist and sacramental ontology, analogical speech about God is, in fact, possible and meaning is not only inherent in the universe but is also at least partially accessible to the human intellect.[36] Giles Hibbert points out that, in order for human

35 Thomas F. Torrance, *The Trinitarian Faith: The Evangelical Theology of the Ancient Catholic Church* (Edinburgh: T&T Clark, 1995), 26.

36 The unredeemed human intellect, of course, is much more limited in its ability to apprehend truth than the intellect informed by revelation and guided by the Holy Spirit.

language to function analogically, words "must have the possibility of being open, being able to point beyond themselves, beyond the sphere and context of their own immediate origin; or in other words by way of analogical predication they must have the possibility of metaphysical realization."[37] Matthew Levering cites Hibbert in the context of arguing that metaphysics is necessary to a Christian theological description of God.[38] I would argue that some sort of realist metaphysics is necessary to sustain analogical talk of God, a conclusion with which I believe Levering (and the great tradition generally) would agree. A certain account of creation (which, I contend, needs to be described in metaphysical terms as the Augustinian-Thomist tradition does) also is necessary for a coherent doctrine of analogy.

This, however, does not mean that human beings always interpret the knowledge of God that they have correctly. Although Paul says that non-Christians *have* knowledge of God apart from special revelation, he explicitly denies in Romans 1 that they use it to form a true knowledge of God. Instead, they "suppress" the truth (Romans 1:18–24). This is significant because you cannot suppress what you do not in some sense have and, in order to be able to do what Paul says the pagans do, one obviously must be able both to perceive and distort the truth simultaneously. This paradox is what one would expect if we were sinners who inhabit a sacramental universe that "declares the glory of God" (Psalm 19:1).

The great tradition thus has room both for apophatic theology that proclaims that God is ultimately unknowable in the depths of his being and also for creeds making true statements about God's nature (for example, that the Father, Son and Spirit are *homoousios*). Is this contradictory? Not at all, for a statement may be true while failing to be exhaustively true. What we know, we know in part; "we see in a mirror dimly" (1 Corinthians 13:12). Because of the incarnation of God in Jesus Christ, we can share in a limited and creaturely way in God's own self-knowledge

---

37 Giles Hibbert, O.P. "Mystery and Metaphysics in the Trinitarian Theology of Saint Thomas Aquinas," *Irish Theological Quarterly* 31 (1964):187–188.

38 Matthew Levering cites it in the context of making a similar argument to mine in *Scripture and Metaphysics: Aquinas and the Renewal of Trinitarian Theology* (Malden: Blackwell Publishing, 2004), 5.

and thus we can be sure that we know God truly, that is, we can know that the tiny bit we know about God is true knowledge of God.[39] This is the significance of the incarnation for the knowledge of God.

Conclusion

I have now described the meaning of the phrase "sacramental ontology" by speaking of this ontology as having three characteristics: (1) metaphysical realism; which leads to (2) the universe having a sacramental character; and therefore, (3) the method of analogy being both possible and necessary in speaking truly about God. I hope it is clear that only such an ontology can undergird and make conceptual sense of a sacramental theology of baptism, although space does not permit the development of a theology of baptism here.

I wish to conclude with a quotation from John Webster, who was Stan Fowler's and my *doktorvater*, a theologian whom both of us respect as one of the most insightful and faithful theologians at work today:

> First, however disapproving its postmodern neighbours may be, however sheerly atavistic it may seem, a Trinitarian dogmatics of the holiness of God will be an exercise in ontotheology. For its concern is—with fear and trembling—to give a conceptual depiction of the Church's confession of the works and ways of the Holy Trinity. *And such a depiction necessarily requires an ontology.* This ontology must certainly be resolutely dogmatic, that is, governed by the gospel's annunciation of the history of God with us; and it must, therefore, of necessity, be engaged in a dispute with metaphysical theism about the nature of God. But dogmatics ought to be unpersuaded that Christian theology can long survive the abandonment of ontotheology and ought to think long and hard before it hands over the doctrine of God for deconstruction. *The undeniably corrosive effects of*

---

39 Torrance, *The Trinitarian Faith*, 54.

> *certain traditions of metaphysics are best retarded, not by repudiating ontology, but by its fully Christian articulation.*[40]

The "fully Christian articulation" of a sacramental ontology is the great need of the present day for those who wish to be evangelicals in the great tradition of Christian orthodoxy.

---

40 John Webster, *Holiness* (Grand Rapids: Eerdmans, 2003), 32–33. Emphasis mine.

7

Come let us read together: The role of the church in reading Scripture for Christian ethics

BY GUENTHER (GENE) HAAS

Evangelical Christians have frequently understood Christian ethics in the following terms: Having become Christians through faith in Christ, believers are called to a life of obedience to the specific commands and general ethical principles of God's Word. These commands are found in the moral laws of God revealed in the Old Testament, especially the Ten Commandments, and in the particular ethical instructions found in the New Testament. Through the guidance of the Spirit, Christians discern biblical ethical principles in the Bible, whether these are explicitly stated or implied in the various writings.

This approach views Christian ethics as primarily *deontological*, that is, about ethical laws and principles. Some refer to this as divine-command ethics.[1] This approach also recognizes that laws and principles must be related to specific situations, which means that believers need to make proper applications into the settings and circumstances of their lives. In all situations, biblical laws and principles remain authoritative.[2]

Such a view of the nature of evangelical ethics has a tendency to be deistic, reflecting the influence of a number of Enlightenment themes: that one reads Scripture individualistically, that the Bible functions primarily to provide principles for morality and that ethical insights result from using methods of biblical interpretation and of application to life situations. Also, the emphasis here can become anthropocentric, implying objective neutrality in the use of Scripture. While evangelicals may acknowledge the need for the guidance of the Holy Spirit in discernment and application, the method of Christian ethics can effectively become a purely human activity. This can marginalize the agency of the Spirit working in and through the Bible, and the role of the Spirit-directed church in guiding believers in their ethical decisions.

The key question is: How do we avoid reading the Bible for ethical instruction in such a deistic and anthropocentric fashion? To put the question in a positive form: *How should Christians read the Bible in the community of the church so as to be transformed by the Spirit through Scripture to gain ethical guidance for their lives?* This chapter attempts to answer the latter question by unfolding various aspects of the church's role in Christian ethics in which it takes seriously Christ's work by the Spirit to create a redeemed community as the central agent in interpreting and embodying Scripture for Christian morality.

By way of introduction, we should note two recent developments in evangelical theology and ethics which highlight the importance of the Spirit-directed church in ethics. First, there has been an increasing appreciation of virtue ethics in evangelical circles over the past few decades. The writings of the Catholic

---

1 Richard Mouw defends divine-command ethics in *The God Who Acts: A Study in Divine Command Ethics* (Notre Dame: University of Notre Dame Press, 1990).

2 J.I Packer makes this point in "Situations & Principles," in *Readings in Christian Ethics, Vol. 1: Theory and Method*, eds. David K. Clark & Robert V. Rakeshaw (Grand Rapids: Baker, 1994), 155–156.

philosopher Alasdair MacIntyre[3] and the Protestant ethicist Stanley Hauerwas[4] have both played major roles in promoting the value of virtue ethics in Protestant and evangelical circles.[5] Virtue ethics emphasizes the role of virtue, character and community in shaping the moral life of people. For Christians, the church is the key institution in the moral formation of Christians by discipling them to live in ethical obedience to God. Of course, for evangelicals there remains the question of the proper role of the Word and the Spirit in this calling of the church. And we will explore this later in this chapter.

The second important theological theme that has gained prominence in recent years is union with Christ. While this is also not a totally new theological insight, theologians such as J. Todd Billings,[6] Robert Letham[7] and Michael Horton[8] have brought this biblical theme to our attention in their recent books.[9] Union with Christ functions as the central doctrine to orientate the lives of Christians to God, the church and their neighbours. All the benefits accomplished by Christ in his redemptive work become ours through our union with him. This gives a wholistic account of the gospel as the foundation and dynamic of the Christian life.[10]

---

3 Notably, Alasdair MacIntyre's influential book, *After Virtue: A Study in Moral Theory*, 2nd ed. (Notre Dame: University of Notre Dame Press, 1984).

4 Stanley Hauerwas has published many books on virtue. The most influential are: Stanley Hauerwas, *Character and the Christian Life: A Study in Theological Ethics* (1975; reprint, San Antonio: Trinity University Press, 1985); *The Peaceable Kingdom* (Notre Dame: University of Notre Dame Press, 1983), *A Community of Character* (Notre Dame: University of Notre Dame Press, 1985).

5 Protestant ethicists who have embraced virtue ethics include Gilbert Meilaender, Robin Gill, Rodney Clapp, Stephen Fowl, L. Gregory Jones, Brad Kallenberg, D. Stephen Long and Jonathan Wilson.

6 J. Todd Billings, *Union with Christ: Reframing Theology & Ministry for the Church* (Grand Rapids: Baker, 2011).

7 Robert Letham, *Union with Christ: In Scripture, History and Theology* (Phillipsburg: P & R, 2011).

8 Michael Horton, *The Christian Faith: A Systematic Theology for Pilgrims on the Way* (Grand Rapids: Zondervan, 2011), chapter 6: "Union with Christ," 587–620.

9 All three note that this is an important theme in John Calvin's theology. See John Calvin, *Institutes of the Christian Religion*, ed. John T. McNeill, trans. Ford Lewis Battles, *The Library of Christian Classics*, vols. 20-21 (Philadelphia: Westminster Press, 1960), 3.11.6,11; 3.13.15.

10 Billings, *Union with Christ*, 9.

Union with Christ is generally understood by evangelicals as central to our reconciliation to God through justification by faith alone. This is clearly stated in passages like Romans 3:21–26 and Romans 5:12–21. What has been less prominent—which recent works on union with Christ have brought to our attention—is the centrality of union with Christ for the sanctifying work of the Holy Spirit in believers. Paul teaches this in biblical passages such as Romans 6:1–14 and Galatians 2:20. Union with Christ maintains the integral connection between justification and sanctification.[11] In fact, our union with Christ in justification becomes the basis for the transformative process of sanctification, and, thus, sanctification is the necessary fruit of justification.

The centrality of union with Christ for the Christian life becomes crucial in resisting the practical deism of evangelical ethics. Paul declares that we are being conformed to the likeness of Christ (Romans 8:29), a transformation that is accomplished by the power of the Spirit (2 Corinthians 3:18). To be united to Christ is to participate in, and therefore to be characterized as, a new creation (2 Corinthians 5:17). Paul contrasts the Spirit from God with the spirit of the world (1 Corinthians 2:12). Because of our union with Christ, the old sinful way of life as the controlling power within us has "passed away." Now, the Spirit enables us to live out of the new reality that union with Christ has produced in us.

Just as we belong to Christ when the "Spirit of Christ" lives in us (Romans 8:9), so also the Spirit of God's Son unites us with the family of God, the church (Galatians 4:4–7). In Ephesians 4:1–16, Paul unfolds the calling of the church to grow up in its union with Christ as the members are progressively transformed by the Spirit of Christ and equipped with the gifts Christ pours out. The goal is that the members of the church resist the transient fads of the teachings and practices of sinful society, and grow up into Christ, the Head of the church (Ephesians 4:14–16).[12]

The Gospel of John connects the Spirit's work of uniting believers to Christ to their submission to the Spirit-inspired Word

---

11 Noted by Letham, *Union with Christ*, 2.

12 For a discussion of this see Michael Horton, *Pilgrim Theology: Core Doctrines for Christian Disciples* (Grand Rapids: Zondervan, 2011), 236–241.

of God. Jesus promises to send the Spirit of truth to his disciples to guide them "into all truth" (John 16:12–14). The Spirit does this through the "God-breathed" Scripture (2 Timothy 3:16). Thus, union with Christ by the power of Spirit unites us with Christ's body—the church—through which the Spirit guides by means of the Spirit-inspired Scriptures.

This brings us to the key issue of this chapter. How should we read the Bible for ethical guidance so that we encompass the importance of the transformative reality of our union with Christ at work in us by the power of the Spirit through the teaching of the Scripture within the church as the body of Christ? A more expansive form of this question is: How do we understand the church's appropriation of Scripture for the ethical life so as to draw upon the insights of the virtue tradition with its emphasis on community and character, and the recovery of the importance of seeing the ethical life as the transformative reality of our union with Christ?

It seems to me that the answer to this question must highlight specific features that should characterize our communal reading of the Scriptures for ethical guidance. These characteristics reflect the important insights of the key role of the church in shaping character and virtue, and the transformative aspect of our union with Christ. The rest of this chapter expands upon what I contend are six key characteristics.

First and foremost, it is the church as the body of Christ which is the primary agent in reading the Bible for moral insight. As the Head of the church (Colossians 1:18), and the Lord over all things for the sake of the church (Ephesians 1:22), Christ builds his church (Matthew 16:18) by pouring out the Spirit upon it. The church is "the pillar and foundation of the truth" (1 Timothy 3:15), within which believers attain maturity, "the whole measure of the fullness of Christ" (Ephesians 3:19). The Spirit is the divine author of Scripture (*inspiration*), and he enables the church to understand and apply the Scriptures (*illumination*) to issues that its members face (1 Corinthians 2:10–16).[13]

---

13 For a discussion of inspiration and illumination, see Horton, *Christian Faith*, 155–168.

The story of Christ's rule as it is accomplished by his redemption is the story of the church.[14] He is the Lord who is the Saviour, and his redemption as revealed in Scripture is his work of gathering a people to himself. While he fills the whole universe in every way (Ephesians 4:10), in a special way he fills his body, the church (Ephesians 3:19). The indwelling Spirit fills the members of the church, enabling them to know and to serve Christ (Ephesians 4:3–6).

As the Spirit through the Scripture shapes the church, it becomes the community which embodies the good news of Jesus Christ in its witness to the world.[15] The church is only able to bear witness to the good news "by Christ's own dwelling in the church through union with Christ." And the church bears witness to Christ by all the members of the church "through displaying the 'oneness' of the people united to Christ."[16] This "oneness" involves a unity in confessing and proclaiming the gospel, and a unity in discerning the life of obedience that flows out of our new lives as those united to Christ.

An individualistic witness always falls short of the complete witness to Christ to which the church is called (1 Corinthians 12:4–6). While the Spirit is promised as a gift to each believer (Acts 2:38), the goal is to bring about a vital connection with the church. Christ pours out gifts to prepare God's people for works of service to produce a unity in the faith and a maturity in manifesting the fullness of Christ in the body (Ephesians 4:11–14). The gifts that all believers receive have as their goal a growth into Christ, which promotes the unity and mutual service that bears witness to Christ (Ephesians 4:15–16). Individual Christians cannot bear witness to mutual service and unity achieved by Christ.

The second characteristic of the communal reading of Scripture is that the church must interpret the Bible as Christian Scripture, to be read prayerfully and with moral seriousness. It may seem self-evident to say this, but it warrants underscoring. Scripture is the revelation of Christ that addresses the members of his kingdom to remind them both of who they are as new creatures in Christ and of the way of life to which they are called

---

14 Hauerwas, *Community of Character*, 51.

15 Hauerwas, *Community of Character*, 55.

16 Billings, *Union with Christ*, 163.

as such new creatures. The Bible is not merely a collection of texts which the church has determined to be important documents from which to draw its theology and ethics. Rather, it is the words of our Saviour-King who makes normative claims on his subjects. Constantine Campbell, in his exegetical-theological exposition of union with Christ in Paul's epistles, notes that for Paul our new status in Christ is equivalent to being in and under Christ's realm, the "new creation" indicated in 2 Corinthians 5:17.[17] Christ, our Lord, addresses us in these words, and we as his renewed people are called to be attentive to his words. Scripture functions not merely as Christ's instrument of speaking to us, but also of his giving of himself to us, and of his transforming us due to his union with us and our union with him. As already noted, Christ gives the Spirit to enable us to hear him, receive him and be transformed by him.

But we know all too well our tendency to domesticate the Bible—that is, to make it subject to our control and management. There is abundant evidence in church history, and in our own day, for this tendency, and the negative consequences that result from this. In Colossians 2:16–19, Paul warns against those who appear to have great insight into biblical teaching but are merely promoting "idle notions." The basic problem is that they have lost connection with the Head of the church. Only as believers receive his Word by remaining rooted and built up in him will they grow as a unified body according to the purposes of God (Colossians 2:6–7,18–19). This requires the church to be a community of repentance, evident in humility and submission before the converting power of the gospel and the renewing work of the Spirit. Campbell rightly contends that our way of submission to the Word of God is analogous to the relationship of the incarnate Son to the Father who sent him, namely, the way of "obedience and utter dependence."[18] While this may be cultivated in personal spiritual disciplines, it is primarily fostered in the worship, communal life and practices of the church.[19]

---

17 Constantine R. Campbell, *Paul and Union with Christ: An Exegetical and Theological Study* (Grand Rapids: Zondervan, 2012), 115–120.

18 Campbell, *Paul and Union with Christ*, 132.

19 For a good description of such practices in the life of the church, see James K.A. Smith, *Desiring the Kingdom: Worship, Worldview and Cultural Formation* (Grand Rapids: Baker, 2009), especially chapter 5, "Practicing for the Kingdom," 155ff.

The third characteristic of the communal reading of Scripture is that the church's discernment of Christian ethics from Scripture is not primarily about method, but about fostering a community of faith and love that delights to do God's will, even when it is personally or socially difficult to do so. This means that techniques of hermeneutics alone are not sufficient to discern the will of God. Of course, there must be principles of interpretation that guide the exegesis of Scripture to understand the will of God for his people. But the variety of principles that relate to the interpretation of the biblical texts requires the interpreter, and the interpretive community, to determine which principles have priority, which ones apply to specific texts and which biblical texts are relevant to particular ethical issues. While not all biblical ethical teachings have equal clarity, the divergence of the conclusions that exist between liberal and evangelical ethicists on issues such as abortion, same-sex relations and divorce and remarriage indicates that there are deeper issues than hermeneutical methods that shape the selection, weighing and exegesis of biblical texts. In large part, these basic issues are about the church's willingness to submit to the ethical demands that Christ makes of his people, even if these are contrary to the beliefs of the surrounding culture.

It is characteristic of those transformed through union with Christ that they delight to do the will of God. Believers' understanding of the gracious nature of God's redemptive work in uniting them to Christ is manifested in their delight to deny themselves and serve God.

> God is love. Whoever lives in love lives in God, and God in him (1 John 4:16).

> We love because he first loved us (1 John 4:19).

In Galatians 5:6, Paul states that "in Christ, neither circumcision nor uncircumcision has any value. The only thing that counts is faith expressing itself through love." As Campbell notes, what is of primary importance in the moral calling of those who have been liberated from the curse of the law through union with Christ is faith working through the practices of love.[20] Paul also connects faith and love to union with Christ in his words of exhortation to Timothy in 2 Timothy 1:13: "What you have heard from me, keep as the pattern of sound teaching, with faith and love in Christ Jesus." The goal for God's people is that their words and deeds are to be characterized by faith and love.[21]

How do believers learn those faithful, loving practices that are characteristic of their union with Christ? They learn these in the community of character, the church. Paul's letters are full of instructions to churches as to how they are to function as the family of God. Their communal life is to reflect their new membership in the body of Christ. Paul exhorts them, "Be devoted to one another in brotherly love. Honor one another above yourselves" (Romans 12:10). James Thompson notes in Paul's exhortations throughout his epistles

> the two dimensions of communal identity that shape the moral conduct of the readers: readers are to respond to "one another" without a concern for differences in social position, and they are to regard all fellow members as equal in status.[22]

Scripture makes clear that for those who are in Christ, and part of the family of God, there is no dichotomy between love and law.

> We know that we have come to know [Christ] if we obey his commands.... But if anyone obeys his word, God's love is truly made complete in him (1 John 2:3,5).

> This is love for God: to obey his commands (1 John 5:3).

Scripture also connects faith in and union with Christ to the gift of the Spirit, a life of love, and obedience to the commandments in 1 John 3:23–24:

---

20 See comments on this theme by Campbell, *Paul and Union with Christ*, 145.

21 Noted in Campbell, *Paul and Union with Christ*, 108–109.

22 James W. Thompson, *Moral Formation according to Paul: The Context and Coherence of Pauline Ethics* (Grand Rapids: Baker, 2011), 58.

> And this is his command: to believe in the name of his Son, Jesus Christ, and to love one another as he commanded us. Those who obey his commands live in him, and he in them. And this is how we know that he lives in us: We know it by the Spirit he gave us.

So, while this does not solve all the hermeneutical issues that arise in discerning God's commands, it does describe the foundational motivation of those united to Christ—that they delight to know and submit to God's revealed commandments as his way of guiding their expression of love to him and to their neighbours.

In this context, due to the fact that some in the virtue tradition have depreciated the place of law in the Christian life, it is important to underline the ongoing relevance and authority of the commandments of God for his people. To emphasize the priority of virtue in ethics some have essentially subsumed ethical principles and rules into the virtues. For example, Joseph Kotka in *The Christian Case for Virtue Ethics* maintains that the rules and laws of communities "work as summaries of previous wise decisions." They are a reference point for future judgements. He insists that "rules serve the virtues; the virtues do not serve the rules. Rules and principles assist in the acquisition and execution of the virtues."[23] This view of principles as summaries of previous wise decisions begs the question, If the church refers to previous decisions as wise ethical ones, must it not have used a rationale to consider them wise, since there were other ethical decisions made that were not deemed wise? Furthermore, in facing new ethical decisions one must be able to interpret the factors in these new situations such that the relevant criteria apply in taking a specific moral action. Both of these involve an appeal to moral principles.[24] The necessary conclusion is that both virtues and principles must have a place in Christian morality. Principles cannot be absorbed into the virtues.

---

23 Joseph J. Kotka, Jr., *The Christian Case for Virtue Ethics* (Washington: Georgetown University Press, 1996), 35–36. This weakness is also noted by L. Gregory Jones, Jr., in his book, *Transformed Judgement: Toward a Trinitarian Account of the Moral Life* (Notre Dame: University of Notre Dame Press, 1990), 1–18.

24 Jean Porter, *Moral Action and Christian Ethics*, New Studies in Christian Ethics, ed. Robin Gill (Cambridge: Cambridge University Press, 1995), 157–159.

Another way that virtue ethics has undermined the normative role of Scripture for Christian ethics is by viewing moral norms, not as the laws and commandments taught by the Bible, but as the social practices of a community shaped by Scripture. Cahill argues: "The contribution of the Bible to ethics is at the level of community formation, not primarily at that of rules or principles."[25] She quotes with approval Allan Verhey's comment that the final test of a moral proposal's authority is "the Christian community's experience of Scripture's authority in the context of its own moral life."[26] Moral norms are not drawn directly from Scripture, but from the moral practices of the believing community. But this is a confusion of the source of ethical normativity with the appropriation of this normativity by the community. Certainly, the church adopts the biblical teaching into her community life, and teaches this in the process of discipleship. This is usually how people are taught and mentored in moral obedience. But this appropriation is always a human activity, subject to modification and correction. It is not the inspired source of ethical teaching, even though it may be motivated by faithful obedience to Christ. Only the Scripture is the authoritative revelation of God's will for his people. Any church appropriation of biblical ethics remains subject to analysis and revision in light of the Word of God.

The fourth characteristic of the church's reading of the Bible for ethical guidance is that it is attentive to and appropriates insights from its tradition of ethical instruction. While evangelicals frequently have an allergy to tradition, they need to understand that it always plays a role in the church's moral discipleship and teachings, and it should do so. So, how exactly does tradition function in the church's calling to guide believers into ethical obedience?

Ethical traditions arise as the church discerns certain moral practices to be faithful practices that express submission to the ethical commands of God's Word. These traditions involve both a discernment of the biblical teaching and an understanding of

---

25 Lisa Sowell Cahill, "The New Testament and Ethics: Communities of Social Change." *Interpretation* 44 (October 1990): 395.

26 Cahill, "The New Testament and Ethics," 387.

the context in which such commands are to be embodied. This is the ethical aspect of what Billings calls the indigenization of the gospel in particular and historical contexts.[27] The result of such discernment is the contextualization of ethical norms to produce Christian obedience in the particular social and cultural situations in which Christians find themselves. An example of this is the early church's condemnation of the widespread practice of abortion and infanticide, especially of female infants or those born with physical defects. The church determined that the sixth commandment, "You shall not murder," required Christians to protect all life in the womb, and to care for all infants born, whatever their gender or physical condition.[28] The church prohibited abortion and infanticide for Christians, and promoted the care and nurturing of all infants and children, even those discarded by parents. The historical missional practice of the church continued this tradition of rescuing discarded infants from death. This general tradition of placing value on all human life led the church to care for the sick and handicapped, the elderly and the dying. All life is a gift of God and is to be accepted and valued with loving care. Thus, when Christians seek to understand what it means to obey the sixth commandment in various historical and social contexts, they are guided by the life-affirming and life-saving teachings and practices of the church.

Hauerwas rightly understands tradition to be "the history of a community's sharing of [moral] judgements as they have been tested through generations."[29] This does not mean that the church accepts uncritically all past traditional practices. But it does mean that the church receives them as historically proved practices that have stood the test of time, and which should provide insight and guidance to the ethical obedience necessary to God's people in the particular situations that they face.

Of course, there is a danger here, namely, to locate ethical authority in the traditions of the church—to establish a Protestant *magisterium* for ethical behaviour. One finds this tendency in

---

27 Billings, *Union with Christ*, 132.

28 Rodney Stark, *A History of Christianity: How the Obscure, Marginal Jesus Movement Became the Dominant Religious Force in the Western World in a Few Centuries* (San Francisco: HarperCollins, 1997), 124–125.

29 Hauerwas, *Community of Character*, 62.

Hauerwas' ethics. He argues that the church should commit to these moral traditions as central and authoritative for its life.[30] There are several problems with this view of tradition.[31] First, church traditions have changed over time, even within more authoritarian, hierarchical institutions such as the Roman Catholic Church.[32] Second, there is a great deal of diversity that exists in the traditions of the various Christian communities and denominations, especially in our modern era. Finally, the church itself has often been influenced by the forces of the larger culture and society in its perspectives and practices. For example, in Western society today the forces of secularism, pluralism, tolerance and consumerism have had an impact on some churches. These churches have embraced doctrinal and ethical pluralism and relativism in their teachings. We do not find the unity and consistency in the church's moral traditions that Hauerwas seems to imply. Thus, Scripture must have the final authority by which all traditions of the past, as well as the newly formed modern "traditions," are evaluated. Scripture alone provides the constant and universal ethical truths for church practices. Without such an appeal to norms, the two extreme dangers for a church community are that its traditions and virtues can degenerate into mere superstition,[33] or that it can resort to authoritarian control to enforce its traditions and virtues.[34]

The full range of the canon must be at work in all the church's ethical teachings, and the church cannot ignore those texts that stand in tension with a church's construal of the Christian tradition.[35] The church must always allow the whole of the Word of God to be the final authority in ethics. Hays rightly notes that

---

30 Hauerwas, *Community of Character*, 66–68.

31 Robin Gill makes the following three points in "Moral Communities and Christian Ethics," *Sudies in Christian Ethics* 8:1 (1995): 6–13.

32 John T. Noonan points out that over time the Roman Catholic Church has changed its moral teachings on usury, marriage, slavery and religious freedom. "Development in Moral Theology," *Theological Studies* 54 (1993): 662–677.

33 Noted by Gilbert Meilaender, *Faith and Faithfulness: Basic Themes in Christian Ethics* (Notre Dame: University of Notre Dame Press, 1991), 4–5.

34 Noted by Philip Goodchild, "Christian Ethics in the Postmodern Condition," *Studies in Christian Ethics* 8:1 (1995): 17–18.

35 Richard Hays makes this point in *The Moral Vision of the New Testament: A Contemporary Introduction to New Testament Ethics* (New York: HarperSanFrancisco, 1996), 260–264.

tradition, reason and experience can "function instrumentally to help us interpret and apply Scripture," but their insights must always be judged and corrected in the light of Scripture.[36]

This can be illustrated by the variations in cultural traditions that Christians have developed for grown children's honouring of their parents in obedience to the fifth commandment. In some Asian cultures it is the firstborn male who has the responsibility to care for his parents, especially when they are elderly, often by providing living space in his home for them. In Western cultures, we tend to view honouring parents as frequently visiting them, either when they are still living in their own residences, or when they are living in a facility that provides care for them. The point here is that variations in Christian traditions on honouring parents can clarify both the essence and the flexibility of obedience to the fifth commandment. The church can give guidance to its members in discerning how to do this appropriately.

The fifth characteristic of the communal reading of Scripture is that Christians learn humility and perseverance in studying the difficult ethical parts of Scripture. The church guides believers to see that the "strangeness" of some biblical teachings is not due to the distance between the biblical horizon and our own, but rather due to the gap between the ways of God and our ways. It is all too easy for Christians today to simply ignore or reject certain biblical injunctions because they seem foreign to our modern social and cultural situation. Some may appear to be relatively benign, such as the command in 1 Corinthains 11:3–10 that a man pray with his head uncovered and that a woman pray with her head covered as a sign of authority. Other commands appear more important, such as the exhortation in 1 Corinthians 8:4–13 not to eat food that has been sacrificed to an idol so as not to be a "stumbling block" [*skandalon*] to a fellow believer with a weak conscience. In the secular and individualistic culture of Western society, this latter command seems irrelevant. But the key principle here is to embrace a loving regard for the impact of our actions on fellow believers—so as not to lead them to violate their consciences. The passage also challenges both our individualistic view of our Christian obedience and the secular perspective of

36 Hays, *Moral Vision*, 296.

our culture that dismisses the dangers of idolatry. The church's calling is to guide believers into a way of life that not only grasps the freedom that is theirs in Christ but also to exercise that freedom in such a way that builds up the body of Christ. As Paul states in Galatians 5:13, believers need to learn to use their freedom not to indulge the sinful nature, but rather, to "serve one another in love."

A key point in the role of the church in teaching believers to submit to Scripture with humility and perseverance is to disciple them into seeing the Bible primarily as a redemptive narrative or story. This is the primary framework for letting the Bible address us "in all its historical oddness and otherness." The writings of N.T. Wright have had a major impact in the evangelical world to lead us to read Scripture as the true story of the world, culminating in God's redemption through Jesus Christ of a people, and of the renewal of all creation. This counteracts the tendency of many believers to read the Bible from their own cultural perspective as a sourcebook of timeless rules and principles which they can apply to their own situations. Wright, among others, has stressed that to appropriate Scripture morally in this way is to misunderstand how the authority of Scripture functions.[37] Scripture functions primarily to get us to see that the biblical story, not our cultural story, is the narrative by which we need to see ourselves, our world and our callings. In effect, the Bible becomes the means that the Spirit uses to enable us to understand and live out of that true story. The church has a key role in instructing, discipling and directing its members in this. The church tells the story in various ways—in liturgy, in reading Scripture, in sermons, in Sunday School and in pastoral guidance. When the church does this faithfully, the question no longer is: How can we relate the biblical teaching, especially the odd and difficult parts, to our situation today? Rather, the question becomes: How can we live out the true story of the Bible—what God is doing today—in the context in which we live?

37 A concise statement of N.T. Wright's argument is found in the article, "How Can the Bible Be Authoritative?" *Vox Evangelica* 21 (1991): 7–32. See also N.T. Wright, *Scripture and the Authority of God: How to Read the Bible Today* (New York: HarperOne, 2011), 24.

Our vocation is to indwell the biblical story as those called into God's kingdom purposes. As we do so, we strive with the help of the Spirit to view and act in the world according to God's kingdom purposes. This does not mean that all the difficult parts of the Bible become clear. Nor does it mean that all the challenges of ethical obedience today will be resolved. But it does mean that we draw upon the rich resources of Scripture, tradition and the contemporary wisdom of the church to guide us in ethical obedience. Not only is the Scripture—both the understandable and the challenging parts—the key instrument of the Spirit in ethical guidance, but also the church is the institutional means that the Spirit uses to direct Christians into humble and obedient submission to Christ in our day.

The sixth characteristic of the communal reading of the Bible is that the church reads Scripture with the expectation that Christ through his Spirit always has new insights and judgements to teach us. Wright uses the analogy of a five-act play to describe the calling that Christians have in living out the biblical narrative.[38] The Bible reveals the first three acts of the divine narrative of creation, fall and redemption, reaching its fulfilment in Jesus Christ. The book of Acts and the epistles provide an account of the church's mission in light of the first three acts. Wright designates this as Act Four, Scene One. The final act, which is the consummation of God's redemption resulting in the renewal of all things, is revealed in the book of Revelation, as well as in other New Testament passages that point to this. The church is living out Act Four, Scene Two. This is directed by the first three acts, and by the goal and end of history in the fifth act. The first part of the fourth act serves as both example and instruction to us as to how we are to live out that mission. This scriptural direction must be accomplished in the context of our historical and socio-cultural context. This calls for, what Wright calls, "improvisation" on the part of the church.[39]

Another term for this task of the church is contextualization.

---

38 Wright, "How Can the Bible Be Authoritative?" 18. The following widely used book expands Wright's analogy of the metanarrative of the Bible into a six-act play: Craig G. Bartholomew and Michael W. Goheen, *The Drama of Scripture: Finding Our Place in the Biblical Story*, 2nd ed (Grand Rapids: Baker Books, 2014).

39 Wright, "How Can the Bible Be Authoritative?" 20.

Contextualization involves embodying the Christian faith in particular historical and cultural contexts such that our ethical lives are both faithful to the biblical narrative and teachings and relevant to the situations in which we live. Both are necessary. If one emphasizes faithfulness and ignores relevance, one's Christianity, and the proclamation of the gospel, become irrelevant. If we emphasize relevance and abandon faithfulness, the result is syncretism—essentially accommodating the Christian message to the culture. Both faithfulness and relevance are essential for contextualization so that the church fulfils her mission to witness to, and embody a life that reflects, the gospel of Christ.[40]

The Christian life of obedience must always be contextualized in particular situations. Samuel Wells makes use of the theatrical theme of improvisation in explaining how Christians should live out their ethical callings in the framework of Wright's paradigm of a narrative with multiple acts.[41] Believers' performance of the Christian life in light of Scripture is not merely repetition of the ethical behaviour revealed in the Bible, but means improvisation so that Christians act ethically in ways appropriate to the circumstances. This can only occur as believers participate in the communal life, worship and ministry of the church. They are trained in the practices of improvisation—contextualization—in and through these ecclesial practices so that, when they are living in the many other spheres of their lives, they have the knowledge, skills and imagination to embody faithful ethical practices there.[42] This obviously involves interaction with other Christians in the same callings or professions—business, medical care, government and so on.[43] Christians who are knowledgeable practitioners

---

40 For a good brief discussion of these aspects of contextualization see Michael W. Goheen, *Introducing Christian Mission Today: Scripture, History and Issues* (Downers Grove: InterVarsity Press, 2014), 264–270.

41 Samuel Wells, *Improvisation: The Drama of Christian Ethics* (Grand Rapids: Brazos, 2004), 50. The weakness of Wells' paradigm is that he collapses the Fall into Creation (57). This weakens both the sense of the goodness of God's original creation and the understanding of redemption as the renewal and restoration of the goodness of creation.

42 Wells, *Improvisation*, 65–84.

43 A helpful distinction here is between the church as *institution* and the church as *organism*. The latter refers to Christians involved in the various spheres and activities of their lives outside of institutional church activities. See Gordon J. Spykman, *Reformational Theology: A New Paradigm for Doing Theology* (Grand Rapids: Eerdmans, 1992), 432.

in an area are able to learn from and to interact with each other to discern faithful ethical obedience in the specific context of their callings. Here, Christians are discerning ethical obedience that reflects their union with Christ and their character and virtues that flow out of the communal life of the church. But they are discerning the specific ethical virtues and practices that reflect faithful contextual expressions of the Christian life of believers in those callings and situations. Those who think and act in these areas are the best ones to carry out this calling of contextualization.

In conclusion, if the Christian life is essentially grounded in our union with Christ, and if union with Christ necessarily involves our union with the church as the body of Christ, then Christian ethics can be neither individualistic nor anthropocentric. That is, it cannot be the result of individual Christians' making use of their knowledge and methodological expertise to discern the ethical themes and principles revealed in Scripture which they then apply in a self-directed manner to the issues and decisions that arise in their lives. To view Christian ethics in this manner, whether in theory or in practice, is effectively to ignore the significance of the work of the Spirit in uniting believers with Christ and with the church. Concomitantly, such a perspective ignores the work of the Spirit as he is sent by Christ to his church to nurture, disciple and guide believers in the process of maturity in their moral lives.

Put in positive terms, Christ sends his Spirit to his church so that those united to him by his Spirit may be shaped within this unique institution to embody lives of ethical obedience. The church serves as the body in and through which the people of God engage in communal reading of Scripture. I have argued that this involves at least six characteristics: to read Scripture for moral insight, to interpret the Bible prayerfully and with moral seriousness as Christian Scripture addressed by Christ to his people, to foster a theologically attuned community that delights to do God's will, to be guided by the living tradition of the church in ethical judgements, to study with humility and perseverance the difficult ethical teachings of Scripture and to have the expectation that through the illumination of the Spirit Christ always has new ethical insights and judgements to teach his church in the particular social and cultural contexts in which it is situated.

This is essentially what it means for the church of Christ to live out of the biblical story and let the ever-living Word of God both shape our characters and direct our decisions by the ongoing work of the Spirit. The Spirit who inspired the biblical authors is also the Spirit who illuminates the people of God in bringing the Word of God to bear upon their lives. And, as this chapter has argued, the Spirit does this in and through the communal life of the church. Only as believers submit to Christ by being a part of his body on earth can they live moral lives of faithfulness to Christ and of relevance to their context. Only as active members in Christ's church can Christians truly fulfil their ethical calling to manifest in a tangible manner the presence of the kingdom of God.

8

Introduction to New Testament distinctives of worship

BY DOUGLAS A. THOMSON

This paper will explore the biblical and historical foundations of New Testament worship and will seek to discover what makes New Testament worship distinctive from worship in the Old Testament by exploring a systematic and comprehensive study of New Testament worship theology and practice. Three New Testament topics that I have purposely omitted are baptism, communion and eschatological worship. This is not an omission because they are not important to New Testament worship. On the contrary, they are so important that they are subjects of which much is written and therefore are beyond the scope of this paper in terms of length.

So much of what Christians understand about worship develops from the practice of worship to which we have grown accustomed. In the past few decades in North America, we have allowed trends to shape our worship practices which have as their primary goal to increase the attendance of the local church. This attractional goal is a biblically questionable motive for altering the shape of our corporate worship. The goal of this chapter is to assemble the biblical and theological teaching of New Testament worship so that its content can inform our worship.

Harold Best is one of many writers who help us to understand that as the New Testament church we need to re-adjust the trajectory of our worship practices to keep them in line with the New Testament. He tells us that in spite of the fact that it has become popular to say all of life is worship, the Sunday morning worship gathering continues to serve as the primary venue for worship. Further misunderstanding is evident when people refer to the opening segment of the service as the worship portion and when they use the word worship as a synonym for music.[1]

Studying the distinctives of worship under the new covenant should enliven our hearts to appreciate God's goodness and mercy to us with doxology to God for the blessings we derive from this "better covenant," as the writer of Hebrews calls it (Hebrews 7:22; 8:6; 12:24). This study will highlight these amazing new covenant benefits that God, through Christ, has afforded us and thus serve as a motivator to worship him with even greater thankfulness and fervour.

I have identified four New Testament worship distinctives, which this chapter will examine. They are: Christ, the Holy Spirit, Christian lifestyle and the church.[2] Each of these distinctives contains at least threads of continuity with the old covenant but each is significantly unique. These four features of new covenant worship have the potential to equip us for and excite us to new heights of worship and devotion to God through Jesus Christ, the central figure in New Testament worship.

A word regarding my use of the term "distinctives"

I have used the term "distinctives" in this paper to describe New Testament worship ideas and practices which are new or different

---

[1] Harold M. Best, *Unceasing Worship: Biblical Perspectives on Worship and the Arts* (Downers Grove: InterVarsity Press, 2003), 9–10.

[2] A fifth distinctive would be our eschatological hope. Due to page limitations this distinctive will not be covered in this essay.

from Old Testament ideas and practices. I have used the words "perspectives," "principles" and "concepts" synonymously. There is no single passage in the New Testament where the principles or concepts of worship under the new covenant are succinctly and systematically laid out, but the reality that the new covenant has brought with it a transformation in worship is clearly evident and sprinkled throughout the entire New Testament. These distinctively new worship concepts represent what I want to explore. David Peterson recognizes the reality of such concepts when he writes that

> more than any other New Testament document, Hebrews makes it clear that the inauguration of the new covenant by Jesus means the fulfillment and replacement of the whole pattern of approach to God established under the Mosaic covenant.[3]

Borchert, writing in *Worship in the New Testament* also testifies of a new pattern of worship by saying

> worship is no longer confined to an old stone temple, but is evidenced in a new context—God's new sanctuary (*naon*)—epitomized in God's people, the place where God now "dwells" (*katoiketerion*) by the Spirit. Moreover, Christ Jesus is to be regarded as the "cornerstone" (*akrogoniaiou*) of the new pattern of worship (Ephesians 2:20–22).[4]

In defining the "distinctives" of new covenant worship, I have borrowed from Peterson's definition, which sums it up in these words: "New-covenant worship is essentially the engagement with God that he has made possible through the revelation of himself in Jesus Christ and the life he has made available through the Holy Spirit."[5]

---

3 David Peterson, *Engaging with God: A Biblical Theology of Worship* (Downers Grove: InterVarsity Press, 1992), 228.
4 Gerald L. Borchert, *Worship in the New Testament: Divine Mystery and Human Response* (St. Louis: Chalice Press, 2008), 133.
5 Peterson, *Engaging with God*, 100.

New Testament worship is reoriented by being Christocentric (Colossians 1:15–20)

One of the most important distinctives of worship under the new covenant is the new way God requires us to approach him. At the very core and essence of Christian worship is the fact that we now worship God the Father through his Son.[6] We focus on the one sacrificed rather than on the old covenant sacrificial system itself (Hebrews 7:25–27; 9:25–28).[7] Jesus Christ is the central figure of Christianity and is the embodiment and personification of salvation, and thus, our divine Redeemer who is worthy of our singular worship.

Jesus talks openly in terms of a new covenant at the Last Supper when he interprets the cup as the new covenant in his blood (Luke 22:20; cf. 1 Corinthians 11:25). As Barry Liesch explains, "When Jesus inaugurated the Lord's supper and charged his disciples to 'do this in remembrance of me,' He effected a permanent change. It was a watershed statement for Christian worship."[8] Jesus associates his sacrifice on the cross for us with the Old Testament sacrificial system (1 Corinthians 5:7) while simultaneously initiating a completely new covenant.[9]

This new covenant predicted by the prophets (Jeremiah, Ezekiel and Isaiah) allows its adherents to know God in a way Israel was never able to know him (Hebrews 8:8–12) because Christ teaches them much more about God than was previously revealed. Christ, the embodiment of the new covenant, does not contradict the old, but completely absorbs and supersedes the old (Hebrews 8:13ff.), which is just a picture or shadow of the new.[10]

Christ is not only the embodiment of the new covenant. Paul, in Colossians 1:15–29, tells us that Christ is the image of God himself. Scholars consider this passage to be an ancient hymn

---

6 Geoffrey W. Bromiley, "The Essence of New Testament Worship" in *The Biblical Foundations of Christian Worship*, vol. 1, Complete Library of Christian Worship (Nashville: Star Song, 1993), 110.

7 Bryan Chapell, *Christ-Centered Worship: Letting the Gospel Shape Our Practice* (Grand Rapids: Baker Academic, 2009), 109.

8 Barry Liesch, *People in the Presence of God: Models and Directions for Worship* (Grand Rapids: Zondervan, 1988), 42.

9 Allan P. Ross, *Recalling the Hope of Glory: Biblical Worship from the Garden to the New Creation* (Grand Rapids: Kregel, 2006), 396.

10 Borchert, *Worship in the New Testament*, 180.

which presents Christ as the preeminent object of our worship. It helps us to recognize Christ's supremacy because, as the image of the invisible God, he is both the creator and the sustainer of creation, he is our Redeemer, the head over the church, and his sovereignty is absolute.[11]

Jesus is the visible representation of God's glory (John 1:14–15). Since no person could actually look upon the Almighty (Exodus 33:20), God provided various alternative means for his people to recognize his presence as he progressively revealed more of himself over time. In the new covenant, not only God's presence but also his Spirit, word, wisdom and glory are most completely and perfectly represented in Jesus.[12] Thus, it is through Jesus that the triune God chooses to be worshipped, making Jesus the central focus of worship in the New Testament.[13] This enables us as new covenant believers to know and worship God more fully because Christ more fully reveals the Father to us (John 1:18).

The Colossians' hymn validates the supremacy of Christ as the creator and sustainer of the universe. Further, Jesus validates his role and identity when he declares himself greater than the temple (Matthew 12:6). In making this claim, he compares himself to the presence and dwelling place of God. God continues to dwell among his people under the new covenant as Emmanuel (God with us). In this way, God dwells in flesh and blood, in Christ himself, thus eliminating the need for a physical temple.[14] Similarly, Jesus asserts to the Samaritan woman that the argument over the place of worship has become superfluous because the Father has sent the Son, the long awaited Messiah. Worship will now be centred in a person, Jesus, not in a building (John 4:21–24).[15]

God demonstrates his acceptance of Christ-centred worship by tearing the veil of the temple in two, symbolically allowing

11 Andrew T. Lincoln, *The Letter to the Colossians: Introduction, Commentary, and Reflections*, The New Interpreter's Bible: A Commentary in Twelve Volumes (Nashville: Abingdon Press, 2000), 11:597.

12 Borchert, *Worship in the New Testament*, 45.

13 Peter T. O'Brien, *Colossians, Philemon*, Word Biblical Commentary (Waco: Word Books, 1982), 44:53.

14 Noel Due, *Created for Worship: From Genesis to Revelation to You* (Fearn: Christian Focus, 2005), 126–131.

15 Ross, *Recalling the Hope of Glory*, 384–385.

believers direct access to God through Christ's atoning work (Matthew 27:51; Mark 15:38). This signifies that God is no longer with the old institutions. The Gospel writers intend to emphasize that Jesus fulfils all the Old Testament prophecies relating to the coming of the Messiah. He is the one who is ordained to usher in the new covenant era. Thus as New Testament believers we worship him.

Christ, the image-bearer of God who came to live among his people, renders obsolete some of the former worship practices that foreshadow his coming while others he reinterprets Christologically.[16] The writer of Hebrews, in particular, notes the similarities between the two covenants, but proclaims that in Jesus Christ, the system of beliefs of the past has become unnecessary (Hebrews 8:13).[17] This cessation of ritual forces the early church to discern carefully what aspects of Old Testament worship end with Christ and what aspects should remain and be Christologically reinterpreted.

One of the important roles that Jesus fulfils and replaces as the image-bearer of the invisible God of the Old Testament is the high priestly ministry of the Mosaic Covenant (Hebrews 8:8–12).[18] The writer of Hebrews establishes that the ministry of Jesus is superior to that of the priesthood instituted by Moses under the Sinai Covenant. Not only is he the crucified, resurrected and ascended Son of God (Hebrews 7:15–17) who is forever seated at God's right hand (Hebrews 8:1–2; 1 Peter 3:22), but he is also mediating a better covenant (Hebrews 7:22).[19] In fact, Hebrews makes it clear that the most significant categories of Old Testament discourse on the duties of the high priest (sanctuary, sacrifice, altar, priesthood and covenant) are manifested in the person and accomplishments of Jesus.[20] No longer do we approach God through the mediation of a human priest, but God has made himself more "approachable" by allowing us to communicate directly with his divine Son who not only

16 Liesch, *People in the Presence of God*, 42.

17 Due, *Created For Worship*, 154–155.

18 David G. Peterson, *Transformed By God: New Covenant Life and Ministry* (Downers Grove: InterVarsity Press, 2012), 77.

19 Peterson, *Transformed by God*, 78.

20 Peterson, *Engaging with God*, 228.

mediates for us but sympathizes with our weaknesses (Hebrews 4:15–16) and considers us family (Matthew 12:46–50).

Being in God's image emphasizes Christ's relationship to God, but the second title presented in the Colossians passage, "firstborn of all creation" (Colossians 15:1), emphasizes his relationship to the creation. One might conclude that Christ is simply the first of all the created beings.[21] But firstborn is frequently used to denote both temporal priority and sovereignty of rank.[22] In this case, the expression points to the latter, signifying the special place Christ enjoys in the Father's love.[23] The context implies Christ's uniqueness from creation, not his union as part of creation, for he both predates creation and has supremacy over it as its creator and Lord.[24]

The theme of Christ's supremacy of rank introduced in Colossians 1:15 is further emphasized in verse 16 which depicts Christ as not just the agent of all things but also the goal of creation, indicating that all things were created for him (cf. Hebrews 1:2–3).[25] The hymn in Revelation 5:13 gives us a glimpse of the mutual reign of the Father with the Son over the entire universe. Such a reign is well deserved since they are its creators. Further, all these pieces fit together to help us understand what Jesus meant when he said, "I and the Father are one" (John 10:30). Suddenly, the greatness of Jesus becomes evident. We are overwhelmed with the privilege of his self-revelation and his stature, and we worship him!

In similar fashion, Christ's supremacy extends to the church as indicated in Colossians 1:18. Paul uses the metaphor of a human body to describe the church's relationship with him and with each other. Christ is the head of the body, and his supremacy and authority over it are evident.[26]

In further connection with the church, Paul calls Christ the "beginning," then he follows that title with the clarifying phrase "firstborn from among the dead." As the firstborn from the dead,

---

21 O'Brien, *Colossians, Philemon*, 43.
22 O'Brien, *Colossians, Philemon*, 45.
23 O'Brien, *Colossians, Philemon*, 44.
24 O'Brien, *Colossians, Philemon*, 45.
25 O'Brien, *Colossians, Philemon*, 47.
26 Lincoln, *The Letter to the Colossians*, 599.

Christ is the founder of the resurrection age and, as the first to rise from the dead, he guarantees the future resurrection of others (1 Corinthians 15:20,23).[27] The resurrection, as Gerald Borchert explains, is the "hinge point of Christianity."[28] Without the resurrection Christ is not who he claims to be. In his own resurrection, and in raising Lazarus and others from the dead, Jesus wants the Jews (who generally believed in the resurrection at the end of the age) to know that he alone will raise them up.[29] Therefore, he declares, "I am the resurrection and the life. He who believes in me will live, even though he dies; and whoever lives and believes in me will never die" (John 11:25–26). By saying this, Jesus identifies himself as the resurrection and thus the correct focal point for Christian worship.[30]

Once again, Jesus is identified with God in Colossians 1:19 where Paul says, "God was pleased to have all his fullness dwell in him [Christ]." Not only is Christ the image of God but that image contains the fullness of God.[31] There are two points of significance to this statement. First, God is pleased to dwell or take up residence in the person of Christ. This is most likely a veiled reference here to the temple as the dwelling place of God in the Old Testament. Now, in the New Testament, God has moved his dwelling place to Christ.[32]

The second point of significance revolves around the word "fullness." Just as humanity was created by God "in his own image" (Genesis 1:26–27), Christ embodies the fullness of that image, making Jesus divine. The fullness of God refers to all of his attributes and activities including his Spirit, Word, wisdom and glory, which are perfectly displayed in Christ.[33] Colossians 2:9 verifies this concept by explaining that "in him all the fullness of deity dwells bodily."[34]

In Colossians 1:20 Paul continues to elucidate to his readers

27 O'Brien, *Colossians, Philemon*, 50–51.

28 Borchert, *Worship in the New Testament*, 114.

29 D.A. Carson, *The Gospel According to John* (Grand Rapids: Eerdmans, 1991), 412, cited in Ross, *Recalling the Hope of Glory*, 387–388.

30 Ross, *Recalling the Hope of Glory*, 387–388.

31 Lincoln, *The Letter to the Colossians*, 599.

32 Per O'Brien, *Colossians, Philemon*, 53.

33 F.F. Bruce, *Commentary on the Epistle to the Colossians*, The New International Commentary on the New Testament (Grand Rapids: Eerdmans, 1957), 207.

34 O'Brien, *Colossians, Philemon*, 53.

the relationship between God and Jesus. The verse clearly states that God has chosen to reconcile everything to himself, and he will do it through the work of Christ. Christ is not *a* means to be reconciled to God; Christ is *the only* means, because he is the only perfect sacrifice that can fulfil the requirements of God. No longer can one achieve redemption through ritual sacrifices and washing, genealogical descent from Abraham, study and adherence to the law or even personal piety. Redemption, from this point forward, comes only from repentance and faith in Jesus.[35] Christ becomes our Redeemer and thus central to New Testament worship.

Jesus also talks of the singularity of his work of reconciliation when he says, "I am the way the truth and the life. No one comes to the Father except through me" (John 14:6). Luke reiterates this in Acts 4:12 when he writes, "Salvation is found in no one else, for there is no other name under heaven given to men by which we must be saved." By stating this, they both highlight that the only worship acceptable to God the Father is that which begins by accepting Jesus as the Messiah.[36]

Jesus, speaking to Nicodemus (John 3:1–18), affirms that everyone who believes in him will have everlasting life. Drawing from the prophets, Jesus reiterates the need for spiritual renewal in order to find a place in the world to come. That renewal comes by faith in him alone who is the unique Son of God and singular Messiah; there is no forgiveness apart from him.[37]

Inherent in the concept of Christ's reconciliatory work is his willingness to be submissive and obedient to his Father's will (John 4:34) which includes being "obedient to death—even death on a cross!" (Philippians 2:8). It is clear from the statements of Jesus that he focuses his entire earthly life on obedient service to God, worshipping him through every word and deed in order to glorify his Father.[38] He is, therefore, simultaneously the true example of a dedicated and joyous worshipper of God

---

35 Ross, *Recalling the Hope of Glory*, 387.

36 Richard E. Averbeck, "Worshiping God in Truth," in Herbert Bateman IV, ed., *Authentic Worship: Hearing Scripture's Voice, Applying Its Truths* (Grand Rapids: Kregel, 2002), 111.

37 Ross, *Recalling the Hope of Glory*, 387.

38 Due, *Created for Worship*, 142–145.

and the one shown to be the object of worship.[39] Like Christ, our joyous and thankful worship response to God's provision of salvation is to serve and obey God.

Included in the context of Christ's reconciliatory work is the implication that Christ made "peace through his blood, shed on the cross" (Colossians 1:20). This account certainly harkens back to the statement that God will reconcile all things to himself through Christ. Christ not only makes peace between God and humanity because of the cross but because he ascended to the Father's right hand he continues to make peace on our behalf as mediator and high priest.[40]

Paul, having explained in this passage that Jesus is the image of God and that the fullness of God dwells in him, leaves us wondering about the exact nature of this relationship in terms of the oneness of Jesus and the Father (Colossians 1:19; John 10:30). If Christians believe that there is only one true God and yet follow the historic Christian pattern of giving reverence and worship to Christ, then some kind of insightful inclusion of Christ within God seems required.[41] The issue of Christocentric worship in the new covenant demands an understanding of God's triune nature. It is only through Jesus, who brought us a more complete knowledge of God (John 17:25–26; Matthew 11:27) that we have an awareness of the three persons of the Trinity.[42]

It is clear from Scripture that God is the source of all power and authority, and that Christ is given authority by God to carry out God's will (Matthew 28:18–20; John 1:1,14; 3:34–35; 5:26–27). By giving Christ all power and authority, it is God the Father who makes our worship Christ-centred, by redeeming us through the work of his Son.[43] Christocentric New Testament worship does not diminish the honour of any other member of the Trinity, rather, Christ presents the Father and Holy Spirit to

---

39 Due, *Created for Worship*, 139.

40 Cf. Peterson, *Engaging with God*, 238.

41 Larry W. Hurtado, *At the Origins of Christian Worship: The Context and Character of Earliest Christian Devotion* (Grand Rapids: William B. Eerdmans, 1999), 102.

42 Due, *Created for Worship*, 142–145.

43 James B. Torrance, *Worship, Community and the Triune God of Grace* (Downers Grove: InterVarsity Academic, 1996), 24, 36; Michael Horton, *A Better Way: Rediscovering the Drama of God-Centered Worship* (Grand Rapids: Baker Books, 2002), 149, quoted in Chapell, *Christ-Centered Worship*, 113.

us in his ministry. Jesus reveals God to us and represents the Father's power and love (John 14:9). Jesus is the object of the Spirit's ministry in that the Spirit illuminates the work of Christ (John 15:26). Each person of the Godhead participates in our redemption, but because redemption is the major theme of Christian worship, the ministry of the one who accomplishes our salvation is the focus of that worship.[44] We honour Father, Son and Holy Spirit when our worship is in the context of the redeeming work in which they all participate, but ultimately our worship culminates in Christ.[45]

Colossians and the entire New Testament proclaim Christ as the central figure of new covenant worship. He is both the agent of and reason for creation, and as such, he is the ruler and sustainer of everything created. He is the pre-existent and preeminent one. He is both the image and the fullness of God and thus has equality with God. He is the head of the church for whom he was crucified, buried and resurrected and is now enthroned on high as God's agent of redemption and reconciliation. He is the object of the church's worship and hope.[46]

New Testament worship is enabled by the Holy Spirit (John 16:5–15)

The second distinctive of New Testament worship is the third person of the Trinity, the Holy Spirit. New Testament worship is trinitarian, which in its most basic understanding is the worship of God the Father through God the Son and in and by the Holy Spirit.[47] True worship has always been both spiritual and in the Spirit; but with the coming of the Holy Spirit in the new covenant era, the fullness of the Spirit is made more complete.[48] Under the old covenant the Spirit especially empowers the prophets and

---

44 Chapell, *Christ-Centered Worship*, 113.

45 Torrance, *Worship, Community and the Triune God*, 24, 36; Horton, *A Better Way*, 149, cited in Chapell, *Christ-Centered Worship*, 113.

46 Todd D. Still, *Colossians*, The Expositor's Bible Commentary, rev. ed. (Grand Rapids: Zondervan, 2006), 12:265.

47 Geoffrey W. Bromiley, "The Essence of New Testament Worship" in *The Biblical Foundations of Christian Worship*, vol. 1, The Complete Library of Christian Worship (Nashville: Star Song Publishing Group, 1993), 110.

48 Bromiley, "The Essence of New Testament Worship," 110.

other leaders; but God promises that someday all his people will be empowered by the Spirit (Joel 2:28–32).[49]

The Spirit (the *Paraklete*) is described as being sent and given by God in John 14:16 and 26, and by Jesus in John 16:7. The Spirit is the vital link between the historical ministry of Jesus and the future life of the church after Jesus' death.[50] When Jesus returns to the Father, he sends the Paraclete or "helper" to the early Christians in order to continue the work that he has begun. When Christ departs to sit at the right hand of God, the Spirit is to be a substitute "in them" for Jesus who has been "with them" (John 14:16–18).[51] The Spirit now permeates every part of our spiritual experience.[52]

The Holy Spirit is integral to everything that God does because God is one—Father, Son and Holy Spirit. At the time of regeneration, the Spirit of God somehow takes up residence in our lives so that our bodies become the temple (the "most holy place") of the Holy Spirit (1 Corinthians 6:19). Once the Spirit has entered our lives and brought us into the family of God, he remains as the pledge or seal of eternal life (Ephesians 1:13–14). Bromiley summarized the Spirit's work in the New Testament by affirming that the Holy Spirit convinces us of sin, guides us in righteousness, focuses our attention on Christ, produces in us the fruit of the Spirit and intercedes for us.[53]

Jesus teaches his disciples about the Holy Spirit in John 16:5–15, where he implies that the end of his physical presence and earthly ministry will usher in a new and better era in the life of the new covenant community because the Holy Spirit will come (verse 7). The coming of the Spirit means that not only the disciples but also all future generations of believers will be able to experience the presence of God because the Paraclete takes the experience of God and extends it beyond the limits of Jesus'

---

49 G. W. H. Lampe, "The Holy Spirit in the Writings of St. Luke," in D.E. Nineham, ed., *Studies in the Gospels: Essays in Memory of R. H. Lightfoot* (Oxford: Blackwell, 1957), 162, quoted in Peterson, *Engaging with God*, 142.

50 Gail R. O'Day, *The Gospel of John*, The New Interpreter's Bible: A Commentary in Twelve Volumes (Nashville: Abingdon Press, 1995), 9:776.

51 Borchert, *Worship in the New Testament*, 52.

52 Bromiley, "The Essence of New Testament Worship," 110.

53 Bromiley, "The Essence of New Testament Worship," 110.

physical life. The Paraclete makes Jesus present to all believers, even though Jesus is now physically absent.

Jesus relays to the disciples in John 16:8–11 that when the Holy Spirit comes, his role in the world will be to convict and judge the world regarding its sin and guilt.[54] Under the new covenant, the Holy Spirit convicts unbelievers, making them aware of sin and righteousness and judgement (John 16:8). Jesus confirms the Spirit's role in regeneration when he tells Nicodemus, "Very truly, I tell you, no one can enter the kingdom of God without being born of water and Spirit. What is born of the flesh is flesh, and what is born of the Spirit is spirit" (John 3:5–6). Jesus again says that it is "the Spirit that gives life" (John 6:63). It is only through the inward working of the Holy Spirit that God's saving acts can become personal to us.[55]

John 16:9 implies that the specific sin of not believing in Jesus is at the heart of the world's sin. Mounce states, "The heavenly prosecutor will prove that the world is guilty for its rejection of Jesus and its distorted ideas of righteousness and judgment."[56]

In John 16:12–13 Jesus turns from discussing the Spirit's work in relation to the world to speaking of the Spirit's role in continuing to guide the disciples into truth. Jesus also implies that without the Spirit's help, the disciples are not prepared to hear the full message that he would like to impart. In order to bear what is coming, as verse 12 states, the disciples need to wait for the arrival of the Spirit and the power that he will provide. Jesus may be referring to the gifts and the boldness the Spirit will give them to carry out their task of spreading the gospel of Christ in the face of great opposition (cf. John 15:26; 20:22–23;[57] Acts 1:4, 8).[58] We see this in Acts 4:31 when, after being filled with the Spirit, the disciples speak the word boldly.[59] The effectiveness and reality of the Spirit's indwelling is evident when compared

54 Andreas J. Köstenberger, *John*, Baker Exegetical Commentary on the New Testament (Grand Rapids: Baker Academic, 2004), 471.

55 Segler and Bradley, *Christian Worship*, 53–54.

56 Robert H. Mounce, *John*, vol. 10 of The Expositor's Bible Commentary, rev. ed. (Grand Rapids: Zondervan, 2007), 587.

57 Jesus gave the Holy Spirit to the disciples when he appeared to them after his resurrection per John 20:19–23).

58 Mounce, *John*, 588.

59 Mounce, *John*, 587.

to the fear they evidence just before the crucifixion when they desert Christ (Mark 14:50).[60]

All believers have the anointing of the Holy Spirit as the disciples did, and are therefore enabled to serve the Lord with the effectiveness of the Spirit (1 John 2:20).[61] On our own, we are unable to produce any spiritual outcome without the Spirit's working.

In addition to anointing his people, the Spirit distributes spiritual gifts to us (Romans 12:1–8; 1 Corinthians 12:1–31; Ephesians 4:7–13; cf. Psalm 68:18). The Holy Spirit bestowed these gifts on the Day of Pentecost to complement the missionary task that Jesus gave to the disciples. The gift of prophetic speech and tongues make obvious the arrival of the Spirit on the Day of Pentecost. These gifts were given for the purpose of proclaiming the gospel to people from every nation.[62] All Christians have at least one spiritual gift, which they are expected to use with liberality to glorify God and bless the body.[63] Unfortunately, the exercise of the gifts in the Corinthian church caused disorder in the services. As a result, Paul admonished the believers at Corinth to respect the variety of gifts given by the Spirit, to exercise the gifts in an orderly fashion for the edification of the saints and, most importantly, to recognize that the expression of gifts has little significance unless accompanied by the love that also comes from the Spirit.[64]

The Paraclete is given the title "Spirit of truth" (John 16:13), which underscores the reliability of the Spirit to point to the truth. This designation also emphasizes his link with Jesus, who is the truth (John 14:6). As the Spirit of truth, the Spirit's role in the future life of the community is to guide the disciples and all believers into all truth (John 16:13). This ministry of guidance is evident in the Old Testament such as when the Spirit led Israel in the wilderness (Isaiah 63:14).[65] In the new covenant, however, the Spirit's ministry of guidance and teaching has to come to its fulness in the life of the faith community. The combination of guidance with truth is a direct echo of John 14:6, where Jesus

---

60 Mounce, *John*, 587.

61 Ross, *Recalling the Hope of Glory*, 421.

62 Peterson, *Engaging with God*, 143.

63 Ross, *Recalling the Hope of Glory*, 421.

64 Ross, *Recalling the Hope of Glory*, 423–424.

65 Köstenberger, *John*, 472.

declares: "I am the way, the truth, and the life." The truth that the Spirit will guide us into is the truth of Jesus.[66]

The Spirit does not speak his own truth or on his own authority. Just as Christ claims that as the Son he speaks only what he hears from the Father (John 8:26–28; 12:49; 14:10), so too is the Spirit limited in his teaching ministry.[67] The Spirit will lead the disciples into a deeper understanding of the person of Christ, and into a full comprehension of the principles which Christ has taught them. Merrill Tenney notes that within the promise to guide the disciples into all truth "lies the germinal authority of the apostles' writings, which transmit the revelation of Christ through his disciples by the work of the Holy Spirit."[68] In other words, the Spirit has guided them into the truth written in the New Testament.

The phrase, the Spirit will take "from what is mine and make it known to you," found in John 16:14, expands on what has just been stated regarding the Spirit's role in revealing truth. The possession of Christ that the Spirit takes, according to Andreas J. Köstenberger, is the full revelation of God (John 1:18; 5:19–20). The Spirit draws on this reservoir of knowledge to enlighten the disciples. He does not advance the revelation given by Jesus since Jesus, not the Spirit, is "the Word" (John 1:1).[69]

Both Son and Spirit clearly identify the Father as the ultimate source of the truth. Here we see the continuity between the ministries of the Son and the Spirit. Just as the Son brings glory to the Father by revealing the Father through his words and actions (John 1:14,18; 7:18; 17:4–6) so the Spirit will bring glory to Jesus.[70] Mounce states, "The full significance of spiritual truth cannot be grasped apart from the illuminating work of the Spirit."[71] By combining prayerful reflection on the works and words of Jesus (recorded in the New Testament) with the illuminating work of the Spirit, the worshipper will attain a deeper appreciation of

66 O'Day, *The Gospel of John*, 773.

67 Mounce, *John*, 589.

68 Merrill C. Tenney, *The Gospel of John*, vol. 9 in The Expositor's Bible Commentary (Grand Rapids: Zondervan, 1981), 158.

69 Köstenberger, *John*, 474.

70 Köstenberger, *John*, 474.

71 Mounce, *John*, 589.

Jesus and a new sense of wonder concerning his person and work. In this way, the Spirit brings glory to the Son.[72]

It is critical, when considering the truth into which the Spirit guides us, to recognize that the truth is to be interpreted in community, because the Spirit was given to the church as a whole. According to O'Day and others, the Paraclete is not a private possession. He states:

> Because the Paraclete is the presence of Jesus after Jesus' departure, it is not simply a subjective experience of "God," but is always linked to the revelation of God made known in the incarnation. The Paraclete keeps the community grounded in Jesus' revelation of God, not in an individual's private experience of God. The Paraclete is thus the unifying mark of Christian community, because it gives all believers access to Jesus.[73]

Under the new covenant, the age of the Holy Spirit, the sanctifying power of the Spirit regenerates people from within. The person who is born of the Spirit, and led by the Spirit, is one who is able to express acceptable worship to God in actions and attitudes by the power of the Spirit.

The Spirit is central to the spiritual life of the New Testament worshipping community. When we choose to follow God, we do so through the work of the Spirit who supernaturally dwells within us (1 Corinthians 3:16; 2 Timothy 1:14). Paul exhorts us to be continually filled with or controlled by the Spirit (Ephesians 5:18) so that his guidance and sanctifying power will be at work in our hearts. We are to be vigilant not to grieve or quench the Holy Spirit's influence in our lives (Ephesians 4:30; 1 Thessalonians 5:19) but to exhibit the fruit of the Spirit and exercise the gifts of the Spirit in our public lives, ministry and worship. The presence and influence of the Holy Spirit in the New Testament is both distinctive and profound.

---

72 Mounce, *John*, 589.

73 O'Day, *The Gospel of John*, 776–777.

New Testament worship is evidenced by a holy and obedient lifestyle (Romans 12:1–2)

In our North American evangelical culture, people often equate worship with the singing of songs, the raising of hands and other demonstrations of adoration to God; but true worship begins with obedience.[74] Without obedience, every other act of worship is meaningless, and God rejects it. This concept is not unique to the New Testament. The Old Testament is riddled with warnings against ritual obedience and reminders that God desires a genuine response of love and thankfulness which prompts an engagement with him characterized by submission and respect (see Isaiah 1:10–16; 29:13; Amos 5:21–27; Micah 6:6–8).[75] Of all the New Testament distinctives of worship, this one holds the most continuity to the Old Testament; however, it does have some distinctive features.

Before God would accept Israel's worship, his people had to prepare their hearts by repenting of their sin and disobedience (Joshua 3:5). In that regard, the new covenant is much the same as the old; God will never accept our worship until we first repent of our sins.[76] Romans 12:1–2 can instruct us in relating acceptable, obedient living to our worship of God.

In this text, Paul urges us to give ourselves completely to God, in fact to sacrifice ourselves to God, not to die for him but to live for him, as living sacrifices. Paul uses the language reminiscent of the old sacrificial system to forge a connection with the new covenant to which the temple has always pointed. Paul's use of cultic terminology does not signal the return to traditional Judaism, but rather illustrates how God has reinterpreted and replaced, the old system.

No longer are rites, rituals and sacrifices required, for Christ has purchased our redemption with the sacrifice of his life, once for all. Paul's is urging the followers of Christ to offer themselves, rather than animal sacrifices, as an expression of their worship to the one who has died for their salvation. As recipients of the gift

---

74 Vernon M. Whaley, *Called To Worship: The Biblical Foundations of Our Response to God's Call* (Nashville: Thomas Nelson, 2009), 52.

75 Peterson, *Engaging with God*, 175.

76 Whaley, *Called To Worship*, 94.

of God's grace believers should respond with a similar action of worship (1 Peter 4:11).[77]

The reference to our bodies in Romans 12:1 does not merely refer to the receptacle for the soul as the Greeks thought but conveys the Hebraic concept of the human being as a whole. Thus, Paul is not urging the dedication of the body alone but essentially our body, soul, mind and spirit. In contrast to the dead animal sacrifices of the old covenant, the re-born Christians of the new covenant are able to continue to offer themselves to God through the new life found in Christ and the power of the Holy Spirit (Romans 6:4).

The sacrificial offering of our lives to God appears often in the writings of Paul. In Romans 6:1–10, he makes it clear that "baptism into Christ means baptism into his death, in order to live with him and for him (cf. 2 Corinthians 5:15)."[78] When Christians enter into fellowship with Christ they also enter, by the power of the Spirit,[79] into his own total self-surrender to the Father. According to David Peterson, "The moral implication of this is to live out the new obedience which baptism into Christ's death entails (Romans 6:11–23; cf. 12:1–2)."[80]

Paul does not say that offering ourselves to God will make us *acceptable* "living sacrifices." He does say that the offering of our lives to God is our *fitting and acceptable* worship response, based on God's mercy. We know that we are not acceptable to God based on anything we've earned, but we are acceptable only through Christ. Nevertheless, God is pleased by and accepts the submissive action of offering ourselves.[81] We are not pleasing to God because we are obedient, but because we have faith in the righteousness God provides for us (Romans 10:1–3).

Even though Christ declares us righteous, the human side of the covenant agreement demands our utmost determination to flee from sin. In Romans 6:1, Paul demands that we no longer live in sin, since being alive in Christ means being dead to sin.

---

77 Donald A. Hagner and Everett F. Harrison, *Romans–Galatians*, vol. 11 in The Expositor's Bible Commentary, rev. ed. (Grand Rapids: Zondervan, 2008), 182.

78 Peterson, *Engaging with God*, 173.

79 Peterson, *Engaging with God*, 174.

80 Peterson, *Engaging with God*, 174.

81 Chapell, *Christ-Centered Worship*, 109.

The latter part of 1 Peter 1 similarly talks about being holy just as God is holy (1 Peter 1:16; cf. Leviticus 11:44) since the professed people of God ought to be like their God.

Paul states to his readers that offering our bodies as living sacrifices to God is a spiritual, or reasonable, act of worship. The rendering of the word translated "spiritual" or "reasonable" is debated, but the message is clear: because God showed great mercy toward humanity, our response in offering ourselves as living sacrifices is both reasonable and spiritual. Further, Dunn argues that Paul's description of worship in the new community as spiritual or rational makes it "*distinct* from cultic hallmarks of traditional Judaism."[82] He explains that the "cultic language of sacrifice and worship that Paul uses is transformed from its orientation of fulfilling the requirements of the law to fulfilling the will of God."[83]

The term *latreia* (usually translated "worship") at the end of verse 1 is most often understood as the cultic activities performed by the Old Testament priests. Here Paul "spiritualizes it, or transforms it to a new level of meaning"[84] so that it refers to a "spiritual *action* or *service* of worship" (NASB, emphasis mine). According to Hagner and Harrison, the context embraces "not merely the idea of the adoration of God but covers the entire range of the Christian's life and activity (cf. Deuteronomy 10:12)."[85] Thus, in the New Testament, a reasonable response to God's love and mercy is a worship that is characterized by holy living, verbal praise and service to God, which are inextricably connected (cf. Hebrews 13:15).[86]

Whereas Romans 6:1 has called believers to make a decisive commitment, verse 2 warns against the negative influence of the world which could hinder that commitment. There is a significant threat to the Christian that comes from "this world," or this "present evil age" (Galatians 1:4), which has Satan as its god (2 Corinthians 4:4). The danger is in consciously or unconsciously

---

82 James D.G. Dunn, *Romans 9–16*, vol. 38B in Word Biblical Commentary (Dallas: Word Books, 1988), 711.

83 Dunn, *Romans 9–16*, 708.

84 Hagner and Harrison, *Romans–Galatians*, 183.

85 Hagner and Harrison, *Romans–Galatians*, 183.

86 Dunn, *Romans 9–16*, 183.

conforming to the sin that is prevalent in the world. Christians are expected to be "in" this world but not "of" this world; we are in the world for witness not for conformity (1 Corinthians 7:31)[87]

The negative injunction, to avoid being conformed to the world, is followed by a complementary positive call to be "transformed by the renewing of your mind." Dunn states that "the present tenses are used here, which indicates that the processes are ongoing—a continual renunciation and renewal."[88] In speaking to a different audience, Paul challenges the immature Corinthian Christians, who are still oriented to the ways of the world, to follow the ways of the Spirit of God—to be a holy people because the Spirit is resident in them (1 Corinthians 2:14–3:3). The reality of the Spirit's indwelling should spur us on to moral behaviour (1 Corinthians 3:4–23).[89]

According to Romans 12:2, the process of being transformed is contingent upon having our *minds* renewed. This implies the necessity of focusing our minds on the theological truths of the faith (Joshua 1:8; Philippians 4:8).[90] The mind, though central to Paul's perspective here, is not meant to be the exclusive focus. By using the term *latreia*, Paul calls for the obedience of faith by those whose minds are being renewed by God, so they no longer conform to the values, attitudes and behaviour of "this age" (Romans 12:2; cf. Colossians 3:9–10; Ephesians 4:22–24).[91] Peterson suggests that having heard Paul express the fullness of obedient worship, and now having understood more fully the repercussions of the gospel, it may, in retrospect, make sense to recognize that the adjective modifying "worship" in the previous verse could legitimately be translated "understanding." Hence, offering ourselves to God is "the service rendered by those who truly understand the gospel and its implications."[92]

It is obvious that new covenant worship is concerned with, among other things, Christian lifestyle and relationship. This involves a balance between our personal commitment and the

---

87 Dunn, *Romans 9–16*, 183.

88 Dunn, *Romans 9–16*, 184.

89 Borchert, *Worship in the New Testament*, 103.

90 Borchert, *Worship in the New Testament*, 103.

91 Peterson, *Engaging with God*, 176.

92 Peterson, *Engaging with God*, 176.

Spirit's divine enabling.[93] Jeremiah prophesies of such a time (Jeremiah 31:31–34), and his promise of a new covenant appears to be fulfilled in the renewed worship of God's people imbued with the Holy Spirit.[94]

It is clear from Romans 12 and the other passages cited above, that true worship leads to a life of faith and obedience. It is the purpose of worship, on the human side, to inspire a consistent life of faith and devotion to the Lord, which is the emphasis of the prophets, and the teaching of Jesus and the apostles. Romans reminds us of our covenant responsibility to live holy lives, a task which is achievable in the New Testament by the power the Spirit.[95] Further, our genuine and obedient worship will prompt us to help the poor and the oppressed, to champion justice and equity in society, and to do the work of evangelism and missions. With these and other serious matters, says Allen Ross, "we may test whether worship has fully achieved what God has designed it to achieve."[96]

New Testament worship is energized by the corporate experience (Acts 2:43–47)

Worship in the early church is not simply a matter of inward attitude or individual expression; it is the corporate experience of a covenant people coming before the Lord who has called it into being.[97] The church is a distinctively New Testament institution, marked by the coming of the Holy Spirit upon the believers as they gather together as described in Acts 2. The church is a major doctrinal theme running through the entire book of Acts.[98] To the surprise of the Jewish converts, the church of the new covenant embraces both Gentiles (Acts 10:44–46; 1 Peter 2:11–12) and Samaritans (Acts 8:17), verified by the coming of the Holy Spirit

---

93 Dunn, *Romans 9–16*, 707.

94 Peterson, *Transformed by God*, 78–79.

95 Ross, *Recalling the Hope of Glory*, 467.

96 Ross, *Recalling the Hope of Glory*, 468.

97 Richard C. Leonard, "Terms Referring to the Practice of Christian Worship" in *The Biblical Foundations of Christian Worship*, vol. 1, of Complete Library of Christian Worship (Nashville: Star Song, 1993), 17.

98 Jaroslav Pelikan, *Acts*, Brazos Theological Commentary on the Bible (Grand Rapids: Brazos Press, 2005), 58.

upon these previously outcast peoples.[99] God is doing something new in expanding the community of his people, as evidenced through the presence of the Spirit in their worship.[100]

The emerging church, largely a Jewish sect, naturally models its ministry in part on patterns borrowed from the synagogue.[101] The early Christians' relationship to the synagogue remains strong, and the opportunity for the apostles to expound the Scriptures makes the synagogue a logical place for evangelism (Acts 13). Because the early Christians interpret the Scriptures Christologically, they are soon unwelcome in the synagogues and the temple. As a result they begin meeting on their own in places like the upper room (Acts 1:13; 4:31; 12:12),[102] in homes (Acts 2:46; cf. Philemon 2) and in larger gathering places, for teaching, fellowship and prayer. The church soon develops a liturgical calendar of its own, based principally on major events in the life of Christ, but also drawn from Israelite feasts which they easily interpret Christologically. The Lord's supper, for example, is the covenant meal of the church, which partly absorbs the significance of the Passover; and the Jewish Sabbath is supplanted by Sunday worship, the Lord's Day (Revelation 1:10, the day of Christ's resurrection[103]

The New Testament gives little detailed information regarding the form of these early worship gatherings. A gathering is recorded in 1 Corinthians 14 where those in attendance are free to contribute a psalm, a doctrine, a tongue, a revelation or an interpretation, though with an emphasis on edification and order. Although there is no indication that a recognized structure has emerged at this period, the features of prayer, praise, exposition, perhaps

---

99 Borchert, *Worship in the New Testament*, 192.

100 Borchert, *Worship in the New Testament*, 69.

101 Richard A. Bodey, "Bishops, Elders, and Deacons" in *The Biblical Foundations of Christian Worship*, vol. 1, of Complete Library of Christian Worship (Nashville: Star Song Publishing Group, 1993), 171.

102 Geoffrey W. Bromiley, "Worship in Acts and the Epistles" in *The Biblical Foundations of Christian Worship*, vol. 1, of Complete Library of Christian Worship (Nashville: Star Song, 1993), 105.

103 Richard Leonard, "Background to the Christian Festivals" in *The Biblical Foundations of Christian Worship*, vol. 1, of Complete Library of Christian Worship (Nashville: Star Song, 1993), 194.

reading of the Scriptures and the Lord's supper are evident in their corporate gatherings.[104]

The Greek word *ekklēsia*, usually translated "church," is used to describe both the believers who constitute a local assembly and the universal church whose constituents are all the believers, past, present and future. It never refers to the location or building where the church meets. At times, it is very difficult to determine which meaning the New Testament writers have in mind.[105]

It is evident that the apostles direct the life of the infant church. But as Christianity grows, evangelists and prophets assist them in spreading the gospel. As the expansion of Christianity continues, the official orders of elders and deacons evolve to guide and lead local churches, and structures become more formal.[106] What concrete evidence exists regarding church leadership and polity comes from the second century documents such as the *Didachē*, or *Teaching of the Twelve Apostles*, and the *Apology of Justin Martyr*, in which we find a president of the congregation who officiates at the Lord's supper. In the New Testament church, both theologically and practically, it is Christ himself who is the leader of the family, "head over everything for the church, which is his body" (Ephesians 1:22–23). Jesus tells his disciples, "One is your Father, He who is in heaven. Do not be called leaders; for One is your Leader, that is, Christ" (Matthew 23:9–10 NASB).[107]

The latter portion of Acts 2 not only shows that the fledgling church is starting to meet as a group of believers but also gives some indication of the contents of its emergent liturgy, namely the apostles' teaching, fellowship, breaking of bread and prayer. Direction concerning offerings for the poor is added later (Acts 2:45), which gives it import, but it does not seem to be part of the liturgical structure. This passage bears witness to the church's vertical relationship with God, along with a strong horizontal relationship among believers.

---

104 Bromiley, "Worship in Acts and the Epistles," 106.

105 Comfort, "The House Church and Its Worship," 153.

106 Bodey, "Bishops, Elders, and Deacons," 171.

107 Richard C. Leonard, "Worship Leadership in the New Testament" in *The Biblical Foundations of Christian Worship*, vol. 1, of Complete Library of Christian Worship (Nashville: Star Song, 1993), 169.

The first of the worship elements listed in Acts 2:42 is instruction. The early believers devote themselves to the teaching of the apostles, who are, in the early days of the church, the principal successors to Jesus and his teaching as well as the primary conveyors of the Spirit's power.[108] The miraculous signs they perform as a result of their baptism with God's Spirit bear witness to their spiritual authority (Acts 1:1–2),[109] and their teaching is considered authoritative by the early Christians.[110] As the church grows, written materials by the first eyewitnesses are created, which consolidates the developing theology and underscores that theological variants are already beginning to emerge.[111]

The biblical record of the early believers' devotion to learning about Jesus through the apostles' writings should cause us to realize that submitting ourselves to the teaching of Scripture is an essential aspect of what may be termed "congregational worship." Compliance to God's Word is itself an act of worship and a service designed to glorify God.[112] Without this instruction it is impossible to live the holy and obedient lifestyle described in Romans 12:1–2. Dedicating ourselves to the study of the Scriptures should motivate us to acceptable worship in the form of consistent prayer, praise and obedience in our everyday life.[113]

In addition to learning from the apostles, the believers are dedicated to sustaining a strong community relationship, according to Acts 2:42. The fellowship in the early church includes not only sharing meals but also sharing life. Although the term *koinōnia*, translated "fellowship," appears only this once in the book of Acts, it occurs nineteen times in the New Testament.[114]

---

108 Robert W. Wall, *The Acts of the Apostles: Introduction, Commentary, and Reflections*, vol. 10 in The New Interpreter's Bible: A Commentary in Twelve Volumes (Nashville: Abingdon Press, 1995), 71.

109 Wall, *The Acts of the Apostles*, 71.

110 Richard N. Longnecker, *Luke–Acts*, vol. 10 in The Expositor's Bible Commentary, rev. ed. (Grand Rapids: Zondervan, 2007), 756.

111 Richard Leonard, "External and Internal Problems of the Worshiping Community" in *The Biblical Foundations of Christian Worship*, vol. 1, of Complete Library of Christian Worship (Nashville: Star Song, 1993), 152.

112 Peterson, *Engaging with God*, 153.

113 Peterson, *Engaging with God*, 153.

114 Darrell L. Bock, *Acts*, in Baker Exegetical Commentary (Grand Rapids: Baker Academic, 2007), 150.

For Paul, this "fellowship" is a uniquely important bond in the faith community bestowed upon the newly initiated believers because of the Holy Spirit (cf. Philippians 2:1–4) who is a transforming presence that unites the different believers into a common *koinōnia*. Robert Wall describes the fellowship of believers as a group that shares "more than common beliefs and core values; they feel a profound regard for one another's spiritual and physical well-being as a community of friends."[115] The communion that the early church shares with God and each other as a result of the Spirit being upon them is different from anything humanity (including Israel) has ever experienced.[116] This makes the church a distinctly New Testament institution.

The extent of mutual caring is further highlighted in Acts 2:44–45 as the believers are described as being "together" and sharing "everything in common." The holding of material possessions in common is possibly intended to demonstrate the new values of the kingdom of God, where the implications of wealth and social status have minimal significance.[117] It also indicates the depth of fellowship, mutual care, love and compassion at work in a community that is functioning in a godly fashion.[118] Similar exhortations to contribute to the needs of the saints (Romans 12:13), to bear each other's burdens (Galatians 6:2), and to do good to fellow believers and others (Galatians 6:10) are found throughout the New Testament.[119]

A similar theme is found in 1 Corinthians 1 where Paul emphasizes that unity in Jesus is an essential element of the church (1 Corinthians 1:10). That believers are quarrelling about which leader to follow causes Paul to remind them that their focus should be Christ (1 Corinthians 1:17), which enhances unity, not superficial differences that encourage division. We need to

---

115 Wall, *The Acts of the Apostles*, 72.

116 Edith M. Humphrey, *Grand Entrance: Worship on Earth as in Heaven* (Grand Rapids: Brazos Press, 2011), 44.

117 Richard Leonard, "Characteristics of the Church" in *The Biblical Foundations of Christian Worship*, vol. 1, of Complete Library of Christian Worship (Nashville: Star Song, 1993), 148.

118 Bock, *Acts*, 152.

119 Richard C. Leonard, "Internal Life of the Worshiping Community" in *The Biblical Foundations of Christian Worship*, vol. 1, of Complete Library of Christian Worship (Nashville: Star Song, 1993), 152.

curb our propensity to elevate human leaders. Only God is transcendent and worthy of worship (1 Corinthians 1:26–29).[120]

The blessing of fellowship and unity in the community of faith is rooted in and guided by the Spirit, the mainstay of its existence.[121] The New Testament, as the beginning of a new covenant, is characterized by a new commandment given by Christ, often referred to as the law of love. Our commitment is not only to love God with all our being, but to love others in the same way we love ourselves (Matthew 22:37–40). Authentic Christianity and worship are characterized by this genuine love and without it both our worship and our contribution to the work of God are worthless (1 Corinthians 12:3–13:13).[122]

Acts 2:42 describes the believers breaking bread together, the meaning of which continues to be a source of debate. The phrase "breaking of bread" is used biblically to mean both a common meal and the paschal love feast.[123] The idea of a sacred meal would be a common notion to Jews and may have taken on some of the characteristics of the Passover meal, as it does for the disciples as they celebrate it with Jesus on the night he is betrayed. In the early church era, Christians celebrate the Lord's Table within the context of a larger meal.[124] Richard Longnecker says that he finds it difficult to believe that "Luke meant only an ordinary meal (in Acts 2:42), placing the expression, as he does between two such religiously loaded terms as 'the fellowship' and 'prayer.'"[125] Either way, the phrase "breaking bread" suggests the intimate interaction that is a positive component of community life.[126]

Prayer is also one of the activities in which the early believers engage as they assemble. A community at prayer is something Luke emphasizes in the early church. Prayer seeks God's direction and demonstrates dependency on God. Darrell Bock suggests that "the plural with the article (the prayers) could suggest that

---

120 Borchert, *Worship in the New Testament*, 103.

121 John B. Polhill, *Acts*, vol. 26 in The New American Commentary: An Exegetical and Theological Exposition of Holy Scripture (Nashville: Broadman Press, 1992), 121.

122 Borchert, *Worship in the New Testament*, 112–113.

123 Longnecker, *Luke–Acts*, 757.

124 Bock, *Acts*, 150.

125 Longnecker, *Luke–Acts*, 757.

126 Bock, *Acts*, 151.

some set prayers were used."[127] In this early stage, it is probable that if this is true, their form would have come from the synagogue. The early believers would understand them to be full of new meaning in light of Christ. It is likely that extemporaneous prayers are also used.[128]

The last verse of Acts 2 indicates that the community of believers enjoys the favour of all the people. The implication seems to be that the mutual love experienced within this early community of believers and their acts of service to those around them has the effect of drawing in many who do not yet believe. These believers are truly the manifestation of the body of Christ on earth as Christ intended.[129]

The biblical picture of the community of believers presented in Acts 2 goes counter to Western culture's narcissistic tendency by focusing not on what we can receive from the church community (although we do, of course, receive), but on what we give and how we contribute to it. The portrait of the early church in Acts shows that the emphasis on community and the welfare of the group is a high priority. This attitude is an indication of spiritual maturity and reflects a consistency of message and authentic practice. This simultaneous inward and outward engagement of Christian values has a positive effect on both the community and the mission and reflects true worship and obedience.[130]

At its birth, the church is a distinctively New Testament institution inextricably linked to the coming of the Holy Spirit upon the believers, enabling the church in its worship, service, fellowship and witness. It is through the mutual indwelling of the Holy Spirit that the church experiences a special bond of *koininia*,[131] and where individual members exercise spiritual gifts in an orderly fashion for the edification of the body (1 Corinthians 14).

Although enabled by the Spirit, the church is distinctive in that its worship revolves around Christ who has taken the church to be his bride. Christ, the ultimate subject of the church's celebration, is the head of the church, the body and physical manifestation of

---

127 Bock, *Acts*, 151.
128 Longnecker, *Luke–Acts*, 757.
129 Bock, *Acts*, 155.
130 Bock, *Acts*, 155.
131 Wall, *The Acts of the Apostles*, 71.

Christ on earth. The sacraments, which are also distinctively New Testament and Christocentric, are practiced in the context of the community of believers.

The church is comprised of not only people gathered in a local assembly but, as the "church universal," all people past, present and future who are part of God's family. The church is not a physical building, but a spiritual building whose cornerstone is Christ, made up of people who are the living stones, whose important task is to represent light in the midst of darkness (1 Peter 2:9).[132] The Christian church extends itself in two directions in the power of the Spirit: toward God through Christ, and toward brothers and sisters in Christ and neighbours, which fulfils the great commandment.[133]

Summary and conclusions

The four distinctives of New Testament worship presented in this paper, namely Christ, the Holy Spirit, Christian lifestyle and the church are vital components to understanding and transforming our corporate worship and the worship of our everyday lives.

New Testament worship, as this chapter illustrates, is Christocentric, but it is equally trinitarian. Each person of the Godhead participates in the New Testament redemptive activity. The Father, who is the source of all power and authority, sends the Son on whom he bestows his own authority. Jesus reveals the Father to us and, because he is willing to be obedient to the Father's will, executes the Father's plan of redemption. The Spirit, also sent by God, illuminates the work of Christ and continues among us to enlighten, inspire and empower our corporate and private worship and enables us to live the holy and obedient lifestyle that is the expected product of our genuine response to God. Each person of the Godhead participates in our redemption, but because redemption is the major theme of Christian worship, the ministry of the one who accomplishes our salvation is the focus of that worship.

---

132 Borchert, *Worship in the New Testament*, 192.
133 Bock, *Acts*, 154.

This chapter also makes clear that we act out and ratify our vertical relationship with God horizontally, among the community of Christ-followers called the church, the physical manifestation of Christ on earth. This distinct people group, whom Christ loves, he calls his bride and his body, of whom he is the head. These truths should inform and transform our worship and our daily lives.

Historical

9

The sacrament of baptism among the first Baptists

BY ANTHONY R. CROSS

The question of Baptist baptismal sacramentalism, examined and explored so carefully by Stan Fowler in his *magnum opus*,[1] continues to generate considerable interest,[2] and often polarized views. So, on the one hand, we have Lloyd Harsch who claims, "It seems clear that from their infancy, Baptists have been non-sacramental

1 Stanley K. Fowler, *More Than a Symbol: The British Baptist Recovery of Baptismal Sacramentalism* (Carlisle: Paternoster Press, 2002).

2 See Anthony R. Cross, *Should We Take Peter at His Word (Acts 2:38)? Recovering a Baptist Baptismal Sacramentalism* (Oxford: Regent's Park College, 2010); Brandon C. Jones, *Waters of Promise: Finding Meaning in Believer Baptism* (Eugene: Pickwick Publications, 2012); and Brian C. Brewer, "Free Church Sacramentalism: A Surprising Connection between Baptists and Anabaptists," in *Interfaces, Baptists and Others: International Baptist Studies,* ed. David Bebbington and Martin Sutherland (Milton Keynes: Paternoster, 2013), 3–28.

in their understanding of baptism,"[3] adding, "the evidence currently suggests, that even the earliest Baptists espoused a non-sacramental view."[4] On the other hand, Stephen R. Holmes states categorically, "Baptists, in their origin, were sacramentalists."[5]

For many the juxtaposition of the words *Baptist* and *sacramentalism* is an oxymoron, though in his 2003 study of this Fowler demonstrates that this need not be so: in fact, there are compelling historical, biblical and theological reasons for them.[6] For others, the suggestion that Baptists can legitimately be sacramentalists is a betrayal of historic Baptist convictions, an abandonment of biblical faith and sound theological convictions.[7] Harsch, for example, asserts that it is "a commonly accepted belief that Baptists observe ordinances, not sacraments," and that it is only since the turn of the present century that "some Baptists have questioned the historical accuracy of that belief and introduced a new perspective on the ordinances." Further these "Baptist Sacramentalists" assert that seventeenth-century Baptists "were more sacramental in their understanding of baptism than has been commonly accepted," and that they also claim this view disappeared during the eighteenth and nineteenth centuries.[8] These are, however, dogmatic statements, not historical ones. Tom Nettles takes this position further when he declares that Baptist sacramentalism has "a corrupting influence on Baptist ecclesiology and soteriology" because it separates "the historic work of Christ on the cross and the present event of baptism,"[9]

---

3 Lloyd Harsch, "Were the First Baptists Sacramentalists?" *Journal for Baptist Theology and Ministry* 6.1 (Spring, 2009): 25–43 (40).

4 Harsch, "Were the First Baptists Sacramentalists?" 41.

5 Stephen R. Holmes, *Tradition and Renewal in Baptist Life* (Oxford: Whitley Publications, 2003), 29.

6 Stanley K. Fowler, "Is 'Baptist Sacramentalism' an Oxymoron?: Reactions in Britain to Christian Britain," in *Baptist Sacramentalism*, ed. Anthony R. Cross and Philip E. Thompson (Carlisle: Paternoster Press, 2003), 129–150.

7 See Tom Nettles, *The Baptists: Key People Involved in Forming a Baptist Identity*, 3 vol. (Fearn: Christian Focus, 2005–2007), 3:311; Christopher Moody, *American Baptismal Sacramentalism?: Toward a Sacred Theology of Baptism in the Context of Transatlantic Baptist Disagreement* (Saarbrücken: VDM Verlag Dr. Müller Aktiengesellschaft, 2009); and the extreme David H.J. Gay, *Baptist Sacramentalism: A Warning to Baptists* (Biggleswade: Brachus, 2011).

8 Harsch, "Were the First Baptists Sacramentalists?" 25. Another is Joe Early, Jr, *The Life and Writings of Thomas Helwys* (Macon: Mercer University Press, 2009), xvi, 48.

9 Nettles, *The Baptists,* 3:311. Fowler's answer to such a charge—and with which I

and that this is "real idolatry."[10] These so-called historical claims[11] have been conclusively answered by Fowler in his doctoral dissertation in which he traces a constant, though at times minority, stream of those who have understood baptism in sacramental terms throughout their 400 year history.[12] That some Baptists have so understood baptism, admittedly in different ways, bears witness to the diversity of Baptist[13] origins,[14] practices,[15] and

---

completely agree—"It is the separation of baptism from conversion by many Baptists which creates the impression of multiple conditions of salvation" (Fowler, *More Than a Symbol*, 205). See also his discussion of baptism and faith, 199–209 and *passim*. See Anthony R. Cross, *Recovering the Evangelical Sacrament: Baptisma Semper Reformandum* (Eugene: Pickwick Publications, 2013).

10 Nettles, *The Baptists*, 3:311. Fowler, *More Than a Symbol*, 193, however, notes that "The debate over sacramentalism is not about the ultimate cause of human salvation; it is about the instrumental cause(s), specifically the role of baptism as an instrument."

11 The historical claims are my main concern here.

12 Fowler, *More Than a Symbol*, 10–155. Also Philip E. Thompson, "A New Question in Baptist History: Seeking a Catholic Spirit among Early Baptists," *Pro Ecclesia* 8.1 (Winter 1999): 51–72 (66–68); and Anthony R. Cross, "The Myth of English Baptist Anti-Sacramentalism," in *Recycling the Past or Researching History?: Studies in Baptist Historiography and Myths*, ed. Philip E. Thompson and Anthony R. Cross (Milton Keynes: Paternoster, 2005), 128–162.

13 A diversity of which those, like Nettles, *The Baptists*, 3:378, disapprove.

14 On the variety of European Baptist origins (note the plural "Beginnings" in the title), see Ian M. Randall, *Communities of Conviction: Baptist Beginnings in Europe* (Schwarzenfeld: Neufeld Verlag, 2009); on the period covered by this chapter, see 13–35; and internationally, see Albert W. Wardin, ed., *Baptists around the World: A Comprehensive Handbook* (Nashville: Broadman & Holman, 1995).

15 Harsch, "Were the First Baptists Sacramentalists?" 27, will only concede that Smyth and his congregation were "proto-Baptists" on account of their adoption of affusion. This, however, is to identify immersion as a *sine qua non* of being Baptist. It is a dogmatic position, not an historical judgement, in that it anachronistically projects onto the first Baptist congregations prior to 1635 a later definition of what a Baptist must do in order to be a true Baptist. The significance of 1635 is the claim made by Champlin Burrage, *The Early English Dissenters in the Light of Recent Research (1550–1641)* 2 vol. (1912; reprint, New York: Russell & Russell, 1967), 1:378–379, that William Britten's 1654 *Moderate Baptist*, includes the author's recollection (65–67) that he "found one Baptist" of Arminian convictions whose church practised the "Ordinances according to Gospel manner," which for baptism meant immersion, as he understood *Baptizo* as "*immergo*, to plunge, dip, in, or overwhelm." However, in the edition of William Britten, *The Moderate Baptist, briefly shewing scripture-way for that initiatory sacrament of Baptism* (London: J. Collins, 1654), held in Christ Church Library, University of Oxford [A.72 (4)], this passage does not appear on pages 65–67 as Burrage claimed, nor does it appear to be anywhere in this edition of the work. This does not mean that it is not in the other extant edition of the work. The reason for this discrepancy between Burrage, who believed that he had the only copy of the work, and the Christ Church edition requires further investigation. But if it is accurate,

convictions.[16]

The focus of this study is on the emergence of the first Baptists in Amsterdam and England between 1609 and the late 1620s, and what their leaders and writers—John Smyth, Thomas Helwys, John Murton, Leonard Busher, Elias Tookey and several others—believed on this matter. It is offered, then, in honour of one of the most important Baptist theologians rigorously to have explored in recent years the rite which has given our tradition its name, and is intended to be neither a polemic nor an apologetic for a particular view on this question, but to be a study in history, specifically Baptist history, seeking to ascertain the answer to the question whether the first Baptists believed baptism to be a sacrament or not.[17] Its focus, therefore, is what the first Baptists wrote on baptism, not what subsequent generations have said about it.[18]

The story of how John Smyth, Thomas Helwys and a group of English Separatists emigrated, reaching Amsterdam and its environs by mid-1608, has been told many times, and need not be rehearsed here. Nor, indeed, does Smyth's self-baptism, then his baptism of Helwys, and together their baptizing the rest of their congregation who had parted company with other Separatists, among them Francis Johnson's congregation which

---

then 1635 is a significant date in the history of Baptist baptismal practice. I am grateful to Dr. Cristina Neagu of the Special Collections, Christ Church Library, Oxford, for her help in exploring Britten's work.

16 Robert E. Johnson, *A Global Introduction to Baptist Churches* (Cambridge: Cambridge University Press, 2010), 3, lays open "global Baptists' nature as a culturally polycentric movement characterized by elements that are too diverse to permit the movement's identity to be contained under a singular cultural vista." See also Baptist World Alliance, *We Baptists: One Lord, One Faith, One Baptism* (Franklin: Providence House, 1999), 52, "Anyone attempting to identify practices which are universal to Baptists is either unusually courageous or simply uninformed! Diversity has always been one of our glories."

17 This is something previous studies into this question have only tangentially attempted, including Fowler, *More Than a Symbol*, who only discusses John Smyth on seven pages, Thomas Helwys twice, while John Murton, Leonard Busher, Richard Overton and Elias Tookey not at all. This is similarly the case with Cross, "The Myth of English Baptist Anti-Sacramentalism" and Harsch, "Were the First Baptists Sacramentalists?"

18 Given this concern, wherever possible the original publications have been consulted (only quoting from transcriptions and translations when the originals are no longer extant or readily available for their translation), and the original spelling and punctuation is retained. Most of the titles have also been shortened for convenience.

remained in Amsterdam and comprised the Ancient Church, and John Robinson's congregation which settled in Leiden. Our concern here is not with Smyth, Helwys and the others' baptismal theology,[19] but specifically on whether their understanding of baptism was sacramental, compatible with sacramentalism or anti-sacramental.

The sacrament of baptism according to John Smyth

Discussion here of Smyth's views on baptism as a sacrament are based on his two major "Baptist" works written in 1609,[20] *Paralleles, Censvres, Observations*, and *The Character of the Beast*,[21] as from 1610 he became increasingly influenced by the local Waterlander Mennonites in both his churchmanship and baptismal theology.[22] *Sacrament* and *sacraments* appears fifty-one times in *Paralleles, Censvres, Observations* and seventeen in *Character of the Beast*, and while many of these appear within the context of his citing the arguments of his opponents,[23] others are his own. The former

---

19 See W.H. Burgess, *John Smith the Se-Baptist, Thomas Helwys and the First Baptist Church in England, with Fresh Light upon the Pilgrim Fathers' Church* (London: James Clarke, 1911), *passim*; Champlin Burrage, *The Early English Dissenters in the Light of Recent Research (1550–1641)*, 2 vol. (1912; reprint, New York: Russell & Russell, 1967), 1:221–280, and 2:167–168 and 172–259; B.R. White, *The English Separatist Tradition: From the Marian Martyrs to the Pilgrim Fathers* (Oxford: Oxford University Press, 1971), 116–141; Stephen R. Brachlow, *The Communion of Saints: Radical Puritan and Separatist Ecclesiology 1570–1625* (Oxford: Oxford University Press, 1988), 150–156; James R. Coggins, *John Smyth's Congregation: English Separatism, Mennonite Influence, and the Elect Nation* (Waterloo: Herald Press, 1991), 61–67; Jason K. Lee, *The Theology of John Smyth: Puritan, Separatist, Baptist, Mennonite* (Macon: Mercer University Press, 2003), *passim*; Stephen Wright, *The Early English Baptists, 1603–1649* (Woodbridge: The Boydell Press, 2006), 1–110; and Anthony R. Cross, "The Adoption of Believer's Baptism and Baptist Beginnings," in *Exploring Baptist Origins*, ed. Anthony R. Cross and Nicholas J. Wood (Oxford: Regent's Park College, 2010), 1–32.

20 Reasons for this position are set out in Cross, "The Adoption of Believer's Baptism and Baptist Beginnings," 3–4.

21 Iohn Smyth, *Paralleles, Censvres, Observations* (s.l.: s.n., 1609), and Iohn Smyth, *The Character of the Beast or the False Constitvtion of the Chvrch* (s.l.: s.n., 1609).

22 It should be noted, however, that he continued to refer to baptism as a sacrament in these "later" writings. In *Corde credimus, et ore confitemur* [ACA, B1348] (otherwise known as *Smyth's Short Confession of Faith in XX Articles* by John Smyth [1610]), Article 13, states that Christ has delegated the church power to administer the sacraments, which Article 16 states are dispensed by its ministers. For the English translation, see William L. Lumpkin and Bill J. Leonard, ed., *Baptist Confessions of Faith* 2nd. rev. ed. (Valley Forge: Judson Press, 2011), 93–95.

23 See Smyth, *Paralleles, Censvres, Observations*, 6, 81, 90, 98 (Richard Bernard), and

need not detain us, but the later are informative.

In *Paralleles, Censvres, Observations* we see that for Smyth the sacraments in general and, for our concern, baptism in particular are intimately related to his ecclesiology. Fowler and others have rightly noted that for seventeenth-century Baptists, the terms *ordinance* and *sacrament* "were often used synonymously."[24] *Ordinance* was the broader term indicating things God has ordained, while *sacrament* was used of two particular ordinances, baptism and the Lord's supper. Evidence for this is clear in Smyth's work when he counters those who "scoffe at the doctrine of the constitution of the true Church," and asserts that the Baptists

> doe constantly & bouldly defend that out of a Church truly constituted (when a man can & may joyne therto) *no ordinance of God* can be accepted, neyther preaching, nor praying, *nor Sacraments*, nor any other religious action. what the Lord accepteth in secreat that we dispute not: but what the word of God teacheth vnto vs to be acceptable that wee speak of.[25]

Though he does not use the phrase "the marks of the church," he denies that either "the word truly preached" or "the Sacraments duely adminstred" are "properties of a true church." Although it is true that "whersoever the word is truly preached...& the Sacraments rightly administred, ther is a true Church," nevertheless he denies the converse, "That whersoever ther is a true Church, the word is truly preached, & the Sacraments are rightly administred."[26] It is, rather, "the powre of Chriſt to have & vse al

Smyth, *Character of the Beast*, 23, 29, 32 (Richard Clifton).

24 Fowler, *More Than a Symbol*, 14; also 6, 17, 19, 31. See Philip E. Thompson, "Practicing the Freedom of God: Formation in Early Baptist Life," in *Theology and Lived Christianity*, ed. David M. Hammond (Mystic: Twenty-Third Publications, 2000), 119–138; and Cross, "The Myth of English Baptist Anti-Sacramentalism," 136, 143.

25 Smyth, *Paralleles, Censvres, Observations*, 13 (italics added). See also Smyth, *Character of the Beast*, 49.

26 Smyth, *Paralleles, Censvres, Observations*, 81. Later Smyth rejects the argument that just because the Church of England "have the Word, Sacraments, Censures, prayers, &c. therefore you are a true Church," and neither are their use indications of the true properties of a true church, because even the Roman Catholics and heretics "vse the Word, Sacraments, Censures, prayers, but they are not therfore a true Church" (91). The only way Smyth can be seen not to be inconsistent here is to note that he does not

the holy things of God" that are "the true property...& infallible token of a true Church."[27] However, God has "indeed commaundeth uſ to pray, heare the word, & to communicate in the Sacraments," and these are "actions of communion," that is, corporate. In their performance, two things are to be respected: first, communion is to be with true Christians as described by the New Testament, namely, "members of the visible Church which is the mystical body of Christ"; and secondly, these actions are to be performed as taught in the New Testament. Regarding baptism this means "administred simply as Christ teacheth without Godfathers, the crosse, questions to infants."[28]

Smyth does not succumb to the spirit-matter dualism that is so evident among Baptists today.[29] As Christ's kingdom is outward and visible yet also spiritual and invisible, as people are bodily, that is visible and sensible, they are also chiefly and principally soul, that is invisible, so, according to Smyth echoing Calvin's second definition of a sacrament,[30] "the true Sacraments are not only the outward Elements, but the inward grace also, & that most especialy," and also the visible church is not only the outward communion but especially and chiefly the inward and spiritual fellowship "which the Saynts have with Christ, & one another." This receives biblical mandate from Ephesians 4:5 and 1 Corinthians 12:13.[31] In the face of Richard Bernard's objections,

---

say that Richard Bernard, the Church of England, the papists or heretics practise "the word *truly* preached" or "the Sacraments *duely* adminstred" or "*rightly* administred" (italics added). See also page 106, and using the same reasoning on pages 139–140, where he is addressing Mr A.S., who had been with Smyth at Cambridge (137).

27 Smyth, *Paralleles, Censvres, Observations*, 82.

28 Smyth, *Paralleles, Censvres, Observations*, 79.

29 See Fowler, *More Than a Symbol*, 93–94, 233–234.

30 John Calvin, *Institutes of the Christian Religion*, trans. Henry Beveridge, 2 vol. (London: James Clarke, 1949), 4.14.1, "a testimony of the divine favour toward us, confirmed by an external sign, with a corresponding attestation of our faith towards Him." Calvin then admits that neither of his definitions differs from that offered by Augustine of "a visible sign of a sacred thing, or a visible form of an invisible grace."

31 Smyth, *Paralleles, Censvres, Observations*, 21. In this Smyth is careful to distinguish the outer and the inner while keeping them together and maintaining the primacy of the inner, Spirit-baptism. "Water is not the matter of baptiſme, but onely the instrument of baptiſme" (Smyth, *Character of the Beast*, 54). It is important for contemporary scholars to realize that none of the earliest Baptist writers formally define either *sacrament* or *ordinance*. The meaning of both terms has to be inferred from the way the writers use the words. It is also important to note the complementarity of the two

Smyth maintains that the corporate dimension of being the true church also means the whole church has the "powre of Christ" "to Preach, to administer the Sacraments, & to exercise the censures of the Church."[32] This, however, is not to suggest that anyone can take these responsibilities to themselves because preaching, administration of the sacraments and government are given by God to some, and both the office and officers are given to the church which has the power, *under Christ*, to appoint.[33]

The relationship between ecclesiology and baptism also provides Smyth with a defence of his much criticized act of self-baptism.[34] He argues,

> Now for baptising a mans self ther is as good warrant, as for a man Churching himself: For two men singly are no Church, joyntly they are a Church, & they both of them put a Church vppon themselves, so may two men put baptisme vppon themselves: For as both those persons vnchurched, yet have powre to assume the Church each of them for himself with others in communion: So each of them vnbaptized hath powre to assume baptisme for himself with others in communion.[35]

It follows, therefore, that "each of them vnbaptized hath power to assume baptiſme for himself with others in communion," a position he supports by appeal to Abraham and John the Baptist, and all proselytes who followed Abraham's example and "did administer the Sacrament vppon themselves." Therefore, "any man raised vp after the Apostacy of Antichrist, in the recovering of the Church by baptiſme, administer it vppon himself in communion with others."[36]

---

terms for the first Baptists, and, therefore, to resist the anachronistic translation of later definitions back into their writings.

32 Smyth, *Paralleles, Censvres, Observations*, 40.

33 Smyth, *Paralleles, Censvres, Observations*, 59 (though mis-numbered as page 61 in the original).

34 His critics included Richard Bernard, *Plaine Euidences: The Chvrch of England is Apostolicall, the Separation Schismaticall* ([London]: T. Snodham, 1610), 17–20; and Iohn Robinson, *Of Religious Commvnion Private, & Publique* (s.l.: s.n., 1614), 48.

35 Smyth, *Character of the Beast*, 58.

36 Smyth, *Character of the Beast*, 58–59.

Not only are the sacraments related to ecclesiology, but also soteriology, and it is clear that he includes the sacraments as means God uses for salvation. Again in dialogue with Bernard, Smyth sets out what for him are "the propertyes of the true Church":

> the first and principal essential property of a true Church is interest and title to al the Holy things, which is extant in divers particulars as parcels of that general and whole property. therefor a people declaring their faith and repentance by Seperating themselves from all vncleanenes, & by resigning themselves wholy to the Lord to become his people, have God for their Father, & Christ for their King, Preist, and Prophett, and so with Christ have title to all the meanes of Salvation: and this title consisteth in the Word, Sacraments, Censures, Prayers, Almes, and al other parts of Spirituall visible communion whatsoever.[37]

The true sacrament of the Lord's supper is not the breaking of bread and drinking of wine "performed by any persons, after any manner," and neither is "washing with water likewise" a true sacrament. Rather for a true sacrament there must be "a concurrence of other matters," and for baptism this means "a baptized person, must baptize into the true Faith of Christ, a person capable of baptisme."[38] This connection between salvation and baptism also comes out explicitly when he notes that "vpon their conversion & baptisme [mē] became Christs Disciples to learne & practise whatsoever he should afterward teach them."[39] It follows, then—and on this Smyth is quite clear—on who are the proper recipients of the sacrament of baptism, for at one point in his dialogue with Richard Clifton, he declares that "the Sacrament of baptisme is profaned when it is adminstred vppon a wrong subject."[40]

The sacrament of baptism according to Thomas Helwys

Once Helwys had adopted Baptist convictions he retained them to the end of his life, so the whole corpus of his work is open to

37 Smyth, *Paralleles, Censvres, Observations*, 90.
38 Smyth, *Paralleles, Censvres, Observations*, 91.
39 Smyth, *Paralleles, Censvres, Observations*, 98.
40 Smyth, *Character of the Beast*, 45.

us, though baptism receives far less attention from Helwys than it does from Smyth, chiefly because his four major works[41] were written after the two friends parted company on the question of whether they should seek membership with the Waterlander Mennonites. The divisive issue was the validity of Smyth's self-baptism, and while they diverged on what boiled down to the issue of baptismal and ecclesiastical successionism, Helwys did not attack Smyth's sacramental understanding of baptism.

In the 1611 *Declaration of Faith*, Helwys uses *ordinance* twelve times, and *sacrament* not once, nevertheless he does define the church of Christ as "a compainy off faithful people…ſeparated frō the world by the word & Spirit off GOD…*being kint* [knit] *vnto the LORD, & one vnto another, by Baptiſme*…Vpon their owne confeſſiō of the faith."[42] As Smyth echoes Calvin's sacramentalism,[43] so does Helwys when he describes baptism as the external sign of forgiveness, mortification and regeneration: it is "the outward sign of the forgiveness of deadly sins, and the regeneration of life," though he obviously departs from Calvin when he concludes that "it is therefore not applicable to infants."[44]

Another possible allusion to mortification comes in the *Declaration of Faith*, when Helwys describes baptism as "the outward manifeſtacion off dieing vnto ſinn."[45] These examples suggest Helwys' openness to the possibility of sacramental theology given that he nowhere explicitly rejects it, though nothing more can be made of these instances than that.

In his 1612 *The miſtery of iniquity*, Helwys does use the word *sacrament* on several occasions. One such is in his account of the Anglican Thomas Bilson in his dispute with the Brownist

---

41 [Thomas Helwys], *A Declaration of Faith of English People Remaining at Amsterdam in Holland* (s.l.: s.n., 1611 [in the York Minster Library]); Thomas Helwys, *An Advertisement or admonition, unto the Congregations, which men call the New Fryelers* (s.l.: s.n., 1611); *A Short and Plaine proofe by the Word and Workes off God* (s.l.: s.n., 1611); and *A Short Declaration of the miſtery of iniquity* (s.l.: s.n., 1612).

42 *Declaration of Faith*, Article 10, A4v (italics added).

43 See Calvin, *Institutes*, 4.15.16 (forgiveness and mortification of the flesh); 4.16.4 (forgiveness and regeneration); 4.15.5 (mortification); and 3.3–7 (regeneration).

44 Thomas Helwys, *Synopsis Fidei, veræ Christianæ Ecclesiæ Anglicanæ, Amsterodamiæ* (1610 [ACA, B1350]), Article 10. Translation by Antony D. Rich, "Thomas Helwys' First Confession of Faith, 1610," *Baptist Quarterly* 43.4 (October 2009): 235–241.

45 *Declaration of Faith*, Article I4, A5r.

Separatists over their sacraments.[46] In rejecting, as Smyth had done before him, the Separatists' claim to be a true church, practising true sacraments, Helwys simply pronounces that false sacraments are no sacraments.[47] On both occasions, Helwys makes no comment on the word *sacrament* itself.

There is evidence, however, which indicates that Helwys' understanding of the ordinance of baptism was not devoid of what is widely recognized as sacramental theology. He concludes the third major section of his *The miſtery of iniquity*:

> iff you followe not Chriſt in the regeneration, that is, if you bee not borne againe of water & of the Spirit, & ſo enter into the Kingdome off Heaven, all is nothinge, as you ſee by the example of this Ruler. And Cornelius Act 10. *If he had not bene baptized with the holy ghoſt and with Water*, for all his praiers and almes he had not, nor could not have entred into the kingdom off Heaven.[48]

Starting a new paragraph he immediately continues, and in doing so indicates the interconnection between doctrines, which subsequent Baptists and others have often separated, but for him stand in intimate relationship—new birth, pneumatology,[49] the inner and outer dimensions of baptism,[50] soteriology and ecclesiology.

---

46 Helwys, *The miſtery of iniquity*, 132.

47 Helwys, *The miſtery of iniquity*, 134.

48 Helwys, *The miſtery of iniquity*, 122 (italics added). On salvation, regeneration, water and Spirit baptism, see also 171. Cf. 139, where he talks of "the Baptiſme of amendment of life, for the remiſſion off ſinnes" on the basis of Mark 1:4, and understands John 3:5 and Hebrews 10:22 as baptism, bringing together Spirit and water with entry into the kingdom (ie. salvation), and the washing of the body with pure water and forgiveness and assurance of faith.

49 Later, in his denial that infant baptism is the seal of the covenant under the law, Helwys insists that water baptism is not the seal, rather the Holy Spirit is (cf. Ephesians 1:13 and 1 Corinthians 12:13). Helwys, *The miſtery of iniquity*, 174–175.

50 In spite of the difficulties of doing so, Helwys argues that the inward and outward aspects of baptism, of Spirit and water, are one baptism. In *The miſtery of iniquity*, 134, he cites Ephesians 4:5 against his opponents' claims that "there is a true baptiſme, a falſe Baptiſme, and no Baptiſme," and asserts that "there is but one baptiſme." On page 139, he sets down "the true Baptiſme," namely, "the Baptiſme off amendement off life for the remiſſion off ſinnes," specifically that "men muſt bee waſhed, which is water, and the holie Ghoſt, that is pure from an evil conſcience, and waſhed with water: Therefore can you not devide the water, and the ſpirit in this Baptiſme, Chriſt

> Thus entered all the people off God of whoſe entrance the Scriptures give testimonie, either by rule or example, and therefore if there bee anie other entrance found out, it is not, nor cannot bee of God: this onelie is the doore which Jeſus Chriſt hath set open for all to enter in at, that enter into his kingdome John. 3.5. and the Lord ſanctifie al your harts with grace, that you may enter thereby: *for no other way of ſalvation hath Chriſt appointed but that mē firſt believe and bee Baptized.* Mark. 16.16.[51]

Helwys picks up Mark 16:16[52] early on in the fourth section of the book, and following reference to both Acts 2:38 and Galatians 3:27, he states that there is "no other way to come, and be ioyned to Chriſt Jeſus," whether they are "infidels and unbeleevers" or Brownists (i.e. those he is addressing in this part of the book), "*onely by believing and being baptized.*"[53] Helwys later develops the theme of the covenant and baptism,[54] declaring "the Covenant on his peoples behalf which they are to keepe and performe is, to believe the Goſpel and bee Baptized."[55] Covenant and baptism are then shown in their relation to ecclesiology, for Helwys asserts "that there can none bee under the Covenant, but they which believe and are Baptized."[56]

---

hath joyned them together, and he that denies waſhing, or is not waſhed with the ſpirit is not baptized, and hee that denies waſhing, or is not waſhed with water, is not Baptized, because wee ſee the Baptiſme of Chriſt, is to bee waſhed with water and the holie Ghoſt." This means that Separatist infant baptism (as that of the Roman Catholics and Anglicans) is no baptism (152).

51 Helwys, *The miſtery of iniquity*, 122 (italics added).

52 Mark 16:16 figures prominently in his argument that the new covenant is one of life and salvation only to those who believe and are baptized, Helwys, *The miſtery of iniquity*, 175–177 and 179–180, with allusions to it on pages 184–185.

53 Helwys, *The miſtery of iniquity*, 124 (italics added). So, too, "their was, nor is, no way for you to ioyne unto Chriſt, but to amend your lives, & be Baptized, and by Baptiſme to put on Chriſt." He also argues that, in fact, the Brownists are "infidels and unbeleevers" because they hold to, among other things, "a worldly baptiſme brought out of the world, and Ordinance of the world, and not the baptiſme and Ordinance of Chriſt" (125). See also page 126.

54 Helwys, *The miſtery of iniquity*, 165–185.

55 Helwys, *The miſtery of iniquity*, 165. On this basis, he contends that in this covenant there is no divine requirement for infant baptism (166, 168).

56 Helwys, *The miſtery of iniquity*, 169.

The sacrament of baptism according to John Murton

In the year Helwys died[57] an anonymous Baptist defence of religious freedom and liberty of conscience was published. *Obiections: Anſwered by way of Dialogue* is either the work of Helwys or his fellow member of the congregation which had returned to London in 1612 and who succeeded him as pastor, John Murton.[58]

Written as a dialogue between three protagonists, Antichristian, Christian and Indifferent Man, the author's preference is clearly to use *ordinance*, especially in the section in which he rejects infant baptism in both the Church of Rome and Church of England.[59] However, *Obiections* has Christian argue that the law of the land can only claim civil obedience even from those who, like the Baptists, "receiveth not the Sacraments" from the Church of England,[60] then records that when "many thouſãds" refused to go "against their conſciences...to receive your Sacraments" they were persecuted.[61]

The author also refuses to accept any form of Spirit–matter dualism which can result from too sharply distinguishing between the outward and inward dimensions of religion,[62] for we "muſt glorifie God with our bodies, & with our ſpirits, for they are his,"[63] and he appeals to Christ's saying (Matthew 3:15) that "It becometh him & all his to fulfil all righteouſnes in outward ordinãces as washinge with water."[64] He also follows the common

---

57 See Cross, "The Adoption of Believer's Baptism and Baptist Beginnings," 1 n.3 and 28.

58 [Thomas Helwys or John Murton], *Obiections: Anſwered by way of Dialogue* (s.l.: s.n., 1615). On authorship, see, Wright, *Early English Baptists*, 45, and *Early English Books Online*, who take Helwys to be the author, while E.B. Underhill, *Tracts on Liberty of Conscience and Persecution 1614–1661* (1846; reprint, New York: Burt Franklin, 1966), 87–90, following John Robinson, *A Defence of the Doctrine Propounded by the Synode of Dort* (s.l.: s.n., 1624), takes it to be Murton. For our purposes authorship doesn't matter, as either way *Obiections* helps us see the earliest Baptists' views of baptism and sacraments. So, too, Wright, *Early English Baptists*, 45 n.3.

59 See the passage in *Obiections*, 58–62.

60 *Obiections*, 35.

61 *Obiections*, 41. Another two occurrences of "the word and sacraments" appears on the lips of Indifferent Man (50), but again no comment is made on the legitimacy of the word *sacrament* itself.

62 *Obiections*, 48.

63 *Obiections*, 50.

64 *Obiections*, 49.

pattern noted already that use of *ordinance* did not preclude the use of *sacrament*, for while Christian states that the Church of England has its own "imitations of Gods' ordinances, as water, bread and wine, ād other thinges," the Baptists, "Gods' people" have "the word and Sacraments."[65]

However, no question of authorship surrounds Murton's *A Discription of what God hath Predeſtinated* (1620), a reply to John Robinson's views on baptism, which takes the form of a dialogue between a searcher, Ereunetes, and his guide, Odegos, who directs him toward a more Arminian theology.[66] In an extended discussion of the "diuers Baptiſmes" in the New Testament[67] (that of John the Baptist, and Christ, but also of affliction[68]), Murton elucidates the pattern seen in Acts of those who receive the word, and are baptized after they believe.[69] Against Robinson, Murton believes that the seal of God's "gracious pardon" is "*the holy Spirit of Promiſe*, which *is the worke of God*," not "Baptiſme with water."[70]

In his discussion of baptism in the catechism of the Synod of Dort,[71] Murton uses the word *sacrament*, but his only objection is to infant baptism, not the term used to describe it.[72] While there are also suggestions of a more sacramental view of baptism, Murton is clearly happier speaking of the Corinthians having "Chriſts ordinances,"[73] though even this term does not occur with any frequency.

There are tensions within Murton's baptismal theology. The majority of the time, his views are not sacramental (which is different from non- or anti-sacramental), but at others they are more than this: calling them sacramental, however, is perhaps

---

65 *Obiections*, 50.

66 [John Murton], *A Discription of what God hath Predeſtinated Concerning Man* (s.l.: s.n., 1620), 154–176, though his discussion of baptism begins earlier. See Robinson, *Of Religious Commvnion*, and his reply to Murton, *A Defence of the Doctrine Propounded by the Synode of Dort*.

67 [Murton], *A Discription*, 129. On pages 126–127, he quotes Hebrews 6:1 with its plural "baptisms."

68 [Murton], *A Discription*, 138–139.

69 [Murton], *A Discription*, 130.

70 [Murton], *A Discription*, 176.

71 See [Murton], *A Discription*, A2.

72 [Murton], *A Discription*, 132–134.

73 [Murton], *A Discription*, 141–142, 148

too much. For example, on the basis of 1 Peter 3:21, he believes that "the Baptiſme that ſaueth vs, is not the putting away the filth of the Fleſh; but in that a good Conſcience maketh requeſt vnto God"; though on the basis of Titus 3:5 he is compelled to assert that "the waſhing of the body with pure water, is that whereby wee come to God. It is the waſhing of the new birth, and renuing of the holy Ghoſt," and this is being "borne of the Spirit."[74] Priority, then, rests on the Spirit, for "the Apoſtles had the Spirit of God, before they had *Chriſts* Baptiſme."[75]

He also discusses regeneration, but restricts its meaning to turning to God from sin,[76] and God's promise to all those God calls. This "Couenant or Promiſe is the couenant of ſaluation, by *Chriſt* made vnto the Children of *Abraham*, vpon the ſame Condition, that it is made to *Abraham* himſelfe; namely, vpon repentance and Faith in *Chriſt*."[77] Both the baptism of Moses (1 Corinthians 10:2) and Noah's ark (1 Peter 3:20) are figures "of the Baptiſme that saueth," yet, "Euen ſo true Baptiſme ſaueth them that are in it, or put on Chriſt by it, from the deſtruction of Hell."[78] Addressing Robinson directly, Murton declares that "the members and Churches of *Chriſt*, are ſo made; both by *Faith* and *Baptiſme*, and not by the one only."[79] By faith we are made sons of God, and by baptism we put on Christ.[80] In fact, so strong is their connection that he declares, "The manifeſtation of Faith and Baptiſme, hath Chriſt ioyned together, and what is mortall man that he ſhould ſeparate them?"[81]

That Murton was not anti-sacraments comes out in correspondence six years after *A Discription* was published. As we will see later, by the mid-1620s Murton's and four other churches entered into correspondence with the Waterlander Mennonites

---

74 [Murton], *A Discription*, 132. Among other passages appealed to are Hebrews 10:22; Titus 3:5; John 3:5. See page 155, "wee are all by one Spirit, baptiſed into one body," and cites 1 Corinthians 12:13 and John 3:5.

75 [Murton], *A Discription*, 139–140.

76 [Murton], *A Discription*, 134.

77 [Murton], *A Discription*, 135 (italics original). For more on covenants, see pages 145–151.

78 [Murton], *A Discription*, 142.

79 [Murton], *A Discription*, 154 (italics original). Also page 155.

80 [Murton], *A Discription*, 155.

81 [Murton], *A Discription*, 156.

over a split which had seen eighteen of their number form a new church under the leadership of one of them, Elias Tookey.[82] In a letter sent by two couriers from the five churches comprising "a number in England of undoubtedly 150 persons" associated with the London congregation led by Murton and Thomas Denys,[83] they acknowledge "that the ministering of the holy sacraments unseparately is united with the ministering of the Word, and that not every member of the body may minister the sacraments." However, "when the bishops [ministers/pastors] are not present" those who "also are servants of the body" but who had not been "installed in the episcopal office" by the laying on of hands, but who "preach, convert, baptize, and build churches and perform other public actions with the consent of the church," may also administer the sacraments.[84] In their discussion of the magistracy, a matter on which they differed from the Waterlanders,[85] the five churches say that when it does not hinder people being a Christian it is "a good ordinance" established by God, and therefore it is permissible for Christians to hold such public office. They ask,

> Must we compel a man who desires to become a Christian, to leave anything else but sin? Baptism, for which we resist the world, is *a baptism of conversion to the forgiving of sins which all those are to receive who repent for their sins and believe in the doctrine of the Gospel.* Shall we make or suspect a sin in their eyes which is a good ordinance of God? This be far from us.[86]

---

82 See Anonymous (but probably Elias Tookey) letter to Hans de Ries, Renier Wybrant and the elders of the Amsterdam church, dated "March 17, 1625" (o.s., so 17 March 1626 n.s. [ACA, B1371]), in Benjamin Evans, *The Early English Baptists*, 2 vol. (London: J. Heaton & Son, 1862–1864), 2:37–40.

83 So the letter by Cornelis C. Claesz to Hans de Ries, dated 13 November 1626 [ACA, B1373], in Evans, *Early English Baptists*, 2:24–25.

84 Letter on behalf of the five churches, dated 18 November 1626 [ACA, B1372], in Evans, *Early English Baptists*, 2:26–30.

85 See Anthony R. Cross, "'Christ Jesus…exalted…farre aboue all principalities and powers': Baptist Attitudes to Monarchy, Country, and Magistracy, 1609–1644," in *Freedom and the Powers: Perspectives from Baptist History*, ed. Anthony R. Cross and John H.Y. Briggs (Didcot: The Baptist Historical Society, 2014), 3–22 (esp. 16–18).

86 Letter dated 18 November 1626, Evans, *Early English Baptists*, 2:29 (italics added). Here is another example of the broader understanding of ordinances.

The sacrament of baptism according to Richard Overton and an anonymous Baptist

The folder of early Baptist writings held by the Amsterdam City Archives (ACA) enigmatically includes a confession of faith in Latin by Richard Overton, to which the date 1615 has been attributed. When this confession was written is unknown, and there are serious obstacles to it being as early as 1615,[87] nevertheless its inclusion among the earliest manuscripts of confessions, handwritten book drafts, letters and minutes held in the ACA at least raises the possibility that it was written six years after the establishment of the first Baptist congregation. It is worth noting, therefore, that according to Overton's confession, the true church is entered into "by baptism," immediately after which he states,

> I believe that there are but two sacraments to be administered and embraced in the church of Christ, *viz.* Baptism and the Lord's supper, and these sacraments are to be administered to, and participated by, those who are penitent and manifest faith; so that both of them are to be denied to all infants and all unbelievers, because they do not belong to such.[88]

In 1618, however, an anonymous Baptist work directly addressed the issue of baptism. Though it is a translation "out of the Dutch tōgue," presumably Anabaptist, possibly Mennonite, its interest lies in the fact that it was translated and published in England by Baptists, those "Falſtly called Ana-Baptiſtes."[89]

---

87 Overton flourished between 1640–1663, see, B.J. Gibbons, "Overton, Richard (fl. 1640–1663), Leveller and pamphleteer," in *Oxford Dictionary of National Biography* (Oxford: Oxford University Press, 2004); http://ezproxy-prd.bodleian.ox.ac.uk:2167/view/article/20974; accessed October 8, 2014. He remarks that if 1615 is accurate then Overton was born before 1600. He further notes that other evidence for the date of the confession suggests a date as late as 1643.

88 Richard Overton, *Credo corde & confiteor ore* (n.d. [ACA, B1353]). This translation appears in Evans, *Early English Baptists*, 2:254–256.

89 *A Verie plaine and well grownded treatiſe Concerninge Baptisme* (s.l.: s.n., 1618), 7 (original in italics). The name *Anabaptists* was used of the Baptists as a derogatory and scandalous epithet intended to discredit them, and was frequently repudiated by them. See Robert B. Hannen, "Historical Notes on the Name 'Baptist,'" *Foundations* 8.1 (January 1965): 62–71, who also explores other names used by them and of them.

A Verie plaine and well grownded treatiſe expounds "the right Comanndement and ordinance of our Lorde Ieſus Chriſt concerning Baptiſme, as alſo the true vſe thereof by the holie Apoſtells & firſt Church"[90] as confirmed by "the wittnes of the Anncyent and latter teachers,"[91] for the sole purpose of bringing to light the truth "which hath beē ſo manie yeares obſcured by the distroyer" on "the principall Ground and meaninge of our Lorde Ieſus Chriſt concerning baptiſme," namely that "thoaſe that weare baptiſed weare firſt taught and inſtructed in the fayth."[92]

Several times in the epistle to the reader the author, about whom we can glean no details,[93] uses the word *mystery*, a term which itself has an ancient pedigree in connection with the sacraments.[94] For instance, in the opening of his first chapter he quotes Jerome (*Hieronimus*) that Jesus commanded the Apostles that they should instruct and teach all nations and "afterwards ſhould baptiſe thoſe that weare inſtructed in the miſteries of fayth. For yt cannot be that the bodye ſhold receive the Sacramente of Baptiſme, vnles the Sowle have received before the true fayth."[95] He also cites Luther to the same effect, that faith must precede receiving either sacrament, though he qualifies this with the righteous are not to live by the sacrament "but by faith in the Sacrament that vivifieth and iuſtifieth for manie receive the Sacrament which are not thereby quickened and bettered, but who ſo ever beleeveth is both vivified & bettered," as confirmed by Mark 16:16. He asserts, "whithout faith the Sacraments profit nothinge yea they are not onlie in vayne but

---

90 *A Verie plaine*, 5.

91 *A Verie plaine*, 3.

92 *A Verie plaine*, 37.

93 In the "Conclusion," *A Verie plaine*, 37, the author writes "beloved Reader I praye thee," and on page 38 there is a comment, "That you maye reade this *our* finale worke and true ſervice of *our* love" (italics added). Whether the original was the production of several, a community, or just one person, and, either way, whether the latter is a reference from those falsely called Anabaptists in England is a matter for conjecture. The style and spelling of the English is not like any other early Baptist work of this period, so it is possible it was translated by someone whose English was not their first language. The original author, however, as is clear from his wide knowledge of the early church fathers and Reformers, was clearly well-educated.

94 Cross, *Recovering the Evangelical Sacrament, passim.*

95 *A Verie plaine*, 8.

bringe damnation alſo to the receivers."[96] And faith, "which we have in our hartes," must be confessed and made known to the church, and for this "the Sacramente is inſtituted externallie to be vſed," hence with the mouth the gospel is confessed and the sacrament is "for a witness or ſigne that the world maye knowe that weare Chriſtians."[97] He also refers to the "Sacrament of regeneration" which was administered only at Easter and Pentecost.[98]

While *sacrament* and its plural occurs in the passages he cites from the early church fathers and Reformers, not the scriptural passages, it is clearly a term he accepts as a valid way of speaking of believers' baptism.

The sacrament of baptism according to Leonard Busher

Another enigmatic figure about whom we know little, is Leonard Busher, an Englishman who in 1611 was noted by two members of Francis Johnson's Ancient Church, Matthew Saunders and Cuthbert Hutten, to be a third sort of Anabaptist to Smyth and Helwys.[99] He had only one work published in our period, an important call for religious toleration addressed to James I, though it appears Busher never returned to England.

Though baptism is not a major subject in *Religions Peace*, nevertheless it does receive brief discussion. The word *sacrament* doesn't appear at all, while *ordinance* is sometimes used as a general term, sometimes with positive connotations, others with negative ones.[100] Other times it is used in more familiar ways. In the first, he brings the ordinances, which we should understand in the broader sense

96 *A Verie plaine*, 10. So also page 19.

97 *A Verie plaine*, 26.

98 *A Verie plaine*, 20–21. See also page 24. On page 36 he quotes Dionysius on the bath of regeneration, the only problem of which is not the theological concept but that it should be used on young children who "neither vunderſtande nor can learn the miſteries of God."

99 See Christopher Lawne, John Fowler, Clement Sanders and Robert B[u]lward, *The Prophane Schisme of the Brownists or Separatists* (s.l.: s.n., 1612), 56.

100 Leonard Busher, *Religions Peace Or A reconciliation, between princes & Peoples, & Nations* (Amsterdam: s.n., 1614): "God giveth a bleſſing onely to his owne ordinance" (2); "Antichriſt's ordinance" (3), while latter, page 23, speaks of "antichristian doctrines and ordinances" (see also page 27); submission to the "Biſhops' ordinances" (10); and "Chriſt hath onely ſet us free from al eccleſiaſtical laws and ordinances, which himſelf hath not commanded in his laſt will and Teſtament" (27; this is repeated a few lines later).

than just baptism and the Lord's supper, when he refers to "Gods' holy word" as "the onely order and ordinance Chriſt hath appointed, for the gathering of his Church together."[101]

Busher also brings the ordinances into relation with soteriology when he warns those who "offend" Christ's "little ones" that it would be better if a millstone drowned them (Matthew 18:6), for they are persecuting "thoſe that cōfeſſe with the mouth, & believe with the heart the Lord Ieſus, & that God rayſed him from the dead: whoſe laws and ordinances they are carefull to keep and obey! Chriſt ſaith that ſuch shalbee ſaved."[102]

Busher entreats James I to reform the statutes of the land by listening to Busher "put him in mynd of thoſe things that do[e] concerne the glory of God," and that when he reads the New Testament, following Josiah's example, he will find "a great alteration of the Apostoliq faith, & change the laws & ordinances of Chriſt, within his dominions."[103]

Busher says little on baptism, and what he does say is not incompatible with the kind of sacramental understanding we have already encountered. He connects baptism with proclamation of the gospel, salvation in terms of new birth by the word and Spirit, forgiveness of sins, ecclesiology and that baptism is participation in the death of Christ.

He exhorts James I and his government to understand that according to Scripture, "the one true religion is gottē by a new birth, even by the word and ſpirit of God." They should, therefore, repeal those laws which force the religion of the Established Church. In their place they should establish the law of Christ, which, according to Matthew 28:19 and Mark 16:16, is that "Chriſt wil haue his miniſters to preach and teach the people of al nations, the things that concerne the kingdom of God, & the name of Ieſus Meſiah, repentance & remiſion of ſins, & to baptiſe in his name, ſuch as doe believe."[104] In Old Testament times the Lord did not want offerings that had been forced, but which were given freely from the heart,

101 Busher, *Religions Peace*, 17.
102 Busher, *Religions Peace*, 17–18.
103 Busher, *Religions Peace*, 22.
104 Busher, *Religions Peace*, 1.

> ſo now in tyme of the goſpel, he wil not have the people conſtrayned, but as many as receave the word gladly, they are to be added to the Church by baptiſme: and therfore Chriſt commanded his diſciples to teach al nations, & baptiſe them, that is to preach the word of ſalvatiō to evry creature, of al ſorts of natiōs, that are worthy and willing to receave it. And ſuch as ſhal willing and gladly receave it, he hath commanded to be baptiſed in the water, that is dipped for dead in the water, ād therfore the apoſtle. ...ſaith: we are buried thē with him by baptiſme &c.[105]

The sacrament of baptism according to Elias Tookey

In the 1620s there developed Baptist churches in five English towns, London, Lincoln, Sarum (Salisbury), Coventry and Tiverton, though the congregation in London split over Christology,[106] the one church being led by Murton and Denys, the latter more latitudinarian by Elias Tookey. Both congregations entered into correspondence with the Waterlander Mennonites led by Hans de Ries and Renier Wybrant, and between 1624 and 1631 a total of eight letters were exchanged.[107]

Tookey only twice mentions the sacraments. In the first he opines that "a private brother is allowed to minister the sacraments, when the congregation calls him to it," but that when the congregation has a minister "a private brother may by no means do it."[108] In his second over a year later, he acknowledges that his congregation had not ministered the sacraments or church discipline as they had promised the Amsterdam church. The fact he only uses *sacrament* and not *ordinance* shows that Tookey was happy with the term; as to his baptismal theology specifically, there is no evidence beyond this.

---

105 Busher, *Religions Peace*, 23.

106 See Tookey to De Ries, dated "March 17, 1625/6," in Evans, *Early English Baptists*, 2:38.

107 This correspondence is kept in the ACA, but translations appear in Evans, *Early English Baptists*, 2:21–51, while the letters have been transcribed by Burrage, *Early English Dissenters*, 2:222–257. The latest of these letters comes from the church in Lincoln, and from James and Isabell Toppe of the Tiverton church, and are dated 5 September 1630 [ACA, B1376], and 5 June 1631 [ACA, B1377] respectively. Baptism, and the sacraments more generally, do not feature in all these.

108 "Elias Tookey, and the others," letter dated "Jun. 3, 1624" [ACA, B1368], in Evans, *Early English Baptists*, 2:21–24.

Conclusion

At times, therefore, the earliest Baptists do adopt both sacramental terminology and sacramental theology in their explication and defence of believers' baptism. But even when it is not overtly present there is sacramental theology but without the word or its cognates, or there is a sufficient amount of material that is not inconsistent with a sacramental view. Perhaps the tensions between non-sacramental and sacramental views of baptism are nothing more than the anachronistic projection of later distinctions and sensibilities which the first Baptists simply wouldn't have understood, which is why their baptismal theologies evince, at times, contradictions, and, at others, tensions with which Baptists have wrestled for four centuries.

What the first Baptists exemplify is the desire to restore the true church, a position at which they arrived through their reading of Scripture and their commitment to be faithful to it in both belief and practice. We must also recognize that the views of these earliest Baptists are not normative for Baptists who are heirs of the tradition they pioneered; but then neither should we regard our views as normative either for our Baptist forebears or those Baptists in different countries. We are part of a dynamic and diverse movement of Christ's people guided by the Spirit who blows where he determines; a tradition which from the earliest days believed that one of God's gracious gifts is universal religious freedom and toleration and liberty of conscience before him.

We should no more feel the need to abandon the word *sacrament* than we should abandon the word *baptism* simply because many Christian traditions mean something very different by it than we do. The first Baptists often both readily and unapologetically employed the word *sacrament* in regard to baptism and the Lord's supper because they found it a helpful theological term which enabled them to understand, practise, propagate and defend their beliefs in the face of opposition and persecution. Similarly they felt no impulse to abandon other terms used by their opponents, such as *preaching*, *the Word*, *prayer* and *censures* (church discipline). In fact, the two great influences on the early Baptists were Calvinism (Smyth, Helwys and company were, after all, Puritan Separatists before they were Baptists[109]) and Arminianism, which itself is a form Calvinism.[110]

The conclusion of this chapter, then, is unusually decisive, and vindicates the claims Stan Fowler makes in his important *More Than a Symbol.* The first Baptists simply did not share the antipathy toward the word *sacrament* and baptismal sacramental theology that we find in some recent and contemporary scholars, whose work seems fuelled more by later theological disputes and concerns, and dogmatic, even ideological, presuppositions than by rigorous historical research. Those who categorically state that the first Baptists were non-sacramental in their theology of baptism, and that baptismal sacramentalism was a later innovation are, quite simply, wrong.

---

109 See, eg, K.R. Manley, "Origins of the Baptists: The Case for Development from Puritanism–Separatism," in *Faith, Life, and Witness: The Papers of the Study and Research Division of the Baptist World Alliance 1986–1990,* ed. William H. Brackney and Ruby J. Burke (Birmingham: Samford University Press, 1990), 56–69.

110 See Roger E. Olson, *Arminian Theology: Myths and Realities* (Downers Grove: IVP Academic, 2006), 44–60; and F. Stuart Clarke, *The Ground of Election: Jacobus Arminius' Doctrine of the Work and Person of Christ* (Milton Keynes: Paternoster, 2006). Even if this is not accepted, for our purposes what is significant is that both Calvin and Arminius, and Calvinism and Arminianism are sacramentalist.

10

Christian community in German pietism: Gottfried Arnold and Johanna Eleonora Petersen on the church, with special attention to the place of women

BY DOUGLAS H. SHANTZ

A neglected factor in the rise of early evangelicalism is the influential movement known as German pietism. Pietist beginnings can be dated to the 1660s and 1670s in the urban settings of Bremen, Frankfurt, and Leipzig. Shaped by an eclectic mix of ideas drawn from the Reformation radicals, the spiritual alchemy of Jakob Böhme, Dutch Calvinism and Jean de Labadie, German pietism represented a dramatic shift away from the Reformation of Luther and Calvin. The pietists were marked by conventicle gatherings for Bible study and prayer, their theology of new birth, post-millennialism, social activism and world mission—all departures from sixteenth-century Protestant reform. In recent years, scholars have significantly revised our understanding of pietism and its connections with the Enlightenment and with evangelical religion in England and America.[1]

An important feature of the German pietist paradigm was its "experimentation with new forms of religious association."[2] A new understanding of the church is evident among both church pietists and radical pietists. "Hierarchical, state-supported structures, based on confessional unity, were minimized or set aside in favour of free associations of true believers, independent of confession and the state."[3] Late seventeenth and early eighteenth century pietists looked for a "Philadelphian" church age marked by deliverance from divisions and polemics in Christ's post-millennial kingdom. Pietists were convinced that the community of the reborn is best nurtured in small, informal gatherings where believers act as prophets and priests to one another in study and application of God's Word.

Women were clear beneficiaries of this new model of church. In Lutheran churches, women remained subject to their husbands and excluded from pastoral leadership, as they had been among the Catholics. But in the informal gatherings of the pietists, women quickly rose to prominence. The first pietist conventicle to break away from the Lutheran Church was led by two Frankfurt noblewomen—Maria Juliana Baur von Eyseneck (1641–1684) and Johanna Eleonora Petersen, nee von Merlau, (1644–1724). In their conventicle, women were free to read and interpret the Bible for themselves, and to engage in theological discussions with each other and with men.

Orthodox Lutheran critics of German pietism, such as theologian Johann Heinrich Feustking (1672–1713), focused their scorn on three influential pietist figures: Gottfried Arnold, Johanna Eleonora Petersen and her husband Johann Wilhelm Petersen. Books by Arnold and the Petersens were bestsellers in Germany in the eighteenth century.[4] In this study, I examine the

---

1 See W.R. Ward, *Early Evangelicalism: A Global Intellectual History, 1670–1789* (Cambridge: Cambridge University, 2006), and my book, *An Introduction to German Pietism: Protestant Renewal at the Dawn of Modern Europe* (Baltimore: The Johns Hopkins University Press, 2013), 1–7, 279f.

2 Jonathan Strom, "Introduction," *Pietism and Community in Europe and North America, 1650–1850* (Leiden: Brill, 2010), 2.

3 Martin Greschat, *Christentumsgeschichte II: von der Reformation bis zur Gegenwart* (Stuttgart: Kohlhammer, 1997), 94.

4 Johann Heinrich Feustking, *Gynaeceum Haeretico Fanaticum* (Frankfurt, 1704), ed.

notion of Christian community in Gottfried Arnold and Johanna Eleonora Petersen, with special attention to the place they granted to women within the church. In *Die Erste Liebe*, Arnold used the early church as a standard for judging the Lutheran Church of his day, and called for re-establishing early church practices. He observed that the early church did not judge godliness according to gender, but according to the heart. Petersen lamented that Protestants had fallen into sectarian divisions, and wrangling with one another. Petersen defended her right as a woman to use God's gifts for his glory and for the good of her neighbour.

German pietist ecclesiology—a neglected field of research

Scholarly discussions of radical German Protestantism are typically divided into two main fields of research: the radical Reformation of the sixteenth century and German pietism in the late seventeenth and eighteenth centuries. Two classic studies of radical Reformation ecclesiology are those by Fritz Heyer and Franklin Littell.[5] Littell argues that sixteenth-century Anabaptists were marked by their "primitivism," a concern for restitution of the true church of the apostles which had fallen away after the reign of Constantine.[6] Heyer suggests that the visible, true church of the radicals had three marks: a pure church, separated from the godless; a church of those who determine to live godly lives; and a church preserved through adult baptism, church discipline and the ban.[7]

Heyer notes the conviction of radical Reformers that the "true church" would appear on earth in the last days. Determined to

---

Elisabeth Gössmann (Munich: Iudicium Verlag, 1998); Shantz, *An Introduction to German Pietism*, 148. Feustking denounced Gottfried Arnold for undermining the Lutheran Church and its pastoral leadership.

5 Fritz Heyer, *Der Kirchenbegriff der Schwärmer* (Leipzig: M. Heinsius Nachfolger, 1939), and Franklin Littell, *The Anabaptist View of the Church: A Study in the Origins of Sectarian Protestantism*, 2nd ed. (Boston: Beacon Press, 1958).

6 Geoffrey Dipple observes that "discussion of the place of historical visions in the Radical Reformation has been dominated for the last half century by the interpretation of Franklin H. Littell." Dipple's own recent study reexamines Littell's thesis and arguments. See Geoffrey Dipple, "Just as in the Time of the Apostles," *Uses of History in the Radical Reformation* (Kitchener: Pandora Press, 2005).

7 Heyer, *Der Kirchenbegriff der Schwärmer*, 50.

discover when and where it would appear, they became convinced that the history of salvation would witness its last act solely in Germany. The Schwenkfelders, for example, identified Caspar Schwenckfeld and Valentin Crautwald as the two witnesses of Revelation 11 who would gather the restored church of new men.[8] Radical Protestants in Moravia also shared this conviction: "In the last age of this world, God has desired to bring forth the light of his truth in its fullness especially in the German nation and lands."[9] Within the boundaries of the German empire, some radical believers identified one German city as the favoured site, while others identified another. In his *Prague Manifesto*, Thomas Müntzer assured the people of Bohemia, "Here the new church will arrive." "In your land, the new apostolic church will approach." Balthasar Hubmaier, however, assured Anabaptist believers in Nikolsburg that their city had a special significance for God. "Just as Christ, after his resurrection, made his way to Emmaus, so now, after the present day resurrection of his word, will he make his way to Nikolsburg." Melchior Hoffman prophesied the arrival of Christ's kingdom in Strasbourg, while the Anabaptists in Münster were confident that their city was the one favoured by God. "Only in Münster would there be peace and security; it would be the city of the Lord and of the new Jerusalem."[10]

Also problematic was the radicals' tendency to rely upon charismatic leaders, rather than ordained clergy, as spokesmen for God. This dependence upon charismatic figures and their sense of calling brought a degree of instability to radical communities, often with disastrous consequences. Bader called himself "a king, sent by God." The peasant Claus Ludwig von Tüngeda claimed that he was Christ. Some radical leaders became overwhelmed by the responsibility, and resigned from their leadership role.[11]

An up-to-date survey of eighteenth-century pietist ecclesiol-

---

8 This was the view of Gregor Tag in 1549. See Valentin Crautwald, "Ein kürz Außlegung Der Offenbarünge Johannis (ca. 1536)," CS XIX, 260f, 318; Douglas H. Shantz, *Crautwald and Erasmus* (Baden-Baden: Valentin Koerner, 1992), 57 n.153, 168.

9 Heyer, *Der Kirchenbegriff der Schwärmer*, 99–100.

10 Heyer, *Der Kirchenbegriff der Schwärmer*, 100–101.

11 Heyer, *Der Kirchenbegriff der Schwärmer*, 102–103.

ogy does not yet exist. As Hans Schneider noted, "Ecclesiology has not been a favorite subject of research on Pietism...monographs dealing with the Pietist understanding of the church are rare."[12] However, helpful discussions of the pietist understanding of the church can be found in a 2010 work edited by Jonathan Strom, while a 2015 study by Ryoko Mori offers insight into Pietist conventicles.[13] Strom notes that there was no one expression of pietist community; Ernst Troeltsch found pietists in all three types of religious groups: church, sect and mystic. This variety includes gatherings of the devout within existing church structures; religious communities that separated from established churches; and spiritualist "Philadelphian" groups with neither clergy nor sacraments.[14]

Hans Schneider likewise finds a "spectrum of options" in pietist efforts to reform the state church. Following the *Augsburg Confession*, Article 7, Philipp Jakob Spener believed the church existed wherever the pure gospel was preached and the sacraments were rightly administered. To this he added the mark of a godly life and love toward one's neighbour. Spener called upon pastors to lead an exemplary Christian life, to read the works of Thomas á Kempis and Johann Arndt, and to preach sermons that edified their hearers. He called for revitalization of Luther's notion of the priesthood of all believers, whereby godly laypeople would form a "church within the church"—*ecclesiola in ecclesia*—and edify one another through spiritual conversation.[15]

In contrast to the "church pietism" of Spener, various radical groups broke away from Lutheran and Reformed state churches, convinced that one must flee the "Babylon" of corruption and ungodliness. There is a certain irony here, as these radical pietists used the same language to describe Reformation churches

---

12 Hans Schneider, "Understanding the Church: Issues of Pietist Ecclesiology," in *Pietism and Community in Europe and North America, 1650-1850*, ed. Jonathan Strom (Leiden: Brill, 2010), 15.

13 Jonathan Strom, ed., *Pietism and Community in Europe and North America, 1650–1850* (Leiden: Brill, 2010); Ryoko Mori, "The Conventicle Piety of the Radicals," in *A Companion to German Pietism, 1660–1800*, ed. Douglas H. Shantz (Leiden: Brill, 2015), 201–224.

14 Jonathan Strom, "Introduction," in *Pietism and Community in Europe and North America*, 2.

15 Schneider, "Understanding the Church: Issues of Pietist Ecclesiology," 24.

as Luther and other Reformers had once used in describing the Catholics. Schneider finds two competing models among the radical pietists: mystical spiritualism and legalist biblicism. These two models reflect George Williams' distinction between Reformation spiritualists and Anabaptists.[16]

For spiritualist pietists such as Johann Conrad Dippel, the true church was the invisible, spiritual community of the reborn, scattered among the many Christian confessions. True believers require neither church, nor sacraments, nor clergy, nor even the external word of the Bible. God speaks the "inner word" to believers by his Spirit. True Christianity is "spiritual, internal and free, not bound to a certain place, time or set of circumstances." Spiritualist pietists preferred the option of "religion without a church."[17]

Some radical pietists formed gathered communities of the reborn, marked by varying degrees of organization and ritual. The Community of True Inspiration, under Eberhard Gruber and Johann Friedrich Rock, received the inner Word of God through the utterances of their prophets. Initially they rejected not only the state churches but the formation of new sects as well. Eventually the Inspired changed from a network of informal gatherings to an organized community with a set of rules.[18] In the new world, the Inspired established the Amana Colonies in Iowa.[19]

---

16 Schneider, "Understanding the Church: Issues of Pietist Ecclesiology," 26. I have recently argued for a four-fold typology of various kinds of radical pietists: the "Spiritualist," "Millennialist," "Conventicle" and "Sect" models of radical pietism. See Shantz, *An Introduction to German Pietism*, 154–158. On Williams' distinction between Reformation spiritualists and Anabaptists, see George H. Williams, "Introduction," *Spiritual and Anabaptist Writers*, ed. George H. Williams and Angel M. Mergal (Philadelphia: Westminster, 1957), 19–36.

17 Schneider, "Understanding the Church: Issues of Pietist Ecclesiology," 25–29, 35.

18 Schneider, "Understanding the Church: Issues of Pietist Ecclesiology," 29.

19 The website reads: "The Amana Colonies are a group of settlements of German Pietists in Iowa, comprising seven villages. Calling themselves the Ebenezer Society or the Community of True Inspiration, *die Gemeinde der wahren Inspiration*, they first settled in New York state near Buffalo in what is now the Town of West Seneca. However, in order to live out their beliefs in more isolated surroundings they moved west to the rich soil of east-central Iowa (near present-day Iowa City) in 1855. They lived a communal life until the mid 1930s." See http://www.amanacolonies.com/about-amana-colonies/; accessed July 9, 2016.

An example of highly organized Biblicist pietism is Alexander Mack's Schwarzenau "New Anabaptists." Mack established a community in which believers' baptism and the love feast were practiced as they sought to revive the life and experience of the early church. Outward baptism of believers was the entryway to their community, signifying new birth and commitment to a holy life.[20] The influence of earlier Anabaptists and Mennonites is clearly in evidence in Mack's group of pietists.[21]

Ryoko Mori's study examines the rise of pietist conventicles, the informal gatherings of German believers in homes, outside of regular church services. Mori describes the controversy over conventicles that arose in the city of Leipzig in 1690, as well as the sense of community among those who belonged to pietist conventicles and the way in which these gatherings nurtured an independent, confident "Pietist self."[22]

Home gatherings of believers were a foreign concept among German Lutherans and Reformed. The authorities saw them as subversive because they were run by lay people, not overseen or endorsed by clergy. In fact, the distinction between laity and ordained clergy was generally ignored in pietist conventicles. Participants, both men and women, shared interpretations of Scripture with one another, traditionally the sole privilege of pastors, and discussions of the Sunday sermon often turned to mockery and ridicule. Ministers complained that conventicle members "behaved stubbornly" toward their pastors and promoted views that are "adverse to church doctrine."[23]

Church and civic leaders were further concerned that pietist conventicles included both men and women from various social classes. Members called one another "brother" and "sister" without observing the social formalities and distinctions of age, gender and class. There was concern that pietist meetings encouraged extra-marital affairs.[24]

---

20 Schneider, "Understanding the Church: Issues of Pietist Ecclesiology," 31–33.

21 See Marcus Meier, *Die Schwarzenauer Neutäufer. Genese einer Gemeindebildung zwischen Pietismus und Täufertum* (Göttingen: Vandenhoeck & Ruprecht, 2008).

22 Roko Mori, "The Conventicle Piety of the Radicals," in *A Companion to German Pietism, 1660–1800*, ed. Douglas H. Shantz (Leiden: Brill, 2015), 203, 216.

23 Mori, "The Conventicle Piety of the Radicals," 208–210.

24 Mori, "The Conventicle Piety of the Radicals," 209.

Those attending pietist home gatherings experienced an intense bond of fellowship. Lay people found encouragement in their pursuit of "true Christianity," as they exchanged experiences of faith and the fruits of Bible study. Women especially valued the opportunity to pray, discuss the Bible and preach.[25] During the "second wave" of pietism, from 1689 to 1694, roving women visionaries and prophets created a mood of prophetic excitement in pietist conventicles throughout northern Germany, above all in Leipzig, Erfurt and Quedlinburg.[26] Johanna Eleonora and Johann Wilhelm Petersen were key figures in promoting this radical, charismatic, millenarian expression of pietism among Leipzig students and their associates.[27]

Gottfried Arnold's view of the church in *Die erste Liebe* (1696)

Gottfried Arnold (1666–1714) is generally recognized as the leading representative of radical pietism.[28] Arnold authored the influential *Impartial History of Churches and Heretics* (1699–1700), where women figure prominently.[29]

Arnold's history of the early church, *Die erste Liebe—The First Love, that is, a true Portrait of the first Christians according to their Living Faith and Holy Life* (1696), is a massive study, some 1,100 folio pages in length. In *Die erste Liebe*, Arnold portrays the first Christians as a community without clergy, hierarchy, dogmas, confessions of faith, formal liturgy or church buildings and observes a falling away from these ideals under Constantine, and loss of its original innocence. *Die erste Liebe* will be the focus of this discussion of Arnold's view of the church.

Arnold makes clear at the outset of *Die Erste Liebe* that his purpose is to use the early church as a standard for judging the

25 Mori, "The Conventicle Piety of the Radicals," 212–213.

26 Mori, "The Conventicle Piety of the Radicals," 216–218, 221. Mori notes that, "From New Year's eve 1692 to Pentecost 1693, more than forty people had ecstatic experiences of God" (217).

27 Shantz, *An Introduction to German Pietism*, 112, 115.

28 Shantz, *An Introduction to German Pietism*, 148.

29 Shantz, *An Introduction to German Pietism*, 200–201. As noted above, Lutheran theologian Johann Heinrich Feustking was convinced that Arnold and the pietists had given over leadership in the church to women. Arnold had not only exalted women's place in the church but undermined the Lutheran church, its clergy and theologians.

church of his day and for re-establishing early church practices.[30] He cites the words of "a famous person":

> The majority of the acts of the apostles are not mere examples, but holy instructions which are set forth from God's counsel for us to follow. They hold within themselves divine principles according to which all the worship and duties of their descendants are to be established.

Arnold further notes the comment of Erasmus: "The ancient, godly men, because they were closer to the times of the Apostles, and held to a pure Christianity, untainted by the world, wrote many things that strongly challenge the mindset of the present time."[31] Tertullian explained that the closer the church comes to the fountain of the truth, the more pure it is. Jerome commented that one must seek to imitate the church in which "the blood of Christ was still warm" and in which faith was more fierce and zealous. For Arnold, the main evidence that the church of his own day had fallen away from the faith was its departure from the ways of the ancient, true church.

Arnold is concerned, then, to provide more than just a history. He explains that his history of the early church is not a typical history at all, but one which examines the history of the early church by setting forth those matters which are especially instructive and exemplary for "the present time." He writes for those who read with an open and illumined heart. "Everything that can be found in the original writings of the first Christians is presented for such people, without partiality."[32]

In Book I of *Die Erste Liebe*, Arnold emphasizes that the early church was marked not just by true confession, but by the fruits of faith. The mark of a true Christian was the ability to love those

---

30 Hans Schneider, "Nachwort," in Gottfried Arnold, *Die Erste Liebe, herausgegeben von Hans Schneider*ed (Leipzig: Evangelische Verlagsanstalt, 2002), 192, 203.

31 Gottfried Arnold, *Die Erste Liebe, Das ist, Wahre Abbildung Der Ersten Christen, Nach Ihren Lebendigen Glauben und Heiligen Leben, aus der ältesten und bewährtesten Kirchen-Scribenten eigenen Zeugnissen, Exempeln und Reden, Nach der Wahrheit der Ersten einigen Christlichen Religion* (Franckfurt am Mayen und Leipzig: Verlegt in Christian Genschen Buchhandlung, 1712), "Vor-Rede an den Unpartheyischen Leser," 2.

32 Arnold, *Die Erste Liebe*, 3. "Solchen Gemüthern wird ohne Partheylichkeit alles vorgeleget was in denen Uhrkunden der ersten Christen sich findet."

one formerly hated, and to hate what he formerly loved. The spirit of believers must be renewed and changed "from the earthly condition into the divine nature."[33] They must become new men. The mouth of the godless now offers true worship to God. The life of Christ must be the Christian's rule of life.[34] Once they were born again, early Christians believed they could attain perfection. They called those Christians "perfect" (*vollkommen*) who had advanced far in Christian godliness. The ancients recognized three stages of growth: "If you follow your lusts in all things, then you are entirely fleshly; if you do not follow them, then you are one who fights and battles against them; but if you have no evil lust at all, then you are perfect."[35]

Book II of *Die Erste Liebe*, almost 200 pages in length, is devoted to worship in the early church. Arnold covers the following topics: prayer, singing, places of worship, the role of the laity, the role of women, the calling and responsibilities of those who teach, preaching, catechism, baptism and the Lord's supper. In the section on prayer, Arnold cites Tertullian's reflection, that prayer must be joined to observance of God's commands.[36] His rule of thumb was that we are never further from God's ears than we are from his commands. Prayer is without effect when the one praying persists in sin.

Arnold cites the hymn of Prudentius:

We know Christ only by faith,
And when we come before God,
Then the purity and simplicity of the dove
Must take hold of our mind;
Then we learn to sing sweet hymns,
And to pray with a godly voice.
If we come before him with tears,
And bow to him with heart and knee,

33 Arnold, *Die Erste Liebe*, 9.

34 Arnold, *Die Erste Liebe*, 68.

35 Arnold, *Die Erste Liebe*, 87.

36 See Paul Wagner, "Gottfried Arnold on Worship: A Translation from *Die Erste Liebe* (1696)" (M.A. thesis, Wilfrid Laurier University, 1989). Wagner translates and discusses just the first chapter of Book 2 on worship. The chapter, 14 pages in length in an eighteenth-century German edition, deals with prayer in the early church.

Then the Father cannot deny his help
To our laments and pleas.[37]

The custom arose that believers joined with one another in common petition to God. They felt assured of God's help when they prayed together with one accord. As Ignatius wrote: "Come together in prayer: there should be one prayer, one desire, and one hope in untainted love and joy, for Christ is one. There is nothing more precious than this."[38]

Prayer in the early church was from the heart, in spirit and in truth. Their practice of prayer called for retreating to a quiet place, and withdrawing to the innermost recesses of the heart, rather than praying with loud words in public. Arnold noted the daily use of the Lord's Prayer among the first Christians, as well as use of the Psalms. Besides these prayers, Christians were generally free to pray according to the desires of their heart and the freedom of the Spirit.[39]

Arnold notes that singing was obviously important to the early church, following the precedent set by Israel and their use of the Psalms. A multitude of sources provide evidence that the early Christians were composing their own hymns. Eusebius, for example, observed that they wrote down spiritual songs and hymns of every sort in praise to God. Sozomenus noted that in order to win the Syrians, Ephrem had composed rhymes and verses for them to sing, and that they were singing them enthusiastically up to the time of writing. It became customary for the early church to include singing of hymns at all their gatherings, whether for public worship, or love feasts, or other occasions. In the beginning, it was common for lay people to lead the singing. Eusebius reported that the Emperor Constantine would sometimes lead in congregational singing.[40]

When, over time, early Christians built places of worship, they did not treat them as something holy. In fact, they did not hesitate to use them for other purposes. But with the "papists," an

37 Arnold, *Die Erste Liebe*, 147.
38 Arnold, *Die Erste Liebe*, 148.
39 Arnold, *Die Erste Liebe*, 152.
40 Arnold, *Die Erste Liebe*, 159–161.

idolatrous attitude soon arose, as they attached a holy awe to church buildings and called those who diminished their value "heretics." Groups such as the Waldensians, however, called church buildings mere "houses of stone," and considered them no more holy than a barn. It would be better to clothe the poor than use money to build great buildings for worship. Arnold cites a host of early Christian teachers who taught that the only true temple of God is the believer himself. Augustine wrote, "Do you wish to pray in a temple? Then pray within yourself, and may it always be that you are the temple of God."[41] Arnold notes that after the time of Constantine, attitudes changed. Arnold quotes from a proverb: "At one time Christians had wretched, dark churches but bright hearts; now they have bright, beautiful churches but dark hearts.... They had wooden chalices but golden priests; now there are golden chalices but wooden priests."[42]

In the time of the early church, Arnold writes, it is clear that all believers, not just their leaders, were enriched with the gifts of the Holy Spirit. It was not uncommon for lay people to demonstrate the miraculous gifts of prophecy, healing and exorcism. Tertullian refers to a Christian soldier who drove away an evil spirit, and parents who did the same for their children. As one ancient wrote:

> Do not worry that you are a layperson. God does not regard the status of people. Heaven stands open for the layperson who keeps God's commands just as much as for the clergy and monks. For all in equal measure can demonstrate the virtues of faith, love, and hope, and serve God from the heart.[43]

John Chrysostom observed that the first apostles were fishermen through whom Christ brought the gospel to all the nations and peoples of the world. They were poor in terms of wealth but rich in their innocent nature; lowly in social standing but high in holiness; commoners in terms of worldly profession but some-

---

41 Arnold, *Die Erste Liebe*, 175–176.

42 Arnold, *Die Erste Liebe*, 180.

43 Arnold, *Die Erste Liebe*, 198–199.

thing special in their calling from God. They believed in and practiced the priesthood of all believers.

As for women in the early church, Arnold observes that the church did not judge godliness according to gender, but according to the heart. When people are born anew in Christ, there is no longer male and female. In the Acts of the Apostles, there is mention of women among the disciples from the very beginning. And Paul makes mention of Lydia, Priscilla, Phoebe, Mariam, Tryphenam and Tryphosam. A young Christian woman from the early church stated: "We are created as much in the image of God as men. A woman prepared by the master worker is just as capable of godliness."[44] Tertullian believed that women were fully as capable of suffering for Christ as men were. Martyr histories are full of examples of heroic women who suffered for the name of Christ. And it is well known that the early church had the custom of ordaining women as deacons. There are also cases of women being ordained to the ministry, and having hands laid upon them.[45] But a day came when the rights of women and laity to minister were withdrawn from them. Women were later forbidden to sing and to approach the altar.

Arnold discussed the early church's use of Scripture in worship and preaching. He showed that the early church considered the New Testament to be more important and edifying for Christian worship than the Old Testament. This was because the Lord himself speaks to us in the New Testament and because the New is the fulfilment and completion of the Old. Gottfried Arnold, Philipp Jakob Spener and other pietists followed this ancient view; they encouraged German Christians to read the New Testament, especially, because it was easier for lay people to understand.[46] Arnold stirred up controversy when he argued that early Christians made use of Apocryphal books in their reading and worship, such as Siriac, The Book of Wisdom, Tobias, Judith and Esra, and that they even included these in the canon. The early church also read the letters and writings of the apostolic

---

44 Arnold, *Die Erste Liebe*, 209–210.

45 Arnold, *Die Erste Liebe*, 213.

46 Phillip Jakob Spener, *Pia Desideria: Deutsch-Lateinische Studienausgabe*, ed. Beate Köster (Giessen: Brunnen Verlag, 2005), 114, 116.

fathers in their services. Finally, early Christians were concerned that the common people should hear and read the Bible in their own language. Jerome translated the Bible into Latin so his countrymen could understand it.[47]

Preaching consisted of commentary on selected passages of Scripture and admonitions to Christian living and growth in faith and love. Tertullian wrote: "We come together to hear the words of holy Scripture: we feed our faith with its holy words; we set our hope on them; we receive the discipline of God's commands with many admonitions."[48] There was no emphasis upon oratorical skill, or upon rational argument based on human wisdom. Effective preaching was marked by simplicity and dependence upon the grace of the Holy Spirit. Sermons were generally "short and sweet" (*kurz und gut*), lasting a quarter hour or half an hour.[49] The pietists drew upon these precedents in criticizing orthodox Lutheran preachers and their displays of learning and scholarship in sermons.

Concerning the sacrament of baptism, Arnold observes that the early church baptized adults after they had been instructed in the faith. There is no evidence for baptism of children in the two centuries following the time of Christ and the apostles.[50] Early Christians associated baptism with conversion and new birth, because they could testify to having had these experiences, and could demonstrate the fruits of the Spirit.[51]

In discussing the Lord's supper, Arnold shows that the early church was careful not to admit any godless people to the celebration. He contrasts this with the practice in his own day: "It is very different with hypocritical Christians today, for one permits those who shame the Christian name [to participate]."[52] In the early church, sinners had to confess their fault before the whole church and perform works of satisfaction before being admitted back into fellowship and communion in the Lord's supper. Arnold notes that the first Christians "broke bread" daily (Acts

47 Arnold, *Die Erste Liebe*, 275.
48 Arnold, *Die Erste Liebe*, 276.
49 Arnold, *Die Erste Liebe*, 280, 287, 289.
50 Arnold, *Die Erste Liebe*, 305, 307.
51 Arnold, *Die Erste Liebe*, 315.
52 Arnold, *Die Erste Liebe*, 327.

2:46), so great were their love and devotion to Christ and his memory. For the ancients, the main benefits of the Lord's supper were union with Christ and fellow believers and strengthening of the new man.[53]

In summary, Arnold's picture of the early church contrasted sharply with the Lutheran and Reformed churches of his day. It was a church of believers who were advanced in godliness. Their prayers and singing, encouragement of the laity and women, and observance of preaching and the sacraments made them a model for later Christians.

Johanna Eleonora Petersen's view of the church in *Anleitung zu gründlicher Verständnis der Heiligen Offenbarung Jesu Christi* (1696)

Johanna Eleonora Petersen, nee von Merlau, (1644–1724) was the most influential female pietist of her day and author of fifteen books. Her writings reveal her to have been "an extraordinarily capable, educated, self-confident and class-conscious woman."[54] Her accomplishments included mastery of both Greek and Hebrew.[55] She always identified herself as Johanna Eleonora von und zu Merlau, reflecting her noble family background. She was one of the first pietists to compose an autobiography.[56]

Probably the greatest influences on von Merlau's thinking about the church were the Frankfurt separatist Johann Jakob Schütz (1640–1690), the writings of the English Philadelphian Jane Leade (1624–1704) and von Merlau's husband Johann Wilhelm Petersen (1649–1726). In May 1672, von Merlau happened to meet Schütz while on a ship to Mainz, and they had a conversation lasting several hours. They discussed issues of eschatology and the importance of serving Christ in simplicity

---

53 Arnold, *Die Erste Liebe*, 333, 335.

54 Prisca Guglielmetti, "Nachwort," in Johanna Eleonora Petersen geb. von und zu Merlau, *Leben, von ihr selbst mit eigener Hand aufgesetzet* (Leipzig: Evangelische Verlagsanstalt, 2003), 91–92.

55 Ruth Albrecht, *Johanna Eleonora Petersen: Theologische Schriftstellerin des frühen Pietismus* (Göttingen: Vandenhoeck & Ruprecht, 2005), 63.

56 Petersen's autobiography has recently been translated into English. See Barbara Becker-Cantarino, ed. and trans., *The Life of Lady Johanna Eleonora Petersen Written by Herself: Pietism and Women's Autobiography in Seventeenth-Century Germany* (Chicago: University of Chicago Press, 2005).

and holiness. In 1675, she moved to Frankfurt and joined Schütz as part of a group known as the Saalhof Pietists, who met on Sunday afternoons and during the week for edifying conversation and Bible study. The group eventually separated from the Lutheran Church, feeling they could no longer worship alongside those who were manifestly ungodly. The Saalhof pietist experience had a lasting impact on von Merlau.

In 1680, von Merlau married Johann Wilhelm Petersen, a Lutheran theologian and pastor. From 1678 to 1688, Petersen served as court preacher in Eutin. During this period of ministry, Petersen demonstrated little evidence of specifically pietist activity. However, his writings began to indicate strong spiritualist and separatist inclinations. In his 1685 *Spruchkatechismus*, a catechism supplemented by Bible texts, or *Bibelsprüche*, Petersen felt free to depart from Luther's catechism, observing that Luther was fallible, and his writings were not directly inspired by God.[57] Petersen's goal in the catechism was to nurture mature Christians who could argue for their faith from Scripture, without relying upon the help and authority of pastors. Petersen's catechism leaves out any discussion of confession to the pastor; for Petersen, the outer ministries of the church are unimportant in relation to the born again believer's inner relationship with God.[58]

In 1685, the Petersens became convinced of the truth of "the blessed thousand year kingdom" of Christ after reading a book by Jane Leade. In 1692, Johann Wilhelm began to produce what became an avalanche of works in defence of chiliastic teaching.[59] He soon came into conflict with Lutheran authorities over his millenarian preaching, and in January 1692 was dismissed from his pastoral position in the city of Lüneburg. Thereafter, he and his wife lived in relative peace and security on an estate in Niederndodeleben, near Magdeburg. Here they devoted much of their time to writing. The estate became a "communications

---

57 Markus Matthias, *Johann Wilhelm und Johanna Eleonora Petersen. Eine Biographie bis zur Amtsenthebung Petersens im Jahre 1692* (Göttingen: Vandenhoeck & Ruprecht, 1993), 152.

58 Matthias, *Johann Wilhelm und Johanna Eleonora Petersen*, 160.

59 In 1719 Petersen reported 67 printed books and over 100 works in manuscript ready for publication. See Johann Wilhelm Petersen, *Lebens-Beschreibung Jo. Wilhelmi Petersen, Die zweyte Edition* (1719), 397–402.

Johanna Eleonora Petersen (1644–1724)

center" for radical pietists, as a host of pietist figures visited them for extended periods, seeking advice and encouragement from the Petersens. Among the visitors was Gottfried Arnold, in May 1698.[60] The Petersens were greatly in demand as speakers in pietist conventicles in northern Germany.

Johanna Eleonora Petersen's 1696 book, *Anleitung zu gründlicher Verständniß der Heiligen Offenbahrung Jesu Christi* (Guide to a more in-depth understanding of the holy Revelation of Jesus Christ), is her most extensive discussion of chiliastic/millenarian ideas. Johanna later identified the *Anleitung* as the most important of all her works. The commentary is a valuable source for understanding Johanna Eleonora Petersen's attitude to the church of her day, and her hopes for the renewed church of the future.

In the Foreword to her commentary, Johanna Eleonora Petersen anticipates that many will criticize her for writing a work of biblical interpretation, because she is a woman. They will cite Paul's words in 1 Corinthians 14:34 and in 1 Timothy 2:12, that it is not fitting for a woman to teach in the church. Her reply is remarkable, and worth quoting at length:

> They should know that these words do not apply to me.... For I also know this: that in the distribution of grace and the Spirit, there is neither male nor female, Galatians 3:28, and that the grace and gift of God in a woman should not be quenched and suppressed according to Paul's instruction in 1 Thessalonians 5:19. For all the gifts of the Spirit, whether in men or women, have value and should be used for the common good, 1 Corinthians 12:7.... So while I know how to govern myself with proper submission in the Church of God, I also know that I have not received the gift

---

60 Hans Schneider, "Der radikale Pietismus im 18. Jahrhundert," in *Der Pietismus im achtzehnten Jahrhundert*, ed. Martin Brecht and Klaus Deppermann (Göttingen: Vandenhoeck & Ruprecht, 1995), 114–115; and Ruth Albrecht, *Johanna Eleonora Petersen: Theologische Schriftstellerin des frühen Pietismus* (Göttingen: Vandenhoeck & Ruprecht, 2005), 104–105. Their visitors included Anna Margaretha Jahn from Halberstadt in 1695; Adelheid Sybilla Schwartz and her husband in 1697; Gottfried Arnold in May 1698; the Swiss pietist Samuel König in summer 1700; and the Hessen radical theologian Heinrich Horch.

> of God to hide it under a bushel, but to use it to His honour and to the benefit of my neighbour…I know that I have been awakened by the urging of his Spirit to share these his gifts solely to his praise and to the good of my neighbour, in humility and love. I hope that this book may be a blessing to many souls in the present time and in the future.[61]

And so Petersen broke new ground as a Lutheran woman, in writing and then publishing a biblical commentary under her own name. To those who will say that she should have published it under her husband's name, she replies that she would have done so had her husband suggested it. But he was not so prideful as to think that he should prevent God's truth from being proclaimed by a weak, womanly vessel. By publishing the *Anleitung* under her own name, the world could see what the Lord had accomplished "through a weak, small and despised instrument."[62]

In her *Anleitung*, or Guide, Johanna Eleonora Petersen interprets the Book of Revelation as portraying the whole history and condition of the New Testament church, both in its humiliation and in its glory, which is soon to break forth at the end of time. This history is summed up by the seven churches of Revelation 2 and 3. For Petersen, this message should offer great encouragement to Christians, as they see how miraculously God's plan for the church will unfold.[63] The main focus of hope and encouragement for Petersen lies in the soon-coming Philadelphian age of the church, which offers a foretaste of the fullness of Christ's kingdom. In the Philadelphian age, the church will be marked by brotherly love and be blessed with the Spirit and power.[64]

But before the sixth Philadelphian age, the church must suffer greatly. "For when the little ship of the church of Christ suffers great deprivation in the waves of the sea of antichrist's kingdom, only then will Christ come and calm the sea."[65] The fifth age of the church, the Church of Sardis, is dominated by the papacy

---

61 Johanna Eleonora Petersen, *Anleitung zu gründlicher Verständnis der Heiligen Offenbarung Jesu Christi* (Frankfurt: Johann Daniel Müller, 1696), "Vorrede."

62 Petersen, *Anleitung zu gründlicher Verständnis der Heiligen Offenbarung*, "Vorrede."

63 Petersen, *Anleitung zu gründlicher Verständnis der Heiligen Offenbarung*, 4.

64 Petersen, *Anleitung zu gründlicher Verständnis der Heiligen Offenbarung*, 9.

65 Petersen, *Anleitung zu gründlicher Verständnis der Heiligen Offenbarung*, 14.

and scholasticism, which by human reason hides and destroys God's Word.[66] The angel says to this church, "I know your works, that you have the reputation of being alive, but you are dead" (Revelation 3:1). Petersen observes,

> This is an accurate description of its condition. For the blind Papacy prides itself as possessing the purity and truth of the first apostles and as being the true church. In fact, it is the mother of all fornication and perversion on earth, and has taken the holy scripture out of the hands of the poor people, and replaced it with human traditions. It has exchanged the saving words of our Lord Jesus Christ and the teaching of godliness with useless questions and battles of words and scholastic arguments.[67]

As imperfect as this age of the church may have been, there remained a small remnant within it who had not bowed down to Baal. Among these Petersen includes the Waldensians, Taborites and Hussites.

Noteworthy features of the Philadelphian age of the church include brotherly love, unity in the Spirit of Christ and disregard for sectarianism and divisions. This age of the church dawned initially with the Reformation and Martin Luther. But soon after Luther, there came a period of testing and falling away, and the simple truth of the gospel was perverted. The Protestants fell into sectarian divisions, and wrangling with one another, making their doctrinal statements the standard of Christian truth. And so Petersen concludes that, as great as the Reformation was, a greater and more glorious period is still to come.[68] Petersen observes that it is evident, in her day, that the Philadelphian age has begun to dawn in fullness, and that "many have been awakened by God to behold the deep mysteries of God, and to understand Scripture and the mysteries of the last days."[69] In the Philadelphian age there will be a separation of those who are

---

66 Petersen, *Anleitung zu gründlicher Verständnis der Heiligen Offenbarung*, 39.

67 Petersen, *Anleitung zu gründlicher Verständnis der Heiligen Offenbarung*, 51.

68 Petersen, *Anleitung zu gründlicher Verständnis der Heiligen Offenbarung*, 52–53, 294.

69 Petersen, *Anleitung zu gründlicher Verständnis der Heiligen Offenbarung*, 57.

Christians in deed and in truth from those who are Christian only in name and appearance.[70]

Conclusion

This study has examined the notion of Christian community in Gottfried Arnold and Johanna Eleonora Petersen, with special attention to the place they granted to women within the church. They both represent the spiritualist tendency within radical German pietism; for them, the born-again believer's personal relationship with Christ is paramount; church involvement and the sacraments are always secondary.

Gottfried Arnold offered sharp contrasts between the early church and the Lutheran and Reformed churches of his day. In the early church, believers were advanced in godliness. Their practice of prayer and singing, encouragement of the ministry of laity and women, and observance of preaching and the sacraments made them a model for later Christians. The early church did not judge godliness according to gender, but according to the heart.

It was clear to Johanna Eleonora Petersen that, soon after Luther, there came a period of falling away and the simple truth of the gospel was perverted. Protestants fell into sectarian divisions. Petersen looked for a church comprised of those who are Christians in deed and in truth, rather than Christian only in name and appearance. Petersen eloquently defended her right as a woman to use God's gifts for his glory and for the good of her neighbour, with humility and love.

The pietists' experimentation with new forms of religious community, and their theology and practice of the priesthood of all believers, would live on in the early evangelicalism of John Wesley and the Methodists. The pietist tendency to see the outer ministries of the church as unimportant in comparison with the born again believer's inner relationship with God continues to mark evangelical religion in England and North America. The pietist view of the church represents an important precursor to the evangelicalism that we know today.

---

70 Petersen, *Anleitung zu gründlicher Verständnis der Heiligen Offenbarung*, 140.

11

"To reconcile a Trinity of persons with the Scripture unity of God": Edward Sharman and his quarrel with Andrew Fuller

BY MICHAEL A.G. HAYKIN

In the late 1740s, the American divine Jonathan Edwards (1703–1758) described the intellectual *mentalité* of his day as "an age, as is supposed, of great light, freedom of thought, and discovery of truth in matters of religion, and detection of the weakness and bigotry of our ancestors, and of the folly and absurdity of the notions of those that were accounted eminent divines in former generations." As far as Edwards was concerned, however, the reality was there had never been "an age, wherein religion in general was so much despised and trampled on, and Jesus Christ and God Almighty so blasphemed and treated with open daring contempt."[1] Central among the ideas

It is a pleasure to be able to dedicate this essay on the most important theological truth of the Christian faith to my dear friend and colleague, Stan Fowler, a truly evangelical theologian.

1 Jonathan Edwards, *Humble Attempt in Apocalyptic Writings*, ed. Stephen J. Stein

held in extremely high regard by "eminent divines in former generations" was the doctrine of the Trinity. Since its creedal codification in the fourth century at the Councils of Nicaea (325) and Constantinople (381), trinitarianism had been fundamental to Christian theology. The exaltation of human reason as the primary epistemological determinant of truth in the long eighteenth century, however, raised major questions about this foundational doctrine, along with other key aspects of the Christian faith. A number of theological authors dismissed the doctrine of the Trinity as a philosophical and unbiblical construct of the post-apostolic church, and turned to classical Arianism as an alternate perspective, while others simply ridiculed it as utterly illogical and argued for Deism or Socinianism.[2] This concerted and heavy attack on the concept of a triune God ultimately led to what Philip Dixon has called a "fading of the trinitarian imagination."[3]

The Particular Baptists: a trinitarian community

Now, throughout this period of the long eighteenth century, the Particular Baptists in the British Isles had tenaciously confessed a trinitarian understanding of the Godhead and so, while other communities, such as the Presbyterians and General Baptists largely ceased to be trinitarian,[4] the Particular Baptists continued to regard themselves, and that rightly, as a trinitarian community.

(*The Works of Jonathan Edwards*, vol. 5; New Haven/London: Yale University Press, 1977), 359.

2 G.L. Bray, "Trinity" in *New Dictionary of Theology*, eds. Sinclair B. Ferguson, David F. Wright and J.I. Packer (Downers Grove: InterVarsity Press, 1988), 694. See the helpful overview of this era's trinitarianism and anti-trinitarianism by Stephen R. Holmes, *The Holy Trinity: Understanding God's Life* (Milton Keynes: Paternoster, 2012), 165–181.

3 See especially William C. Placher, *The Domestication of Transcendence. How Modern Thinking about God Went Wrong* (Louisville: Westminster John Knox Press, 1996), 164–178; Philip Dixon, *'Nice and Hot Disputes': The Doctrine of the Trinity in the Seventeenth Century* (London/New York: T & T Clark, 2003). The quote is from Dixon, *'Nice and Hot Disputes,'* 212. On the rise of Socinianism, see also Sarah Mortimer, *Reason and Religion in the English Revolution. The Challenge of Socinianism* (Cambridge: Cambridge University Press, 2010).

4 For the loss of trinitarianism among the General Baptists, see the helpful overview by Curtis W. Freeman, "God in Three Persons: Baptist Unitarianism and the Trinity," *Perspectives in Religious Studies*, 33 (Fall 2006): 324–328.

Their earliest confessional document, *The First London Confession of Faith* (1644/1646), had declared this about God:

> In [the]...Godhead, there is the Father, the Son, and the Spirit; being every one of them one and the same God; and therefore not divided, but distinguished one from another by their several properties; the Father being from himself, the Son of the Father from everlasting, the Holy Spirit proceeding from the Father and the Son.[5]

B.R. White has argued that this confession gave these early Baptists an extremely clear and self-conscious sense of their community's distinct identity and *raison d'être*.[6] And yet, as this specific paragraph also reveals, these Baptists were desirous of declaring their complete solidarity with the mainstream of classical Christianity that was rooted in the fourth-century trinitarian creedal declarations and that also included the mediæval Western church's commitment to the *Filioque*. The other major Particular Baptist confession of the seventeenth century, *The Second London Confession of Faith* (1677/1689), was equally forthright in its trinitarianism—in the words of Curtis Freeman, its "words...resonate with Nicene orthodoxy"[7]—and firmly linked this core Christian doctrine to spirituality. The "doctrine of the Trinity," it affirmed, "is the foundation of all our communion with God, and comfortable dependence on him."[8]

Throughout the long eighteenth century this community unhesitatingly maintained that this doctrine is, in the words of

5 *The First London Confession of Faith* 2 in William L. Lumpkin, *Baptist Confessions of Faith*, rev. Bill J. Leonard, 2nd rev. ed. (Valley Forge: Judson Press, 2011), 144. The spelling has been modernized.

6 See, in particular, the following publications by White: "The Organisation of the Particular Baptists, 1644–1660," *Journal of Ecclesiastical History*, 17 (1966): 209–226; "The Doctrine of the Church in the Particular Baptist Confession of 1644," *The Journal of Theological Studies*, ns, 19 (1968): 570–590; "Thomas Patient in Ireland," *Irish Baptist Historical Society Journal*, 2 (1969–1970): 36–48, especially 40–41; "The Origins and Convictions of the First Calvinistic Baptists," *Baptist History and Heritage*, 25, no.4 (October, 1990): 39–47; and *The English Baptists of the Seventeenth Century*, rev. ed. (London: The Baptist Historical Society, 1996), 59–94.

7 Freeman, "God in Three Persons," 331.

8 *The Second London Confession of Faith* 2.3 in Lumpkin, *Baptist Confessions of Faith*, 237.

Benjamin Wallin (1711–1782), the "first and grand principle of revealed truth and the gospel."[9] In 1690, the London Baptist layman Isaac Marlow (1649–1719), for example, published a treatise on the Trinity in which he stated his conviction that of those elements of divine truth that redound most to the glory of God and best further the fellowship of believers, "the blessed doctrine of the holy Trin-unity is the chiefest."[10] Nearly fifty years later, the renowned preacher Joseph Stennett II (1692–1758) similarly affirmed that "the doctrine of the ever blessed Trinity, is of the greatest importance to his [that is, God's] glory."[11]

The challenge of Socinianism

The major challenge to Particular Baptist trinitarianism came from Socinianism, which was the leading form of heterodoxy within English dissent in the last quarter of the eighteenth century.[12] In large part, this was due to the vigorous campaigning of Joseph Priestley (1733–1804), whom Michael R. Watts, in his study of the early history of British nonconformity, has dubbed the "Leonardo da Vinci of Dissent."[13] By his early twenties, Priestley was proficient in physics, philosophy and mathematics as well as a variety of modern and ancient Near Eastern languages. During the 1760s and 1770s his reputation as England's

---

9 *The eternal Existence of the Lord Jesus Christ considered and improved* (London, 1766), iv–v.

10 "To the Reader" in his *A Treatise of the Holy Trinunity* [*sic*] (London, 1690), [i–ii]. For a brief discussion of this work, see Freeman, "God in Three Persons," 332–333.

11 *The Christian Strife for the Faith of the Gospel* (London, 1738), 78, cited Roger Hayden, "The Contribution of Bernard Foskett" in *Pilgrim Pathways: Essays in Baptist History in Honour of B. R. White*, ed. William H. Brackney and Paul S. Fiddes with John H.Y. Briggs (Macon: Mercer University Press, 1999), 197.

12 H.L. Short, "Presbyterians under a New Name" in C.G. Bolam, et al., *The English Presbyterians from Elizabethan Puritanism to Modern Unitarianism* (London: George Allen & Unwin Ltd., 1968), 229–233.

13 *The Dissenters* (Oxford: Clarendon Press, 1978), 1:472. For the biographical details of Priestley's career, I am especially indebted to *The Memoirs of Dr. Joseph Priestley*, ed. John T. Boyer (Washington: Barcroft Press, 1964); Robert D. Fiala, "Priestley, Joseph (1733–1804)," *Biographical Dictionary of Modern British Radicals* (Hassocks, Sussex: Harvester Press/Atlantic Highlands, New Jersey: Humanities Press, 1979), 1:396–401; Erwin N. Hiebert, "The Integration of Revealed Religion and Scientific Materialism in the Thought of Joseph Priestley" in *Joseph Priestley: Scientist, Theologian, and Metaphysician*, ed. Lester Kieft and Bennett R. Willeford, Jr. (Lewisburg: Bucknell University Press, 1980), 27–61.

foremost experimental scientist was established by his publication of a weighty history of electrical experimentation and his discovery of ten new gases, including oxygen, ammonia and sulphur dioxide. Alongside this illustrious career as a scientist, Priestley was also a prolific and profound theological author. In fact, he regarded his work as a theologian as his true vocation.

After his conversion to the Socinian cause, which probably took place in 1769,[14] Priestley devoted much of his time to theological writing "with no other view," he baldly stated on one occasion, "than to make proselytes."[15] "An unflagging and often pugnacious controversialist," Priestley sought to establish his position not on nature and human reason, as did the Deists, but on a serious and rational investigation of the Scriptures and history.[16] As a Dissenter he had inherited the Protestant commitment to the Scriptures as a sufficient source of religious truth. "Revelation," as Martin Fitzpatrick has noted, "lay at the core of his religion."[17] This attachment to the Scriptures, though, was yoked to a deep-rooted conviction that the "plainest and most obvious sense of the Scriptures is in favour of those doctrines which are most agreeable to reason."[18] In other words,

---

14 Robert E. Schofield, "Priestley, Joseph (1733–1804)," *Oxford Dictionary of National Biography* (Oxford: Oxford University Press, 2004; online ed., May 2007 [http://www.oxforddnb.com.libaccess.lib.mcmaster.ca/view/article/22788]).

15 *Defences of Unitarianism, for the Year 1786* (1787) (*The Theological and Miscellaneous Works of Joseph Priestley*, ed. J.T. Rutt [New York: Klaus Reprint Co., 1972], 18:372). Later references to the corpus of Priestley will cite these works as *Works of Joseph Priestley*.

In a lecture that Fuller's friend Robert Hall, Jr. (1764–1831) gave "On the Spirit of Socinianism" in 1823, the Baptist preacher took note of the Socinians' "zeal for proselytism" (*The Works of the Rev. Robert Hall*, ed. Olinthus Gregory and Joseph Belcher [New York: Harper & Bros., 1854], 3:24).

16 For Priestley's threefold appeal to reason, Scripture and history, see his *Defences of Unitarianism, for the Year 1786* (*Works of Joseph Priestley*, 18:350); *An History of Early Opinions concerning Jesus Christ* (1786) (*Works of Joseph Priestley*, 6:7). The description of Priestley is that of Martin Fitzpatrick, "Toleration and Truth," *Enlightenment and Dissent*, 1 (1982): 25.

17 "Toleration and Truth," 29, n.119. On the commitment of Socinianism in general to Scripture, see Klaus Scholder, *The Birth of Modern Critical Theology. Origins and Problems of Biblical Criticism in the Seventeenth Century*, trans. John Bowden (London: SCM Press/Philadelphia: Trinity Press International, 1990), 32–38.

18 *An Appeal to the Serious and Candid Professors of Christianity* (1770) (*Works of Joseph Priestley*, 2:385). See also J.G. McEvoy and J.E. McGuire, "God and Nature: Priestley's Way of Rational Dissent," *Historical Studies in the Physical Sciences*, 6

the Scriptures do indeed contain divine revelation, but their interpretation is to be determined by what is in accord with sound reason.

Priestley did not deny that there were certain affirmations of Scripture which were beyond the grasp of human reason. He admitted, for example, the historicity of many of the miracles of the apostolic era, including the bodily resurrection of Christ.[19] What he refused to countenance, though, were interpretations of Scripture which, to his mind, entailed a logical contradiction. This explains why orthodox trinitarianism bore the brunt of Priestley's theological polemic.[20] Priestley was convinced that the doctrine of the Trinity not only had no scriptural foundation, but it was also a mathematical impossibility, "since three cannot be one, or one, three."[21] From Priestley's perspective, if there is one divine being, there must perforce be one person and thus one God; if there are three divine persons, then there must be three divine beings and so three gods. Hence Priestley made "a strict Patrolatry...[a] central and distinguishing" feature of his theological system. [22]

The threat that Socinianism posed to trinitarian orthodoxy among the Particular Baptists is well illustrated by three incidents taken from the life of the leading Baptist apologist of the late eighteenth century, Andrew Fuller (1753–1815). When Fuller came to write the memoirs of his friend Samuel Pearce (1766–1799), the pastor of Cannon Street Particular Baptist Church in Birmingham, he included a letter which Pearce had written to his friend William Steadman (1764–1837) on February 1, 1793.

(1975): 325–326; Fitzpatrick, "Toleration and Truth," 4–5.

19 *An History of the Corruptions of Christianity* (1782 ed.; reprint, New York/London: Garland Publishing, 1974), II, 440.

20 Cf. Scholder, *Modern Critical Theology*, 40; Geoffrey Gorham, "Seventeenth- and Eighteenth-Century Intellectual Life" in *The Routledge Companion to Theism*, ed. Charles Taliaferro, Victoria S. Harrison and Stewart Goetz (New York/London: Routledge, 2013), 129–130.

21 *Defences of Unitarianism, for the Years 1788 and 1789* (1790) (*Works of Joseph Priestley*, 19:108). See also his *Appeal to the Serious and Candid Professors of Christianity* (*Works of Joseph Priestley*, 2:395); *History of Early Opinions concerning Jesus Christ* (*Works of Joseph Priestley*, 6:33–37); *Letters to the Members of the New Jerusalem Church* (Birmingham, 1791), 2.

22 Alexander Gordon, *Addresses Biographical and Historical* (London: The Lindsey Press, 1922), 276.

In it Pearce mentioned that he had been "much perplexed about some doctrinal points, both Arminian and Socinian" through the close reading of the writings of Priestley among others. Happily, Fuller noted, his perplexity was but transient, and "by the overruling grace of God, [it] tended only to establish him more firmly" in trinitarian convictions.[23] On the other hand, James Lyons (1768–1824), the pastor of the Particular Baptist Church in what is now Kingston Upon Hull, became a Socinian in 1807 through the writings of Richard Wright (1764–1836), an ardent propagator of Socinianism. Despite the fact that Fuller sent Lyons a number of pamphlets to help him maintain a firm grasp on trinitarian doctrine, Lyons became "convinced that there are no such doctrines in the sacred Scriptures as that of the Trinity, [or] the equality of Jesus Christ with his Father" and he subsequently resigned his pastorate.[24]

Edward Sharman's attack on Fuller's trinitarianism

A decade or so earlier, Edward Sharman (fl.1780–1800) had also been converted to Socinian principles. Sharman was originally a member of the College Street Church in Northampton under the powerful, though eccentric, ministry of John Collett Ryland (1723–1792).[25] In 1781 he was dismissed to help found Guilsborough Baptist Church in Northamptonshire, and by 1790 he had become the pastor of the Baptist work in the village of Moulton, William Carey's (1761–1834) first charge. In the fall of 1792 he was one of the founders of the Baptist Missionary Society. Two years later, though, he was asked various queries about the Trinity by a day-labourer for which he was unable to

23 *Memoirs of the Rev. Samuel Pearce* in *The Complete Works of the Rev. Andrew Fuller*, ed. Joseph Belcher (1845 ed.; reprint, Harrisonburg: Sprinkle Publications, 1988), III, 374 and 431. These volumes will be cited as *Works of the Rev. Andrew Fuller.*

24 H.D. Roberts, *Matthew Henry and His Chapel 1662–1900* (Liverpool: The Liverpool Booksellers' Co., 1901), 204–206, n.1. On the career of Richard Wright, see Gordon, *Addresses*, 311–339.

25 For what follows on the career of Sharman, see John Taylor, *History of College Street Church, Northampton* (Northampton: Taylor & Son, The Dryden Press, 1897), 86; John Rippon, *The Baptist Annual Register* (London, 1793), 1:10; John Rippon, *The Baptist Annual Register* (London, 1797), 2:10; John Rippon, *The Baptist Annual Register* (London, 1800), 3:28; Timothy D. Whelan, transcribed and ed., *Baptist Autographs in the John Rylands Library of Manchester, 1741–1845* (Macon: Mercer University Press, 2009), 446.

provide a satisfactory answer. He later claimed that it was these questions that prompted him to search the Scriptures, to question his previous trinitarian convictions and to come to the view that the Socinian perspective better fit the biblical evidence.

When Sharman began to share his new-found views with some of his fellow Baptists, including John Webster Morris (1763–1836), the printer-pastor of Clipstone, Northamptonshire, and Andrew Fuller, he found himself in the midst of what he described as "a dreadful storm." Some called him a heretic as he had "forsaken the only foundation of the saints," while others like Morris considered him "a little deranged."[26] Sharman's response was to publish a series of four tracts on the subject of the Trinity, in one of which he personally took Morris to task for remarks the latter had written to him in a letter.[27] In another of these pieces he expressed the opinion that his differences with trinitarians like Fuller were really over a matter "so very trifling," though his subsequent argumentation reveals that this was hardly a tertiary issue for Sharman himself.[28] The final tract, published in 1800, was addressed to Fuller himself and entitled *A Second Caution against Trinitarianism; or, An Inquiry whether that System has not some tendency to lead people unto Deism and Atheism. In a letter addressed to the Rev. Mr. Fuller, Kettering.*[29]

In this piece Sharman did not hesitate to affirm that Christ was a "finite dependant character" and that only God the Father, being "the only one Almighty God and supreme Governor of all," was worthy of worship. It was, therefore, shameful for Fuller and other trinitarians to worship Christ, who was but a servant and "inferior messenger," for they were guilty of "dethroning Jehovah from the government of his own world."[30] Far from be-

---

26 *A Letter on the Doctrine of the Trinity; Addressed to the Baptist Society, at Guilsborough, Northamptonshire* (London: J. Johnson, 1795), 4–9. See also Andrew Fuller, Letter to William Carey, May 2, 1796 (cited Whelan, transcribed and ed., *Baptist Autographs*, 446).

27 *A Letter on the Doctrine of the Trinity*, 3–13.

28 *A Second Letter on the Doctrine of the Trinity* (Market Harborough: W. Harrod, 1796), 7–9.

29 *A Second Caution against Trinitarianism; or, An Inquiry whether that System has not some tendency to lead people unto Deism and Atheism. In a letter addressed to the Rev. Mr. Fuller, Kettering* (Market Harborough: W. Harrod, 1800).

30 *Second Caution against Trinitarianism*, 7, 9, 11.

ing a man wise in his understanding of the God of the Scriptures, Fuller was actually ignorant of the Bible, for, Sharman argued, the "mystical plan that Mr. F. had taught me, to reconcile a trinity of persons with the scripture unity of God, I now found to be real polytheism in disguise." In other words, the embrace of Fuller's trinitarian worship, "instead of deserving the name of promoting Christianity...will lead me into Deism and Atheism!"—hence the title of this final tract.[31] To add insult to injury, Sharman argued that his new perspective on Christianity was the result of adhering to Fuller's principle that "we must learn what is divine truth immediately from the oracles of God" and we have to "let what God has revealed be the only standard to determine what is right."[32]

Responding to Sharman?

Four years earlier, after Sharman had published but one of his four anti-trinitarian tracts, Fuller had written to William Carey that though "it be a blundering performance, it must be answered."[33] But Fuller never did get around to writing an answer to Sharman, for the simple reason that he was far too busy with other vital ministries. What might he have said and how might he have argued?

First of all, Fuller regarded Socinianism's denial of Christ's deity as being akin to Deism, and this could only lead to the total ruination of the virtuous life.[34] As he put it in a sermon he preached in 1801: "The person and work of Christ have ever been the corner-stone of the Christian fabric: take away his Divinity and atonement, and all will go to ruins."[35] Christ's deity and his atoning work are "the life-blood of Christianity"; deny them and there is only death.[36] Fuller would thus have insisted

31 *Second Caution against Trinitarianism*, 12, 24, 27.

32 *Second Caution against Trinitarianism*, 27, 33.

33 Andrew Fuller, Letter to William Carey, May 2, 1796 (cited Whelan, transcribed and ed., *Baptist Autographs*, 446).

34 *Calvinistic and Socinian Systems* (*Works of the Rev. Andrew Fuller*, II, 220–233).

35 *God's Approbation of Our Labours Necessary to the Hope of Success* (*Works of the Rev. Andrew Fuller*, I, 190). See also *Calvinistic and Socinian Systems* (*Works of the Rev. Andrew Fuller*, II, 183); *The Backslider* (*Works of the Rev. Andrew Fuller*, III, 637).

36 *Christian Steadfastness* (*Works of the Rev. Andrew Fuller*, I, 527). See also *Calvinistic and Socinian Systems* (*Works of the Rev. Andrew Fuller*, II, 183, 191–192).

that without the confession of the deity of Christ, one simply cannot be counted as a Christian, for "the proper Deity of Christ...is a great and fundamental truth in Christianity."[37]

Fuller probably would not have emphasized the divinity of the Holy Spirit, though he did believe that the Scriptures "expressly call...the Holy Spirit God" in Acts 5:3–4 and he did not hesitate to assert that "every perfection of Godhead" has been ascribed to the Spirit.[38] While Fuller, like others impacted by the evangelical revivals of the eighteenth century, had a robust understanding of the Spirit's work and ministry,[39] Priestley, Sharman and the other apostles of Socinianism focused their attention overwhelmingly upon Christ and not the Holy Spirit. And that is where Fuller would have defended the faith. On one occasion when Fuller referred to the first principles of Christianity he believed were the focus of the Socinian controversy, he listed the doctrine of the Trinity, the deity of Christ and the atoning death of the Lord Jesus,[40] not the distinct deity of the Spirit. Fuller's defence of the deity of Christ and the propriety of worshipping him is therefore akin to the way that Athanasius argued in the fourth century. The Egyptian church father also spent most of his time and energy defending the full and essential divinity of Christ in the face of the Arian onslaught against Christ's person. Only near the end of his life did Athanasius turn his attention to the Spirit.[41] However, Fuller was also aware that the Spirit's

37 *Calvinistic and Socinian Systems* (*Works of the Rev. Andrew Fuller*, II, 180); Justification (*Works of the Rev. Andrew Fuller*, I, 284); *Calvinistic and Socinian Systems* (*Works of the Rev. Andrew Fuller*, II, 183, 191–192); *Defence of a Treatise Entitled The Gospel of Christ* (*Works of the Rev. Andrew Fuller*, II, 458); "Decline of the Dissenting Interest" (*Works of the Rev. Andrew Fuller*, III, 487); "The Deity of Christ" (*Works of the Rev. Andrew Fuller*, III, 693–697); *Calvinistic and Socinian Systems* (*Works of the Rev. Andrew Fuller*, II, 180).

38 "Defence of the Deity of Christ" (*Works of the Rev. Andrew Fuller*, III, 698); "Remarks on the Indwelling Scheme" (*Works of the Rev. Andrew Fuller*, III, 700). See also *Letters on Systematic Divinity* (*Works of the Rev. Andrew Fuller*, I, 711); "Mr. Bevan's Defence of the Christian Doctrines of the Society of Friends" (*Works of the Rev. Andrew Fuller*, III, 758).

39 See, for example, his *Causes of Declension in Religion, and Means of Revival* (*Works of the Rev. Andrew Fuller*, III, 319–320, 324) and *The Promise of the Spirit the Grand Encouragement in Promoting the Gospel* (*Works of the Rev. Andrew Fuller*, III, 359–363).

40 *Socinianism Indefensible* (*Works of the Rev. Andrew Fuller*, II, 249).

41 See his *Letters to Serapion*, written in the late 350s. Athanasius died in 373. See further my *The Spirit of God: The Exegesis of 1 and 2 Corinthians in the Pneumatomachian*

Andrew Fuller (1753–1815)

overarching new covenant ministry is the glorification of the Lord Jesus—the "Holy Spirit is not the grand object of ministerial exhibition; but Christ, in his person, work and offices"—and this is a key reason why "much less is said in the Sacred Scriptures on the Divinity and personality of the Holy Spirit."[42]

Finally, with regard to statements about the Trinity, Fuller would have argued that the Scriptures affirm the existence of three divine persons—the Father and the Son and the Holy Spirit.[43] These three are never to be considered three separate beings, but one God. As Fuller put it: "in a mysterious manner, far above our comprehension, there are in the Divine unity three subsistences."[44] How they are one has not been revealed—and so to believe it steadfastly requires faith and humility.[45] Moreover, this is a truth that must be regarded as being above reason, not against it nor a contradiction. As long as Christian theology does not make the mistake of the Socinians, which is to regard God as unipersonal, it can affirm this truth without fear of being irrational. In this Christians need to "regulate [their] ideas of the Divine Unity by what is taught us in the Scriptures of the Trinity; and not those of the Trinity by what we know, or think we know... of the Unity."[46]

Fuller's convictions upon baptism might also have been used to support his defence of trinitarianism against Sharman. His main piece on this ordinance was *The Practical Uses of Christian Baptism*, a highly significant tract on the meaning of baptism.

Controversy of the Fourth Century (Leiden: E.J. Brill, 1994).

42 *Letters on Systematic Divinity* (*Works of the Rev. Andrew Fuller*, I, 711).

43 See *Jesus the True Messiah* (1809) (*Works of the Rev. Andrew Fuller*, I, 219); "Passages Apparently Contradictory" (*Works of the Rev. Andrew Fuller*, I, 668); "Remarks on the Indwelling Scheme" (*Works of the Rev. Andrew Fuller*, III, 700); "The Doctrine of the Trinity" (*Works of the Rev. Andrew Fuller*, I, 707–708). In the last of these passages Fuller cites a catena of trinitarian texts, including Matthew 28:19; 1 John 5:7; Romans 15:30; Ephesians 2:18; Jude 20–21; 2 Thessalonians 3:5; and 2 Corinthians 13:14.

44 "The Doctrine of the Trinity" (*Works of the Rev. Andrew Fuller*, I, 708).

45 *Nature and Importance of an Intimate Knowledge of Divine Truth* (1796) (*Works of the Rev. Andrew Fuller*, I, 163–164).

46 *Letters on Systematic Divinity* (*Works of the Rev. Andrew Fuller*, I, 708); "Remarks on the Indwelling Scheme" (*Works of the Rev. Andrew Fuller*, III, 700). Cf. *Walking by Faith* (1784) (*Works of the Rev. Andrew Fuller*, I, 124–125): "It is one thing to say that Scripture is contrary to right reason, and another thing to say that it may exhibit truths too great for our reason to grasp."; "Trial of Spirits" (*Works of the Rev. Andrew Fuller*, I, 654).

Fuller argued that since baptism is to be carried out, according to Matthew 28:19, "in the name of the Father, and of the Son, and of the Holy Spirit," submission to the ordinance entails an avowal of the fact that God is a triune Being. Well acquainted with the history of the early church at this point, Fuller rightly stated that this baptismal formula was widely used in that era to argue for the doctrine of the Trinity.[47] To relinquish the doctrine of the Trinity is thus tantamount to the virtual renunciation of one's baptism.[48]

Fuller tied baptism to the Trinity again, and also to worship, in another small piece entitled "The Manner in which Divine Truth is Communicated in the Holy Scriptures." He wrote:

> The doctrine of the Trinity is never proposed to us as an object of speculation, but as a truth affecting our dearest interests. John introduces the sacred Three as witnesses to the truth of the gospel of Christ, as objects of instituted worship, into whose name we are baptized; and Paul exhibits them as the source of all spiritual good: "The grace of the Lord Jesus Christ, the love of God, and the communion of the Holy Spirit be with you all. Amen." [2 Corinthians 13:14]. Again, "The Lord direct your hearts into the love of God, and into the patient waiting for Christ." [2 Thessalonians 3:5].[49]

What is noteworthy about this text is the refusal to see the Trinity as merely a "metaphysical mystery," or as Fuller put it, "an object

47 *The Practical Uses of Christian Baptism* (*Works of the Rev. Andrew Fuller*, III, 340). The very same point had been made a quarter of a century earlier by John Collett Ryland. Also writing in a circular letter for the Northamptonshire Association, Ryland had observed that "the true doctrine of the Trinity" had been "kept up in the Christian church" by the ordinance of baptism "more than by any other means whatsoever" (*The Beauty of Social Religion; or, The Nature and Glory of a Gospel Church* [Northampton: T. Dicey, 1777], 10, footnote).

48 *Christian Baptism* (*Works of the Rev. Andrew Fuller*, III, 340). For other instances of Fuller's trinitarian exegesis of Matthew 28:19, see *Calvinistic and Socinian Systems* (*Works of the Rev. Andrew Fuller*, II, 236); "On the Sonship of Christ" (*Works of the Rev. Andrew Fuller*, III, 705–706).

49 "The Manner in which Divine Truth is Communicated in the Holy Scriptures" (*Works of the Rev. Andrew Fuller*, III, 539).

of speculation."[50] Rather, Fuller emphasized that the doctrine has a bearing on our "dearest interests," namely, the truth as it is in the gospel, worship, and "all spiritual good." The first item, the truth of the gospel, is supported by an allusion to 1 John 5:7, the famous *Comma Johanneum*, which Fuller evidently regarded as genuine.[51] For the third point, "all spiritual good," Fuller has recourse to 2 Corinthians 13:14 and 2 Thessalonians 3:5. The use of the latter Pauline text is fascinating. Fuller's trinitarian reading of it ultimately goes back to Basil of Caesarea (*c.* A.D. 329–379), who employs it in his argument for the Spirit's deity in his classic work, *On the Holy Spirit*.[52] Fuller most likely found this reading of the Pauline verse, however, in John Gill's commentary on 2 Thessalonians 3:5, where Gill follows Basil's interpretation.[53]

It is with regard to the second point, the Trinity as the object of adoration, that Fuller mentions baptism: "the sacred Three" are described "as objects of instituted worship, into whose name we are baptized." Fuller was presumably thinking of Matthew 28:19. The reason why doctrinal confession of the triunity of God is vital is because it lies at the heart of Christian worship. Fuller clearly saw baptism into the name of the triune God as not only the initiatory rite of the church—what made it a "trinitarian community"—but also the beginning of a life of

---

50 For the phrase "metaphysical mystery," I am indebted to Stephen Holmes. See "The Quest for the Trinity: An Interview with Stephen R. Holmes," *Credo Magazine*, 3, no.2 (April 2013): 49.

51 See his extended argument in *Letters on Systematic Divinity* (*Works of the Rev. Andrew Fuller*, I, 708–709).

52 See Basil of Caesarea, *On the Holy Spirit* 21.52.

53 Here is the relevant section of Gill's comments on this verse: "The phrase of directing the heart to God...is not to be done by a believer himself, nor by the ministers of the Gospel: the apostle could not do it, and therefore he prays "the Lord" to do it; by whom is meant the Spirit of God, since he is distinguished from God the Father, into whose love the heart is to be directed, and from Christ, a patient waiting for whom 'tis also desired the heart may be directed into; and since it is his work to shed abroad the love of God in the heart, and to lead unto it, and make application of it; and which is a proof of his deity, for none has the direction, management, and government of the heart, but God,...and in this passage of Scripture appear all the three Persons [of the Godhead]; for here is the love of the Father, patient waiting for Christ, and the Lord the Spirit." John Gill, *An Exposition of the New Testament* (1809 ed.; reprint, Paris: The Baptist Standard Bearer, 1989), III, 265. See also John Gill, *The Doctrine of the Trinity, Stated and Vindicated* (London: Aaron Ward, 1731), 198–199.

worshipping the Trinity that would ultimately culminate in the beatific vision of the Trinity.

Such might have been the shape of Andrew Fuller's reply to Edward Sharman, his "once intimate friend."[54]

---

54 These are Sharman's words for Fuller: see his *Second Caution against Trinitarianism*, 72.

Practical

12

"For the good of the Baptist interest": The work of the Particular Baptist associations

BY JAMES M. RENIHAN

Baptist associations have been, from their inception in the 1640s, working associations.[1] More than simply ministerial fraternals, they came into existence as a means of mutual encouragement and support in the face of overwhelming opposition, and even after

1 Slayden A. Yarborough, "The Origin of Baptist Associations among the English Particular Baptists," *Baptist History and Heritage* 23, no.2 (April 1988): 14–24; B.R. White, "The Doctrine of the Church in the Particular Baptist Confession of 1644," *Journal of Theological Studies* n.s., 19, no.2 (October 1968): 583ff; White, "The Organization of the Particular Baptists, 1644–1660," *Journal of Ecclesiastical History* 17, no.2 (October 1966): 216ff; Geoffrey F. Nuttall, "*The Baptist Western Association 1653–1658*," *Journal of Ecclesiastical History* 11 (1960): 213–218; Walter B. Shurden, *Associationalism among Baptists of America 1707–1814* (New York: Arno Press, 1980); Shurden, "Minutes of the Philadelphia Baptist Association," *The Center for Baptist Studies*; http://centerforbaptiststudies.org/resources/philadelphia.htm; accessed March 19, 2015. Some of the material here is from James M. Renihan, *Edification and Beauty* (Milton Keynes: Paternoster, 2008), 173ff.

periods of persecution ended, continued to be of great blessing to the churches.

Baptist ecclesiology developed out of the matrix of English Puritan and Separatist churches of the sixteenth and seventeenth centuries.[2] In the slow and gradual emergence from Rome, questions were continually asked about doctrine and practice. The most important issues as perceived by the reformers—justification by faith alone, or the authority of Scripture alone—were the first to receive careful attention. But as these matters were settled and consensus developed, other doctrinal issues surfaced for examination. For more than a century after the initial stages of reformation, discussion and debate marked the life of the churches of northern Europe. The doctrine of associations must be understood as part of this process.

While many consider the medieval Roman church to be a great monolith, the situation was somewhat more complex. Certainly authority focused on the papacy, but it must be recognized that churches were frequently identified closely with political jurisdictions, or perhaps it is better to state that "locally run churches"[3] existed, one often being different from another. Each of these "national" churches (and we must remember that the idea of "nation" was somewhat different 500 years ago) maintained a certain amount of autonomy. So long as they figuratively bowed to Rome, they were allowed to develop along their own trajectories. In 1500, just prior to the Reformation, the church in England, for example, would have been very different from the church in Spain.

The reformers inherited this notion of churches identified with political entities, as seen, for example, in both Lutheran and Presbyterian ecclesiologies. While the American versions of these have been altered somewhat, most of the older European versions continue to think of themselves as the church in whatever country they happen to be located.

By the late sixteenth century in England, a growing separatist movement was developing. The men of this movement, some-

---

[2] Renihan, *Edification and Beauty*, 1–36.

[3] Diarmaid MacCulloch, *The Reformation* (New York: Viking, 2003), 41–50, especially 49–50.

times called "hasty puritans" were unwilling to wait for progress to come through the slow process of reform advocated by the leadership of the national church. They believed that the Bible provided a blueprint for the church, and that it should be followed without hesitation or delay. When it became clear that the hierarchy was not amenable to this program of reform, these men took the daring step of separating from the Church of England, and forming independent congregations outside of its authority. This was not an easy step—perhaps it is difficult for us to realize just how painful such an act would have been, and why it was viewed with such horror—but these men believed that conscience and not convenience must have priority. One by one, these congregations emerged, often faced with severe hardship, opposition and persecution. Many fled to Holland, others were hounded by the authorities and forced into hiding, or even out of existence.

Coming out of this national church environment, they recognized that there was another end of the spectrum, and they found that place as unattractive as the one from which they had come. The opposite end was isolation. While these separatists rejected external control of their church, they also rejected the notion that churches were entities to themselves, without any kind of mutual obligation between congregations. This is addressed in the Separatist *True Confession* written in 1596, a document which served as the basis for the *The First London Baptist Confession* (1644):[4]

> 38 That though Congregations bee thus distinct and severall bodyes, every one as a compact Citie in it self, yet are they all to walk by one and the same rule, & by all meanes convenient to have the counsell and help one of another in all needfull affayres of the church, as members of one body in the common Faith, under Christ their head.[5]

---

4 James M. Renihan, *True Confessions: Baptist Documents in the Reformed Family* (Palmdale: Reformed Baptist Academic Press, 2004), 3–58.

5 Williston Walker, *The Creeds and Platforms of Congregationalism* (New York: Charles Scribner's Sons, 1893), 71.

This language is almost exactly repeated in *The First London Confession of Faith* (1644). Independency did not mean the rejection of inter-dependency. It simply meant that new and hopefully more scriptural forms must be developed to ensure that churches walk by the same rule, and may counsel and help each other in their lives as churches. While the separatists rejected national churches in the sense of Episcopacy or Presbyterianism, they recognized that there was still, of necessity, a place for significant inter-church cooperation, on the basis of geography.

The Particular Baptists, who came directly out of this separatist environment,[6] adopted this idea and turned it into what may be called *associationalism*. It is the recognition that there are some kinds of ties, providentially placed on churches, which bind them together in mutual obligation. The great question is simply, how did this work in practice? In order to handle this topic simply, I wish to present two general categories: 1. The work of associations at their general meetings; 2. The work of associations outside their general meetings. Using these two divisions, we shall be able to describe the functions of Baptist associations.

The work of associations at their general meetings

Perhaps the best place to begin is with the London General Assembly of 1689. When the Act of Toleration was passed, and persecution was ended, it was generally recognized that serious deficiencies existed in many of the churches. The first generation of ministers was almost gone from the scene (only William Kiffin, Hanserd Knollys and Henry Forty remained from the signers of the First Confession), several other important leaders had died during the years of persecution, and in some churches reluctance to give financial support to their pastors had taken hold. It was these problems, among others, that led to the call for a General Assembly issued by London ministers in July 1689. In the letter sent out to call for the Assembly, the London pastors state,

---

6 James M. Renihan, "'Truly Reformed in a Great Measure': A Brief Defense of the English Separatist Origins of Modern Baptists," *The Journal of Baptist Studies* 3 (2009): 24–32 [http://baptiststudiesonline.com/276-2/renihan-english-separatism/; accessed July 11, 2016].

> the great neglect of the present ministry is one thing, together with that general unconcernedness there generally seems to be, of giving fit and proper encouragement for the raising up an able and honourable ministry for the time to come; with many other things which, we hope, we are not left wholly in the dark about, which we find we are not in a capacity to prevent and cure (as instruments in the hand of God, and his blessing attending our christian endeavours) unless we can obtain a general meeting here in London.[7]

This letter argues that there are several pressing issues, especially the lack of pastoral support and the need for pastoral training, which could only be remedied by a "general meeting."

When the London elders called for the first national General Assembly in 1689, they requested of the churches around the country, "that you would be pleased to appoint two of your brethren—one of the ministry, and one principal brother of your congregation with him—as your messengers."[8] The 1689 General Assembly *Narrative* records the names of 155 individuals in its account of the churches that attended or communicated with the Assembly.[9] At least 79 of the men present were preachers and teachers in the churches. The majority of the other 76 attendees were probably laymen.[10] This makes the mixture at the initial General Assembly to be almost exactly what the London elders had asked for in their letter.[11]

---

7 Joseph Ivimey, *History of the English Baptists* (London: B.J. Holdsworth, 1811), 1:478–480.

8 Ivimey, *History of the English Baptists*, 1:479.

9 *A Narrative of the Proceedings of the General Assembly of Divers Pastors, Messengers and Ministring-Brethren of the Baptized Churches, Met Together in London, from Septemb. 3. To 12. 1689, from Divers Parts of England and Wales: Owning the Doctrine of Personal Election, and Final Perseverance* (London: n.p., 1689), 19–25.

10 Crosby says, "I cannot but observe…the prudent conduct of the ministers of the English Baptists, who, in all their publick administrations, either in general assemblies, or particular associations, have always required two or more judicious gentlemen of the laity, from each church, chosen by the congregation, to assemble with them, to aid and assist in all their debates and determinations." Thomas Crosby, *History of the English Baptists* (London: John Robinson, 1740), 3:295–296. While he overstated the number of laymen requested, the point is well taken.

11 This does not mean that every church sent one minister and one "principal brother." Many sent only one representative, while some of the London churches

The initial London General Assembly met for eight days. The first day of the Assembly was spent in "humbling ourselves before the Lord, and to seek of him a right way to direct into the best Means and Method to repair our Breaches, and to recover our selves into our former Order, Beauty, and Glory."[12]

The second day was spent in organizing and determining the bylaws of the Assembly, and in reading letters from the churches. Seven rules were agreed upon for the proceedings. The messengers disavowed any kind of "superiority," "superintendency," "authority," or "power" over any churches,[13] and refused to allow differences over open and closed membership to divide them. In the case of offenses between churches or individuals, they would not allow discussion until "the rule Christ hath given"[14] was applied and both parties consented to have the issue discussed. No decisions would be binding on any churches until they themselves gave consent; that all decisions be supported by Scripture; that the report of the meeting would be published; that the only messengers allowed to sit in the assembly would be those "recommended by a Letter from the Church;" and that speakers would only be allowed by general consent.[15] No mention is made of an individual moderator, or of any sermons preached during the week.

Beginning on the third day, proposals and recommendations were made. A fast day was called in all the churches, to be observed on October 10. They unanimously adopted the 1677 *Confession of Faith*, and urged all the members of each church to familiarize themselves with its contents. Similarly, they declared their "Approbation" of the anonymously published book *The Gospel Minister's Maintenance Vindicated* and urged that every church obtain a copy.[16]

---

sent as many as 4.

12 *1689 Narrative*, 9.

13 This is in contrast to the General Baptists who practiced a more centralized structure. See J.F.V. Nicholson, "The Office of 'Messenger' amongst the British Baptists in the Seventeenth and Eighteenth Centuries," *The Baptist Quarterly* 17 (1957–1958): 212–213; John Inscore Essick, *Thomas Grantham: God's Messenger from Lincolnshire* (Macon: Mercer University Press, 2013), 70ff.

14 Presumably, this refers to the process of settling offenses in Matthew 18:15–17.

15 *1689 Narrative*, 10.

16 *1689 Narrative*, 7, 18.

Perhaps the most important item of business discussed by the messengers was what would later become known as the Particular Baptist Fund. This fund was established as a means to help poor ministers and encourage young men to pursue the ministry. It was to be administered by a committee of nine men from different London churches. These men were authorized to solicit, receive and distribute financial contributions from the member churches for the support of poor pastors and young men desiring to train for the ministry. The churches were strongly urged to participate in this fund.[17] In the *Narratives*, one notices that much of the discussion at the assemblies was taken up with organizing and promoting the fund. At the 1690 Assembly, they modified the working of the fund, and expanded the board of trustees to twelve (although five was a quorum).[18] The *Narrative* from that year stated that preachers were sent out at the expense of the fund, and were well received in Essex and Suffolk, so much so that "divers were baptized, and two Churches are like to be gathered."[19] The *1691 Narrative* is mostly taken up with matters relating to the fund, especially exhortations to churches to give liberally,[20] and the *1692 Narrative* similarly continues the emphasis on the importance of the fund.[21] Cooperative effort was considered a primary function of the general assemblies.

In addition to the establishment of this fund, the Assembly did what virtually every Baptist Association has done: they debated a series of theological and practical questions, seeking to ascertain from the Scriptures answers to these queries from the churches. In all, eight days were filled with these matters.

---

17 *1689 Narrative*, 10–12.

18 *A Narrative of the Proceedings of the General Assembly of the Elders and Messengers of the Baptized Churches Sent from Divers Parts of England and Wales, Which Began in London the 9th of June, and Ended the 16th of the Same, 1690* (London: n.p., 1690) 7.

19 *1690 Narrative*, 5. See also Murdina MacDonald, "London Calvinistic Baptists 1689–1727: Tensions Within a Dissenting Community Under Toleration" (D.Phil. thesis, Regent's Park College, Oxford University, 1982), 42.

20 *A Narrative of the Proceedings of the General Assembly of the Elders and Messengers of the Baptized Churches Sent from Divers Parts of England and Wales, Which Began in London the 2d of June, and Ended the 8th of the Same, 1691* (London: n.p., 1691), 4–11.

21 *A Narrative of the Proceedings of the General Assembly, Consisting of Elders, Ministers and Messengers, Met Together in London, from Several Parts of England and Wales, on the 17th Day of the 3d Month, 1692, and Continued unto the 24th of the Same* (London: n.p., 1692), 4–5, 7–8.

Beyond the London General Assemblies, there have been a host of association meetings in both the United Kingdom and America. Records from many of these meetings are available to us today, both in manuscript and printed forms. From them, we are able to learn much. The procedural details of most of the association meetings themselves are seldom explicitly stated in the extant records. They were convened by messengers appointed by the churches for the specific gatherings. Business was conducted according to the priorities of each association. The Hampshire Association records state that a "moderator" or "mouth of the assembly" was chosen to preside in their meetings.[22] Beginning in 1761, the Philadelphia records speak of both a moderator and a scribe or clerk.[23] It may be assumed that this was the case in the other gatherings as well. The 1694 Bristol, or Western, Association meeting included a "sermon suitable to the occasion."[24] This may have become a standard part of the Bristol Association's proceedings, as several of the following meetings incorporated sermons.[25] It is fascinating to note that preaching had a very small role in the association meetings. There is no record of preaching at the London General Assemblies, and seldom does it occur at other meetings. The Philadelphia Association meetings always began with a sermon, the preacher (one of the ministers of member churches) having been appointed by the association the year before. Preaching was not the focus, association meetings were taken up with business.

---

22 Marion Cox, transcriber, A Collection of Manuscript Letters Relating to the Calvinistic Baptist Church at Whitchurch (The Angus Library, Regent's Park College, Oxford), 19 number A5; 23 number A6.

23 A.D. Gillette, ed., *Minutes of the Philadelphia Baptist Association* (reprint; Atlas: Baptist Book Trust, n.d.), 81.

24 J.G. Fuller, *A Brief History of the Western Association* (Bristol: I. Hemmons, 1843), 22. According to Fuller, this is "the first instance recorded, of preaching constituting any part of the Association services." The minutes of the 1693 Bristol Association request that one of the London messengers preach at the 1694 Bristol meeting, but there were no London representatives at that meeting. Ivimey, *History of the English Baptists*, 1:529, 534–535. One might expect that preaching was common at these meetings, but the extant minutes do not mention it. The Whitchurch Manuscript notes that Richard Chalk was chosen to preach at the October 1701 meeting of the Hampshire Association. Whitchurch Manuscript, 26, number A6.

25 Fuller, *Western Association*, 23.

The local association meetings seem to have lasted from one to three days.[26] The records indicate that these groups had two primary orders of business: listening to reports from the churches, and the discussion of questions proposed by the messengers from the member churches.[27] Both doctrinal and practical in nature, they range across the whole spectrum of theology and practice. Among the theological issues discussed were matters such as the presence of scriptural rules for the proper ordering of a church,[28] the relative nearness of the coming of Christ,[29] the validity of a baptism "performed in a standing pool and not a river,"[30] the nature of God's covenant,[31] sanctification and good works,[32] eternal justification[33] and the abiding validity of the Lord's Day Sabbath.[34] Among the many questions addressed to the Philadelphia Association in 1748 is one that is strangely contemporary: "Whether to deny the foreknowledge of the eternal God, concerning all future evil as well as good, be not a fundamental error?" Their answer is to the point: "We look upon such an opinion to be directly repugnant to Scripture; there fore exceeding erroneous and pernicious."[35] The Philadelphia Baptists answered the question 250 years before open theism hit the marketplace!

More commonly, the questions were practical in nature. They addressed issues relating to church membership,[36] the ordinances,[37]

---

26 B.R. White, ed., *Association Records of the Particular Baptists of England, Wales and Ireland to 1660*, 3 vol. (consecutive pagination) (London: The Baptist Historical Society, 1971–74), *passim*; Whitchurch Papers, *passim*; Stephen Copson, ed., *Association Life of the Particular Baptists of Northern England, 1699–1732* (London: The Baptist Historical Society, 1991), *passim*.

27 The General Assemblies also incorporated questions and answers into their deliberations.

28 Copson, *Northern Association*, 82.

29 Copson, *Northern Association*, 86.

30 Whitchurch Manuscript, 23, number A6. The baptism was judged valid.

31 Copson, *Northern Association*, 94.

32 Copson, *Northern Association*, 93–94.

33 *1689 Narrative*, 14; Copson, *Northern Association*, 91.

34 *1689 Narrative*, 16.

35 Gillette, *Philadelphia Minutes*, 58.

36 Whitchurch Manuscript, 19, number A5, 24-25, number A6; Copson, *Northern Association*, 82–83 and *passim*; *1689 Narrative*, 14.

37 Copson, *Northern Association*, 89; Whitchurch Manuscript, 20, number A5; *1689 Narrative*, 18.

discipline,[38] marriage,[39] inter-church relationships,[40] ministerial activity,[41] relations with paedobaptist churches and ministers[42] and a host of other subjects.[43] The answers to these questions were offered as "advice"[44] to the churches, and were not considered binding until the churches had given consent. The *Confession* clearly stated that the messengers when assembled "are not intrusted with any church-power properly so called; or with any jurisdiction over the churches themselves, to exercise any censures either over any churches or persons; or to impose their determination on the churches or officers."[45] A vigorous doctrine and practice of interdependence did not undermine a similarly vigorous doctrine of independence. The conclusions of messengers could not have binding authority over local churches. Only the churches themselves could determine what course of action should be followed.

In the confessional statement, holding communion provided the means for the giving of advice in "matter[s] of difference" in the churches. Several examples are extant. In 1696, a dispute arose in the Bromsgrove, Worcestershire church between the pastor, John Eckells, and the people of the church consisting of charges of disorderliness against Eckells and his family.[46] The contention dragged on for four years. In 1697, the church sought

---

38 Copson, *Northern Association*, 88; Whitchurch Manuscript, 19-20, number A5; W.T. Whitley, *Baptists of Northwest England, 1649–1913* (London: The Kingsgate Press, 1913), 77–78.

39 Copson, *Northern Association*, 93; *1689 Narrative*, 13.

40 Copson, *Northern Association*, 83; *1691 Narrative*, 11–12; Whitchurch Manuscript, 21, number A5.

41 Copson, *Northern Association*, 84, 89; Whitchurch Manuscript, 14, number A3; Ivimey, *History of the English Baptists*, 1:527.

42 Copson, *Northern Association*, 86, 93; *1689 Narrative*, 13.

43 The extant association records are replete with discussions of a wide variety of topics.

44 *1689 Narrative*, 10; *1690 Narrative*, 7; Whitchurch Manuscript, 11, number A2.

45 *A Confession of Faith. Put Forth by the Elders and Brethren Of Many Congregations of Christians (Baptized upon Profession of their Faith) in London and the Country* (London: n.p., 1677), 93–94.

46 Bromsgrove Baptist Church Record Book, 69–107 (134–170). The double pagination is in the original. It is difficult to determine the exact nature of the incidents precipitating in the dispute. When it was finally resolved it was decided that "all papers should be burnt to ashes or obliterated," 106 (169), and this seems to have been applied to the Church book, as there are many gaps in the transcript.

the help of the local association, and sent a long letter explaining the circumstances. The association responded with an equally long and detailed letter specifically addressing the problems and sorting out the sins of the various individuals concerned. They called for repentance and asked all of the churches in the association to observe a day of prayer and fasting. Sadly, a division ensued, and Eckells and a group of supporters denounced the majority and claimed to be the church in Bromsgrove. Appeal was made to the association a second time, wherein it was ruled that the original church continued to be the church. In 1699, a third appeal to the association was made because Eckells had refused to heed the advice given earlier, and had sought help from a "higher court,"[47] the elders in London. From all appearances, the London elders made a judgement based solely on Eckells' testimony and asserted that the church members had severely wronged their pastor. Benjamin Keach wrote a letter vindicating Eckells and charging the church with schism.[48] The association responded in no uncertain terms:

> 'Tis our opinion, that Mr. Eckells and those who went out with him departed from ye Church of Christ and do lie under ye guilt of schisms. Whatsoever our London Elders may judge, we humbly conceive that we had a proper call to examine this matter, receiving appeals from ye Church respecting that difference, with ye cases and circumstances upon evidence, we herein have a greater advantage to find out ye breach, than our London Brethren have or possibly can, they having heard but one side.[49]

In 1700, the matter was finally settled when both parties acknowledged wrong and decided to exist as two distinct churches with "no more disputing on either side."[50]

In this case, the local association claimed a right to rule on the matter of schism after appeal had been received by the aggrieved

47 Bromsgrove Baptist Church Record Book, 99 (160).
48 Bromsgrove Baptist Church Record Book, 100 (161).
49 Bromsgrove Baptist Church Record Book, 103 (166).
50 Bromsgrove Baptist Church Record Book, 106 (169).

church. They addressed the specific issues involved, urged a course of action to take, and protested when others became involved.

Another attempt at settling a church division is contained in the minutes of the Hampshire Association. In 1701, a separation took place in the Broughton church. Both parties were present at the April 22 meeting of the association, at which time each had opportunity to express their concerns, and were "examined face to face" with a "full enguairie into all yt could be produced on either side."[51] The disputants left the room, and the assembly reduced the issues to the main points, determined a course of action, and called the dissenting parties back in order to give their advice. They ruled that the church should strive to show "meekness, gravity and love" to the dissidents, that those who separated should "mistrust their own case, and endevor as much as in them lieth after a reunion," and that both parties should meet together for fasting, prayer and humbling themselves, seeking to "live together in love as Xns."[52]

The Philadelphia Association was concerned that "complaints, queries, or grievances" be handled carefully. They were not to be included in the letters written by the churches and read in the general meeting, but were to be for the private meetings of the Association.[53]

To summarize, the work of the associations at their general meetings consisted of: prayer, reports from the churches, business proposed by churches and theological discussion. A sermon was often included. In every case, these associations were lively, and they were busy.

The work of the associations after their meetings

At the meetings of messengers of churches, the associations often determined that action should be taken for the benefit of the churches and the kingdom. It was not enough for them to meet together, listen to reports, pray, discuss and dismiss. Difficulties of administration (to use the language of the *Second London Confession of Faith*, chapter 26:15) had to be settled. As they

---

51 Whitchurch Manuscript, 24, number A6.

52 Whitchurch Manuscript, 24–25.

53 Gillette, *Philadelphia Minutes*, 28.

considered the issues before them, they sought for means to address those difficulties and provide remedies. While they took action on many issues, such as the publication of confessions and catechism, it is possible to consider the work of the associations under generic headings. Broadly speaking, four general categories of action may be identified: benevolence, ministerial training, political action and missions (both foreign and domestic). We will consider each of these briefly.

1. Benevolence

Benevolence is perhaps the first and most obvious issue addressed by the associated churches. Virtually all of the associations found some means by which to give assistance to those in need. We have already noted that it was the dual issues of ministerial support and training that precipitated the 1689 General Assembly, and the associated churches took decisive steps to remedy the perceived problem. The Particular Baptist Fund, reorganized in 1707, continues to this day. At other times, the churches were urged to assist poor ministers after fires or natural disasters or for other causes. In 1766, the Philadelphia Baptists began a fund to help the Konoloway church (Township of Air, Cumberland County, Pennsylvania), a tiny assembly of 6 members. Twelve pounds, 6 shillings and 1 pence were collected and distributed to the church. By 1768, they had grown to 25 members. In that same year, the association "ordered to give the sum of £14...for the use of Charles Thomson, a student in Rhode Island College."[54] In 1795, Philadelphia took up collections to help build a meeting-house in Savannah, Georgia, to accommodate hundreds of blacks.[55] It would not be difficult to multiply the examples. One-time grants could be made by act of the association proper, while funds on deposit required supervision by appointed trustees. Both cases are abundantly testified in the literature.

2. Ministerial training

As we have seen, the London churches were concerned with the provision of a continuing ministry, and sought to collect funds

---

54 Gillette, *Philadelphia Minutes*, 97, 101, 106.

55 Gillette, *Philadelphia Minutes*, 307.

to this end. The Bristol Baptist College, a school that produced the best Particular Baptist ministers of the eighteenth century, was assisted by these churches. In America, the Philadelphia Baptists sought to encourage the work of the Hopewell Academy, New Jersey, even writing to the trustees of the Particular Baptist Fund in London to solicit financial support. They argued that this school evidenced the prospect of supply for destitute pulpits.[56] Likewise, Rhode Island College was an early recipient of the support of the associations. As soon as it was chartered by the Rhode Island government, the Philadelphia Association urged its churches to be "liberal in contributing" toward the establishment of the school.

Later in the eighteenth century, the churches started an education fund as a means to assist in the training of men. In 1800, for example, their records state that $40 was to be provided "for the instruction and assistance of Thomas Jones, a young man lately from Wales of promising gifts." Along with Philadelphia, the Charleston Association and the Warren Association (Rhode Island) were deeply involved in ministerial training projects. One author says that "prior to 1750 the number of college-trained Baptist ministers in America was extremely few.... By 1814 this situation had been altered."[57] While frontier churches tended to decry the emphasis placed on an educated ministry, it was the associations that led the way forward.

3. Political action

While it may seem unexpected, the early associations, both in England and America, were actively involved in the political arena. In both places during the seventeenth century, Baptists suffered under tremendous disadvantages, and even persecution. The joint actions of associated churches gave to these minorities a greater voice, and produced significant benefits for the churches and their members. Isaac Backus, the great Baptist leader from Middleboro, Massachusetts, lobbied successfully to end the religious taxation forced upon farmers by the government of the Commonwealth of Massachusetts. Since the Congregational

---

56 Gillette, *Philadelphia Minutes*, 74, 76, 77, especially 84.

57 Shurden, *Associationalism among Baptists of America*, 182.

churches were the established churches of the state (until 1833), every landowner was by law to pay a tax which was used to provide support to the local congregational minister. Such a practice galled the Baptists, as they desired to support their own ministers, and not the parsons of the "Standing Order." The Warren Association minutes for 1769 state, "Many of the letters from the churches mentioned grievous oppressions and persecutions from the 'Standing Order'; especially the church from Ashfield, where religious tyranny had been carried to great lengths." The Association took decisive action, formed committees to investigate the circumstances, represent the aggrieved, and pursue relief. "For Baptists, the organization of the Warren Association was the most important step toward achieving religious freedom in New England."[58]

The circumstances in Virginia were similar, though there Episcopalianism was established by law. *The History of the Ketockton Baptist Association* details the difficulties endured by the Baptists in this commonwealth.[59] It was especially the formation of the General Association of Separate Baptists in 1771 that provided Baptists with a voice loud enough to begin the process of toleration and freedom. On these occasions, the united action of Baptists paved the way for freedom.

4. Missions

The last, and perhaps most important, general category of Baptist association work is missions. By this, I speak of both foreign and domestic work. The latter is, of course, the earlier of the two, since Baptists were not involved in foreign missions until 1792, and in America not directly until 1814.

So soon as it was begun, the Particular Baptist Fund was used to pay the expenses of ministers itinerating in places where Baptist churches were not found. The records of the London General Assemblies record the successful labours of men such as Benjamin Keach and Richard Tidmarsh. In the middle of the eighteenth century, the American associations were concerned

58 Shurden, *Associationalism among Baptists of America*, 210–211.

59 William Fristoe, *A Concise History of the Ketockton Baptist Association* (Staunton: William Lifford, 1808), 58–88.

with sending ministers into "destitute" places, and collected money to support such causes. The men sent were always pastors of settled churches, but sometimes they were away from their own congregations for extended periods. Here are examples from the minutes of the Philadelphia Association:

> 1766, That it is most necessary for the good of the Baptist interest, that the Association have at their disposal every year a sum of money. Accordingly it was further agreed: That the churches, henceforth, do make a collection every quarter, and send the same yearly to the Association, to be by them deposited in the hands of trustees; the interest whereof only to be by them laid out every year in support of ministers travelling on the errand of the churches, or otherwise, as the necessities of said churches shall require.
>
> 1771, Item #6: A motion being made in the Association, relative to the appointment of an Evangelist, it was universally agreed that such an appointment promised much advantage to the Baptist interests. Five ministers were put in nomination for the office, *viz.*: Rev. Messrs. John Gano, Benjamin Miller, Samuel Jones, David Jones, Morgan Edwards. The choice fell on the last, which he accepted on the conditions then specified.
>
> 1773, Item #14: The usefulness of a travelling minister on this continent appearing more manifest by trials, and Brother Morgan Edwards declining the office, it was agreed, that Brother John Gano be a messenger of the churches for this year; and that the treasurer do pay him the interest of the Association fund, to help defraying his expenses.
>
> 1774 (May 25), Item #8: A motion being made, that Brother John Gano should give an account of his travels to the southward: he accordingly did, by which it appears he has been indefatigable in his labors, and that a minister, travelling annually, according to the plan proposed, may answer very valuable purposes.

> 1774 (Oct. 12–14), Item #17: Voted, That Brother Gano be paid by the treasurer the interest due on the Association fund, towards defraying his expenses in travelling the last year: accordingly he received £12.[60]

Apparently, the Philadelphia Association saw no conflict between their existence as an association and the opportunity to send out men and compensate them for their expenses. They did not turn to any one particular church to meet the need (and it must be remembered that in the instance of John Gano, he was the pastor of the First Baptist Church of New York at this time), they took upon themselves the right and responsibility to send men out to preach and plant new congregations. They established this fund for the purpose of assisting the work of the association of churches. From 1793 onward, this type of work was extended to include regular fundraising to help support William Carey and his labours in India.

According to Walter Shurden, "the Bowdoinham Association in Maine was probably the earliest association to organize a permanent home missionary project."[61] In 1799, it took up an offering, appointed a committee to superintend the work, elected a treasurer, and sent elder Isaac Case to unchurched areas of eastern Maine. From this point on, examples may be easily multiplied. The eyes of the associated churches were lifted to see the needs of the vast continent, and find means to reach those places. The Shaftsbury, Vermont; Charleston, South Carolina; and Elkhorn, Kentucky associations all became active at the beginning of the ninteenth century.

Probably the first full-time employee (if we may use such terms appropriately) of any association was Luther Rice. He had been a companion of Adoniram Judson, and like Judson, came to Baptist convictions during the sea voyage to the orient. After being baptized at Serampore, he returned to the United States to rally support for the Judsons, who had been cut off by the Congregational missionary society which sent them. The Baptists in America were pleased to have such an opportunity, and in

---

60 Gillette, *Philadelphia Minutes*, 97, 119, 130, 135, 142.
61 Shurden, *Associationalism among Baptists of America*, 171.

1814 the Triennial Convention was born (its full name was the General Missionary Convention of the Baptist Denomination in the United States of America). Richard Furman of Charleston served as moderator of the formational meeting, held in Philadelphia. This organization, the earliest equivalent of a national association, appointed 21 men to serve as commissioners, with William Staughton, a pastor from Philadelphia who had been present at the formation of the Particular Baptist Missionary Society in 1792, as the first corresponding secretary of the board. It has been said that "after Rice returned to America...a literary avalanche of circular letters on the subject of foreign missions appeared."[62] The associations (at least the majority of them in the east—there were anti-missions groups, especially in the frontier territories) were at the forefront of the missionary movement. Rice, the official travelling "agent" of the Convention, spoke to local associations, churches and any group that would listen. Through him, foreign missions (as well as ministerial education) received growing support from the American Baptist churches.

By these means, churches working together were enabled to accomplish far more than any one church could do on its own. These unions of churches were always careful to maintain and respect the rights of their local churches, but they did not view autonomy and independency as antagonistic to cooperation across a wide spectrum of activities. Some men were appointed to visit churches in order to help them establish settled ministries, others to solicit, receive and distribute funds in the name of the Assembly, others to go out to dark places and plant churches. They sought to work together for ministerial education, the settling of disputes and, eventually, to support foreign missions. But in many ways, these associations were active and alive. Fellowship in itself was a good thing, but prayer and friendship did not satisfy the level of "communion" required from the body of Christ. Mutual recognition, principled cooperation and financial support were important components of true communion.

---

62 Shurden, *Associationalism among Baptists of America*, 177.

How did associations work? When they were together, they did their business. When they were apart, their appointed agents did the work assigned. Whether that was printing their *Confession* or travelling to strengthen churches, the associations exerted great effort. As the emissaries of the associations, their agents reported back the labour that they accomplished. This may have been done personally, or by letter. But in every case, their responsibility to the assembled messengers of the churches required accountability. The Particular Baptist associations serve as a useful model for cooperation between churches in the extension of the kingdom of Jesus Christ.[63]

63 Congratulations to Dr. Fowler on his seventieth birthday!

13

Reviewing recent trends in congregational worship: It is time for a mid-course correction

BY GRANT GORDON

The last thirty years has seen remarkable changes in congregational worship, especially for those in the Free Church tradition, like Baptists, who can establish their own liturgy. When I served for fifteen years as an intentional interim pastor (now often called transitional pastor) in seven churches, and consultant to other churches, I was thrust into what became known sadly as the worship wars. All but one congregation were embroiled in this conflict. Yes, there were other issues, but this was the prominent one, at least on the surface. As a church historian, I was aware that there have always been struggles over changes in worship and congregational life. For example, in 1911 Thomas Wright lamented that a new hymnbook omitted numerous valued eighteenth-century hymns which he labelled "neglected gold."[1] Furthermore, the compilers mutilated many hymns they did include and added newer songs; many of which he described as doggerel. So what we are experiencing today is not a new phenomenon. But there has never been a time in church history when there has been such a deep infatuation with new praise songs coupled with strong opposition to older hymns and songs. Donald Hustad, who was a longtime professor of church music and worship at Southern Baptist Theological Seminary, observes that "popular music styles have changed with each generation, yet this is the first time they have threatened to divide families at the worship hour."[2] Though in most cases the intensity of the struggle is subsiding, it does not mean that all is well and healthy. Therefore, now is a good time to assess where we are, to acknowledge the gains and learn from the losses so our churches can move ahead.

Our churches have gained from many aspects of contemporary worship (hereafter CW). In many churches, upfront leading and assisting in services are more extensively shared. The pastor is not the only one leading, praying, serving communion and baptizing.[3] Worship teams and bands have increased fervour in our services. Technology has enabled us to project songs and visual clips onto a screen and amplify our sound. Praise choruses have led us to give our praise to God, rather than mostly speaking about God as is typical of most hymns. Youth and young adults are more actively involved in worship. The worship mood is one of celebration.

However, in the process, there have been subtle shifts and losses. In many churches where they adopted what some have called "music driven worship," the services have changed shape considerably. John Stackhouse, until recently of Regent College,[4]

---

1 Thomas Wright, *The Life of Augustus M. Toplady and Contemporary Hymn Writers* (London: Farncombe & Son, 1911), xvi.

2 Donald P. Hustad, *Jubilate II: Church Music in Worship and Renewal*, rev. ed. (Carol Stream: Hope Publishing Co., 1993), 307. This is a helpful revision of his book that was formerly titled, *Jubilate: Church Music in the Evangelical Tradition* (1981).

3 In some of our Free Churches, non-ordained staff and laity are invited by their pastors to baptize, especially where that person has a special connection with the baptismal candidate.

4 He is now the Samuel J. Mikolaski Professor of Religious Studies and Dean of Faculty at Crandall University in Moncton, New Brunswick, Canada.

observes that it is "pretty bad and actually regressing."[5] He laments that "nowadays the trend setting churches seem to have fallen back into two halves—singing and preaching—which among other bad consequences, has put a very heavy burden on worship leaders and preachers to perform at a high standard, since that's pretty much all there is to the service."[6] Therefore, I give the following recommendations so that, hopefully, our services will be stronger and more complete.

Music issues

1. Expand our focus in worship singing

Donald Hustad, points out that "full worship is more than words of adoration."[7] Unfortunately, CW services are often limited to praise songs, with "no gospel songs of experience, no hymns of thanksgiving, no didactic songs of the faith, no expressions of confession, petition, or submission—*just praise*, in the narrowest-possible understanding of the word!"[8] He emphasizes that "Above all, submission to God is the ultimate praise."[9] This is frequently expressed in historic worship hymns (hereafter HW) such as Isaac Watts' "When I Survey the Wondrous Cross." After meditating on Christ's sacrifice, he determines "Love so amazing, so divine, / Demands my soul, my life, my all." CW songs are predominately upbeat and triumphant. They focus much on Christ as Victor and little on the Suffering Servant. Marva Dawn observes that consequently when the 9/11 tragedy occurred, most CW churches had no songs of lament to sing.[10] In other words, present CW worship does not reflect the whole of our earthly experience. Because of what God has done, and continues to do, our mood ought to be marked by celebration and

---

5 John Stackhouse, "Worship Sandwich," *Leadership Journal* (Winter 2015): 14.
6 Stackhouse, "Worship Sandwich," 14.
7 Hustad, *Jubilate II*, 296.
8 Hustad, *Jubilate II*, 286 .
9 Hustad, *Jubilate II*, 297 .
10 Marva Dawn said this at a worship seminar I attended at Redeemer College, Ancaster, Ontario, about ten years ago. See Marva J. Dawn, *Reaching Out Without Dumbing Down: A Theology of Worship for the Turn-of-the Century Culture* (Grand Rapids: Eerdmans, 1995).

confidence in God (e.g. "In Christ Alone"[11]). But there also needs to be expressions of our frailty and pain and our need of forgiveness and God's help. A recent comparison of HW and CW concludes that HW emphasizes our pilgrimage on earth toward heaven, whereas CW stresses immediate praise at the throne of heaven.[12] Since our journey can be messy and stressful, some of our songs need to acknowledge this and help us express our faith in the midst of our journey.[13] This is expressed powerfully in Horatio Spafford's hymn "It Is Well with My Soul"[14] when he declares his hope, and the reason for it, in the midst of his deep pain.[15] And, its melody by Philip Bliss, especially when sung with strong feeling, and not sentimentality, enhances the lyrics. In contrast, the bouncy tempo in the popular CW song "My Lighthouse"[16] unfortunately overshadows the admissions of "my wrestling...my doubts...my failures" in the lyrics.

---

11 Keith Getty and Stuart Townend © 2001 Thankyou Music (admin. by Capitol CMG Publishing).

12 Lester Ruth, "Some Similarities and Differences between Historic Evangelical Hymns and Contemporary Worship Songs," *Artistic Theologian* 3 (2015): 75–76. This is a journal of the School of Church Music at Southwestern Baptist Theological Seminary. You can find it online at: http://artistictheologian.com/journal/artistic-theologian-volume-3-2015/some-similarities-and-differences-between-historic-evangelical-hymns-and-contemporary-worship-songs/; accessed May 4, 2015.

13 This does not mean that HW is always realistic, especially in the gospel songs that focus much on experience. I doubt it is true of HW singers that "I Love Him Better Every Day" by Sydney Cox (1926) or "This is my story, this is my song, / Praising my Saviour all the day long" in Fanny Crosby's "Blessed Assurance" (1873). Aspiration, yes. Reality, no!

14 Lyrics (*c.*1876) by H.G. Spafford and melody by Philip Bliss.

15 Hillsong published a revision of this song in 2011 with two verses and slightly modified the melody. But, for some strange reason, Ben Fielding and Reuben Morgan start with verse 1, omit verses 2–4 that are in most of our hymnbooks and end with a verse ("But Lord, it's for Thee. / For Thy coming we wait.") that is very seldom included. I could only find it in http://cyberhymnal.org/htm/i/t/i/itiswell.htm and in Ira Sankey, *Sacred Songs and Solos of 1200 Songs* (*c.*1890). Hence, the Hillsong revision jumps to the hope of the second coming. Consequently, such statements as, "Though Satan should buffet / Though trials should come" and especially the reason for our hope such as "Christ has regarded my helpless estate" (which could have easily been updated to my poor helpless state) and "my sin, not in part but the whole / is nailed to the cross, / and I bear it no more" are not mentioned.

16 Rend Collective © 2013 Thankyou Music (admin. by Capitol CMG Publishing).

2. *Move beyond the unhealthy conflict between historic worship hymns (HW) and contemporary worship songs (CW)*

Timothy Keller, pastor of the very successful and influential Redeemer Presbyterian Church[17] in New York City, challenges this either/or obsession. Speaking to the CW advocates he warns,

> When we ignore historic tradition, we break our solidarity with Christians of the past. Part of the richness of our identity as Christians is that we are saved into a historic people. An unwillingness to consult tradition is not in keeping with either Christian humility or Christian community. Nor is it a thoughtful response to the postmodern rootlessness that now leads so many to seek connection to ancient ways and peoples.[18]

He also notes that "any worship that is strictly contemporary will quickly become dated."Yet he points out that HW advocates can get just as stuck too. "While strict CW advocates bind worship too heavily to the present culture, strict HW advocates bind it too heavily to a past culture."[19]

We can learn from Keller's solution. He rejects the idea that CW is the only kind of music that attracts non-Christians[20] and

---

17 In 1989, Keller started as the founding pastor with about fifty people and today the average Sunday attendance is about 4,500. It has launched numerous daughter churches and ministry initiatives. http://www.redeemer.com/learn/about_us/redeemer_history; accessed May 14, 2015.

18 Timothy Keller, "Evangelistic Worship" (2001, 2009), 3, 4 n.11. This ten page paper published by Redeemer Presbyterian Church, New York, is available as a free download at www.gospelinlife.com. For an expansion of this article, with more details from church history and theological analysis, along with specific examples, see Timothy Keller, "Reformed Worship in the Global City," in *Worship by the Book*, ed. D.A. Carson (Grand Rapids: Zondervan, 2002), 193–249. See also Timothy Keller, *Center Church: Doing Balanced Gospel-Centered Ministry in Your City* (Grand Rapids: Zondervan, 2012), 297–309. The strict CW extreme is expressed by Rick Warren who says that within a year after Saddleback's decision "to stop singing hymns…[we] attracted thousands because of our music." Rick Warren, *The Purpose Driven Church* (Grand Rapids: Zondervan, 1995), 285. Sadly, many churches desperately wanting to grow have quickly adopted Warren's strategy without examining their context and consequently suffered significant congregational disruption and losses.

19 Timothy Keller, "Evangelistic Worship," 4.

20 See Timothy Keller, "Worship Worthy of the Name," 3. This three-page paper is available as a free download at www.gospelinlife.com. He says, "I am always puzzled

he does not target a specific age demographic.[21] Nor does he attempt a wooden blending of CW and HW. Instead he chooses a third way. His focus is primarily on what he calls *evangelistic worship* through "making worship comprehensible to unbelievers"[22] with the goal of "leading to commitment."[23] It is not an evangelistic service in the traditional sense. Keller emphasizes,

> Christocentric preaching both grows believers and challenges nonbelievers. If the Sunday service and sermon aim primarily at evangelism, they will bore the saints. If they aim primarily at education, they'll bore and confuse unbelievers. If they aim at praising God who saves by grace, they'll both instruct insiders and challenge outsiders.[24]

As to what is sung, the church holds that music style boundaries "are very elastic." Generally speaking, the two styles "set different tones" and "each one conveys certain theological themes better than the other."[25] Keller's church believes a "judicious mixing" of both in a service is "both possible and desirable." However, depending on the service, usually one style is more dominant. "Each piece of music is judged on its own merits."[26]

3. Express our trinitarian faith in our songs

Much of our CW worship is Christocentric but not in a full or balanced sense and lacks a trinitarian focus. This is seen in a

---

when I hear pastors say it is." In fact his more dominant HW service in Manhattan has grown more than their other service with a CW dominant format.

21 For a critique of targeting, see Douglas D. Webster, *Selling Jesus: What's Wrong with Marketing the Church* (Downers Grove: InterVarsity Press, 1992), 58–73.

22 Keller, "Evangelistic Worship," 7–10. The approach is: (a) worship and preach in the vernacular; (b) explain the service as you go along; (c) directly address and welcome nonbelievers; (d) cultivate high-quality aesthetics; (e) celebrate deeds of mercy and justice; (f) present the sacraments in ways that make the gospel clear; and (g) preach grace.

23 See Keller, "Evangelistic Worship," 9–10 for how this is done during and after the service.

24 Keller, Keller, "Evangelistic Worship," 9

25 Keller in Carson, *Worship by the Book*, 237–238.

26 Keller in Carson, *Worship by the Book*, 238. In the morning service at their main site in downtown Manhattan, they follow their Presbyterian liturgical order more closely, predominately using HW. In the evening, CW is more dominant. In the CW-dominant service, "traditional hymn lyrics are either put to contemporary tunes or at least to contemporary arrangements."

recent research team study of the CW songs in the "CCLI's Top 25 lists between 1989 and 2005."[27] Using a specific formula, the team selected and then examined different aspects of seventy-seven of the most popular CW songs.[28] Lester Ruth, formerly of Asbury Theological Seminary and now at Duke Divinity School, meticulously surveyed the references to the Trinity in these songs.[29]He wanted to know the extent to which the most used CW songs "lead Christian Congregations to pray to and worship the Triune God." His findings are quite revealing. He found that none use the word Trinity or triune. Further, "only four[30] explicitly refer to or name all three Persons of the Trinity" and "only one song in addition to these four ('How Can We Name a Love') speaks of God as 'Father.'" There are a few references to the Spirit, but none use the name "Holy Spirit." In contrast, thirty-seven of the songs "make explicit reference to the Son, or Jesus Christ." Other references are unspecified, "but given the stronger tendency to name the second Person of the Trinity throughout the entire body of 77 songs, it is more likely that most of these generic references are to Jesus Christ."[31]

Ruth concludes that "as a whole, this body of 77 songs is what some might call 'functionally unitarian.'" He points out that "few of the songs, unlike the New Testament, explore the internal dynamics of the Father, Son, and the Holy Spirit in their wide range of saving activity. Whereas the New Testament continually explores how the Father, Son, and Holy Spirit have acted in concert on our behalf." Unfortunately, in the popular CW songs, "with respect to the Father and the Son, there is only occasional reference to Christ's saving activity being of the Father. The Holy Spirit as an active agent in our salvation is almost nowhere

27 Christian Copyright Licensing International (CCLI) is the copyright clearinghouse that serves 160,000 churches in North America.

28 The results are in Robert Woods and Brian Walrath, ed., *The Message in the Music: Studying Contemporary Praise & Worship* (Nashville: Abingdon Press, 2007).

29 Lester Ruth, "How Great Is Our God: The Trinity in Contemporary Christian Worship Music," in Woods and Walrath, *Music in the Message*, 29–42. The first ten pages of this chapter can be found at https://www.cokesbury.com/forms/displayImage.aspx?pcid=2050176; accessed February 1, 2015.

30 "Glorify Thy Name"; "Father, I Adore You"; "Shine, Jesus, Shine"; "How Great Is Our God."

31 Ruth, "How Great Is Our God," 30–32.

to be found." This results in the "doctrine of the atonement" being "under-developed in its Trinitarian aspects." Further, there is "little emphasis on present aspects of God's work. There is no emphasis on ongoing mediation, whether it be on the heavenly ministry of Christ or the saving role of the Holy Spirit."[32] He points out that the lack of clarity in lyrics is compounded by the use of "Lord" which is "often used in an ill-defined, generic way." For instance, he says the song "Awesome God"[33] made popular by Michael W. Smith, "complicates the matter by tossing 'God' into the mix: in this song 'God' and 'Lord' appear to be interchangeable names for whoever expelled Adam from Eden, experienced crucifixion ["shed his blood"], and poured

---

32 Lester Ruth, "How Great Is Our God," 33–35. Note that as my research was nearing completion, Ruth published "Some Similarities and Differences between Historic Evangelical Hymns and Contemporary Worship Songs," *Artistic Theologian* 3 (2015): 68–86. He examined the 112 most popular CW songs that appeared in the CCLI top twenty-five songs from 1989 to 2015. He then compared these to the most published hymns (if they appeared in at least one-third of the eighty-six evangelical American hymnals published from 1737 to 1860, compiled by Stephen A. Marini). Ruth found that both lists were robustly Christocentric. Surprisingly, he found that the HW hymns (a total of seventy), similar to his observation in his CW 1989–2005 study, were also in some ways weak in references to the Trinity and the interworking of the persons of the Trinity. However, some pre-1860 hymns, which speak of trinitarian relationships, are not in Marini's popular list; though they did become favourites later. These would include John Bakewell's "Hail, Thou Once Despised Jesus" ("Jesus...Paschal Lamb, by God appointed...Seated at the Father's side"); William Kethe's "All People that on Earth Do Dwell" ("To Father, Son and Holy Ghost, the God whom heaven and earth adore"); and Martin Luther's "A Mighty Fortress Is Our God" ("Were not the right Man on our side / The Man of God's own choosing... The Spirit and the gifts are ours / Thro' Him who with us sideth"). Further, because the list goes up to only 1860, Ruth's study did not include later popular hymns that speak of the interworking of the Trinity. These would include Fanny Crosby's "To God Be the Glory" ("He gave us his Son, who yielded his life an atonement for sin"); Cleland McAfee's "Near to the Heart of God" ("O Jesus Blest Redeemer / Sent from the heart of God"); and William Whiting's "Eternal Father Strong to Save" ("Eternal Father...O Saviour...O Holy Spirit...O Trinity of love and power"). He notices some interesting differences between early American HW and present CW. For example, in contrast to HW, the concept of a gathered community, God's ongoing mission, and eschatology are absent in most CW songs. Also, 16% of the HW hymns use the word *Father* compared to 4% in CW songs. Strangely, Stuart Townend's strong CW song, "How Deep the Father's Love for Us" (1995) did not make the list of most popular CW songs (see list on page 79).

33 Rich Mullins © 1988 Universal Music—Brentwood Benson Publishing (admin. by Brentwood-Benson Music Publishing, Inc.).

out judgment on Sodom."[34] Fortunately, only the chorus from this 1988 song is sung today, if at all.

Ruth makes clear that his conclusions apply only to the seventy-seven songs in the most popular CCLI list and acknowledges that there are less popular CW songs that "have a greater capacity for naming the Persons of the Godhead." He was especially encouraged by Chris Tomlin's "How Great Is Our God" (2004)[35] that appeared near the end of the study period. It declares, "The Godhead three in one: Father, Spirit, Son." Ruth expressed hope that this song would be a sign of better things to come. But nine years later, Tomlin wrote "Once and for All."[36] Because he takes one line from the Nicene Creed ("God from God, Light from Light"), one expects the song would be clearly trinitarian, like the Creed. But Tomlin mentions only the deity of Jesus. The first line of the chorus boldly declares, "We believe our God is Jesus."

One blogger who is a strong CW advocate and worship pastor, likes the song but that line troubles him. "To be clear," he writes,

> we do certainly believe that Jesus is God.... But just as clear: we believe that God is Father, Son, and Holy Spirit. We worship a God who is one in being yet distinct in three persons. Neither the Father, nor the Son, nor the Holy Spirit is any more or less 'God' than the other 'person'. It's a mind-boggling truth, but it's one we embrace, and it's one that this good song, in one little line, makes unnecessarily fuzzy....To say that "our God" is only one person of the Trinity is a bit of shame, particularly in a song that will be downloaded and purchased hundreds of thousands of times, be incorporated into thousands of churches' repertoire, and inwardly digested by the people singing the words on Sunday mornings all over the world.[37]

---

34 Lester Ruth, "How Great Is Our God," 35.

35 Chris Tomlin, Ed Cash & Jesse Reeves © 2004 Sixsteps Songs (admin. by Capitol CMG Publishing).

36 Chris Tomlin, Ed Cash, Jason Ingram & Matt Maher © 2013 Sixsteps Songs (admin. by Capitol CMG Publishing).

37 Blog of Jamie Brown, http://worthilymagnify.com/2013/04/04/we-believe-our-god-is-jesus/; accessed February 3, 2015. To be fair, Charles Wesley's great conversion hymn says something similar about Christ: "Amazing love, how can it be! / That Thou, *My God*, shouldst die for me?" (1738, emphasis mine). But Wesley has a

He states that "in this instance, I think this line slipped past some theological editing that would have made the song a lot better," and he wished the line had said, "We believe our *King is* Jesus."

This blogger expressed his concern to Lester Ruth who replied:

> I don't think that a single line ("our God is Jesus") should disqualify the song, particularly if you can couple it with other liturgical items that bring out a more trinitarian, New Testament way of speaking. Put the song in a good, strong, more balanced context. The line is not wrong per se, but it is not the best way to express things.[38]

That is wise advice to today's worship leaders who want to use a song that is weak or open to misunderstanding.[39]

While our worship is to be robustly Christocentric, it is also to be trinitarian, as clearly stated by our Baptist ancestors in their major *Confession of Faith* (1677).[40] Today Robin Parry reminds us that "the worship of Jesus is central to Christianity, and it is honouring to both the Father and the Spirit," but it must not be done in a way that "[pushes] the Father and the Spirit to the margins."[41] For example, Jesus said that the Father desires and deserves worship (John 4:23). In that sense, we confess "faith in one God, Father, Son and Holy Spirit" and worship "the Father, through the Son in the power of the Holy Spirit."[42]

---

clearer description of the incarnation ("he left his Father's throne above, and emptied himself of all but love"). Further, he is rightly making a statement only about Jesus divinity, without giving the impression that only he is God, which Tomlin's statement "my God is Jesus" could lead others mistakenly to conclude.

38 http://worthilymagnify.com/2013/04/04/we-believe-our-god-is-jesus/; accessed February 3, 2015.

39 A helpful book on the Trinity and worship (by one who is sympathetic to CW) is Robin Parry, *Worshipping Trinity: Coming Back to the Heart of Worship* (Milton Keynes: Paternoster Press, 2005). See "Worshipping with the Trinity," "Worshipping the Trinity" and "Singing the Trinity," 86–146. Forewords by Matt Redman and Keith Getty.

40 The Baptist *Second London Confession of Faith* (1677), article XXII (Of Religious Worship and the Sabbath Day) par.2, states that "religious worship is to be given to God the Father, Son and Holy Spirit" in William L. Lumpkin, ed., *Baptist Confessions of Faith,* rev. ed. (Valley Forge: Judson Press, 1969), 280.

41 Parry, *Worshipping Trinity*, 109.

42 James Torrance, quoted in Carson, *Worship by the Book*, 43. See pages 41–43 for a helpful description of this.

It is encouraging that a tweeter's request for a song written on the Apostle's Creed resulted in Hillsong's recent "This I Believe (the Creed)."[43] In his church tradition, Ben Fielding the co-composer explains that the Apostle's Creed was repeated regularly in his church so he did not want to "mess with words or treat it lightly."[44] His rendition covers some major points of the Creed and in fact makes it stronger than this fourth-century statement by declaring, "Our God is three in One."[45]It is also heartening to see that before his band plays it in concerts, he has the audience read the Apostle's Creed on the screen. That way he says "there is an incredible power in realizing this great history we were joining."[46]

4. *Encourage the worship bands to enable the congregation to sing*

John Stackhouse raises a significant point from church history. "By the time church music matured...in the 16th century, it had become too demanding and ornate for ordinary singers. So Christians went to church to listen to a priest and a choir."[47] He points out that the Protestant Reformation corrected this when the reformers "yanked musical worship away from the professionals and put it back in the pews. Luther composed hymns with simple (and beautiful) tunes and metres.[48] ...This was music in

43 Ben Fielding and Matt Crocker © 2014 Hillsong Music Publishing (admin. by EMI Christian Music Publishing).

44 Interview with Ben Fielding, https://www.youtube.com/watch?v=lqfLu29dSRQ; accessed May 10, 2015.

45 It also wisely leaves out the word *catholic*, since many today misinterpret this to be the Roman Catholic Church.

46 Interview with Ben Fielding.

47 John Stackhouse, "Memo to Worship Bands: Five Sound Reasons to Turn Down the Volume," *Christianity Today*, February 2, 2009 (http://www.christianitytoday.com/ct/2009/february/14.50.html; accessed January 3, 2015).

48 In the original published CT article, this sentence read, "Luther composed hymns based on popular melodies, including drinking songs." But historian bloggers informed him that this is an oft repeated myth. Once convinced of their evidence, he changed the wording of this sentence in his blog and said, "I am persuaded. So I have altered the original post so I will not be guilty of spreading this myth further!" http://www.johnstackhouse.com/2009/02/04/memo-to-worship-bands-turn-it-down-please/; accessed February 20, 2015.

The myth (that both Luther and Wesley used saloon tunes for their hymns) needs to be dispelled for it is often used to support the notion that for the sake of evangelism

which almost anyone could participate."[49] In contrast to this, Stackhouse declares,

> is the modern-day insistence that a few people at the front be the center of attention. We do it by making six band members louder than a room full of people. But a church service isn't a concert at which an audience sings along with the real performers. Musicians—every one of them, including the singers—are *accompanists* to the congregation's praise. They should be mixed loudly enough only to do their job of leading and supporting the congregation.[50]

In his related blog post, which generated much discussion, he states why he had not set a decibel level in that article.

> Sorry, but I don't have a dB rating or anything of the sort. My sense instead is this judgment has to be made contextually and communally. Ask your church through a survey whether the music hurts their ears (I am appalled to hear that some churches hand out earplugs.)[51] or whether they find it unpleasantly loud, or whether they find it too loud for the style, or whether they find it too loud relative to the congregation, or whether they find it too soft for the style, for leading. ...once you get past the question of sheer ear

---

any kind of music can be used. See Dean McIntyre, "Did the Wesleys Really Use Drinking Song Tunes for Their Hymns?" (http://www.umcdiscipleship.org/resources/did-the-wesleys-really-use-drinking-song-tunes-for-their-hymns; accessed March 2, 2015) and Lester Ruth, "History Takes a Hit" in *Discerning the Spirits: A Guide to Thinking about Christian Worship Today*, ed. Cornelius Plantinga Jr.and Sue A. Rozeboom (Grand Rapids: Eerdmans, 2003), 32, 33.

49 Stackhouse, "Memo to Worship Bands."

50 Stackhouse, "Memo to Worship Bands."

51 He is not exaggerating. For example, the webpage for Elevation Christian Church in Aurora, CO, USA (www.elevationcc.com) informs visitors: "We also want to make you aware that we offer earplugs at the doors of the auditorium if you feel like you need extra hearing protection." Similarly, I recently attended an Easter service in a very large chapel with wonderful acoustics. The service included two choirs and instrumental pieces. Sadly, a youthful worship band started the service with their "set" and the volume was so loud I literally could not hear myself sing, or anybody else, so I stopped. Some people ahead of me plugged their ears. To be fair, the organizers were new to the building, but it was evident that they had not done a thorough sound check, nor had they considered the largely older demographic in attendance.

damage, other questions come into play that require Christian virtues of good judgment, concern for others, concern for worship, concern for visitors, the respective roles of leaders and congregants and the like.[52]

Include and/or expand time-honoured components of the worship service

1. *Highlight the Lord's supper, rather than diminish it*

Sadly, there is a trend in some of our churches, especially in seeker-friendly services, to minimize aspects of the Lord's supper and have a very open communion position, with little pastoral instruction or time for self-examination given. Traditionally, in Free Churches there was always a time of introspection before receiving the elements (as required in 1 Corinthians 11:28). Many understood "the purpose of one's self-examination" (for any sin in their lives) "was to become worthy of the Table, lest one come under judgment."[53] Unfortunately, as Gordon Fee points out, this understanding was based on the word in 1 Corinthians 11:27 that the King James Version mistranslated as *unworthily* and this produced "dire threat for generations."[54] In part, this caused many Baptist churches in the past to hold to a closed communion position (only believers baptized by immersion were eligible).[55] The NIV translates it more accurately as "in an unworthy manner," which when taken in context, refers to improper behaviour at the Table.[56] In the present day, with denominational differences being minimized, it is understandable that the Lord's table would be presented in a friendlier way so as to not offend visitors.

It is therefore striking that Willow Creek Community Church in Illinois, the flagship seeker church, which holds an open com-

52 Stackhouse blog at http://www.johnstackhouse.com/2009/02/04/memo-to-worship-bands-turn-it-down-please/; accessed July 11, 2016 .

53 Gordon Fee, *The First Epistle to the Corinthians* (Grand Rapids: Eerdmans, 1987), 560, 560 n.10.

54 Fee, *The First Epistle to the Corinthians*, 560.

55 This was the position held by Andrew Fuller (1754–1815), the influential pastor and secretary of the British Baptist Missionary Society in the eighteenth century, though his close friend and fellow pastor Dr. John Ryland Jr (1753–1825) held to an open position that welcomed non-immersed believers to participate.

56 Fee, *The First Epistle to the Corinthians*, 558, 559.

munion position, places limits on participation. It makes clear that "communion is 'the *believer's meal,*' ...for *Jesus' followers....* Anyone who has *accepted His forgiveness* and *surrendered their lives* to Him is invited to share the Communion table at Willow." In contrast, "Those investigating Christianity who have not yet made a *commitment of faith* through Jesus Christ are encouraged to simply let the Communion plate pass by utilizing that portion of the service to pray and invite God's activity into their investigation of faith (emphasis added)."[57]

The position of Redeemer Presbyterian Church is similar but goes one step further. "If you are not in a saving relationship with God through Christ today, do not take the bread and the cup, but as they come around, take Christ. Receive him in your heart as those around you receive the food. Then immediately after, come up here and tell an [church] officer or a pastor about what you've done, so we can get you ready to receive the Supper the next time as a child of God."[58] To help, a prayer of repentance is included in the bulletin.

In the Free Church tradition, we are able to have non-ordained persons preside at the Lord's supper, if we wish. But because this is such a key moment, it is important to coach them how to lead this so it is in line with biblical guidelines. Rather than turning people off, Keller states that Redeemer's procedure, when presented in a sensitive but firm way, is one of the two main ways in their church services that persons come to faith. That is why he says that when presented "in ways that make the gospel clear ...the Lord's Supper can become a converting ordinance" when "it is explained properly."[59]For unbelievers and believers "there is no more effective way to help a person take a spiritual inventory."[60]

---

57 "Who can take communion?"; http://www.willowcreek.org/southbarrington/go-deeper/baptism-a-communion; accessed January 10, 2015.

58 Keller, "Evangelistic Worship," 9. See also free download paper by Timothy Keller, "Changing the World through the Lord's Supper," © 2002, 2010 Redeemer City to City available at www.gospelinlife.com.

59 Keller, "Evangelistic Worship," 8. The second way in the church service is through a time of guided reflection following the sermon.

60 Keller, "Evangelistic Worship," 8.

2. Reclaim the privilege of public prayer

In earlier days, pastors did most of the praying. Today, it is refreshing to see laity actively leading in prayer. Unfortunately, the variety of the prayers has diminished. In the Free Church tradition, we tend to think that our extemporaneous public prayers are more fresh and spiritual. But John Newton (1725–1807), the former slave trader turned Anglican pastor, observed,

> many who profess to pray extempore, that is, without either a printed or a written form, go so much in a beaten path, that they who hear them frequently can tell, with tolerable certainty, how they will begin, when they are in the middle, and when they are drawing towards the close of their prayer.[61]

Also, today's worship team members often utter prayers that are mere segues between songs. That is, using wording from the song just sung or about to be sung.

Further, our extemporaneity makes us more susceptible to habits that distract, rather than edify the congregation. Kevin DeYoung reminds us that leading in public prayer is different from personal prayer. "*Remember you are praying with and on behalf of others*. Use 'we' and 'our' (as in the Lord's Prayer). This is not the time to confess your personal sins or recount your personal experiences."[62] He also warns us about unhelpful and distracting prayer habits. "*Beware of verbal ticks*. For example: popping your p's, smacking your lips, sighing, ums, mindless repetition of the divine name, overuse of 'just' and 'like,' an over-reliance on the phrase 'we pray' or 'we would pray' instead of simply praying.[63] Similarly, Spurgeon taught his students to avoid what he called "an unhallowed and sickening superabundance of endearing words" such as *Dear Jesus, Blessed Lord* and *Sweet Lord.*[64]

---

61 John Newton, *The Works of John Newton*, vol.5 (1820; reprint, Edinburgh: Banner of Truth, 1985), 11, 12.

62 Kevin DeYoung, "Leading in Prayer…deserves thoughtful preparation," *Leadership Journal* (Summer 2010); http://www.christianitytoday.com/le/2010/summer/leading-prayer.html?share=qsUJ2FqhIZWtQchPnQozEa6w%2fV%2faxdgg; accessed April 2, 2015).

63 DeYoung, "Leading in Prayer."

64 Charles Spurgeon, *Lectures to My Students* (1875; reprint, Lynchburg: The Old-Time Gospel Hour, n.d.), 57.

Gordon MacDonald, bluntly said recently, "Can I be frank? I'm distressed by the low quality of public prayer that is being heard in too many worship services today."[65] He continued,

> I love to be in worship when young men and women are leading. And many of them lead us so well. But when they come to the place where prayer is appropriate, the substance of the prayer sometimes reveals a person who has hardly thought for a minute what they are going to say next... "God...we just want to thank you for this day...that we just could...just...sing to you...that we could...just...love you." Well meant, those words. But they lack thought; they lack power, and they fail to lodge themselves in the souls of their hearers.[66]

The same can often be said of others leading in prayer in the service. When, for example, non-ordained[67] persons offer spontaneous public prayer, if God the Father is addressed in prayer, he is periodically thanked for shedding his blood and dying for our sins. To correct this sloppy thinking, it would help if we kept John 3:16 and Colossians 1:20 in mind.[68]

The difficulty is further compounded when the purpose of each prayer is unclear. Hence, at times it appears repetitious, and often other areas are omitted. MacDonald addresses this in his article, "The Cleansing Power of Public Prayer."[69] He says, "In worship, I

---

65 Gordon MacDonald, "Praying that Makes a Difference," *Leadership Journal* (Spring 2012); http://www.christianitytoday.com/le/2012/spring/makesdifference.html; accessed April 2, 2015).

66 MacDonald, "Praying that Makes a Difference."

67 Here I use the term non-ordained because those ordained are usually required to have formal theological training and hence are not as prone to be unclear regarding the dynamics within the Trinity.

68 Some distinctions are succinctly expressed in the song "There Is a Redeemer" ("Thank You O my Father / For giving us Your Son / And leaving Your Spirit / Till the work on earth is done.") Melody Green © 1982 Universal Music—Brentwood Benson Publishing. For helpful instruction see also "Praying the Trinity," in Parry, *Worshipping Trinity*, 147–159.

69 Gordon MacDonald, "The Cleansing Power of Public Prayer," *Leadership Journal* (Winter 1987); http://www.christianitytoday.com/le/1987/winter/8711056.html; accessed February 3, 2015. Note that the remaining quotes from MacDonald are taken from this article.

discovered, there are at least six kinds of prayer to be offered on behalf of the people. The unknowing leader may confuse the six, mix their purposes, and diffuse [their] effectiveness." For him, there are prayers of: (1) gathering ; (2) sending at the end of the service; (3) focus on God and his dealings with his people; (4) confession; (5) for world needs; and (6) for our people's needs.

MacDonald includes these final four in what is commonly called the pastoral prayer. He admits that when he first began in ministry, he did not value this prayer highly. Like most of us, he had not been taught how nor seen it modelled. Nor had he come to appreciate how people desire to be prayed for in their difficult and stressful situations. But once he did, he changed his approach. "In my pastorates, it became the one prayer of worship I steadfastly refused to delegate as long as I was in the [pastoral] service." He continues, "I deem the pastor's prayer on a par with the pastor's sermon. If the sermon is the pastor's opportunity to hold up the Word of God to the people, the pastor's prayer is the opportunity to hold up the people to God." Charles Spurgeon, that great prince of preachers, went further than MacDonald. He declared that if he had to choose between praying and preaching, he would "sooner yield up the sermon than the prayer."[70] We need to remember that Spurgeon and another great Baptist preacher, Alexander Maclaren, were as much valued for their praying as for their preaching![71] Today, where various people pray in the same service, it is necessary that each prayer's focus be decided in advance so that elements are not missed.

MacDonald reminds us that the pastoral prayer is a holy pastoral moment for the gathered church. "They come each week wearied, muddied, and bloodied. Perhaps the most refreshing thing I can do for them is offer heartfelt prayer.... It is the congregation's opportunity (and, I believe, privilege) to hear their pastor pray for them." All week our people are bombarded with news of natural disasters, horrible butcheries, widespread injustice and economic unrest. "Somehow," he says, "my prayer must

70 Spurgeon, *Lectures to My Students*, 60.

71 See C.H. Spurgeon, *The Pastor in Prayer: A Collection of the Sunday Morning Prayers of C.H. Spurgeon* (Edinburgh: Banner of Truth Trust, 2004) and Alexander Maclaren, *Pulpit Prayers* (New York: Hodder and Stoughton, 1911).

put these things into an eternal perspective and model how to pray in light of such events."[72] While we may value spontaneity from the heart, it behooves us to prepare our minds so we can pray with thoughtfulness too! (I have been challenged by reading MacDonald's articles quoted above and I would encourage pastors and all who pray publicly to read them to see how he understood it and prepared himself for it.)

There is also a trend of providing musical background when prayer is offered. Donald Hustad is critical of this because it creates a "vague, mystical-but-distracted feeling." If the background music is a familiar tune, "the listeners may be directed to the words" and if it is something the musician is improvising the listener may be "following and evaluating the 'instant composing.'" He concludes, "We need no background 'mood music' for talking to God; it really gets in the way of coherent and cognitive worship." He bluntly says that "music should stop" when the person "begins to pray."[73] Of course there can be exceptions to this, but background music need not be the norm for prayer. We need not be afraid of some moments without hearing music.

3. Incorporate more language of the Psalms

N.T. Wright, the noted British bishop and theologian, observes that "in a great many contemporary churches, something very odd has happened, which is that many of the newer churches write their own worship songs—which is wonderful. I'm all in favor of people writing their own worship songs in every possible idiom—but they often simply forget the Psalms." He complains, "You can go to many churches where if you attend week after week, you will never ever sing or read the Psalms."This is quite striking. "There's something very peculiar about that, because in pretty well every branch of the Christian tradition for 2,000 years, the Psalms have been the backbone of Christian worship. Certainly in all traditional denominations, but in many non-traditional ones, as well, it's assumed that the Psalms are the heart of worship." Furthermore, he points out that "the Psalms were the

72 MacDonald, "The Cleansing Power of Public Prayer "and "Praying that Makes a Difference,"

73 Quotations in this paragraph are from Hustad, *Jubilate II*, 497, 498.

prayer book that Jesus Himself used...and the early Christians used them, and it seems to me extraordinary that we would ignore that resource in our own worship."[74] In fact until Isaac Watts (1647–1748) the more liturgical churches sang only from the psaltery. Free Churches did not sing them as much but often read them in the services.[75] For example, in the *Baptist Hymnal*[76] that many Free Churches used in the 1960s, one quarter of the 100 responsive readings were Psalms.[77] Sadly, even Psalm 23 (as well as the Lord's Prayer) is seldom read publicly today, except at funerals.

In a *Christianity Today* interview, Wright explained why the Psalms can be so beneficial in worship. Human beings find themselves overcome with a wide spectrum of deep emotions and perplexing thoughts and "we must have a way of saying 'Yes, that is exactly where I am right now.' The Psalms offer a way of worshipping God amid any and all emotional states."[78] Calvin wisely called the Psalms a mirror of the soul, "for there is not an emotion of which anyone can be conscious that is not here represented as in a mirror."[79] The Psalms include more than expressions of praise, and these need to be sung, read, prayed or quoted if we are going to have authentic worship. Therefore, it is time for some creative ways of reintroducing Psalms (whole or in part) into our services.[80] For example, a UK musician, Matt Searles, has recently produced music for twenty Psalms that include

---

74 Eddie Kaufholz, "N.T. Wright on Why the Psalms Matter," *Relevant Magazine* (January 2014); http://www.relevantmagazine.com/god/practical-faith/nt-wright-why-psalms-matter#comments; accessed March 29, 2015.

75 Hustad, Jubilate II, 203

76 Walter Hines Sims, ed., The Baptist Hymnal (Nashville: Convention Press, 1956).

77 Similarly, the popular inter-denominational *Hymnal for Worship and Celebration* (Waco: Word, 1986), 650–661, has a special section of extensive readings of twenty-six Psalms.

78 "Saving the Psalms: An Interview with N.T. Wright," *Christianity Today* (September 2013): 79. See his full treatment in N.T. Wright, *Case for the Psalms: Why They Are Essential* (New York: HarperOne, 2013).

79 Quoted in Tremper Longman III, "Getting Brutally Honest with God: The Psalms of Lament Invite Us To Voice Our Frustrations—and Provide a Reason To Hope," *Christianity Today* (April 2015): 58.

80 For a guide and resource for the use of all the Psalms see John D Witvliet, Martin Tel and Joyce Borger, *Psalms for All Seasons: A Complete Psalter for Worship* (Grand Rapids: Calvin Institute of Christian Worship, Brazos Press, 2012).

most of each psalm, so that a wider range of psalmists' emotions and thoughts are expressed.[81] His melodies lend well to a meditative time of reflection. They are written in a key that the congregation can sing, and they are also very moving when sung by a soloist as the congregation is bowed in prayer. Further, when sung, it is important periodically to point out that what we are singing is from, or inspired by, a specific Psalm. For example, Matt Redman's "10,000 Reasons" is a popular CW hymn-like version of a portion of Psalm 103.[82] Sadly, in the four settings where I have heard this sung, there was no mention that it was from a Psalm. Hence, people were not pointed back to Scripture.

4. Prominently display the Bible as a key symbol of our faith

In many of our newer church buildings, there are few religious symbols. Generally on church buildings, the cross is still a noticeable symbol of a Christian church. But inside the sanctuary (now usually referred to as auditorium) there is little in our multiple-use space to remind us we are in church, except for our offering plates and, once a month, our communion trays. Pews are being replaced with theatre seats or flexible comfortable chairs. Many have removed the large fixed pulpit to provide more flexibility of movement and improve sightlines.[83] But after the music has stopped and the sermon begun, it looks like the preacher is speaking from an evacuated concert stage cluttered with abandoned music stands, instruments and microphones. Unfortunately, possibly to impress visitors that our congregations are trendy and modern, those upfront often read Scripture from their smartphones. However, it would be more instructive to read from what is obviously a Bible in one's hand, especially when major portions are being read and from which they are preached. This clearly reminds all that our sacred book is the

---

81 From the "River to the Ends of the Earth" (2011) and "Now and Not Yet" (2013). See http://www.mattsearles.org.uk/; https://mattsearles.bandcamp.com/

82 Matt Redman and Jonas Myrin, © 2011 Thankyou Music (admin. at EMICMG-Publishing.com).

83 I am not speaking against this, for twenty years ago in two churches I encouraged them to replace the large ornate pulpits (which a few in one church dubbed the penalty box) with something less overpowering and more movable.

Bible and that it is foundational to our faith and practice.[84] Of course, in our visual age we would do well to consider how to introduce other symbols and images, especially at special times in the church year.

5. Conclude the service sensitively and pastorally

Following the sermon, many contemporary-focused services conclude quickly with a few announcements and a casual dismissal. Unfortunately, this misses key pastoral opportunities. The following would be sensitive ways to respond to the sermon:

(i) Give time for congregants to process what they have heard and to offer their hearts up to God. Since solid preaching is always for a response it is important to provide time for this. This might also include a moment of silence and application prayer by the preacher who has been meditating on that sermon all week.

(ii) It is appropriate for the congregation to sing in response to the sermon. A wisely chosen response song will express something of what people are feeling and wanting to express to God.[85]

(iii) It is fitting to end with a form of benediction. It is noteworthy that giving the Aaronic blessing was the one action God asked of all priests (Numbers 6:23–26). Therefore, one writer laments the casual conclusion of services today that end in only a "charge (instruction as to what we should do)," rather than "a benediction (blessing from God to go forth empowered to live lives worthy of our calling)."[86] This results in our going forth "shut up to our own strength"

---

84 This is especially helpful for those visiting from other faiths that have a sacred book and expect us to have one too.

85 A very helpful and practical book for worship leaders is Bob Kauflin, *Worship Matters: Leading Others to Encounter the Greatness of God* (Wheaton: Crossway Books, 2008). See pages 241–259 on ways worship leaders and pastors can work together.

86 Comments by Marguerite Shuster in Amos Yong, "Which False Teachings Are Evangelical Christians Most Tempted To Believe In?" *Christianity Today* (April 2015): 27.

rather than leaning on God's enabling grace.[87] There is a significant difference.

(iv) Provide an easily found designated location (probably at the front) with prepared attendants where after the service individuals can go for prayer, ask questions about what they have heard or indicate they desire to follow Jesus.[88]

Concluding comments

Sadly, in the recent struggle over worship, the focus quickly degenerated into a conflict over a simplistic choice between music styles of HW and CW. In the process, some changes enhanced our worship, but other aspects developed out of shape, and still others did not receive the attention they deserve. Therefore, we need to address these shifts and losses so that our worship will be more complete. It will require pastors and worship leaders making mid-course corrections and doing this in such a way that their congregations come to value all that a worship service can be.

---

87 Marguerite Shuster in Yong, "Which False Teachings Are Evangelical Christians Most Tempted To Believe In?" 27.

88 This is the approach used by Redeemer Presbyterian Church in New York City (Keller, "Evangelistic Worship," 9).

14

What does a sixth-century Catholic pope have to say to twenty-first century evangelical pastors? An examination of Gregory the Great's *Pastoral Care*

BY BARRY H. HOWSON

Stan and I first met in a theology classroom in 1980, he was the professor and I was the student. It was a first for both of us, his first time teaching theology and my first time taking theology. I don't remember much about the course, but this is where we began a long and precious relationship. Over the following years we crossed paths on numerous occasions. One of those occasions was in the early 1990s when I was considering pursuing post-graduate studies in order to teach in a seminary setting. Stan, as blunt and honest as he is, made it clear that the likelihood of obtaining a seminary teaching position was slim. For a variety of reasons I decided to pursue a Ph.D. in church history at McGill University and subsequently graduated in 2000. It was in the following year that I was interviewed and accepted as the Bible and theology professor at Heritage College, Cambridge, Ontario. Though

Stan's advice was and is still true, I am truly thankful to the Lord that it wasn't true for me.

Though Stan and I had been good friends prior to my coming to Heritage, our friendship has deepened over the fifteen years that we have been colleagues. Stan is truly a kindred spirit and I highly value his friendship. One of those areas in which we thoroughly agree is the place of formal theological education *vis a vis* the church. The college and seminary exists to serve the church. Our goal, our purpose is to help the church fulfil its mandate of glorifying God through making disciples around the world. For this reason, as a professor of church history, I would like to look at one of the great medieval pastors, Gregory the Great, who some 1,400 years ago laid out the role and function of the pastor in his *Pastoral Rule.*[1] We might ask, what can a sixth-century Roman Catholic Pope have to say to twenty-first century evangelical pastors? As we will see, much. In this paper we will give a survey of Gregory's life, followed by a brief explication of his *Pastoral Rule* and conclude with application for pastoral ministry in the twenty-first century.

Gregory's life[2]

Gregory was born into a Christian family of the senatorial aristocracy sometime around A.D. 540. It was at this time that Justinian (A.D. 483–565), the eastern Roman emperor, and his general, Belisarius, were in a campaign against the Goths to recover Italy. By the time Gregory was fifteen years old, the war had left Italy depopulated and impoverished. As much as a third of the population had perished through war, famines and plague. Even though the Goths were defeated and Imperial rule was restored, the fruit of victory was not to be felt by the Roman aristocracy

---

1 The title in Latin is *Regula Pastoralis*. I will be using the English edition from the Ancient Christian Writers series entitled, *St. Gregory the Great: Pastoral Care*, trans. and annot. Henry Davis (Mahwah: Newman Press, 1978).

2 For the details of Gregory's life and thought the most comprehensive study of the life and writings of Gregory comes from the two volume set by F. Homes Dudden, *Gregory the Great: His Place in History and Thought*, 2 vol. (London: Longmans, Green and Co, 1905). Not as comprehensive but an update to Dudden is R.A. Markus, *Gregory the Great and His World* (Cambridge: Cambridge University Press, 1997). Other worthwhile books include J. Barmby, *Gregory the Great* (1879; reprint, Miami: Hardpress Publishing, 2012) and John Moorhead, *Gregory the Great* (Abingdon: Routledge, 2005).

but by Justinian's eastern court officials. In other words, Italy became an eastern Roman colony.

From the 540s onward, most of the surviving ancient families of Rome left the city in pursuit of more fruitful opportunities in the eastern part of the world, particularly in Constantinople. Moreover, since the fifth century the political centre and place of power in Italy had moved from Rome to Ravenna. From here the Imperial Governor of Italy, known as the Exarch, ruled in the emperor's place.

Rome's glory days were long past. This was even reflected in its population decline since the early fifth century. In A.D. 400, the population of Rome was approximately 800,000 but by A.D. 546 it had dropped to just 30,000. The pope had little power, the Roman Senate no longer existed and the former glory of Rome was truly gone. This was the world into which Gregory the Great was born and lived his early years.

Gregory's family had a distinguished tradition of service to the church and the city of Rome. For example, he was the great-great-grandson of Pope Felix III and a relative of Pope Agapitus I. In his early years, he was educated in the traditional schools of grammar and rhetoric, as well as natural science and Roman law. In his early life, Gregory entered into a political career, becoming a prefect of the city in his early thirties. Following the death of his father, who was a *Regionarius* in the church, his mother Silvia became a nun along with three of his father's sisters. It was not unusual at this time for those of the Roman aristocracy to flee from the world into the bosom of the church; and this, in part, reflected the church's power and growing dominance in the West. Considering the times, it was an understandable response to the disasters afflicting Rome. Life in a monastery allowed one to be useful through contemplation, as action seemed futile.

When he was about thirty-five, Gregory resigned from his prefecture and turned his parental home into a monastery, dedicating it to St. Andrew, and submitted himself to the monastic life. His family had extensive estates in Italy and Sicily, and they all passed into the hands of the Roman church for which Gregory established six monastic houses. Gregory spent the next several years in prayer and reflection on Scripture, and he would later recall them as the happiest of his life. It was the contemplative life that Gregory valued the most, and when he became pope he greatly missed it. He writes,

> I remember with sorrow what I once was in the monastery, how I rose in contemplation above all changeable and decaying things and thought of nothing but the things of heaven.... But now by reason of my pastoral care I have to bear with secular business, and, after so fair a vision or rest, and fouled with worldly dust...I sigh as one who looks back and gazes at the shore he has left behind.[3]

In the latter part of the 570s, Pope Benedict I ordained Gregory as deacon, and he was placed in charge of the city's 7th District with the responsibility for its administration and charitable relief. It was at this time that the city of Rome was besieged by the Lombards and the new pope, Pelagius II, sent Gregory to Constantinople to plead for military help and relief from the eastern Emperor Tiberius. He remained there for seven years.

During this time, he lectured regularly on the book of Job, as well as carried out his diplomatic duties for the pope. During these years, he made many connections in Constantinople that would stand him in good stead when he later became pope in the West. These years, however, did not influence his theology; he remained thoroughly Roman and quite suspicious of Eastern theology and liturgy. In his mind, Rome was the eternal city, the dwelling place of the apostles, and so had the primacy in theology.

After seven years in Constantinople, he was recalled to Rome by Pope Pelagius II in order to resolve the Istrian schism, sometimes known as the Three Chapters controversy which related to monophysitism.[4] Subsequent to his arrival in A.D. 589, Rome experienced a dreadful winter in which the Tiber rose and overflowed the city's walls. Churches and granaries were flooded and destroyed, and the food supplies needed for the winter were decimated. Consequently, a plague broke out and Pope Pelagius

---

[3] Quoted in Eamon Duffy, *Saints and Sinners: A History of the Popes*, 3rd ed. (New Haven: Yale University Press, 2005), 61.

[4] Christ does not have two natures but one. The human nature has been subsumed into the divine. This was an ongoing issue from the fifth century and many eastern churches were Monophysite, particularly east of the Mediterranean.

was one of the first to fall. Upon Pelagius' death, Gregory was elected by the clergy and the people to succeed in him as pope.

One of the first significant issues that Gregory addressed as pope was the defense of the city against the Lombards. Strategically, Rome was unimportant (Ravenna was the capital), and it was essentially left up to the popes to defend it. In the past, they had kept the Lombards at bay by buying temporary truces from them; basically, these were bribes that were raised from the church's own resources. As this was the policy of Pelagius II, Gregory continued to do so. In addition, he negotiated treaties with the Lombards, ransoming refugees and providing for their relief. In addition, he had to pay the wages of the Imperial troops who resided in Rome, as well as pay for their provisions. Moreover, he oversaw the monastic communities and encouraged the establishment of new ones. He also sought to raise money for the needy and to make sure that those in charge of church properties were good employers. He even made a detailed register of every poor person in the city of Rome—where they lived, what their names and ages were—and made sure that they got a weekly ration of corn, wine, cheese and oil. This concern for the poor can be seen in his personal life such that every day he shared his dinner table with twelve poor people.

It needs to be understood that by this time the church was the largest single landowner in the West. This was the result of Constantine and his successors, as well as the provision of donations and legacies of great families like Gregory's. The most important of these church holdings were the ones in Sicily which had not been ravished by the wars of the past and had the potential to adequately supply the needs of the people of Rome. Gregory made sure that this would be so by overhauling the administration of these church lands by replacing corrupt local bishops and lay administrators with his own hand-picked members of the Roman clergy. Moreover, he continued to scrutinize their activities, making sure that they were honest, generous and fair in their dealings with the tenants and employees of the land.

Gregory detested the Lombards and their cruel acts, such as taking Roman people to the north of Gaul and selling them as slaves, but he also recognized the need for the Lombards to be saved from the Arian heresy.[5] It was during his tenure that two successive Lombard kings were married to the Bavarian Catholic princess, Theodelinda. This gave Gregory a foothold in the Lombard court and eventually the Lombards renounced Arianism for Catholicism.

During his papacy, Gregory was always willing to work with the emperor in Constantinople. But he was just as willing to stand against him, if he felt that the emperor was overstepping his bounds. For example, in A.D. 593 Emperor Maurice issued an edict that forbade any soldiers from resigning their posts in order to enter monastic life. In response, Gregory wrote a blistering rebuke, accusing Maurice of abusing his power and so locking up the way to heaven for those who wanted to pursue the contemplative life. He even charged him with ingratitude to God who had given him his emperorship, reminding him that he would one day have to stand before God's judgement seat and give an account.

In another instance in A.D. 595, he told Maurice that

> the care of the whole church had been committed to the blessed Peter, Prince of the apostles. Behold he received the keys of the kingdom of heaven; to him was given the power of binding and loosing, to him the care and Principate of the whole church was committed.[6]

Gregory was utterly committed to Roman supremacy. This issue of supremacy came to a head when the patriarch of Constantinople, John the Faster, took the title of "ecumenical patriarch." Even though John meant the title to be no more than "Imperial Patriarch," Gregory opposed John's continued use of the phrase and sought to pressure members of the Imperial family and administration in Constantinople to stop using it. He also wrote to the patriarchs of Alexandria and Antioch, seeking to convince them of the illegitimate use of the word "ecumenical," which Gregory thought implied "universal." It would appear that Gregory was not so concerned about his own power and prestige

---

5 Many of the Germanic tribes were evangelized by Arian missionaries from the eastern half of the empire in the fourth century.

6 Quoted from Duffy, *Saints and Sinners*, 65–66.

but that the papal primacy be based on humility and service. Consequently, his favourite term for his office was "servant of the servants of God." This pastoral vision for leadership was most excellently expressed in his treatise entitled, *Pastoral Rule*, as we will see. The key message of the *Rule* is that the bishop is to be a servant, not a master. In addition, Gregory feared that the devilish desire for power was creeping into the true church through this terminology. And, he blamed the emperor and his pride as one of the reasons the patriarchs of Constantinople had "fallen into the whirlpool of heresy."

The patriarchs of Antioch and Alexandria did not share Gregory's concern, and, in fact, believed that Gregory was using this rhetoric to strengthen his own position of power. When Gregory heard this accusation he was horrified. He wrote, speaking to the patriarch of Alexandria:

> Here at the head of your letter I found the proud title of "Universal Pope," which I have refused. I pray your most beloved holiness not to do it again, because what is exaggeratedly attributed to another is taken away from you. It is not in words that I would find my greatness, but in manner of life. I do not consider that an honor which, as I know, undermines the honor of my brothers. My honor is the honor of the universal church. My honor is the solid strength of my brothers.... Away with these words which inflate vanity and wound charity.[7]

Gregory would have nothing of this seeking of power and prestige in the church.

It should be noted that Gregory's papacy had little influence in Gaul, North Africa, Spain and England, or the church in Ireland. It would appear that Gregory's ministry during these years of his papacy was essentially responding to the material and spiritual needs of the world around him and as they came to his attention. We know that almost two-thirds of his surviving letters are replies to problems, rather than initiatives that Gregory instituted.

He did, however, initiate one very important mission, the

7 Quoted from Duffy, *Saints and Sinners*, 67.

sending of a monk named Augustine (not to be confused with Augustine of Hippo) to Anglo-Saxon England. Essentially, this was the first time that a leader of the Roman church had sought missionary outreach beyond the Empire. Why did Gregory decide to evangelize England? The earliest biography of Gregory, written in England a century after Gregory had died, elaborates on a scene in Rome in which Gregory, as a deacon, saw some handsome, fair-haired Anglo-Saxon boys. When he was told that they were called Angles, he replied, "they are angels of God." From that point, he desired to win England for Christ. We even have record that, by A.D. 595, Gregory was instructing the rector of the papal patrimony in Gaul to purchase seventeen- or eighteen-year-old English slave boys so they could be trained as monks in Roman monasteries. It is not inconceivable that Gregory was thinking of this Anglo-Saxon mission and using these boys as interpreters in England.

In A.D. 596, Gregory sent the prefect from his own monastery at St. Andrew's, known in history as Augustine of Canterbury, to England. Forty monks landed in Kent to serve in the lands of King Ethelbert who was married to a Catholic Christian (the daughter of the King of Paris). Gregory's desire was for Augustine to establish two archbishoprics with twelve subordinate bishops under each in the old centres of Roman rule in Britain, that is, London and York.[8]

It is important to note that the English church saw Gregory as its founding father, first mentioned in Bede's *Ecclesiastical History*.[9] And it was his *Pastoral Rule*, as well as his letters, that were treasured as sources of inspiration and guidance in the English

---

8 It is worthy of note that in terms of liturgical practice, Gregory was open to diversity. For example, he told his friend Leander of Seville who had sought counsel about the correct method of baptizing, that "where there is one faith, a diversity of usage does no harm to the church." Again when Augustine was inquiring about which custom of the mass he should use in England whether Roman or Gallican, Gregory told him to adopt whatever customs seemed likely to be helpful to the Church of England regardless of their source. He wrote, "My brother, you know the customs of the Roman church in which of course you were brought up. But...things are not to be loved for the sake of a place but places are to be loved for the sake of their good things." It is clear that Gregory's heart was primarily for the spread of the gospel to barbarian kingdoms like that of Britain, as we have already seen in his desire to win the Lombards to Christ, not tradition.

9 This is the first history of the church of English people, written in the seventh century.

church. Many Anglo-Saxon churchmen and kings went to Rome for inspiration, and so English reverence for the Roman bishop increased over the centuries. This reverence also extended to all things Roman, from building styles to the style of chanting of the Psalms in the Roman basilicas (Gregorian chant). But the primary focus of the English was on the person of the pope who had "the keys of Peter." Gregory would often send tiny reliquaries to select bishops and even kings, as marks of his favour toward them. These reliquaries were made in the form of a key and contained some filings from the chains of St. Peter. This was a powerful symbol of the power that the popes of Rome possessed in order to bind and loose.[10]

Gregory's influence in missionary endeavours went beyond England long after his death. English clergy of the Roman mould, such as Willibrord, Boniface and Alcuin, spread the gospel and the settling of Christianity in northern Europe in the seventh and eighth centuries. With the spreading of this Anglo-Saxon Christianity came a submission to the Roman bishop as never before. In many ways, this is why Gregory has been considered the first real pope, exercising papal power and influence that would only increase throughout the Middle Ages. Gregory's life and papacy came to an end in A.D. 604.

Gregory's *Pastoral Rule*

Gregory produced several books but the one that we are concerned with in this essay is the *Pastoral Rule*.[11] It was written just

10 This power was clearly manifested at the Synod of Whitby in A.D. 664. King Oswiu, having heard the arguments from both the Roman and Irish clergy regarding the dating of Easter, ruled in favour of the Roman practice because the keys of the kingdom had been given to St. Peter not to St. Columba of Iona. And so the king declared, "Since he is the doorkeeper, I will not contradict him but I intend to obey his commandments and everything to the best of my ability, otherwise when I come to the gates of the kingdom, there may be no one to open them, because he who holds the keys has turned his back on me" (quoted in Duffy, *Saints and Sinners*, 71). So had become the power of the papacy in England by the middle of the seventh century.

11 All of Gregory's extant works, including his letters, come from his years in the papacy. He believed that his teaching of the things of God to others enabled him to understand the things he was teaching better. He writes, "By the generous gift of God it happens that, when I am teaching in your presence what I am learning on your behalf, my understanding becomes greater and pride smaller, because to tell the truth, I am hearing with you many of the things which I say" (*Homilies on Ezekiel* 2.2.1).

Gregory wrote several important works: his commentary on the book of Job, entitled, *Moralia in Job*; *Pastoral Rule* or *Regula Pastoralis*; *The Homilies on Ezekiel*; *Dialogues*; *Forty Sermons on the Gospels*; and *Exposition of the Song of Songs*. In addition, we have 850 extant letters in 14 books, one for each year of his pontificate.

Most likely Gregory's greatest work is his commentary on the book of Job entitled, *Moralia in Job*. This work is based on talks that he had with the group of monks that joined him on his trip to Constantinople as the papal ambassador. He states at the beginning of this work that the monks who accompanied him asked him to expound the words of the history of the book as well as its allegorical meaning. One needs to understand that for Gregory, the deeper meaning, particularly in the Old Testament, was what the text taught concerning Christ and the church. The deeper meaning of the text was more important than the historical (literal) meaning of the text. The monks also wanted him to direct the allegories toward the practice of morality and so not only looking at the text allegorically in order to see New Testament truths present there but also to see how we might live properly. This is why almost all of the works that we have from Gregory are essentially from the Old Testament.

This exposition of Job was fifty times longer than the book itself and was only half completed by A.D. 595. It was a work directed toward those who had given themselves over to the religious life and was not meant for public use. He begins his commentary by describing his method of interpretation. His intention for the whole work was, first, to describe the historical meaning, that is, the literal meaning, then the allegorical interpretation which follows, and finally what it teaches concerning the proper way to live (morality). He begins this way but then ends up very shortly dismissing any commentary on the historical meaning, and moves directly to the allegorical and the moral. Looking back at other great theologians such as Ambrose or Augustine, this was certainly nothing new. The portion that Gregory spends the most time on are the words of God in Job 38 to 41, which takes up nearly 400 pages in a modern translation.

In the early part of his pontificate (*c.* A.D. 593) he preached his *Homilies on Ezekiel* but did not have them published until A.D. 601. It was made up of two books. The first book dealt with chapters 1 to 4, and the second book examined the vision of the temple found in chapter 40. The latter part of Ezekiel made no sense on the literal level and so, for him, it demanded an allegorical interpretation. As with Job, it was the more obscure parts that demanded detailed commentary. This was definitely a scholarly work meant for those who knew their Bibles and even knew the difference between the Septuagint and the Hebrew versions of the Old Testament. Gregory ended the exposition before he finished chapter 40 and asked his readers not to rebuke him for the place where he concluded because at that time the Lombard King Agilulf was on his way to invade Rome.

The more popular of Gregory's works was his *Dialogues*, probably written around the same time as the *Homilies on Ezekiel*. The four books of the *Dialogues* are filled with stories of holy men who had worked miracles, approximately 200 examples in total. The work has a popular and folksy feeling to it, and the purpose of these miraculous stories for Gregory was their signification—they pointed beyond themselves, that is, pointed to the reality of holiness in the person who performed them, or set forth God's will. It should be noted that the entire second book is given over to the life of St. Benedict.

Other works from Gregory's early years as pope, probably A.D. 590 to 592, are his sermons on the Gospels: *Forty Homilies on the Gospels*. As usual, Gregory's exposition and concern was for the allegorical meaning of the text as well as the moral meaning.

after he became pope, and was dedicated to John of Ravenna, a fellow bishop. Its purpose was to help those who were holding episcopal office.[12] Part of this work was sent to the Eastern patriarchs, and copies of the whole work were given to newly appointed bishops over the next centuries.[13] It is divided into four books

---

These sermons were directed to a more popular audience. His love for allegory is transparent in his exposition of the parable of the lost coin in Luke 15. When expounding on the friends and neighbours in verse 9, he proceeds to give a long discussion of the nine ranks of angels.

Gregory also did a short work on the first nine versus of Song of Songs 1. And, as we would expect, it was interpreted in a highly allegorical way.

12 The initial reason behind Gregory's *Pastoral Rule* was essentially his reluctance to take the office of the Bishop of Rome. Some speculate that he composed parts of it while he was at St. Andrew's Monastery but that it didn't reach its final form until his consecration early in A.D. 591 when John of Ravenna's letter occasioned its publication. The Latin title, *Liber Regulae Pastoralis* gives us a hint as to what Gregory had in mind when he wrote this work. The word *regula* is most important. The term had been used in the past for the monastic rules for different monastic houses. For example, Pachomius had a *Regula*, Caesarius of Arles had a *Regula*, and of course the famous Benedict of Nursia had a *Regula*. It is quite likely that Gregory used the *Rule of St. Benedict* in his monastery at St. Andrew's. It would appear then that Gregory's plan was to write a *regula* for the *secular* clergy as a counterpart to the *regulae* for the monastic life. Worthy of note are the number of similarities between Gregory's work and the work of Gregory of Nazianzus (A.D. 329–390), in particular, the second treatise of his *Orations* or *Discourses*. In the latter work, Gregory of Nazianzus gives the reasons behind his desire to flee his ordination, which parallels Gregory's experience.

13 From the day of its publication the *Pastoral Rule* was read by many. He sent a copy to his friend Leander, Archbishop of Seville, and Leander introduced it to the churches of Spain. He sent a copy to the Irish monk and missionary Columban, who received it with great joy. During his lifetime, it was translated into Greek by the Patriarch of Antioch by order of the Eastern Emperor Maurice. And Augustine of Canterbury took this work on his mission to England in the 590s. Several hundred years later, Alcuin wrote a letter to the Archbishop of York and said, "Wherever you go, let the pastoral book of St. Gregory be your companion. Read and reread it often, that in it you may learn to know yourself and your work that you may have before your eyes how you ought to live and teach. The book is a mirror of the life of a Bishop and medicine for all the wounds inflicted by the devil's deception" (Alcuin, *Epistle* 116). Its influence continued in England when at the close of the ninth century, King Alfred the Great had the *Pastoral Rule* translated into West Saxon. The king desired that every bishop in England have a copy of this translation; he wanted this *Rule* to bring about reform in the clergy and laity. It should also be noted that in several synods called by Charlemagne in 813, the study of the *Pastoral Rule* was made obligatory for all the bishops. It was Gregory's treatise that was to train the priests in how to be ministers of the church in order for the laity to grow spiritually. A little later in time, it became customary to give the *Pastoral Rule*, along with the canons of the church, to each bishop at his consecration. They were told to observe this rule in their life, their teaching and their pastoral decisions. F. Homes Dudden outlines the

and, as we would expect, addresses areas of ministry that Gregory felt were important. The first book deals with the difficulties of taking up the pastoral office, as well as the requirements needed for it, that is, how one should become a pastor. The second is on the inner and outer life of the pastor. The third is on how the pastor is to teach and admonish those under him. In the last book, he teaches how the preacher should look to his own life and teaching so he does not become proud.[14]

Counsel from Gregory to twenty-first century pastors

Gregory's *Pastoral Rule* does not really say anything that has not been said before, but it provides reminders and emphases that are worthy of our attention as pastors in the twenty-first century. There are three areas of his counsel that I want to highlight: (1) Counsel to those who are considering the call to pastoral ministry; (2) Counsel to those in pastoral ministry regarding their lives; and (3) Counsel to those in pastoral ministry regarding ministry of the Word. We will look at each one in turn.[15]

1. Counsel to those considering pastoral ministry

The whole of the first part of Gregory's *Pastoral Rule* addresses those who would seek to enter pastoral ministry. And he begins the section with a word of caution:

> No one ventures to teach any art unless he has learned it after deep thought. With what rashness, then, would the pastoral office be undertaken by the unfit, seeing that the government

---

Pastoral Rule's continued influence throughout the Middle Ages in Europe: "Its influence during this period can scarcely be overrated—indeed it is felt even now in its results. The maxims of Gregory have molded the church. They have sensibly shaped the conduct and the policy of the church's rulers, and as a modern writer well expressed it, have 'made the bishops who made modern nations.' The ideal which Gregory upheld was, for centuries, the ideal of the clergy of the West, and through them the spirit of the great Pope governed the church, long after his body had been laid to rest beneath the pavement of St. Peter's" (Dudden, *Gregory the Great*, 1:107–109).

14 It should be noted that much of the material in this work is similar to that in the *Moralia*. The book of the Bible that is most quoted in the *Rule* is the book of Proverbs. Consequently, Gregory's purpose was to give a practical theology to those who were in pastoral ministry.

15 All page numbers for *Pastoral Care* will be provided in the text for the remainder of the essay.

> of souls is the art of arts! For who does not realize that the wounds of the mind are more hidden than the internal wounds of the body? Yet, although those who have no knowledge of the powers of drugs shrink from giving themselves out as physicians of the flesh, people who are utterly ignorant of spiritual precepts are often not afraid of professing themselves to be physicians of the heart, and though, by divine ordinance, those now in the highest positions are disposed to show a regard for religion, some there are who aspire to glory and esteem by an outward show of authority within the holy church. They crave to appear his teachers and covet ascendancy over others, and, as the truth attests: they seek the first salutations in the marketplace, the first places at feasts, and the first chairs in the synagogues (*Pastoral Care*, 1:21–22).

For Gregory, anyone looking for glory in the pastoral office should refrain from entering it. Later in the *Rule,* he has these words for those who have just begun their ministries and are eager to preach, thinking they are quite able to do so. He strongly admonishes them "not to cut themselves off from the way to future progress by hastily arrogating to themselves the burden of so great an office" (1:180). It may be that they will one day have the opportunity to preach, but they must wait for that day without going forth hastily. He writes, "They should be admonished to bear in mind that when fledglings attempt to fly upwards before their wings are fully developed, they fall down from where they tried to soar" (1:180). In this, he reminds his readers that Jesus did not officially begin preaching until he was thirty years of age.

Moreover, Gregory wants those who seek pastoral ministry to make sure they count the cost. Gregory realizes that Paul had stated in 1 Timothy 3:1, "If a man desire the office of the bishop, he desires a good work." Therefore, one who is called to pastoral ministry should have a desire for the office, but Gregory also points out that Paul promptly qualifies this desire by adding a reason for fear, stating, "but it behooves a bishop to be blameless." And then Paul enumerates what it means to be blameless in the following verses. Gregory writes, "the great master in the art of ruling urges subjects on by approving of their desire, but deters them" (1:35). Gregory sees Paul's qualifications for ministry as deterrents. One entering into the ministry must realize this calling is to an exemplary holy life.

What then is the character required of one who comes to the office of pastor? It is necessary that he who desires to rule must devote himself entirely to setting an ideal of living. Gregory writes:

> He must die to all passions of the flesh and by now lead a spiritual life. He must have put aside worldly prosperity; he must fear no adversity, desire only what is interior. He must be a man whose aims are not thwarted by a body out of perfect accord through frailty, nor by any contumacy of the spirit. He is not led to covet the goods of others, but is bounteous and giving of his own (1:38–39).

What does this kind of life mean specifically for Gregory? Two things in particular: an attitude of humility and a giving of oneself to others.

He realizes that those in pastoral leadership will be tempted to pride. One who is governing others must watch that he is not puffed up by the experience of his position. He is to be as Jesus, "to love adversity for the sake of truth and to shrink in fear from prosperity" (1:26). Gregory realizes how easy it is for people in leadership positions to become conceited. Consequently, he uses Jesus as an example who "fled from the exalted glory that was offered to him" and chose the pain of death in order that "his followers might learn to flee from the favors of the world" (1:26).

In order to see if one is fit for this office, therefore, Gregory encourages the one seeking pastoral office to reflect on his past life. In particular, he must consider what his attitude has been when under the authority of others. Did he learn humility? Was he humbly submissive to his superior? According to Gregory, "for a man is quite incapable of learning humility once he is in a position of superiority" (1:37). Consequently, he must learn humility *prior* to taking up the position of bishop. This is an excellent point.

This kind of holy life in pastoral ministry means a giving of oneself to others. Gregory states that the pastor must have a compassionate and sympathetic heart, taken up with the concerns of others. He writes:

> He is [one who is] quickly moved by a compassionate heart to forgive, yet never so diverted from perfect rectitude as to forgive beyond what is proper. He does no unlawful act himself while deploring those of others, as if they were his own. In the affection of his own heart he sympathizes with the frailties of others, and so rejoices in the good done by his neighbor, as though the progress made were his own. And all that he does he sets an example so inspiring to all others, that in their regard he has no cause to be ashamed of his past. He so studies to live as to be able to water the dry hearts of others with the streams of instruction imparted (1:38–39).

Should a pastor be concerned for himself? Certainly. But as a pastor he will have to forgo many of his own interests for the sake of those in his flock. Gregory understood this. His own desire was to live a contemplative life, and so he resisted public life for personal solitude. But he took up public life as bishop of Rome, giving up what he personally desired, for the sake of others.[16]

Gregory also highlights those things that he believes disqualify a person form pastoral office. He cautions anyone who is seeking this office but is weighed down with earthly cares or is controlled by sin; this one should refrain from this calling. He states that one who is allowing vice to reign in him and who is "debased by his own guilt must not intercede for the faults of others" (1:40). He maintains that the one who does not "love the light of heavenly contemplation does not know where to direct the steps of his conduct," and therefore, should not lead others (1:40). If he sees the way that he should go but does not follow that way persistently, he should not take up the office. He uses the analogy of

16 Gregory also warns those who have been gifted with many virtues and talents for the training of other people not to flee from the pastoral ministry for the sake of their own peace. If they are gifted, they are to use these gifts for the sake of others. They also must not hide behind humility, he writes, "for he is not genuinely humble, who understands that the decision of the supreme will is for him to take leadership, and yet refuses that leadership. But when the supreme rule is imposed on him and provided that he is already endowed with those gifts whereby he can benefit others, he ought, in submission to God's dispositions and removed from the vice of obstinancy, to flee from it in his heart and obey, though to obey is contrary to his inclination" (*Pastoral Care*, 32).

the nose and its ability to discern sweet from foul odours. He states that the man with a little nose is unable to discern virtue from sin—this does not become one who leads others. Or, if he is like the one who has a crooked back and is therefore weighed down by the burden of earthly cares so that he never looks up to the things that are above (1:41). Gregory goes on to say about this one,

> If at any time he hears something good about the heavenly fatherland, he is so weighed down by the burden of evil habit, that he does not raise up the face of his heart; he just cannot. The cast of his thought being bowed down by his habitual earthly solicitude (1:41–42).

In addition, one is disqualified if he has not learned to control the thoughts of his mind, allowing them to be controlled by evil thoughts; he calls this one "a ruptured man." He states, "because his mind cannot disengage itself from these thoughts, he consequently lacks the strength to raise himself to the overt exercise of good deeds, because a shameful hidden burden weighs him down" (1:44). Gregory is not suggesting that pastors be perfect in thought, but that they be not controlled by evil thoughts.

He concludes, after delineating those things that disqualify a person from pastoral ministry, by saying that if anyone has these defects he is "forbidden to offer loaves of bread to the Lord"(1:44). The reason is obvious: a man who is still ravaged by his own sins cannot help with the sins of others.

2. *Counsel for the pastor's life*

The second area of Gregory's counsel to be highlighted is advice to his fellow pastors regarding their character and ministry life—in his words, "how he who has worthily undertaken the office ought to live in the exercise of it." The whole of the second part of the *Pastoral Rule* is taken up with this advice. He declares at the beginning of this section, "The conduct of a prelate should so far surpass the conduct of the people as the life of a pastor sets him apart from his flock." He goes on to enumerate what that life is to be like:

> It is necessary, therefore, that he should be pure in thought, exemplary in conduct, discreet in keeping silence, profitable in speech, in sympathy a near neighbor to everyone, in contemplation exalted above all others, a humble companion to those who lead good lives, correct in his zeal for righteousness against the vices of sinners. He must not be remiss in his care for the inner life by preoccupation with the external; nor must he in his solicitude for what is internal, fail to give attention to the external (1:45).

We will highlight several of these areas that I believe are particularly pertinent to twenty-first-century pastors, namely: (1) a life of humility; (2) thought-life; (3) motives for ministry; (4) balance of inner life and outer ministry; and (5) Word possessed.

But, before we look at each one in turn, Gregory gives his readers his rationale for the godly life of the pastor. Gregory believed that the pastor should be exemplary in his conduct because "by his manner of life he may show the way of life to his subjects, and that the flock, following the teaching and conduct of its shepherd, may proceed the better through example rather than words" (1:48). Consequently, his words will penetrate the hearts of his hearers much more effectively if his life commends what he says. According to Gregory the pastor's conduct should be outstanding, not "only doing what is upright in the midst of the wicked, but also surpassing the well doers among his subjects" (1:49). For Gregory, the godly life of the pastor is not only necessary as an example, but also gives credibility to his words when in private counsel and preaching.

So, what are those areas of pastoral life that Gregory believed are becoming of a good pastor? The first, which is prominent in all of Gregory's writings, is *a life of humility*. Gregory realizes that the pastor's position can lead to conceit and pride. He provides Saul as an example of one who began in humility, but by his eminence in power became proud. And so Gregory can say, "When the mind of a man is inflated with a multitude of subjects under him, he becomes corrupted and moved to pride by the eminence of his power which panders to the mind" (1:62). But the good pastor knows how to control this problem of pride while in pastor leadership. Gregory states that this one

> disposes his power aright, who knows how, with great care, both to derive from it what is profitable, and to subdue the temptations which it creates and how, though in possession of it, to realize his equality with others, and at the same time set himself above sinners in his zeal for retribution (1:62).

He gives the example of the apostle Peter, who had the primacy from God in the church.[17] He dealt with godly people on an equal level but, with the ungodly like Ananias and Sapphira, he showed "with what great authority he had been made preeminent over others"(1:63). This demands that "humility must be preserved in the heart and discipline in action" (1:64). Therefore, Gregory writes, "Let rulers, therefore, uphold externally what they undertake for the service of others, and internally retain their fear in their estimate of themselves" (1:64). Consequently, for Gregory, pastors that have this power over others must keep it in subjection "otherwise the mind will be unable to control that to which it subjects itself in its lust for domination" (1:65). And, in this he quotes Jesus in Matthew 20:28 and Mark 10:45ff, that pastors are to be servants of all. He calls the one who uses his power for the purposes of domination a hypocrite.

However, if the pastor deals with his flock as an equal, it should not lead him to cease exercising his duties to the degree that he fails to discipline those who need rebuke in their lives. And yet humility must control his heart in his rebuke so that the one rebuked senses a heart of lovingkindness, as a father lovingly correcting his child. He believed that discipline must not be "too rigid or loving-kindness to lax" (1:66). There needs to be a balance in the pastor's ministry to those under him between gentleness and severity. In fact, "gentleness is to be mingled with severity." As King David said, "Thy rod and thy staff, they have comforted me." And so Gregory states, "It is with the rod that we are smitten, but we are supported by a staff. If, then, there is the correction of the rod in striking, let there be the comfort of the staff in supporting." He concludes by saying,

---

17 Remember, for Gregory, the apostle Peter was the first pastor of the church of Rome, and therefore, had great pre-eminence.

> There should, then, be love that does not enervate, vigour that does not exasperate, zeal not too immoderate and uncontrolled, loving kindness that spares, yet not more than is befitting. Thus, while justice and clemency are blended in supreme rule, the ruler will soothe the hearts of his subjects even when he inspires fear, and yet in soothing them, hold them to reverential awe for him (1:67).

Concerning humility, he also warns the pastor of the danger of the mind flattering itself about its virtue in its fight against vice. He needs to realize that the devil will use this against him. And so he concludes,

> It is necessary that when a wealth of virtues flatters us, the eye of the soul should turn its gaze on its infirmities, and for its own good it should prostrate itself. It should look to the good not that it has done, but that which it has neglected to do, so that while the heart becomes contrite in recalling its weakness, it may be the more solidly established in the eyes of the author of humility. For Almighty God perfects in great measure the minds of those who rule but leaves them partially imperfect for this reason, that when they are resplendent with extraordinary attainments, they may grieve with disgust for their imperfections, and, least of all, exalt themselves for great things, when they have to labor and struggle against very small matters. And as they are not able to overcome the very little things, they should not presume to pride themselves on the great things they accomplish (1:237).

Gregory believes that honest self-reflection of our own failings is one way to be humble. He reminds his readers of Jesus' words in the Sermon on the Mount, where we are to be conscious of the log in our own eye before we remove the speck in our neighbour's eye (Matthew 7:5).

Not only is humility prominent in Gregory's writings but so is his *concern for the pastor's thought life*. The pastor should be always pure in thought. He believed that it was necessary that "the hand that aims at cleansing filth should itself be clean, lest, sordid with clinging dirt, it fouls for the worse everything it touches" (1:46). This will allow the pastor to deal with his subjects properly so that he "allows no mixture of human reason in what he dispenses in the place of God" so that when counselling others, he is not embittered toward them as he seeks to minister to them (1:47). How easy it is to let one's own emotions get hold of oneself when counselling and so fail to provide the right advice! Moreover, Gregory realized that impure thoughts will manifest themselves in the lives of pastors, but that they must hasten to overcome them by repulsing them. This is to be a constant practice for the pastor's own sake. Consequently, the pastor must prevent the sin of impure thoughts that tempts him "by its voluptuous delight... from inflicting a fatal blow because of his too tardy rejection of it" (1:48). Be persistent in dealing with impure thoughts.

Another area of Gregory's concern for pastors is their *motivation for ministry*. He is concerned that this motivation not be to please men. That is, while he is properly caring for both the external and internal needs of his flock, he should always seek the truth more than the admiration and love of his subjects (1:75). The pastor needs to be mindful that while he performs his good works, they are not performed to be loved by the church but rather to be loved by Christ. The danger Gregory sees is clear: if the pastor is more concerned about what he gets out of his ministry for himself, his mind will be diverted into laxity. That is, he will not be willing to speak the truth and, if necessary, correct those of his flock, because he fears losing their love. He will reprove those who hinder his pursuit of temporal glory but will freely rebuke those who are unable to advance him temporally (1:76). This is hypocrisy and unbecoming of a pastor. Pastors are to treat all equally in their congregations, whether rich, poor, important, famous or not. This reminds us of James' counsel to show no favouritism (James 2:1–13). Gregory recognizes that this is a constant temptation for pastors, but that they are to desire and love truth more than themselves or their own personal advancement or gain.

A fourth area of concern for the pastor's life is the *balance between his inner life and outer ministry*. Again this is prominent in all of Gregory's writings, and is the result of his own struggle with this balance, particularly in his role as pastor of the Roman Church, and as the chief churchman of the Western church.

Gregory believed that the pastor needs to keep a balance between his contemplation of heavenly realities and his ministry to help the infirmities of the people he serves. Gregory's ideal is captured in these words,

> [The pastor is one who has already been] introduced to the secrets of heaven and yet by condescending love he gives thought to the bed of carnal men; and though he raises the vision of his heart to invisible things being himself elevated, yet he turns in compassion to the secrets of those who are weak (1:56).

He uses the example of Jacob when he saw the angels ascending and descending on the ladder. He writes, "That this was a sign that true preachers do not only aspire by contemplation to the Holy Head of the church above, namely, the Lord, but also descend to its members in pity for them" (1:57.) Again, he uses the example of Moses who went in and out of the Tabernacle. While in the Tabernacle, Moses is caught up in contemplation, but outside he devotes himself to the affairs of the people. For Gregory, by the pastor's willingness to go out and be among the weak, those of his flock will feel welcome at the pastor's bosom to hear words of comfort and encouragement in the midst of their struggles with sin (1:58).

At the same time, the pastor needs to be careful that in this condescension to the trials and sins of others, he does not succumb to the temptations that he hears. Gregory goes on to provide encouragement, saying, "But the pastor need not fear these things at all, for when God weighs all things exactly, the pastor is the more easily delivered from temptation, as he is the more compassionately afflicted by the temptations of others" (1:59).

Consequently, the pastor's longing for the solicitude of the inner life should not bring about neglect of his external duties. The pastor needs to remember that all of his external duties are to be performed for the sake of the people's souls that he ministers to. Therefore, he is not truly ministering to the real needs of his people if he is blind to the light of the truth because his concern for earthly cares occupies his mind. "Dust, driven by the winds of temptation, blinds the eyes of the church" (1:69).

> Subjects then are to transact inferior matters, rulers to attend to the highest, so that the eye, which is set above all for guiding the steps, may not be dimmed by annoying dust. For all rulers are the heads of their subjects, and surely the head ought to look forward from above, then the feet may be able to go onward on a straight path (1:70).

Gregory goes on to say, "For when anyone resigns himself to earthly activities after a life of constant holiness, reverence for him is ignored and grows dim, as though his lustre had faded in the eyes of man" (1:71). He continues,

> Secular employments, then, are sometimes to be sympathetically put up with, but never sought after out of affection for them. Otherwise, when they oppress the mind of him who is attached to them, he becomes submerged by the weight and sinks down from the concerns of heaven even to the very depths (1:72).

And so, Gregory counsels, the pastor cannot relax the care for his inner life by his preoccupation with external matters.

He also gives counsel to those pastors who have been put in charge of a flock but desire to be free from dealing with the concerns of that flock in order to pursue their own spiritual concerns, and, consequently, don't give any time to external matters. The needy need to know that their pastor cares for them by providing for them in their physical necessities. He writes, "Doctrine taught does not penetrate the minds of the needy, if a compassionate heart is not commended to the hearts of the hearers; but the seed of the word does germinate promptly, when the kindness of a preacher waters it in the hearer's heart" (1:72). Gregory is encouraging pastors to be concerned about their own inner lives, as well as the inner lives of his subjects, but also not to neglect to provide for their physical life. However, he cautions, "Care for temporal concerns must be displayed as much as need be, yet promptly reduced, lest it increase beyond measure" (1:74). For Gregory, the pastor must balance service to others with his spiritual growth in ministry.

So what should a pastor do to keep this balance? This brings us to the final area of concern for Gregory and his counsel to pastors: *they must be people in the Word and of the Word.* They must be in the Word regularly, saturated by it. He strongly encourages pastors to meditate diligently and every day on the precepts of the sacred Word (1:86). The purpose is so that the words of the Lord will restore in him a sense of his pastoral responsibility and provide a healthy check to his own spiritual life, which the constant dealing with people in this world destroys. Gregory writes,

> Actually the heart greatly deteriorates in the midst of human converse, and since it is undoubtedly manifest that, driven by the tumults of exterior occupations, it goes to ruin, it should ceaselessly make it its aim to rise again by the pursuit of instruction (1:87).

He uses examples from the writings of Paul, as well as the words of David and Moses to support his counsel.[18]

In addition, Gregory believed that when the pastor is constantly in the Word, "when his people consult him about spiritual matters, he does not have to go and find out for himself the answer and then solve the problem" (1:88)—he already knows the answer. To make his point, he uses the example of Exodus 25:12–15 which deals with instructions given to Moses about carrying the ark (1:87–88).[19] It is evident that Gregory expected the pastor to be a godly person filled with the Word.

---

18 1 Timothy 4:13; Psalm 119:97.

19 This is a great example of his allegorizing. He writes, "What is symbolized by the Ark but Holy Church? The orders are that it is to be provided with four rings of gold in the four corners—obviously because, being extended to the four parts of the world, it is declared to be equipped with the four books of the Holy Gospels. And staves of setim wood are made and inserted into these rings for carrying, because strong and persevering teachers, like incorruptible timbers, are to be sought out, who, always adhering to the instructions of the sacred volume, proclaim the unity of Holy Church, and, as it were, carry the Ark, by their being let into the rings. Indeed, to carry the Ark with staves is to bring Holy Church through preaching to the untutored minds of unbelievers. Furthermore, they are ordered to be overlaid with gold, that when the sound of their preaching goes forth to others, they may themselves shine in the splendor of their way of life. Regarding them it is well added: And they shall always be in the rings, neither shall they at any time be out of them; for it is evidently necessary that they who devote themselves to the office of preaching should never depart from the occupation of sacred reading. It is to this purpose that the staves are ordered to be always in the rings, that when occasion demands the carrying of the Ark, there should be no delay in inserting them—that is to say, when subjects

3. Counsel for the ministry of the Word

The largest section, almost two thirds of the *Pastoral Rule*, is devoted to the pastor and the ministry of the Word to his parishioners. Gregory sees pastors as "physicians of the soul" who must be about the business of helping all of those under them with their various struggles and sins. He follows the counsel of Gregory of Nazianzus who taught that "one and the same exhortation is not suited to all, because they are not compassed by the same quality of character" (cited in 1:89). And so Gregory the Great comments,

> Often…what is profitable to some, harms others. Thus, too, herbs which nourish some animals, kill others; gentle hissing that calms horses, excites young puppies; medicine that alleviates one disease, aggravates another; and bread such as strengthens the life of robust men, destroys that of little children (1:89).

Consequently, Gregory maintained that whatever a pastor teaches needs to be adapted to the character and needs of the hearer, and at the same time their preaching should never waver from being generally edifying. He concludes his introductory comments with, "Every teacher, in order to edify all in the one virtue of charity, must touch the hearts of his hearers by using one and the same doctrine, but not by giving to all one and the same exhortation" (1:90). This is very important for Gregory: there is one truth, and yet the application and the exhortation can vary according to the individuals to whom he is preaching.

In the first chapter of this section, he lists the different people to whom we preach, and counsels pastors to be able to distinguish between different types. For example, we need to distinguish between men and women, young and old, rich and poor, joyful

---

consult the pastor in any spiritual matter, it is most disgraceful if he should then seek to learn at a time when he ought to solve their problem. Let the staves remain in the rings: let the teachers, ever meditating in their hearts on the sacred word, at once raise the Ark of the Testament, let them teach forthwith when the occasion demands it. Wherefore, the first pastor of the church [Peter] well admonishes all other pastors, saying: Being ready always to satisfy every one that asketh you a reason of that hope which is in you, as if he plainly said: 'Let the staves never be withdrawn from the circles, so that no delay may hinder the carrying of the Ark'" (*Pastoral Care*, 1:87–88).

and sad—he goes on to chronicle a large variety of different types of people.[20] The rest of the chapter deals with these various groups and how we are to preach to them. In total, Gregory makes 36 Admonitions, encompassing a total of 72 different types of people; some of these Admonitions are short and some are long.[21] Most of the Admonitions take up anywhere from a page to several pages in a modern edition. In Admonitions 25 and 26, he even directs preachers on the way they should address fellow preachers.[22]

---

20 Here is a list of all the admonitions: "men and women; young and old; the poor and the rich; the joyful and the sad; subjects and superiors; slaves and masters; the wise of this world and the dull; the impudent and the timid; the insolent and the fainthearted; the impatient and the patient; the kindly and the envious; the sincere and the insincere; the hail (healthy) and the sick; those who fear afflictions and, therefore, live innocently, and those so hardened in evil as to be impervious to the correction of affliction; the taciturn and the loquacious; the slothful and the hasty; the meek and the choleric; the humble and the haughty; the obstinate and the fickle; the gluttonous and the abstemious; those who mercifully give of their own, and those addicted to thieving; those who do not steal yet do not give of their own, and those who give of their own yet do not desist from despoiling others; those living in discord and those living in peace; sellers of discord and peacemakers; those who do not understand correctly the words of the holy law and those who do, but utter them without humility; those who, though capable of preaching worthily, yet are afraid to do so from excessive humility, and those whose unfitness or age debars them from preaching, yet who are impelled thereto by their hastiness; those who prosper in their pursuit of temporal things, and those who desire, indeed, the things of the world yet are wearied out by suffering and adversity. [He continues:] those who are bound in wedlock and those who are free from the ties of wedlock; those who have had carnal intercourse and those who have had no such experience; those who grieve for sins of deed and those who grieve for sins of thought only; those who grieve for their sins yet do not abandon them, and those who abandon their sins yet do not grieve for them; those who even approve of their misdeeds and those who confess their sins yet do not shun them; those who are overcome by sudden concupiscence and those who deliberately put on the fetters of sin; those who commit only small sins but commit them frequently, and those who guard themselves against small sins yet sometimes sink into grave ones; those who do not even begin to do good, and those who begin but do not finish; those who do evil secretly and good openly, and those who hide the good they do, yet allow themselves to be thought ill of because of some things they do in public" (*Pastoral Care*, 1:90–92).

21 For example, a short one is his second admonition where he says, "Young people are to be admonished in one way, old people in another because the former are for the most part guided to make progress by severe admonition, while the latter are disposed to better deeds by gentle remonstrance, for it is written: an ancient man rebuke not, but entreat him as a father" (*Pastoral Care*, 1:92).

22 In Admonition 25, Gregory counsels those who have a right understanding of Scripture to make sure that they speak and teach that Scripture with humility. He

Gregory provides these admonitions because he believed that the pastor should know the issues with which his parishioners struggle so that "he may carefully propose the remedies indicated by the wound in each given case" (1:226). He also acknowledged the difficulty for any pastor when preaching to many hearers, to deal with the variety of issues that need to be addressed. And so, he says, "In this case the address must be formulated with such skill that, notwithstanding the diversity of failings of the audience as a whole, it carries a proper message to each individual, without involving itself in self contradictions" (1:226). And so, for example, when preaching on humility, the message needs to be spoken "to the proud in such a way not to increase the fear in the timorous, and damage their confidence," but at

---

writes, "They, therefore, who do not speak the words of God with humility, are certainly to be admonished, when applying remedies to the sick, to look to the poison of their own infection; otherwise, while seeking to heal others, they themselves will die." He further says, "They must be admonished to take heed that their manner of saying things is not at variance with the excellence of what is said, and not to preach one thing in words, and another in their outward conduct" (*Pastoral Care*, 1:174). Therefore, the teacher needs to be careful not to seek to win the praises of men in their teaching and preaching. In Admonition 26, he counsels people who can preach but do not out of an "inordinate humility." He writes, "Let them, then, consider in what great guilt they are implicated, because by withholding the word of preaching from sinning brethren, they are hiding the medicine of life from souls that are dying" (1:176–177). He strongly warns, "Let them consider what punishment is to be meted out to those who do not minister the bread of grace which they themselves have received, when souls are perishing from hunger for the word." Again he writes, "If men versed in the medical art were to observe a sore that needed lancing, and yet refuses to lance it, surely they would be responsible for a brother's death by their failing to act. Let them see, therefore, in what great guilt they are involved who, while recognizing the wounds of the soul, neglect to heal them by the lancet of words." And again he warns, "Let those therefore, who conceal within themselves the word of preaching, hear with terror the divine judgment against them, so that fear may expel fear from their hearts" (1:177). On the other hand he writes, "A man who goes out and dispenses blessings by his preaching, receives the fullness of interior increase; and while he unceasingly inebriate's the souls of his hearers with the wine of eloquence, he is himself increasingly inebriated with a draft of multiplied grace" (1:178). He also counsels in this admonition, those who for various reasons are not considered able to preach but think themselves able and so seek to undertake it. They are to be admonished "not to cut themselves off from the way to future progress by hastily arrogating to themselves the burden of so great an office" (1:180). It may be that they will one day have the opportunity to preach, but they must wait for that day without going forth hastily. He writes, "They should be admonished to bear in mind that when fledglings attempt to fly upwards before their wings are fully developed, they fall down from where they tried to soar" (1:180). In this, he uses Jesus' example who did not preach until he was thirty years of age.

the same time to correct the proud. Or when preaching to married and unmarried people, he states, "Wedlock is to be preached to the incontinent, but not so as to recall to lust those who have become continent. Physical virginity is to be commended to the continent, yet so as not to make the married despise the fecundity of the body" (1:227). He concludes by saying,

> Good things are so to be preached as not to give incidental help to what is bad. The highest good is to be so praised, that the good in little things is not discarded. Attention should be called to the little things, but not in such a way that they are deemed sufficient and there is no striving for the highest (1:227).

But there is more to the pastor than his public ministry of preaching—*he is also to minister to individuals privately*. Gregory considers this task to be the more difficult one, because it demands more careful investigation to provide the right counsel. For example, Gregory counsels that if a person is assailed by two vices, and one oppresses him more lightly and the other more severely, it is best to address the vice that leads to death more speedily (1:229). So Gregory gives an example,

> A man who does nothing at all to moderate his gluttony, is hard-pressed by temptations to impurity and is on the point of yielding to them. Thoroughly frightened by his struggles, he tries to check himself by abstinence, with the result that he is now harassed by temptations to vainglory. In his case, it is quite impossible to extinguish the one vice unless the other is fostered. Which, then, of the two plagues should be attacked more vigorously? Surely that one which presses with greater danger. It is simply to be tolerated that by the virtue of abstinence arrogance should, for the time being, gather strength in the case of one who is alive; otherwise by his gluttony impurity would cut him off from life utterly (1:230).

Moreover, when in private counsel, the pastor should not overtax the mind of his hearer so that "the string of the soul be strained too much and snap" (1:231).

Most importantly, before, after and during his public or private ministry of the Word to his parishioners, he states unequivocally that "every preacher should make himself heard rather by deeds than by words, and that by his righteous way of life should imprint footsteps for men to tread in, rather than show them by word the way to go" (1:232). They must carefully examine themselves and where they are failing, "make amends by severe penance." And so he concludes,

> Then, and only then, let them set in order the lives of others by their words. They should first take heed to punish their own sins by tears, and then declare what deserves punishment in others; and before they utter words of exhortation, they should proclaim in their deeds all that they are about to say (1:233).

Gregory the Great was truly a physician of the soul and these admonitions show him to be one who understood the human heart and the challenges believers face in this world. An excellent example is his counsel regarding temptation. He addresses those people that have sins of thought. He counsels them to consider carefully, deep down in their minds, "whether it was by pleasure only that they sinned, or by consent also." He goes on to say, "For, as a rule, the heart is tempted and feels pleasure in the sinfulness of the flesh, and yet opposes irrational resistance to the sinfulness, so that in its innermost thought it is saddened by what pleases it, and pleased by what saddens it" (1:201). Gregory realizes that often when we are tempted, our minds are engulfed by the temptation and so we do not resist the evil thoughts. But actually, we deliberately consent to what thrills it with delight and if there was an outward opportunity to act on the thought, we would. He believes that God sees this sort of sin in thought, as also one in deed, and so he writes, "If lack of opportunity defers the external sin, the will has consummated the sin by its act of consent." He gives the example of Adam, and says that sin was committed in three stages: firstly, the suggestion of it; secondly, the pleasure experienced; and thirdly, the consent. He maintains that the first stage comes from the evil one, the second from the flesh and the third comes from our spirit. And so he says, "For he who lies in wait for us suggests the evil, the flesh submits to the pleasure and at last the spirit, overcome by the pleasure, consents." Interestingly, he sees in this first sin: (1) the serpent suggests the evil; (2) Eve who is identified with the flesh, gave herself up to the pleasure; and lastly (3) Adam, who is the spirit, overcome by the suggestion and the pleasure, gives consent. And so he concludes, "We, then, become aware of sin by suggestion, we are overcome by pleasure, and by consenting we are also put in bonds." Consequently, Gregory admonishes those who have evil thoughts only (not acting on them), to be sorrowful for those thoughts so that they will not be led into evil deeds. On the other hand, they should not become despondent with grief over these thoughts because God has absolved his sins of thought "the more readily, in that he does not allow them to issue in deed" (1:202).

So how should one deal with temptation that comes upon him suddenly? He is to realize that

> they are daily engaged in the warfare of this life and to protect the heart unable to foresee wounds with the shield of anxious fear. They are to have a horror of the hidden darts of the Enemy lurking in ambush. They must fortify themselves within the mind's fortress with unceasing vigilance in so darksome a conflict. For if the heart lacks anxious circumspection, it exposes itself to wounds, for the crafty enemy smites the breast more freely, as he catches it unprotected by the breastplate of forethought (1:210–211).

One way that Gregory suggests that one not be overcome by such sudden impulses is to not be overly attached to earthly things. He compares it to the pilot who loses hold of the rudder of the ship—it is like the mind losing hold of the body. And so he says,

> To lose the rudder at sea is to fail to keep attentive forethought amidst the storms of this world. But if a pilot carefully holds fast the rudder, he steers the ship, now against advancing billows, now by cleaving the impetuous winds aslant. So, when the mind vigilantly rules the soul, it now surmounts and treads down some things with forethought, turns aside from others. It thus overcomes the present

dangers with great toil, and by looking forward, gathers strength to face future conflicts (1:212).

On the other hand, those individuals who willfully go into sin must be aware that there will be a severe judgement against them. Gregory says to these ones, "They...who go so far as to bind themselves in willful sin, are to be admonished to infer what kind of retribution will smite them someday, inasmuch as they now become, not the companions, but the princes of, evil-doers" (1:214).

Gregory provides many other examples of wise counsel for pastors as they minister to different types of people.[23]

---

23 He gives some important counsel in Admonition 13 to the healthy. He says the healthy "are admonished not to set aside the opportunity of winning eternal life.... They are to be admonished that if they are unwilling to please God when they can, they may not be able to please him when, too late, they decide to do so." In support he quotes from Proverbs 5:9, "Give not thy honor to strangers, and the years to the cruel." He interprets the "strangers" as evil spirits and so he says, "He, therefore, gives his honor away to strangers, who, being created in the image and likeness of God, devotes the span of his life to the behest of the malignant spirits. He, too, gives his years to the cruel, who expends the span of the life which he has received, according to the will of an adversary who dominates him for evil" (*Pastoral Care*, 1:120–121).

His counsel to the sick is for them to remember that they are sons of God and as sons he disciplines those he loves. He encourages them to focus on the heavenly country; and in order to reach the heavenly country they must endure the struggles of this country as if it were an alien one. He states, "The sick are to be admonished to consider what great health of the heart is bestowed by bodily affliction, for it recalls the mind to a knowledge of itself and renews the memory of our infirmity, which health commonly disregards" (1:123). Again Gregory counsels the sick to consider "how great a gift is bodily affliction, in that it both cleanses sins committed and restrains such as could be committed and that a troubled mind suffers the wounds of penitence inflicted by outward stripes" (1:124). He maintains that "when we are outwardly afflicted our sins are brought to our mind and we bring before our eyes all the evil we have done, and in proportion as we suffer outwardly, the more do we grieve inwardly for our deeds" (1:125). And to encourage the virtue of patience, the sick are encouraged to remember all that our Saviour went through, the blows to his face, the insults to him, the bearing of our sins. And so, he concludes, "Why, then, is it considered hard that a man should endure stripes from God for his evildoing, if God endured so great evil in requital for his own good deeds? Or what man is there of sane mind who is ungrateful for being himself smitten, when he who lived here without sin did not depart hence without a scouraging?" (1:126)

Another example is his counsel to young people regarding sin. In Admonition 29, Gregory counsels those who are innocent of the sins of the flesh to be all the more conscious of the possibility of falling into sin. He says, "We should admonish them to realize that the more conspicuous their position, the more numerous are the arrows hurled against them by him who lies in wait for us. The more stoutly he sees himself worsted, the more energetically does he bestir himself. The more intolerable to him

Conclusion

So what does a sixth-century Roman Catholic pope have to say to twenty-first century evangelical pastors? From this survey of Gregory's *Pastoral Rule*, we can see that he has much to say. Gregory's pastoral counsel is universal, and therefore, he doesn't really say anything new. He follows in the tradition of the apostle Paul, Cyprian, Gregory of Nazianzus and Augustine, and foreshadows the thinking of Luther, Calvin, Spurgeon and John Piper, to name but a few. However, Gregory provides us with fresh counsel of age-old truths, and provides a reminder of what is most important in pastoral ministry. I believe three things in particular stand out: (1) pastors need to be examples of godliness, and so vigilantly attend to their own walk with Christ; (2) they need to know and care for their flock; and (3) they need to be steeped in the Word for their own sakes and for the sake of their parishioners.

---

is his shame of being conquered, the more clearly he perceives that he is opposed by an unbroken barrier of weak flesh." Gregory sees the devil lurking around seeking to destroy this one and stepping up his attack to do so. And so he goes on to say, "They are to be admonished to look unceasingly to their rewards, and then, without doubt they will gladly spurn the toils of temptation which they suffer. For if we regard the happiness which we attain and which does not pass away, then the toil which passes becomes light"(1:195–196). In particular, Gregory is talking about those who have given themselves to virginity and so he says, "Those who are innocent of the sins of the flesh should be admonished to realize that the state of virginity is superior to the state of wedlock; but at the same time they must not extol themselves above those who are married. They should esteem virginity in the first place, but put themselves last. Thus they will the better keep what they prize, and so guard themselves from vainly extolling themselves" (1:197).

Afterword

BY HEINZ G. DSCHANKILIC

It was the Spring of 1991. As the academic year drew to a close, so did my time as a full-time student of divinity at Central Baptist Seminary. As I reflected upon the previous three years, I humorously chuckled at a warning passed on by upper classmen about a particular Systematics professor by the name of Mr. Stan Fowler. (He wasn't a doctor in those days.) To a man, they quoted Proverbs 6:5: "Free yourself, like a gazelle from the hand of the hunter, like a bird from the snare of the fowler." Their warnings were not without warrant.

One of Stan's charms is his quiet, disarming and deadly logical analysis of quotes, quips and comments made by students under his watch care. He has a rapier-like mind for theology and uses it to great effect. I can recall, on more than one occasion, engaging Stan in a discussion of some thorny area of doctrine. I knew I was correct in my reasoning, had all my texts lined up in context and had supporting evidence from other theologians who had commented on the same point of doctrine. I was right! In the space of five minutes he had twisted me into a theological pretzel and caused me to doubt my real birth name was Heinz. I asked him sheepishly, "But sir, I think I did my research correctly. I had the right texts, and the weight of secondary evidence was on my side. Where did I go wrong"? Stan answered, "You didn't. Your research was spot on, your conclusions were biblical and your reasoning was in accord with orthodox doctrine. You did well. I wanted to make sure that you were certain of your facts."

These encounters were causing endless nights of sleeplessness as graduation day loomed ahead. In those days, every student prepared a doctrinal statement of faith. The statement was then submitted to faculty for review. An appointment time was set in which the graduate would have to give an oral defense of his statement in front of two members of the faculty. I had hoped and prayed that I would draw any examiner but Stan Fowler. As was my lot, under the providence of God, my old professor sat across the table from me, and so the final interrogation commenced. I vaguely recall having stream-of-consciousness lapses and stumbling verbally as the combination of adrenalin, nerves and caffeine took its toll. I was doomed! Stan was kind, sympathetic, gracious and generous for the entire hour of that examination. Thankfully, according to Stan, my stumbles and lapses were not sufficient to merit failing. I graduated!

I would be remiss in failing to mention that, in addition to being a merciful teacher, Dr. Fowler played a pivotal role during some harrowing years at Central Baptist Seminary. Between the years 1990 and 1993 and up to the merger with London Baptist Seminary, the future of Central Baptist was bleak. Financially the school was living day to day. Bankruptcy was writ large in everyone's thinking.

At the same time, Stan was in the middle of his Ph.D. program. Doctoral programs are very expensive and must be completed by a specified deadline. In most schools, if the dissertation is not completed within a given time frame, the student loses credit for his work and forfeits the chance to present his dissertation—thus forfeiting the Ph.D. In the midst of this turbulent period, Stan put his personal and career aspirations on hold, stepping up to lead the school when it had no leadership in sight. He placed the kingdom first, with the real knowledge and concern that personal goals might never be fulfilled, sacrificing time and money already spent. This was no easy decision.

As Christians, we understand that all things work out according to God's will. Ultimately, human achievements and successes are within God's providence. However, God does use appointed means to bring about his desired ends. The school, now known as Heritage College & Seminary, with its state-of-the-art campus and burgeoning enrolment, was made possible by Stan stepping into the breach at a critical juncture. At that crucial point in Canadian Baptist history, God used Stan Fowler as an appointed means to bring about a desired end. Had he not been a selfless servant, willing to put aside personal milestones, Heritage might not exist today.

I and countless other alumni thank you, Dr. Fowler, for your service to our risen Saviour and your dedication to Christian education. It was a privilege and honour to have you as a teacher.

Stanley K. Fowler's publications

Books

Rethinking Baptism: Some Baptist Reflections. Eugene: Wipf & Stock, 2015.

More Than a Symbol: The British Baptist Recovery of Baptismal Sacramentalism. Studies in Baptist History and Thought. Eugene: Wipf and Stock, 2002.

Papers, articles, chapters and workshops

"Election, Grace, and Perseverance in Baptist Thought." A paper presented at the Evangelical Theological Society, San Diego, CA, November 2014.

"Baptism and Church Membership: An Evaluation of John Piper's Proposal." A paper presented at the Evangelical Theological Society, Milwaukee, Wisconsin, November 2012.

"An Analysis of Baptist Arguments for Congregational Autonomy." A paper presented at the Evangelical Theological Society, San Francisco, California, November 2011.

"Moral Law and the Law of the Land: Mosaic Case Law as a Paradigm." A paper presented at the Evangelical Theological Society, New Orleans, Louisiana, November 2009.

"Baptists and Churches of Christ in Search of a Common Theology of Baptism." In *Baptist Sacramentalism 2*, edited by Anthony R. Cross and Philip E. Thompson. Carlisle: Paternoster, 2008.

"Unending Destruction and the Justice of Hell." A paper presented at the Evangelical Theological Society, San Diego, California, November 2007.

"Churches and the Church." In *Recycling the Past or Researching History? Studies in Baptist Historiography and Myths*, edited by Anthony R. Cross and Philip E. Thompson. Carlisle: Paternoster Press, 2005.

"Karl Barth the Complementarian." A paper presented at the Evangelical Theological Society, Valley Forge, Pennsylvania, November 2005.

"Can Egalitarians and Complementarians Stay Together? A Canadian Case Study." A paper presented at the Evangelical Theological Society, San Antonio, Texas, November 2004.

"The Problem of Evil: How Can This World Be God's World?" *The Evangelical Baptist* 51, no. 5 (September/October 2004).

"A Second Look at Local Church Autonomy." *The Evangelical Baptist* 51, no. 3 (March/April 2004).

"Is Baptist Sacramentalism an Oxymoron?" In *Baptist Sacramentalism*, edited by Anthony R. Cross and Philip E. Thompson. Carlisle: Paternoster Press, 2003.

"Baptists and Restorationists in Search of a Common Theology of Baptism." A paper presented at the Evangelical Theological Society, Atlanta, Georgia, November 2003.

"God's Law and the Law of the Land." A workshop presented at the national convention of The Fellowship of Evangelical Baptist Churches in Canada, Toronto, Ontario, November 2003.

"Baptists and Churches of Christ in Search of a Common Theology of Baptism." A paper presented at the Third International Conference on Baptist Studies, Prague, Czech Republic, July 2003.

"Evaluating Open Theism." A workshop presented at the national convention of The Fellowship of Evangelical Baptist Churches in Canada, Toronto, Ontario, November 2002.

"Facing the Issues: Church for the Unchurched." *The Evangelical Baptist* 49, no. 4 (May/June 2002).

"Facing the Issues: Dealing with Change." *The Evangelical Baptist* 49, no. 3 (March/April 2002).

"Facing the Issues: What's a Pastor to Do?" *The Evangelical Baptist* 49, no. 2 (January/February 2002).

"Facing the Issues: Christian Unity." *The Evangelical Baptist* 49, no. 1 (November/December 2001).

"Facing the Issues: The Collapse of Christendom." *The Evangelical Baptist* 48, no. 5 (September/October 2001).

"Facing the Issues: Homosexuality." *The Evangelical Baptist* 48, no. 4 (May/June 2001).

"Facing the Issues: The Worship War." *The Evangelical Baptist* 48, no. 3 (March/April 2001).

"Facing the Issues: Religious Pluralism." *The Evangelical Baptist* 48, no. 2 (January/February 2001).

"Facing the Issues: Open Theism." *The Evangelical Baptist* 48, no. 1 (November/December 2000).

"Facing the Issues: Women and the Church." *The Evangelical Baptist* 47, no. 5 (September/October 2000).

“Is ‘Baptist Sacramentalism’ an Oxymoron? Reactions in Britain to Christian Baptism (1959).” A paper presented at the Second International Conference on Baptist Studies at Wake Forest University, Winston-Salem, North Carolina, July 2000.

“John Gill's Doctrine of Believer Baptism.” In *The Life and Thought of John Gill (1697–1771): A Tercentennial Appreciation*, edited by Michael A.G. Haykin. Leiden: Brill, 1997.

“Interpreting the Toronto Blessing.” A workshop presented at the national assembly of The Evangelical Missionary Church of Canada, Waterloo, Ontario, July 1995.

“Signs and Wonders Today: Some Theological Reflections.” *Baptist Review of Theology* 3, no. 2 (Fall 1993): 46–55.

“By Water and Spirit: The Sacramental Language of Early English Baptists.” A paper presented at the Canadian Baptist Heritage Conference, at Ontario Theological Seminary, Willowdale, Ontario, May 1993.

“The Meaning of Ordination: A Modest Proposal.” *Baptist Review of Theology* 2, no. 1 (Spring 1992): 33–36.

“Charismatic Views of Sanctification.” A paper presented at the International Baptist Conference, Toronto Baptist Seminary, October 1990.

“Calvin's Doctrine of Assurance.” A paper presented at the annual meeting of the Canadian Evangelical Theological Association, Ontario Theological Seminary, Willowdale, Ontario, May 1990.

“Eschatology and Israel.” *Faith Today* 7, no. 6 (November/December 1989): 24–25.

Sexual Hierarchy in the Anthropology of Karl Barth. Toronto, Ontario: Central Baptist Seminary, 1989.

“Divorce, Remarriage, and the Church.” *The Evangelical Baptist* 33, no. 1 (November 1985): 11–14.

Deo Optimo et Maximo Gloria
To God, best and greatest, be glory

www.joshuapress.com